Uttara Yogi

Published by
NIYOGI
BOOKS
D-78, Okhla Industrial Area, Phase-I
New Delhi-110 020, INDIA
Tel: 91-11-26816301, 26813350, 51, 52
Fax: 91-11-26810483, 26813830
email: niyogibooks@gmail.com
website: www.niyogibooks.com

Cover Painting: Sri Aurobindo by Arup Mitra
Cover Design: Nabanita Das/Niyogi Books
Editor: Madhuparna Banerjee/Niyogi Books

ISBN: 978-81-89738-55-6

Publication: 2010

Printed at: Niyogi Offset Pvt. Ltd., New Delhi, India

Uttara Yogi

Arup Mitra

NIYOGI
BOOKS

Contents

Preface

Uttara Yogi is a work of fiction in which the creation and portrayal of the characters, the plot and the narrative thread are products of the author's imagination. But this does not mean that everything in the novel is fictitious. Much of it is based on available documents, all of which are listed in the bibliography. Without this storehouse of information—books, letters, newspaper reports, government and police records, career records, biographies, old photographs, city maps and street directories, railway timetables, maritime records, calendars and unpublished manuscripts—this work would not have been possible.

I have also provided a list of historical personalities as well as a glossary of Indian terms and names used in the novel for the benefit of the readers.

I have recounted the story of Sri Aurobindo's life in the form of a novel. Harimohan Datta, whom I have created in a given set of circumstances, meets Sri Aurobindo at different times and places as both their lives happen to come together. Harimohan's narrative carries the reader back to the days of pre-independent India and recreates the mood of the nationalist movement.

As for the historical characters, most of the time, I have referred to their respective published works—though the words, as spoken by them in the narrative, do not always correspond to the actual context in which they were uttered. In the same light, some of the characters in this story say things of which there are no records, but which could have been said by them, if we consider their later writings. Here again, I have taken artistic liberty.

Let me emphasise, however, that there has been no attempt to belittle any historical personality or to cast aspersions on him or her. If, inadvertently, some details are felt to be disparaging, I beg to be pardoned for my unintended error.

Through this fictional work, if I am able to bring to life something of that momentous period in India's history in which the first sparks of national awakening were born, if even some of my readers feel inspired to serve their country more fully, if in their hearts the devotion for Sri Aurobindo has been lit, I would feel that my labour has been richly rewarded.

Acknowledgements

I sincerely thank the Board of Trustees of the Sri Aurobindo Ashram, Puducherry, for allowing me to quote and reproduce information from the collected works of Sri Aurobindo and those of some other inmates of the Ashram.

I also thank the Sri Aurobindo Archives and Research Library of Puducherry for providing me access to the Government of India records, West Bengal State Archives records, Baroda records, India Office (London) records and the unpublished papers of Biren Sen.

I thank the Sri Aurobindo Pathamandir, Kolkata, for allowing me to reproduce Rabindranath Tagore's poem 'Salutation' composed on Sri Aurobindo.

I also thank the National Library of Kolkata, Alipore Court Museum of Kolkata, Museum Library of Baroda, West Bengal State Archives, the West Bengal Secretariat Library (Writers' Buildings), *The Statesman* and the Kolkata Police Commissioner's Office for allowing me to study old records and take notes.

I am indebted to Peter Heehs for allowing me to refer his authoritative book, *The Bomb in Bengal*, for the chronology of events and the interpretation of the history of the period.

I am also very grateful to Sri Nihar Roy, former director of the Kolkata Police Museum, whose constant assistance has been invaluable in unravelling important primary and secondary source documents without which this book would have remained incomplete. I am equally indebted to Mrs Barnali Roy for her valuable advice, guidance and counsel.

Special mention needs to be made of the late revolutionary leader Amarendranath Chatterjee's son Sri Yogabrata Chatterjee, for allowing me to use quotations from his father's unpublished works. This has helped to establish Sri Aurobindo as the actual progenitor of the Swadeshi and the Boycott movements and also as the forerunner in popularising the *Vande Mataram* mantra. Later, these valuable, handwritten manuscripts were donated to the Sri Aurobindo Archives, Puducherry, through me.

The help extended by David, my former English teacher, and the indefatigable Maurice Shukla for patiently scrutinising the text also needs special mention. They gave, over the years, much of their time and attention for the success of this project despite their usual workload. I also thank Sunayana Panda and an unnamed friend of the Sri Aurobindo Ashram, who wishes to remain anonymous.

And last but not the least, the unstinted support from my own family needs special mention, as without their encouragement, help and support, this ambitious project would never have seen the light of the day.

A Short History

The British East India Company conquered India through cunning and guile, taking advantage of a disintegrated Mughal Empire and the constant infighting amongst the Indian princes. Thus, within a century, the Company of traders had transformed itself into an invincible imperial power.

The plunder and loot of the country's wealth that followed thereafter led to impoverishment, culminating in unprecedented famines. William Digby, observed acerbically in his *Prosperous British India* that little more than a century ago even the state of Bengal was wealthier than Britain. Brooks Adams postulated that Britain's Industrial Revolution would not have been possible without the influx of money that followed the conquest of Bengal. He drew attention to the fact that major industrialisation in England began only in 1760, exactly three years after the British had won the Battle of Plassey.

While Indians were made to work for low pay under inhuman conditions in British-owned plantations, benevolent enterprises such as the introduction of the railways and irrigation works were primarily undertaken by the Britishers to help the rulers in the economic exploitation of the country.

The Imperialists were careful not to let Indians rise to the rank of an army officer though they used them as native soldiers to conquer the country. Consequently, trouble broke out all over the land. Although the Mutiny of 1857 was the first large-scale uprising against British rule in India, it failed because the rebel leaders were disorganised and disunited. As a result, in 1858, the British Crown took charge of administering India. While the direct responsibility for governing the country remained in the hands of the viceroy, and his council in Calcutta, everyday business of the Raj was conducted by the thousand members of the prestigious Indian Civil Service (ICS).

Following the Mutiny, the Imperialists ruled the country with an iron grip for the next fifty years. England had become the centre of an empire that included one-quarter of the world's area and population. And, its hold on India, its most valuable possession, seemed permanent. But it was during this same period that a strong current of nationalist feeling prevailed in the country. The second half of the nineteenth century was a time of great suffering in India. During this period, there were as many as twenty-four famines, in which a staggering thirty million people died. Mass protests became inevitable. Reawakening or renaissance stirred India's educated classes. Constitutional agitation began to rise when Surendranath Banerjea began his public career. Viceroy Ripon was more than sympathetic towards Indian aspirations, and in 1883, he asked C P Ilbert, the law member of his council, to draft a bill modifying the Criminal Procedure Code. This legislation would have allowed qualified Indians to have jurisdiction over Europeans and establish a trial by jury, of which only half were to be Europeans. This culminated in the controversial Ilbert Bill which unleashed a storm of racial antipathy.

The Indian National Congress was founded in 1885 as a direct result of the Ilbert Bill imbroglio. It remained the vanguard of the national movement from 1885 till 1947. But simultaneously, an advanced section of nationalists was growing impatient for results. It was not enough, they asserted, to give speeches and pass resolutions once a year in the three-day meeting called Congress. This radical wing found an able leader in Bal Gangadhar Tilak, a brilliant and outspoken journalist, who became a national hero following his internment in 1897.

Ineffective imitation of Western models was not the only defect of the early Congress. Young Aurobindo Ghose authored in 1893 a series of articles called 'New Lamps for Old' in the English journal *Induprakash*, criticising the Congress for its incompetence.

In 1905, Viceroy Curzon brought the Partition of Bengal into effect, an administrative measure aimed at attacking Indian nationalism covertly. As the Partition plan was hastily pushed through, the leaders resorted for the first time to a more active form of resistance—a boycott of British goods. A great number of Bengalis vowed not to purchase cloth, salt, sugar or anything else manufactured in Great Britain. This set forth the Swadeshi Movement, which within a few years electrified the Indian political scene. The sale of British goods plummeted sharply and Indians shunned foreign products with greater determination. Bankim Chandra Chatterjee's *'Vande Mataram'* became the battle cry for the revolutionists.

Throughout 1905 and 1906, the Swadeshi spirit spread rapidly from Bengal to Bombay, Madras and other provinces and signs of a cleavage began to grow evident in the Congress. As the established Congress leaders were afraid of proceeding too quickly, they were labelled as moderates by a group of younger men, who, in return, were called the extremists by their opponents. Led in Maharashtra by Tilak, in Punjab by Lajpat Rai, and in Bengal by a brilliant circle that included Bipin Chandra Pal, Brahma Bandhab Upadhyay and Aurobindo Ghose, the extremists soon made important inroads into Indian politics.

In mid-1906, Pal founded a newspaper called *Bande Mataram*. In it he and his associate Aurobindo Ghose lay down the tenets of the extremist philosophy. Other talented writers such as Tilak and Subramaniam Bharati also contributed similarly in promoting patriotism in journals like *Kesari* of Poona and *India* of Madras, respectively. Finally, it was the moderates' failure to accept complete independence as the goal of the Indian National Congress that led to an open rupture between the moderates and the extremists at the Surat Congress in 1907.

Interestingly, even before the split at Surat, extremists had begun to form secret societies, with its members sworn to the use of physical force to obtain independence for India. Thousands of young Bengalis joined the Anushilan Samiti, which at one time boasted of more than five hundred branches. Another society led by Aurobindo's brother Barin Ghose was the first to collect arms and make preparations for a large-scale uprising. Unfortunately, its activities were nipped in the bud. However, revolutionary actions were to remain a regular feature of life in Bengal through the next decade.

But reacting swiftly to the threats posed by extremists and revolutionaries, the government imposed restrictions on the printing of newspapers and holding of public meetings. Finally, taking advantage of the split between the moderates and the extremists, the government was able to curb the latter's strength.

And by 1910, the extremist party had lost all its leaders. But by then, the extremist's message of Swaraj or Independence was clear; it burned more ardently than ever before within the heart of every patriotic Indian.

PART ONE

The Beginning

Today I know that the one who will lead India to its ultimate fulfilment is present among us. He's the chosen priest for the worship of Mother India. Like all incarnations of the Supreme, he has come to prepare the path and lay the foundation on which the temple of faith shall solidly stand.

Prologue

In the summer of 1870, drought hit parts of the South Indian Peninsula. Lakes and ponds dried up around Tanjore, forcing villagers to move to nearby towns. This district, known for its luxuriant paddy fields, nestles in the fertile delta of the Cauvery. But now, it seemed as if the Creator had wilfully wiped out the exuberance of green from this part of the earth. Ironically, this harsh display of nature was turning a sleepy little village called Nagai within the same district into a place of pilgrimage.

About three decades before the drought a saint named Vasudeva had halted at this village and decided to make it his spiritual home. Soon word went around about his *yogic* feats and the people of Nagai began to revere him as their guru. Sri Vasudeva had another divine gift: he was a rainmaker and people believed that he communicated directly with Lord Varuna, the God of Rain.

A lone gigantic tree stood near the Tirutturaipundi-Mannargudi road connecting Nagai. In the torrid heat of one summer afternoon in 1870, a large group of pilgrims—hungry, thirsty and exhausted—was trudging along to meet Sri Vasudeva. Attracted by the welcoming shade of the tree, they decided to halt for a little respite. However, Ayanar Gounder, the leader of this group, looked worried. They had left their village Ariyalur at dawn, walked over fifteen miles, but were still quite far from their destination. He urged his men to resume their difficult journey and the pilgrims were soon on their feet again.

The last rays of the setting sun rebounding from the fortified walls of Nagai fell on the clouds of dust raised by the dragging feet of the pilgrims. In that golden glimmer the men seemed like silhouettes. As they entered the outskirts of Nagai, the weary eyes of the pilgrims fell happily on the pond Mandakini, famous for its milk-white water. 'This isn't a mirage surely,' they seemed to ask one another. Smiles returned to their faces and hearts filled with hope. With such abundance of water here, inexistent elsewhere in the district, the legend of Sri Vasudeva, the rain-man, became reality once again. The water drew everyone in like a magnet. They plunged into its coolness and revelled in it like happy children. When Gounder's men emerged from the pond recharged and rejuvenated, they were happy to learn that many other men too had come for requesting Sri Vasudeva to make it rain.

Just then an excited murmur went around and everyone rose to his feet. Sri Vasudeva, the spiritual leader of the Nagai Japata came into view accompanied by a group of his disciples. Of powerful build, with long curly hair and a silver-streaked beard, Sri Vasudeva instantly became the focus of everyone's attention. He walked like a saffron-clad rishi of the Vedic age, radiating peace and strength.

He looked at them gently and stated, 'I know why you've come. This year, Lord Varuna has not been as generous as usual. Remember, we are surrounded by falsehood and decadence, more so today as never before. But this Dark Age will soon end. God shall reincarnate again as man and walk on this earth to lift us out of our misery. Therefore chant the name of Narayana, for purification. If you can achieve *shuddhi*, Varuna will be pleased.' The crowd murmured with joy and the Guru's face lit up with a smile. 'Join me in singing the name of the Lord all night. We'll assemble in about two hours.'

His devotees, already exhausted by their journey, felt slightly nonplussed but could not ignore the Swami's invitation. The place where they assembled was a *yantra* shaped platform of occult dimensions. There was an octagonal tiled roof over the central area under which a mystical symbol—the *Pranava Chakra*—was drawn. Almost a thousand men rose as Sri Vasudeva approached. He motioned them to sit. Two enormous torches illuminated the seated Guru and his presence reigned over the gathering. A man stood before a big drum and looked intently at another man holding a pair of gigantic cymbals. Everybody was silent and waited for the signal. The hooting of an owl was heard in that silence while the growing red glow of the the torches began to illuminate the dark faces of the devotees.

Sri Vasudeva's gaze now turned on the man holding the cymbals. A crashing sound followed and the drummer began to play. At the stroke of every eighth beat the cymbal rang. The cycle went on. As the third round began, the well-rehearsed disciples started to recite the *astakshara* mantra: '*O-om Na-mo Na-ra-ya-na*'—its eight syllables matching the eight-beat cycle. The drone of the solemn voices was firm and flawless. Sri Vasudeva sat still with his eyes closed. As time passed, most visitors felt fatigued. Only a few continued with their chanting what now was an unintelligible lisp.

Just then lightning flashed. That tiny burst of light invigorated the tired men. A cool moist breeze began to blow, carrying the musty smell of humid earth. Then a squall broke out. Happiness rent the air and the tired bodies of the pilgrims tingled with joy at this coolness. Flashes of lightning lit up the tall coconut trees which swayed rapturously. At last, the morning star reappeared as the clouds parted and innumerable other tiny flickers began sparkling from the heavenly vault. A much yearned for coolness purified the air. A magnificent magenta dawn gently spread from the east to the far corners of the earth. Then Sri Vasudeva opened his eyes as the magenta turned into gold. For a long time he looked at this mysterious burst of colour. To him it meant something more, a sure symbol of an 'arrival': the descent of the Deliverer, of the saviour from falsehood. He slowly rose and bowed to the Almighty before turning to his disciples.

'My children,' he began, 'I have led you in your spiritual quest for a long time. But it is God's wish that I should now withdraw. However, I'm a little disheartened that no one is ready to carry on my spiritual work.' The disciples remained bewildered as they listened in rapt silence. 'But don't despair. Very soon God shall manifest in this land.' As he said this, his finger pointed towards the east. 'Read God's writing in the sky. Soon a great Uttara Yogi will come and settle down in these parts of the country for his own and the world's spiritual salvation. It is he who will lead you in the future.'

A senior disciple asked, 'How will we recognise him?'

Sri Vasudeva did not speak for some time. Then he answered, 'He'll make himself known through three utterances. He'll take up the integral yoga and it will be the unmistakable prelude to the liberation of our country. But, you mustn't lose patience. He'll arrive only after three decades.'

A strange, inexplicable gloom came over Nagai as the visitors left. They had been witness to the miracle of rain materialising out of thin air in the midst of an unprecedented drought and that alone was a memorable event. Sri Vasudeva's disciples fixed their eyes on the future. They began to wait for the mystic events that their Guru had forecast.

And, as he had predicted, shortly after his vision, Sri Vasudeva left his body and passed into eternity.

The long vigil for the Uttara Yogi had begun.

1

Hurry Mohun Dutt

It was a misty morning. As usual, the native residents of old Calcutta woke up to the lilting music of a kirtan sung by a group of Vaishnav beggars accompanied by harmonium, *khol* and cymbals. But as soon as the men emerged on the wide Baghbazar Street a sudden shriek disrupted their fervent song. The painful cry was coming from Gourmohan's shop where a huge cauldron of boiling syrup had overturned on the sweet-maker's assistant, Baidhar. The accident occurred when Baidhar lost balance while lifting a brass cauldron off the mud oven, spilling the hot syrup all over himself. Kaviraj Moshay, grimly shook his head and confirmed that the youth's life was in grave danger. Nevertheless, he dutifully applied fresh aloe vera juice all over Baidhar's wounds.

The unfortunate incident momentarily unnerved Gourmohan Datta. For, with just one day to go for the Durga Puja, his own future and particularly that of his shop Sri Tarakeshwar Mistanna Bhandar, now hung precariously on the balance. He had promised Rai Bahadur Pashupatinath Bose to deliver twelve thousand sweets for the following four days of the Puja. It would be impossible to achieve such a gigantic feat without the help of his head assistant, Baidhar. But Gourmohan Datta was a born fighter. He swung back into action soon. First, he sent Baidhar to his nearby rented house on Brindaban Pal Lane. Then leaving him under the care of the Kaviraj, he personally contacted his biggest rival, Nakur Chandra Basak. He wanted to replace Baidhar with Nakur's head assistant. Gourmohan's offer of a cut of ten rupees above the entire month's wages to his assistant for working just four days was too big an offer to turn down. Thus, Gourmohan was able to save his reputation and enjoy the patronage of the Boses.

Baidhar recovered miraculously and resumed work within two months of the accident. Riding on a new wave of popularity for his honesty and hard work, Gourmohan's business soared higher and higher, prompting him to take another bold step. He decided to bring his wife Kattayani and his three sons—Gopimohan, Madanmohan and Harimohan—to the city from their ancestral village Banseye, popularly known as Seiya in the Hooghly District of Bengal.

Six months after his family's arrival in Calcutta and almost a year after the accident, a stroke of luck knocked at Gourmohan's door. One afternoon, a spruce phaeton pulled before his shop from which a short Englishman alighted. He was probably in his late forties. His receding hairline, French-cut beard and whiskers gave him a very respectable look. His large benign eyes conveyed a warmth and friendliness quite uncommon amongst Englishmen living in India.

He came in straight and addressed Gourmohan's youngest son, Harimohan, in faultless Bengali, '*Tomaadiger bhaalo mistanna aamaake khawaaite paaro*? [Will you please serve me some of your best sweets?]'

The Englishman, not used to eating so many sweets, patiently ate a morsel of each sweet and enjoyed the *rossomalai* most. After placing an order for two dozen of them, he courteously began conversing with the young boy. Soon the sahib found out how bright the boy was. His unusual refinement and poise impressed him very much.

When he asked the adolescent what he would like to become, Harimohan replied confidently, 'A big barrister.'

'But you've got to learn English,' Horace Cockerell interjected, 'then travel to England to study law in one of its reputable inns of court to acquire a degree!'

'I'm sure I can do that if I'm given the opportunity.'

'And how old are you now?'

'Sir,' Gourmohan butted in, 'He's only fourteen and ...'

'Would you give me your son, Datta Moshay?' the Englishman impulsively asked, surprising even himself. His wife and he had often thought of adopting a child. 'My name's Horace Cockerell and I live in Rawdon Street in central Calcutta. I think your son has a bright future and I shall be glad to be of any help. He could live with me. As I'm childless, I could take charge of his education and probably make his dream come true.'

Gourmohan was a man of the world and knew how foolish it would be to deny the small sacrifice of parting with his son when such an attractive proposal was offered to him. He gave his consent unconditionally, thereby satisfying both Harimohan and the Englishman.

'Now, if you give me a piece of paper,' Horace said happily, 'I can write down the way to contact me in order to find out how your son is. You'll find me at the Writers' Building.'

Someone instantly brought paper, pen and inkpot and the Englishman neatly wrote: 'Horace Abel Cockerell, Secretary to the Government of Bengal, Judicial and Political Departments, Writers' Building, Calcutta.'

Soon father and son went home to inform Kattayani about Harimohan's departure. But separation from her youngest son was unacceptable to the simple-hearted, illiterate mother and she was in no mood to relent. When all persuasion failed Hari spoke up boldly.

'Ma,' he said, 'just think of my happiness! I shall probably go to *bilait* and become a big barrister and then bring home lots of money!'

Sensing the ingenuity of his son's argument Gourmohan quickly added, 'Besides, Horey can visit us as often as he wishes!'

This finally settled the matter. Harimohan quickly packed up some clothes and touched his mother's feet for her blessings. As Gopimohan and Madanmohan were not at home, Harimohan requested his father to wish them goodbye on his behalf.

'I'll surely tell them.' Gourmohan reassured sadly. 'But remember Horey, we're all uneducated. If you study well and rise, you'll illumine our family.'

Gourmohan's last words were still echoing in his son's ears when the phaeton turned round the corner of Cornwallis Street. He caught a glimpse of his father standing outside his shop, wiping his eyes with one end of his dhoti.

Harimohan could hardly believe his eyes as the carriage cruised past the beautiful Esplanade Square, revealing the full glory of English architecture. A little later, as they turned left on Park Street, Harimohan marvelled at the vast gardens on either side of the road. But on entering Rawdon Street, it was Horace's heart that began to beat faster as they approached his house after passing by the graveyard. He could hardly wait to break the news of the sudden adoption to his wife.

'Julia,' he shouted excitedly upon entering the big drawing room. 'Where are you? Look who's here.'

It took a little while for his wife to come out of her study.

'What is it Horace?' she enquired eagerly, revealing her comely features. Her speech froze as soon as her eyes fell on Harimohan. 'Oh, and who have we here?'

'Darling, this is Harimohan Datta and he has come to stay with us.'

'How can he stay here?' his wife asked knitting her eyebrows.

'I'll explain it later. He can stay in our spare room on the second floor.'

After the boy was taken to his room, Horace continued, 'Hari's father is the owner of the most famous sweet shop in north Calcutta. And this pot of delicious *rossomalai* is a present from him to you.'

The new spelling for his name—Hurry Mohun Dutt—became the first symbol of Hari's new status. At first he could only speak short incoherent sentences but by the end of the second week he astonished his new mother by expressing himself quite adequately. Delighted by Harimohan's progress, Julia began taking a personal interest in teaching him how to read and write English. There was, however, an element of irony as Hari was learning a foreign language without knowing his mother tongue. Horace was the first to understand the problem and took up teaching Bengali to Harimohan. He himself had learned the language during his apprenticeship of the ICS as it was mandatory to learn the language of the natives.

Impressed by Hari's eagerness to learn, one evening Horace told his wife, 'Believe it or not, I have this uncanny feeling that the boy's future is bright and, on his own merit, he'll become someone special.'

~

As Durga Puja was nearing, the Cockerells were planning to visit the countryside and spend the holidays on the outskirts of Hooghly, the principal town of a district of the same name.

The lushness of Hooghly and the sublime luxuriant beauty of its countryside might well have given birth to the description *Sonar Bangla*. But few knew that a mighty mantra would be born from this soil and captured in verse by a great rishi. Bankim Chandra Chatterjee was a member of the first cadre of Indians who became Bengal's prestigious public servants. Bankim's association with the district of Hooghly began when he assumed the office of deputy collector-cum-magistrate in 1875.

Three years after Bankim's posting, Horace came to spend his holiday in the state guest house, situated on a picturesque slope of the Ganges, also known as the Hooghly River. Bankim was deputed to call on him as it was incumbent for an important officer of the local administration to welcome the secretary of the judicial and political department.

Bankim's carriage arrived before the all-white, ten-columned, two-storied stately mansion. The ornate cast-iron gates gave a metallic squeak as they were opened by the uniformed guard. An attendant of the house came running out and warmly welcomed him and showed him into the waiting hall. A little later, Horace came down to meet the visitor. Bankim felt instantly drawn by his host's eyes. There was also an air of informal dignity in his appearance that appealed to Bankim. He quickly rose to his feet to greet Horace.

'Welcome to Hooghly, Sir. I'm the deputy collector. My name's Bankim Chandra Chatterjee.'

The Englishman looked pensive as he examined the striped *shamla* Bankim held in his hand.

'Are you the Bengali author of the same name?' he enquired. 'Well, I've read your novels. A fine talented writer you are. Would you please tell me more about yourself?'

The men sat down on separate divans.

'*Deputy sahab ke liye hookah aur sherbat le aao*, [Get hookah and sherbat for the deputy sahib],' the Englishman instructed a native servant in impeccable Hindi.

'May I ask which of my novels you have read?' Bankim asked politely, holding the long pipe in style and taking in a puff of the aromatic smoke.

'Well, let's see.' Horace spread out his right palm and began counting his fingers. '*Kapalkundala*, *Vishvrikshya*, *Durgeshnandini, Indira* and *Jugalangarya*.'

Bankim was very impressed. Not only was the Englishman's knowledge of Bengali profound, but he also knew the chronology of the books.

'Would you tell me something about your next novel?' asked Horace curiously.

'I'm contemplating something about the eighteenth-century famine in Bengal and the *sannyasi* uprising. I'd like to call it *Ananda Math*.'

Horace was lost in thought.

'I have been in a dilemma for the last two years. You might be able to help me decide. I arrived in India exactly twenty-five years ago and I ought to retire in a few years. You see, I would like to live here till the end of my life and die in this country. I am realising that my involvement with India is growing each day. Its rich culture, its colourful diversity, its natural beauty and above all the people's commitment to religion, are things that have touched me deeply.'

Bankim was visibly moved. The Englishman had just voiced Bankim's own feelings about his motherland – this country was not merely composed of hills, plains, rivers and people, but represented a vibrant embodiment of the divine Shakti, the Mother Herself.'

'Well, since you mentioned India, let me tell you about a sacred poem that came to me about four years ago. It is partly in Sanskrit and partly in Bengali. I would like to incorporate it in *Ananda Math*. Would you like to hear it, Sir?'

For a while Bankim stood still with his head bowed in a sort of intense concentration. Then he raised his head high and in a deep resonant voice began to recite the mantra that had been revealed to him:

'Vande Maataram!
Sujalaam, suphalaam, malayaja shitalaam,
Shashya shyaamalaam Maataram.
Vande Maataram!'

The poem ended but Horace remained seated speechless, immobile. His eyes were glistening.

'This has been the most unforgettable experience of my life,' he said at last. 'Thank you for giving me the answer to my problem.'

Brushing aside protocol, later that evening, Horace introduced Bankim to his wife Julia, and with great warmth personally saw him off.

The next day, Harimohan learnt from the old caretaker that Seiya lay just eleven miles west of Hooghly. He pleaded with his foster parents to let him go there for a day. Although the Cockerells allowed him to go, they urged him to return before nightfall. Harimohan happily accepted the condition and set off the next day at dawn, accompanied by the driver and the coachman. After crossing the villages of Sugandha and Gotu, Harimohan could not suppress his joy, as the scenery began to grow familiar and the tip of the Shiva temple became visible. As the carriage skirted the big pond which belonged to the zamindar, the half-naked young boys who were playing in the fields began shouting and waving and dashed behind the coach. The crowd slowly swelled and by the time Harimohan reached the open field in the middle of his village more than two dozen children and elders had gathered around the carriage. A hush fell and everyone froze as he proudly stepped out of the carriage amongst his acquaintances. Clearly, they had not expected to see a stranger.

Ultimately on recognising Harimohan, the local blacksmith, Ibrahim Mian, said, 'But are you not our Gour Kayet's youngest son?' Making reference to one's caste is an inevitable factor in the countryside.

Everyone was stunned. After an initial lukewarm response, someone from the crowd mockingly uttered, 'But why is he dressed like a monkey?'

Manik Dolui, one of Gourmohan's closest friends, obliquely remarked, '*Arey*, leave him alone! Haven't you heard about Gour's sudden riches? He has bought this carriage and sent his son to show off his newly acquired wealth and mock at us.'

A note of approval went around the crowd and to Harimohan's utter disappointment, everyone dispersed without further ado, ignoring him completely.

Bravely withholding his tears, Harimohan made for the ancestral home on foot to meet his relatives. The way was too narrow to allow the carriage to pass. Harimohan began to feel awkward in his fine European clothes as the villagers stood looking at him curiously. Obviously, he was far too over-dressed for this simple rural milieu. It was not at all strange that he had been dubbed a monkey.

While speaking to his grandfather, Harimohan was saddened to learn that the family was eating only one meal a day as the rains had failed. A sense of guilt kept gnawing at his heart while he narrated the story of his adoption and his father's prosperity to his grandparents. Around three that afternoon, his friends came to see him. From them Harimohan learned that his close friend Dhonu had moved to Calcutta. Somehow, the knowledge that Dhonu was sharing his city life brought unexpected warmth to his heart. Perhaps one day he would come across Dhonu. At four, Harimohan headed back for the carriage. He did not want any family member or friend to see the well-decorated state coach leased out to his foster parents. Midway, a little distance from another cluster of huts, Harimohan heard his name being sweetly called. He turned back and found Saraju smiling at him.

'I saw you from a distance and wondered if it was you.'

'Ah, Saraju, how are you? How's your sister?'

'I'm fine. Didi has had a son, you know. But first, tell me about yourself.'

While narrating his own tale and that of his father's prosperity, Harimohan grew conscious of the big change in Saraju. She had grown more rounded and her complexion had become brighter than before. She looked so much more attractive now. Suddenly, Harimohan felt a bit uneasy in her presence though he could not understand the reason. Earlier, he had never felt this way in the presence of a girl. Interestingly, Saraju was the only person in the village who comforted him by saying, 'How lucky you are, Hari. If the rains fail one more time, death and famine will surely overtake us.'

At this point, Harimohan touched her mouth lightly with a finger and bid her to stop. Then delicately cupping her face in his hands as hot tears clouded his eyes, he said, 'I wish I could lift you all out of this state of despair!'

Saraju spread her palms over his and looking straight in his eyes, replied with dignity, 'We're born to suffer. But you are different. Help us when you can.'

2

The First Meeting

After Christmas, Horace Cockerell got a very special assignment. He was given charge of receiving a new batch of young men from England enrolled for the ICS and introducing them to their surroundings. To the thousands of Englishmen such as Horace, the ICS opened up opportunities for acquiring wealth, honour and social uplift. Indeed, his salary of three thousand three hundred and thirty-three rupees compared very unfavourably with an average Indian clerk's monthly pay of about fifteen rupees in 1878.

Horace met and married Julia, daughter of the honourable Sir Edmund Drummond and the granddaughter of the sixth Viscount Strathallan in India, when he was thirty-one years old. The Cockerells had sailed back to England only twice which shows how much at home they felt in India.

Once, in the course of a soirée, Julia had run into one of her former schoolmates, Annette Susannah Akroyd, who had recently come to India. Annette was a student of London's prestigious Bedford College from where Julia had also graduated. This happy meeting of the two schoolmates had led to a strong friendship.

Later, Annette married Henry Beveridge, a district judge and settled in Rangpur.

Now, seven years later, the Cockerells took Harimohan to meet Annette Beveridge upon receiving an unexpected letter from her informing of her proposed visit to Calcutta. She had put up with a common friend, the Indian barrister Mano Mohun Ghose, at nearby Theatre Road. It was mid-morning of a cloudless, summer Sunday. The beautiful, two-storied house at 4 Theatre Road basked delightfully in the sun. This house had been bought by the barrister only a year earlier. The Cockerells were escorted into a large hall on the first floor.

'What a pleasant surprise, Horace and Julia!' Mano Mohun Ghose exclaimed, welcoming his old friends. 'Did you know that Annette has arrived?'

Just then, one of the doors of the hall flew open and Annette floated in.

'Julia and Horace! How awfully happy I am to see you again,' she said warmly extending her arms towards her friend who eagerly rushed into them. After hugging each other the two ladies sat down together on a large sofa and began chatting earnestly.

'There's another surprise waiting for you,' the barrister told the Cockerells while pointing towards the end of the hall. 'Behold Dr Krishna Dhone Ghose of Rangpur!'

The Cockerells stood up to greet the doctor whom they already knew. Like the barrister, the doctor was also a thoroughly Anglicised gentleman always dressed in European clothes.

'I'm travelling back to England to enrol my three sons in English schools,' Krishna Dhone proudly informed them.

Then Horace steered the conversation to a different topic.

'Doctor,' he said jovially, 'I would like to introduce you to my foster son, Hurry Mohun Dutt.'

Till then no one seemed to have taken notice of Harimohan.

'Oh, but why is he so quiet?' Dr Ghose wondered aloud. 'Where's my wife? Ask my sons to be brought in. Let the boy play with them.'

Swarnalata Ghose, the doctor's wife, was purposely absent, not because she hated company, but because she was pregnant. Besides, she had to look after her two-year-old daughter whom she was still nursing. For long she had also been suffering from mental instability.

When the three boys were brought in, the twelve-year-old Benoybhushan cordially stretched out his hand to Harimohan. The second brother, Manomohan, who had completed ten, stood sullenly, eyeing Harimohan for some time before giving his hand. But Aurobindo, the youngest and the sweetest amongst the three brothers, just stood quietly. Harimohan kneeled down to take a closer look at the seven-year-old who just kept gazing back with his large, tranquil eyes. It took Harimohan a long time to get over the mesmerising spell of those unforgettable, dreamy eyes.

The Puja holidays arrived soon after the Ghoses left for England in August 1879. Just then, Herbert John Reynolds, one of Horace's colleagues, proposed to the Cockerells to accompany his family for a hunting excursion to Hazaribagh, the land of a thousand tigers.

At the station, while Horace and Harimohan were waiting for their train, another train chugged into one of the nearby platforms, raising a clamour and inundating the railway station with thick, black smoke. Impulsively, Harimohan strode off to take a better look at the impressive steam locomotive.

'Take care, don't run through the crowd,' Horace warned from behind.

As Harimohan turned around to catch what his father was saying, he tripped over a huge pile of baggage that he had not noticed and fell on his face. Within a few seconds a man in his mid-fifties and two young men picked him up. Luckily, Harimohan was unhurt.

As Horace arrived hurriedly on the scene, the older man bearing a sublime, priest-like countenance apologised humbly. 'I feel at fault for this huge pile of luggage,' he explained. 'You see, I am shifting with my family from one town to another.'

'Well, let me wish you a happy journey,' Horace said sincerely, extending his hand. 'Your English is impeccable Sir, and permit me to congratulate you for it. My name's Horace Cockerell ...'

'Then you must be the secretary of the judicial and political departments, am I not right?' the older man intervened excitedly even before Horace could complete his introduction.

Horace was pleasantly surprised.

'My name is Rajnarayan Basu. I am an educationist.'

'Ah! You are our friend Dr Krishna Dhone Ghose's father-in-law, the Brahmo leader who sponsored women's education!

'Yes, indeed. I am glad to know that you are Krishna Dhone's friend. But may I ask where are you going?'

'My family and I are on our way to Hazaribagh.'

'Ah! Going for *shikar*!' Rajnarayan cried excitedly. 'Then why don't you stop by at Deogarh for a couple of days? I've recently taken a house on lease there.'

'It is extremely kind of you Mr Basu. Thanks. But you know how short the Puja holidays are for such an extensive tour.'

'Then you must come during Christmas. You will see how we Brahmos celebrate it with a lot of pomp. So do we have a deal, Mr Cockerell?'

'Yes, you have my word Mr Basu; if not for Christmas, then certainly another time.'

A couple of months later, Horace came to spend the Christmas holidays with his family in Deogarh. Horace had been looking forward to meeting Rajnarayan again. The countryside especially along the beautiful Darowa was splendid and the evening walks down its banks coupled with Rajnarayan's lively discourses on religion left an indelible memory on Horace's mind. One evening, Harimohan accompanied them for the walk.

'Well, Mr Basu,' Horace remarked in the course of the stroll, 'I forgot to tell you that when we recently met your son-in-law, we also saw Dr Ghose's children.'

Rajnarayan looked at Harimohan and smiled. He then fondly asked, 'Harimohan, which one among my grandsons did you like most? Ah, the little one? Indeed, there's something mystic about his eyes. I've noticed how different he is from other children. For instance, Auro always remains calm, distant and in-drawn. Once when I saw him sitting alone while others were playing in the courtyard, I casually asked him what he was thinking. Do you know what he replied? "One day, in Darjeeling," he calmly explained, "when I was lying in my bed, I saw a huge cloud of darkness enter into me and cover the whole world. That darkness has never left me since and I'm carrying it with me wherever I go." Then in a peculiar tone that pierced my heart he asked, "What does it signify, Dadu"? "I don't know," I replied. Well, all I can say now about this is that it's a deep spiritual experience. But frankly, the true explanation evades me, just as it eludes little Auro.'

3

A Windfall and a Downfall

A few months passed by and Lakshmi, the Hindu Goddess of Wealth and Prosperity, smiled happily on the Datta family. Gourmohan soon opened a branch of the Sri Tarakeshwar Mistanna Bhandar at the busy Maniktala junction, installing his second son, Madanmohan, as manager. Gourmohan's turnover doubled within just a couple of months and this success prompted him to open a third shop.

The sudden riches went to Gourmohan's head and he took to drinking heavily. Already rumours were rife that he had picked up a pretty, young concubine named Motimala. When the simple Kattayani heard about her husband's downfall, she began to quarrel regularly with him. But when persuasion failed to bring him back to the path of righteousness, she left hope and withdrew to Seiya. Afflicted by depression and a gradual loss of appetite, she developed tuberculosis. Although Harimohan could not leave school to pay a visit to Seiya, he felt distressed by the news that constantly poured in, but not once did he guess that his mother was dying. Kattayani's eldest son Gopimohan was by her side when she finally passed away on a windless afternoon in the month of *Bhadra*. It was his duty as the first son to light her funeral pyre. Almost till the very end she had kept inquiring whether Harimohan had come. Ultimately, however, when Madan and Harimohan reached Seiya, everything was over and the emptiness of their mud house seemed unbearable to Kattayani's youngest son. Gourmohan also broke down, crying uncontrollably for hours.

By then, Harimohan had turned fifteen and had developed a mind of his own. Angered and hurt by his father's carnality, he secretly vowed never to give in to lust and lechery. One evening, he sat alone on the banks of the zamindar's pond, sadly reflecting back on his village days. A sense of guilt was gnawing at his heart for having drifted away from his mother before her death—the time when she needed him most. Torn by grief and remorse, he lost sense of the surroundings and began sobbing helplessly.

It was the magical moment of *godhuli*. And by the time he grew conscious of Sarajubala's presence, it was too late to hide his tears. She spontaneously took his head and pressed it hard against her. But instead of calming down, Harimohan began to cry even more, being spurred on by her sympathy, softness and warmth. Finally, after a long time, Harimohan sat up with a jerk. He felt angry with himself at having betrayed his emotions. But Saraju comforted him.

'The loss of one's mother is the loss of the life-giver. Why should you feel ashamed to express that loss? And then, why hide your sorrow from someone who loves you?' she asked innocently.

'You're right. You're so different from other girls. I've never felt so happy at being hugged before. Saraju, will you promise never to tell anybody?'

'Tell what? That you cried? But it was the most normal thing to do!'

Just then the holy bells at the Mukherjee mansion began to toll, raising an infernal din and drowning their voices. It was time for the deity's evening adoration.

'I must go now,' Saraju shouted before running away into the darkness. 'I'll see you later.'

But Harimohan did not meet Saraju again before leaving Seiya. However, he came to know that she had gone to her elder sister's house. The news dampened Harimohan's spirit. Now, he would have to wait for months to meet her again!

The pressure of studies increased with Harimohan's return to the city. For, he had to work twice as hard to make up an entire month's absence from school because of the *shradh* ceremony that he with his brothers had to perform. One day Harimohan accidentally met Dhonu, his village friend, at Goldighi. From him he learnt that Saraju's elder sister, Sarama, had recently lost her newborn son.

'So that was the reason of Saraju's sudden departure from Seiya,' Harimohan reflected silently. 'She was so happy to give the news of the childbirth.'

'By the way,' Dhonu went on, 'I'm sorry to learn about your mother's death. Please accept my condolences.'

During his conversation with Dhonu, Harimohan came to know that he had lost his job. So he took his friend to their sweet shop and introduced Dhonu to his brother.

'Listen, Chhorda, I need your help,' Harimohan said taking Madan aside. 'I've very little time and have to rush back home. Please take care of my friend Dhonu and promise me to employ him here in your shop. He has eaten very little for the last couple of days.'

A month passed by and Harimohan lost all interest in his family. It was amazing how much Harimohan's life had changed within the last year. While he had acquired plenty of new Indian friends at the college, he had grown more accustomed to the English way of life. And living with the Cockerells had given him a clear edge over his classmates, as his command of English was appreciably better than theirs.

But what had brought about the greatest difference was a thin strip of hair growing over his upper lip, which created in him a growing sense of maturity, poise and independence.

4

The Wedding

Harimohan received an unexpected visit from Dhonu after almost a month.

'Horey, there is news,' Dhonu informed excitedly. 'Saraju is getting married!'

The news was like a thunderbolt! But surprisingly, Harimohan grew calm within seconds. He had anticipated this inevitability and knew that it was impossible to stop or control these events.

'When is the wedding?' he asked steadily.

'It's in the month of *Augrahayan*, in a little over a month's time. You'll never believe it. She's getting married to Nepal Gupta, a balding man in his forties! He has remained unmarried ever since the death of his first wife because no father thought him fit to take charge of his daughter. But from what I heard, Nepal himself has shown keenness to marry her and is even ready to take her home without any dowry. Don't you know the pitiful financial state Kedar Banujje is in after Saramadi's marriage? Or else, how could Saraju remain unmarried at fifteen? She has become a burden for the family and they fear severe ostracism.'

Harimohan understood that what was relatively easy for Nepal at forty-two, would never be possible for him even at a perfectly marriageable age. For, he was a Kayastha, a caste lower in rung than Saraju, hence glaringly disqualified to ask for her hand. But would Harimohan be able to wipe away the sweet memory of Saraju from his heart and mind?

'I must go to the village immediately,' he said. 'Will you come with me? I'll take care of your job and bear your expenses. Meet me here tomorrow.'

Harimohan and Dhonu caught the morning train from Howrah and alighted at Chinsura. Then they hired a carriage and reached Seiya the same afternoon. Meeting Saraju would not be a problem now that her marriage had been fixed. In fact, Harimohan knew that coming from an affluent family, his presence would be quite welcome in Kedar Banerjee's house. As Harimohan did not want Dhonu to hear what he spoke to Saraju, he sent him off to his own house.

As expected, the whole household came alive when Harimohan arrived. Kedarnath went out to get some sweets for him. Saraju looked up at Harimohan for the first time and smiled shyly.

'I have come for some urgent work,' Harimohan lied. 'Actually, we are going to build a pucca house soon.'

'Won't you come for my wedding?' Saraju enquired. 'I won't take "no" for an answer. Come for a couple of days at least.'

'Horey, please carry on your conversation,' Saraju's mother Subodhbala said apologetically. 'It's time for my tulsi puja.'

Left alone with Saraju, Harimohan now looked straight into her eyes.

'Are you happy about this marriage?' he asked directly. 'Don't we all know he's a drunkard?'

'I may be able to change his habits. But do I have a choice?' Saraju asked looking up at him. 'Who will marry a girl like me without demanding a fat dowry? My father is left with nothing. The fields that he had mortgaged to the zamindar for my sister's wedding have now been taken over to pay his debts. My so-called drunkard fiancé has even offered to feed the whole village on our behalf. Naturally, Baba refused, for if he doesn't pay for that obligation, there won't be any respect left for the family!'

'Saraju, you know how beautiful you are. Don't you realise that the man is taking advantage of your poverty and youth to satisfy his lust?'

'Well, so be it,' Saraju retorted, disappointing him. 'Does anyone ever do anything in the world without a selfish motive? At least his selfishness will do a world of good to my family, besides restoring my honour.'

Soon Saraju's parents joined them and Harimohan was given a plate full of sweets. Before leaving, Saraju made him promise that he would attend her wedding. When he left, Kedarnath walked with him up to Harimohan's grandfather's house.

Harimohan spent the whole evening with his grandparents. Aggravated by the failure of the monsoons, the second time in a row, many villagers were moving to the nearby towns in search of jobs. Oddly, what was a source of misery to the villagers was becoming a boon to the townsmen as labour was becoming cheaper by the day. But the villagers' misery had quite the opposite effect on Harimohan's mind—it increased his resolve to stand by his people and uplift them.

The Cockerells were pleasantly surprised by Harimohan's early return. Knowing about the motive behind their son's visit to Seiya, Horace and Julia had feared the worst.

'How did your interview go, son?' Horace asked jokingly.

'Along totally unexpected lines,' Harimohan confirmed. 'Well, the fact is that Saraju is willing to marry the drunkard because she says there's no choice. I'm glad to admit that I'm a little less selfish than before and have learnt to be more useful to others. I gave her father two hundred rupees out of my pocket money. This, I hope, will remove the last obstacle to the marriage and help him to save face by feeding the whole village. But I asked him never to tell Saraju about my gift.

'Good,' Horace said approvingly. 'I'm very proud of you, my dear son!'

Three days before the wedding, Harimohan sent Saraju a beautiful *Benarasi* sari. Saraju became annoyed on seeing Dhonu alone. But Dhonu explained that Harimohan was unable to come because his annual exams were just a fortnight away. Seeing her gift, she broke out into silent sobs, burying her face in the sari. Later she reassured Dhonu that she would wear it for her wedding.

5

Indraneel

The years 1882 to 1884 brought many changes in Gourmohan's life. His father died before the auspicious occasion of Sri Panchami, when the much-publicised *grihapravesh* of his imposing two-storied mansion in Seiya was to be held. His new family abode was meant to establish his economic clout over the region. Having bought hundreds of acres of land for a song from the poor villagers during the recent famine, he had far surpassed the financial status of the zamindar and had established himself unchallenged over the area. Simultaneously, Gourmohan's new-found wealth was improving his standing in Calcutta's elite society.

Beginning cautiously, Gourmohan had soon become a small, innocuous moneylender, advancing his money against movable properties. Encouraged by his success in earning quick profits, he realised that big business lay only in hypothecating immovable properties such as houses, office buildings or industries. Not willing to set off alone on such an ambitious venture, he discreetly joined hands with a wealthy Englishman and a Marwari businessman. Thus, the Bengal Urban Bank Limited, a joint-stock company of limited liabilities, came into existence. The bank advanced working capitals, bridge-loans and long-term loans to big traders, merchants and foreign entrepreneurs.

As a result, within hardly two years, the bank's juniormost partner was able to make several hundred thousand rupees, besides acquiring two imposing houses in Baghbazar and Bhowanipore. After renaming the prim, south-facing, three-storied mansion in Baghbazar as *Datta Kuthi*, Gourmohan moved in with his two sons and their families. His eldest son, Gopimohan, began looking after the affairs of the Bengal Urban Bank as one of its accountants. Madanmohan had become the administrator of the two new branches of the sweet shops. But the main shop at Baghbazar, renovated and widened, was still devotedly run by Gourmohan himself. It had acquired the undoubted status of the largest sweet shop in Calcutta and proudly boasted of the highest sales.

Harimohan was the only member of the family who had so far remained aloof from his family's prosperity. He had completed his entrance examination and obtained his first degree from the Presidency College. At nineteen, he began studying for his degree in law. He was a handsome, eligible young man for whom his father never tired of bringing marriage proposals. But Harimohan repeatedly refused to tie the knot.

~

The sequel to Saraju's marriage had proceeded entirely along expected lines, for such was the boon of his lovely wife's company that the unshaven and unkempt Nepal Gupta was transformed overnight. He put on clean clothes and shaved regularly once a week like other villagers. Initially, Saraju's care did relieve Nepal of his alcoholism, for he did not even touch or contemplate a drink for more than three years. But no sooner had she gone back to her parents' house following her pregnancy than he inevitably gave in to the temptation to drink. The desire had no doubt been spurred by his unbearable loneliness, which seemed ten times worse than before marriage. Sadly, his second affair with the bottle cost him his life.

When Dhonu informed his friend about Nepal's demise, Harimohan instantly decided to break his four-year spell of abstention and pay Saraju a visit in the village. The call would also enable him to see their new house—something that his father had been insisting on for a long time.

When Harimohan arrived at Kedarnath's hut, he was amazed to find Saraju alone. Saraju, wearing all white, did not seem surprised by Harimohan's visit. And, strangely, she did not attempt to hide the bulge of her abdomen.

'I'm sorry to learn about your husband's death,' Harimohan began, 'please accept my condolences.'

'Aren't you happy that everything is happening according to your prediction? I know you didn't come to my wedding because you were angry with me.'

'No. I abstained from attending your wedding because of my own limitations.'

Saraju understood Harimohan's point. 'And what is going to be the fate of my baby? I have a feeling it's going to be a boy.'

'Ah, I think the same too. What name will you give him? How about the name Indraneel? Indraneel Gupta, sounds very nice. But Saraju, wouldn't you like to speak to me about your husband?'

Saraju hesitated for a while and then said evasively, 'He was a good and kind man. He loved me more than anything else in the world.'

'I don't doubt that. What interests me Saraju is how much *you* loved him.'

'I thought you were clever enough to find out.'

'What do you mean? How much do I really know about your personal life?'

'You men are very stupid. Don't you understand that he was no more than a father to me? Or else, how can a girl of fifteen love a man of forty-two?'

'And can life really be intimate under such conditions?'

'Well, I don't think that he ever found out the truth. You rich guys only study external things and aren't taught to look within!' she remarked ruefully. 'When will you discover the world of feelings and sentiments lurking in your heart? Search carefully and you'll know the truth.'

On a misty morning in late *Poush*, Saraju gave birth to a boy. He was named Indraneel, meaning sapphire. Kedarnath knew the basics of astrology and customarily cast the child's birth chart. He was stunned when he read it. The boy would be a renegade who would not only bring tragedy upon himself but cause anxiety to all those around him. But the strangest thing was that in spite of such a negative preamble, the boy would earn extraordinary fame.

When Harimohan came for the first time to see Saraju's son, he gave the child a beautiful diamond ring that created a flutter in the village. Saraju seemed transformed after childbirth and looked radiantly beautiful. As the child kept staring at him with big wondrous eyes, smiling and gurgling occasionally, Harimohan felt a strange sense of pride and fulfilment. The boy was very special, he thought, and seemed attached to him. That day, Saraju made Harimohan promise two things. First, that he, as she had no brother, would perform Indraneel's *annaprashan*. But Saraju's second request surprised Harimohan even more.

'I want you to initiate him,' she said, 'for his *hateykhori* too.' During this ritual, an elder helps to draw a letter of the alphabet on a slate by taking the hand of the child, in which a piece of chalk is held. Naturally, Harimohan gave his consent to both requests.

'What name have you given the boy, Saraju?' he asked casually before leaving.

'Indraneel,' she whispered. 'I told nobody that you had suggested it.'

6

An Awakening

The news that appeared in the Calcutta papers was unusual but not totally unexpected. The *Hindoo Patriot* announced that Sir Augustus Rivers Thompson, the lieutenant governor of Bengal, had not been in good health and may take leave for a month and proceed to Ceylon for the benefit of the sea air. Therefore, the question was who would Sir Rivers' successor be during his absence and a mood of happy expectancy filled the air in the government circles. Horace Cockerell seemed the natural choice. Even a conservative daily such as the *Englishman* enthused: 'We would be glad to see the office made pucca for him.' Horace proceeded to the summer capital of Darjeeling and decided to stay in his own bungalow instead of the official residence of the governor.

During his father's brief tenure in office, Harimohan paid him a visit in Darjeeling. He had, on several occasions, visited him at the Writers' Buildings but all that he had seen earlier stood in no comparison with his new status. The workload, the urgency, the bustling crowd and the security were far greater than before.

One evening, while Horace, Julia and Harimohan were leisurely having a cup of tea in the sprawling living room, a valet brought in a visiting card that surprised everyone. Horace immediately had the visitor brought in.

'Good evening, Mr Governor,' the visitor said taking off his hat and bowing graciously. 'I happened to be in town and couldn't resist the temptation of dropping in. Am I intruding in any way?'

'Good evening, Doctor, what a pleasant surprise!' said Horace, warmly shaking his hand. 'Please make yourself at home.'

'First of all, please accept my sincerest congratulations for the governorship,' said Dr Krishna Dhone Ghose. Then turning towards Mrs Cockerell he said, 'How are you, Julia?'

'Tell me, Doctor,' Horace asked, 'I suppose you are staying in a hotel here. Shall I have your belongings brought? You can stay in our guest room.'

After giving instructions to the chief of the guards to have the doctor's belongings brought from the hotel, the governor leaned back in his sofa and lit a cigar.

'Well, your foster son reminds me so much of my own children,' Dr Ghose spoke nostalgically looking at Harimohan. 'It's been a long time since I last saw them. How old are you, son?'

'I'm twenty-one,' Harimohan replied.

'Well, Beno must be eighteen, Mano sixteen and Auro thirteen. But I think my fate is sealed. Owing to my wife's incurable insanity, I'm not even allowed to visit my only daughter and my youngest son who live with their mother in Rohini. I wanted so much to bring them back with me to Khulna the last time I was with them. But my wife firmly rejected my plea to let them go to school!'

'By the way Doctor,' Horace interrupted, 'which is your favourite son?'

'Auro, the third one,' the doctor replied at once. 'You'll see, my friend, he'll become the greatest administrator after studying ICS. I want Auro to be an able administrator like you, Horace,' he sincerely added, 'and, if possible, someone as humble and upright, too. But my friend, I'm a thoroughly disillusioned man now. At one time I admired everything that was British. Now, I'm sorry to say I no longer wish my children to ape the Englishman. Above all, I want them to become true Indians in their heart and soul. I can't take the atrocities committed on my countrymen any more. You'll please pardon me for being so blunt, but I know you're my friend and will understand my point.'

'But Doctor,' Julia Cockerell interrupted sympathetically, 'don't you understand that the Indians must take from the British what is their rightful due but reject the alien government ultimately with all its might?'

'Can such a thing ever happen? The Indians are too weak to protest or retaliate.'

'That's where the question of responsible leadership must come in,' Horace intervened. 'Why don't you inculcate the spirit of self-determination in your sons, Doctor? They would then have the clear advantage of possessing an analytical Western mind fitted with an Indian spirit.'

'You may be right. But among my three sons, it's only Auro who can do what you ask. I'll do whatever I can to apprise him of the realities.'

'I don't have the slightest doubt that India has to be free to forge ahead. And I'm convinced that India alone can choose its own destiny.'

During Horace's governorship, the council for making laws and regulations assembled for a routine sitting. After the meeting, the governor, who was president of the council, invited his councillors to an open-air tea party in the tidy English garden in front of his bungalow. Fortunately, the weather had cleared that afternoon. As everyone stepped out into the garden, the imposing beauty of the Kanchenjunga could not be ignored. Its peaks glowed, caressed by the golden rays of the setting sun. The air had a mystic tranquillity. Like little children, the men gaped at this impressive sight. Horace remembered an evening he had spent seven years earlier with an Indian poet singing about the divinity of his country. As the sun set, the mood changed and the guests got down to talking.

After Horace, it was Anthony Patrick MacDonnell who was the man to watch out for. He had a promising career ahead of him. He now chatted with the other five English councillors—Reynolds, Macaulay, Garrett, Irving and Colonel Trevor.

The five Indian princes, brightly attired and exuding a dignified air, stood out as they sipped their tea. Some of them wore aristocratic turbans with feathers and the colourful velvet of their princely costumes glistened under their expensive shawls. Two of the princes carried long swords, which nearly touched the traditional upturned shoes that completed their official regalia. Kumar Boykantonath De, Abdul Jabbar and Rai Joy Prakash Lall Bahadoor were the senior members of the council while Ban Behari Kapoor and G C Paul were the new entrants. Soon the governor went across to the Indian circle, and after the usual familiar exchanges, he brought up his meeting with Bankim Chandra Chatterjee and how much he had valued the opportunity of knowing him.

'Why do you say "opportunity" Your Honour? After all he's only an ordinary magistrate,' Kumar Boykantonath said.

'Haven't you read his novels? Well, let me assure you that Bankim Babu is one of the finest writers of today's generation. I've little doubt that he is among the world's greatest authors. *Ananda Math* is his best work.'

The Indians remained speechless with astonishment.

'I have read *Ananda Math*,' said the Rai Bahadoor, putting his right hand across his sword. 'I was struck by the personification of the country as one's real mother.'

Horace looked pleased. He did not know of any other country that had such a wonderful surviving cultural heritage as India. If it were to grow and prosper truly it was logical that it should be ruled by Indians.

'Forgive me for asking you this, Rai Bahadoor,' said Horace. 'What would you have done if your own mother was chained and then imprisoned?'

'Why, I would free her, of course.'

'And how would you react if your own motherland were conquered? Isn't it important then to set it free from the shackles of enslavement?'

The Rai Bahadoor's embarrassment was almost palpable. The other faces turned pink with shame. They felt scandalised and started fidgeting and glancing at the other Englishmen to see if they had overheard Horace. As the Indians retreated into their shells, Horace seemed jolted by this unexpected exchange. He was surprised by the fact that the five councillors who bragged of distinguished lineage and impeccable education lacked in individuality. If this was the mentality of the upper class, Horace shuddered to imagine the state of the illiterate majority. A reawakening was needed and that would possibly require all the strength of a mighty superman.

Horace spent a sleepless night, thinking about the destiny of this mysterious country. He sat at the window watching the moon-bathed Kanchenjunga dominating the vast expanse of the Lebong Valley. But slowly it faded into a haze as if reflecting his disillusionment. He felt a pain as of something snapping and realised that this was to be his farewell night. His long courtship with India was coming to an abrupt end.

7

London and Back

As Harimohan had completed his degree one year before Horace retired, his foster parents decided to send him alone to England. They arranged for his stay with a friend and fellow civilian of the Bengal cadre, Ross Lowis Mangles, who had taken early retirement. With Mangles' help, the twenty-two-year-old Harimohan got himself admitted at London's Gray's Inn, one of the four famous Inns of Court, where Francis Bacon had studied and obtained his degree.

Familiarity with the English way of life and his mastery of the language allowed Harimohan to mix freely with his classmates who were, without exception, all British. However, he began to feel homesick within a couple of months, even though neither the food nor the extreme cold bothered him much. What he missed most was someone to speak to him in his mother tongue. One day he suddenly remembered that Dr Ghose's children were also in London. The doctor had, in fact, mentioned the name of their school, but it was eluding him. About a month later, while taking part in a cortege following the death of a relative of the Mangles, a happy coincidence fulfilled his desire. As the funeral procession was passing through Lillie Road on its way to the Brompton Cemetery,

Harimohan's eyes accidentally fell on the imposing building on the right with its name 'St. Paul's School' displayed prominently. In a flash, he recollected the name that had slipped his mind. After the burial, he walked back to ask the old gatekeeper of the majestic four-storied building whether two Indian brothers studied there.

The next evening, Harimohan apprised the members of the Mangles family of his meeting with Dr Ghose's second and third sons. Although the Mangles had not met Dr Ghose, they knew about him through friends in Calcutta and were aware of his special friendship with the Cockerells.

'I bunked my afternoon session at the Inn,' Harimohan explained jocularly, 'and met the two boys who were among the first to emerge after the day was over. "Excuse me," I addressed the older one, Manomohan, and asked, "Aren't you Dr Ghose's son?" Manomohan instantly became tense and said, "Yes, but who are you?" he asked sceptically. "I'm Harimohan Datta. Do you remember our meeting at Barrister Mano Mohun Ghose's house on Theatre Road, in Calcutta? That was in 1879, I think, just days before you sailed for England. Your father was there too."

'"Pardon me for not remembering the meeting," Manomohan answered. "But yes, indeed, we arrived here in 1879. By the way, I'm Manomohan and this is my brother, Aurobindo," he added, extending his hand. Manomohan explained that they lived in Shepherd's Bush in the western district.

'"Would you like to eat something, my friends?" I enquired in Bengali, obviously hinting at the roasted chestnuts that were being sold in front of the park.

'"Thanks," Mano replied in English. "We wouldn't mind eating, but let's speak in English. You see my Bengali has never been too good. And Auro can't even speak a word of it. Our father was very particular about making us speak in English at home. We were however, allowed to speak in Hindi with the servants."

'He said they walked the entire distance of about two-and-a-half miles back and forth to school. Besides, their clothes also looked quite old and worn out. Then I furtively glanced at their old school bags and unpolished shoes which sadly confirmed my fears. I then turned my attention curiously towards Aurobindo.

'"How are you Aurobindo?" I asked politely. "I suppose you don't remember me?"

'"Yes, I do," Aurobindo replied sweetly. "Your parents are English and your mother is a friend of Mrs Beveridge who lives in Rangpur."

'Now, isn't that incredible? 'How can a seven-year-old note so many details?' Harimohan enquired of the Mangles. 'But then Aurobindo had added calmly, "Besides, as I was very short then, I think you had knelt down to take a closer look at me." That left me stunned. I didn't recollect much about that summer morning except precisely those two things—first, that I had gone to the barrister's house accompanied by my parents and next, that I had actually knelt down to take a closer look at the little Aurobindo.'

'Yes, indeed. The boy surely has a phenomenal memory,' Ross Mangles proclaimed.

'Following our conversation, another interesting development took place,' Harimohan added excitedly. 'It seems that the three Ghose brothers are planning an excursion during the summer vacation, and Manomohan even asked me if I would also like to join them.'

'Of course, Hurry,' Mangles approved smilingly. 'You must go by all means.'

Earlier, during their stay in Manchester, the three brothers had practically no contact with other Indians. Not only had Dr Ghose issued strict instructions to Reverend Drewett, in whose house the children were staying, to dissuade any Indian trying to contact his sons, but they were also not supposed to know anything about the Indian way of life. Understandably, therefore, Harimohan's arrival in their midst assumed a very great significance. In terms of age, Benoybhushan was the closest to him and they became good friends. And in spite of his cavalier temperament, Manomohan was quick to respond to Harimohan's friendship. But undeniably, it was to the young enigmatic Aurobindo that Harimohan was attracted the most. There was something so lovable yet so distant in his nature that Harimohan did not know how to cope with it. Slowly, things began to take shape during their long excursion and the three brothers started looking upon Harimohan as an elder brother.

The four youngsters spent three memorable weeks sightseeing in Keswick. They visited Borrowdale, the Honnister Pass, Buttermere and Newland's Vale. Then Manomohan and Aurobindo attempted to reach the long Windermere Lake. But the beautiful lake was not once visible owing to an obstinate and unrelenting mist. At long last, the weather cleared and they all went over to a small picturesque lake called Thirlmere and came back home, eating a tremendous tea, getting through two considerable loaves.

The next day they went to one of the loveliest places in the Lake District. They walked along Lake Derwentwater and then up the Barrow woods, a steep hill climb into Watendlath. Then they came back very leisurely by the Barrow woods.

The brothers made their new friend vow to meet them often in London. Harimohan began visiting them almost every weekend at their residence at Shepherd's Bush. Mrs Drewett, Reverend Drewett's mother, who had taken charge of the children, was openly sceptical about Harimohan's weekly presence in their house. However, Harimohan did not have to interact with the old lady for too long as something happened that brought a welcome change in the lives of the brothers.

After Reverend Drewett left for Australia leaving the children in the care of his pious mother, the three brothers had to participate in nightly prayers, as the old lady was a devoted Christian. Often, passages from the Bible would be read. One day, as the name of Moses came up for review, Manomohan vehemently opposed any glorification and iterated that Old Moses was well served when the people disobeyed him! And as expected, the old lady was so shaken by the blasphemy that she concluded that living under the same roof with such unworthy heretics would incur the wrath of God, causing the house to fall down! To the great relief of the brothers, she ultimately went away to live elsewhere. After this, the Ghoses lived apart, attending different schools.

The headmaster of St. Paul's School personally examined Aurobindo before admitting him. Aurobindo's proficiency in Latin and other subjects satisfied him but he found his Greek to be weak. Evincing interest in the boy, Dr Walker took him in his special coaching classes where, as a practice, he gathered all promising students who were weak in particular subjects. He seemed to have an eye for a clever student and never lost sight of one once he found him.

Harimohan moved in with the Cockerells when they returned to England in 1887. The Cockerells lived at Beaufort Gardens, adjoining Beauchamp Place, midway between Knightsbridge and

Chelsea. Harimohan's shifting coincided with Aurobindo's and Benoybhushan's moving to Cromwell Road, in the south-west district of London. Fortunately, Cromwell Road lay barely a mile to the west of Beaufort Gardens, allowing him to pay regular visits to his friends.

A year later, Harimohan was called to the Bar. This was a proud moment for the Cockerells. Harimohan would have liked to return to India after the end of his studies but he could not abandon his parents and return home so suddenly. His parents were both old and their attachment to him was evident.

Having rid himself of his moustache and grown remarkably fairer from being away from the tropical sun, Harimohan looked extremely handsome. It was an open secret that Ross Mangles' daughters, Martha and Cynthia, vied with each other for Harimohan's attention. After sitting idle for well over a year, an unforeseeable incident suddenly opened up his passage to India.

Julia's niece, Elisa, who lived in the neighbourhood, was a regular caller at their house. Although married, Elisa had a crush on Harimohan. As Julia had reason to believe that on his part Harimohan was uninvolved, she took the matter to her husband.

'Don't you realise that Hurry is held up here just because of us?' Horace asked, fondly holding her hands. 'He is unable to leave because he doesn't want to hurt our feelings after all that we've done for him. Look, darling, Hurry's twenty-five now. Isn't it our duty to send him back?'

Among his last engagements in London, Harimohan attended the two sessions of the Pauline Literary Society where Aurobindo, a member who took an active interest, spoke on the inconsistency of Swift's political opinions and on Milton. Lacking the domineering voice of some of the earlier speakers, Aurobindo's soft and musical utterance strangely carried forth through the auditorium with a unique resonance.

While returning home, following Aurobindo's last speech at the Pauline Literary Society, Harimohan and his younger friend stopped at a café on Earls Court Road, at the corner of Hogarth Road. Harimohan told him how proud his father would have been to hear him speak from the podium.

'Well, talking of my father,' Aurobindo said suddenly, 'I feel a very big change has come about in him. Earlier, everything British pleased him. Now I find traces of clear disillusionment in his letters. I suppose, it's his aim to awaken in me a consciousness of revolt. But paradoxically, while influencing my mind negatively, he expects me to appear for the ICS exam and be part of the very British administration that he loathes!'

After this meeting Harimohan went to Aurobindo's lodging only once to bid him farewell before sailing back to India. He carried back a letter from Aurobindo to his father at Khulna, which he promised to deliver in person, as Horace had also given him a letter for Dr Ghose.

The penultimate day of Harimohan's stay in England was undoubtedly the saddest one. He had already bought his mother an intricately embroidered shawl in maroon, her favourite colour. Harimohan had also bought for his father a magnificent leather-bound copy of the original publication of the *Voyages aux Indes orientales et à la Chine* by the French savant, Pierre Sonnerat, published from Paris, which he knew his father had desperately searched for but failed to procure.

'Mother … Father, may I come in?' he asked politely. 'I don't know how to thank you both for all the good things that you have given me through these past ten years. Although I understand that it is now that you need me most and however much I would like to be useful to you, I feel that my countrymen need my services more. Please pardon me for being so selfish.' He then handed them their presents.

With a heavy heart, the old couple began opening their gifts. Horace was the first to succeed.

'Hari, you're a genius!' he exclaimed joyfully. 'Where on earth did you find this book?'

Then noticing that his mother was still struggling to open her gift, Harimohan quickly helped her out. And even before she had held the shawl open, he spread it out with a flourish and put it round her shoulders.

'Oh my God, how extraordinarily beautiful!' she acknowledged. 'My child,' she said hugging him tightly, 'I don't think we could ever have been so proud of our own offspring.'

'It's not as if Hurry's disappearing from our lives forever,' her husband lovingly pacified her. 'I'm sure he'll visit us from time to time. Thanks for everything, my son. We also have something special for you,' and he gave him a neat bunch of papers folded length-wise at the middle. To Harimohan's trained eyes, they meant a deed of conveyance.

8

Hurry Mohun Dutt & Co.

After alighting at Princep Ghat, Harimohan realised that it would take a long time to shake off the images of affluence of England from his memory. Within a week of his arrival he met Barrister Mano Mohun Ghose at his chamber at the Ballards Building. Harimohan handed him the deed.

'You've guessed it right, my son,' Horace had said while offering the document. 'This is the deed of conveyance of our house in Rawdon Street. It's our wish that you enjoy living in it just as you did while we were there. We have left the trusted Haripriya in charge of the house and the gatekeeper and the coachman are there as well. Please meet my friend Mano Mohun Ghose and have the deed registered as soon as you can.'

The conveyance was duly registered and the deed handed over to him. Shortly afterwards, he set out to register his own firm, 'Hurry Mohun Dutt & Co.'. Then after inserting an advertisement for office space in several dailies, he bought the premises at the Temple Chambers from an old English barrister who was sailing back to Britain. At a time when there was only a handful of Indian barristers in the country, Harimohan had little difficulty in getting Indian customers, among whom his biological father was undoubtedly the wealthiest and the most reputable. Slowly, Englishmen of lesser munificence also began visiting him for counselling. It was, above all, Harimohan's sense of fair play that endeared him to his clients. Often he acted as an arbitrator and after summoning his client and the opposite party, was able to iron out their differences. Harimohan got his fees, but at least he was able to save his clients the agonies of long delays. Sometimes, being impressed by Harimohan's honesty, some opposite parties also signed him up for their other lawsuits.

Indraneel had just turned eight when Harimohan met him at Seiya. Even though Indraneel had no recollection of the unknown man, he sweetly smiled before repeating the name 'Hari-mama', after his mother.

'Indraneel needs proper education,' Harimohan told Saraju. 'Don't you realise how intelligent he is? Allow me to take him to Calcutta.'

'But how can I think of leaving the village when my father is paralysed?'

'I've an offer. I shall take charge of Indraneel and take him to Calcutta if …'

'Are you mad?' Saraju remonstrated angrily.

'I haven't finished yet Saraju,' Harimohan continued coolly as he addressed Saraju's mother. 'Henceforth, Mashima, you'll work in our kitchen and also take care of my old grandmother. As you're a Brahmin, I don't think there should be any problem. I shall also arrange that whatever food you cook can be brought home to feed the three of you. So besides earning ten rupees a month, you'll also bring home food twice a day …'

'Ten rupees a month!' exclaimed Saraju's father, Kedarnath. So far he had been lying like a corpse on one side of the hut. 'Get some sweets for Horey.'

'But wait,' Harimohan warned, 'my proposition stands only if Indraneel is allowed to travel with me to Calcutta.'

'This is blackmail! I don't want to live away from my child!'

'Let me see. All of you can live in our outhouse. That way you'll enjoy the goodness of a pucca house and there will be no more leakage during the July rains.'

Suddenly, Kedarnath drew everyone's attention by mumbling something loudly.

'He's a renegade,' he muttered, 'who will bring tragedy upon himself and cause anxiety to others.' Then his voice became clearer and he added, 'But somehow the boy will attain fame!'

The others only heard the last sentence due to its clarity. As Kedarnath was widely respected for his astrological predictions, even Saraju suddenly felt elated on learning that her son would become eminent.

'Yes, and for that he needs a good education,' Harimohan asserted quickly. 'I'm sure he'll not lack anything in the city. Saraju, you have my word that he'll be well looked after and he'll come to meet you during his vacations.'

At nine, Indraneel was five years younger than Harimohan was when he left home to join his foster parents. But he looked just as happy and excited as Harimohan was at the prospect of his new life in Calcutta. On his part, Harimohan would have been happier had Saraju come along with her son but he dared not make such a proposition. The child had to be saved first; other things could wait for a suitable opportunity.

Gourmohan was very happy with the arrangement at Seiya and thanked Harimohan for his thoughtfulness. The prosperous Gourmohan now had reached another important milestone. The newly established Hurry Mohun Dutt & Co. had added a new status of honour and respectability to his affluence. But to his consternation, Harimohan continued to oppose all proposals of marriage and lived independently at Rawdon Street.

So sensing that something must be seriously wrong, the wily Gourmohan sent for Dhonu.

'Dhonu,' he began glibly, 'I must ask you for a personal favour. You have to convince your friend to marry or a terrific offer from the Ghose family of Jorabagan will expire like many others before it.'

'Jetha Babu,' Dhonu apologised, 'I think you may be wasting your time.'

'Why? Is something the matter with Horey?'

'The fact is ...,' he paused before blurting out, 'Horey loves Kedar Banujje's daughter.'

'What! the widow of that drunkard? But she's a Brahmin and ... Hmm, I am beginning to understand that sudden decision to employ her and her mother at home. Yes, yes, I see it as clearly as daylight. But why should someone so qualified as Horey have a crush on a village girl?'

Suddenly Gourmohan felt helpless. Kedarnath's wife and daughter were clearly taking advantage of his son's weakness. Through cunning and deceit they had also thrust the widow's son on his foolish boy.

'Give me your solemn word not to tell anybody about this conversation,' Gourmohan told Dhonu before dismissing him.

But now the question was how to proceed? Already Gourmohan's scheming mind was racing ahead. Nepal's young widow was ominously standing in the way of a hundred thousand rupees that had been promised by the Ghoses as dowry for Harimohan. He badly needed the money to pay back a part of the substantial loan that he had drawn from his own bank under the false name of his trusted henchman Panchanan Barat. He had been compelled to draw the money to buy a house in Bowbazar for his beloved Motimala when she threatened to take a rich merchant of Burrabazar as her new lover. He knew that although he had momentarily succeeded in stemming the rot, his own finances were in a state of utter disarray. And if something was not done immediately to pay back the loan, his end would be no different from the bank's customers. Besides, the casualty would be his much-vaunted house at Bhowanipore, which was mortgaged to his own financing institution. But Gourmohan dreaded a far worse consequence that would inevitably follow. The Bhowanipore property stood in Gopimohan's name and he had forged his signature to hypothecate it, knowing well that his elder son would never have allowed it to be pledged. Therefore, should the house actually be attached, he would have to face a serious revolt from his own family. And all this for the sake of a concubine!

Harimohan would have to be kept away from the city for at least a week in order to execute his plan. It did not take much time for the old fox to find a practical way. He had recently purchased a big garden house in Jessore in East Bengal, the acquisition of which had posed some legal wrangling. If Gourmohan could send Harimohan to Jessore, the possession of the property could be taken with the help of the police and the local court and he could buy sufficient time to execute his second and critical plan during Harimohan's absence from Calcutta. That way he could dextrously kill two birds with the same stone.

The next morning, as the high court rose to transact business, Gourmohan's imposing carriage turned around the corner of the Old Post Office Street. Panchanan Barat, his trusted henchman, quickly stepped out and helped the greying Gourmohan out of the carriage. As he descended, he looked up with admiration at the imposing high court looming majestically over his left. Gourmohan began climbing the imposing stairway of the Temple Chambers with visible difficulty.

'Baba, what brings you here so unexpectedly?' Harimohan enquired with some concern as Gourmohan entered his office. 'I was going out to court. I have an important case coming up.'

Gourmohan quickly briefed his son about the Jessore property muddle. 'I suppose, the execution order will have to be first ratified by the local court and served by its bailiff on the respondents. My impression is that you're the best man to handle it.'

'Me? But I can't leave Calcutta now.'

'Of course you can. Wouldn't a short holiday be a welcome relief after six months of gruelling work? I'm ready to finance it fully. Here's five hundred rupees for your expenses,' Gourmohan said haughtily. 'You'll get your fees and whatever other expenses you incur on your return.'

Harimohan consented to undertake the journey purely for a selfish motive. He knew that Jessore was hardly a day's journey away to the north-west of Khulna where Dr Ghose lived. Ironically, his own desire to kill two birds with a single stone spurred him to accept his father's engagement. Being ignorant of Harimohan's other interest, Gourmohan was surprised by the relative ease with which his son took up the assignment. But now, the second and the more critical phase remained to be executed.

At Jessore, Harimohan took only three days to complete his business. The widow's tenants panicked in the presence of a big police force led by a British sergeant and quit without resistance on receiving the court's attachment order.

It was not difficult for Harimohan to find Dr Ghose's residence as everyone in Khulna knew him. Harimohan was received by the doctor's daughter.

'I'm sorry, but Baba will not be back before noon,' Sarojini informed curtly, her thin lips remaining straight without a smile. But mercifully, she spoke fluent Bengali. 'We're here on a short holiday,' she explained. 'Usually, Baba visits us a couple of times each month.'

'Do you mean to say that your father pays visits to Calcutta every fortnight and I have come this long way to meet him just for nothing?'

On realising his faux pas, Harimohan felt a pang of remorse for taking such a hasty decision to come to Khulna. For the first time he realised that his junior could easily have handled his father's case. He wondered why his father was keen to pay so much money when the entire thing could have been settled for one-tenth of the price.

At this point a benign, bearded man walked in looking questioningly at Harimohan. Harimohan quickly got up to greet Dr Ghose. He looked so different now in his flowing beard.

'How are you, Sir?' Harimohan asked, fully enjoying the doctor's firm grip. 'I'm Harimohan Datta. We met in Darjeeling during my father's governorship.'

'Oh, I see. So you're Horace and Julia's adopted child. Yes, yes, I remember now. And how are my dear friends, I mean your foster parents?'

'Well, Father is all right. But Mother is slightly unwell. However, here is a letter from your friends and here is another from Aurobindo.'

'Oh, so you were also in touch with my children in England! Isn't that wonderful?' the doctor remarked while tearing open his favourite son's letter first.

'It's wonderful to receive Auro's letters. I always wonder how he writes so well!' But just then someone called him from outside.

'Bring him here,' Dr Ghose called out to his servant and went in quickly to get his stethoscope. 'What's the matter, Janardhan?'

'My son's body is burning with very high fever, Doctor, and he's shivering.'

'Hmm,' Dr Ghose said worriedly. 'He's got acute malaria. He has to be given quinine immediately. Here take this prescription. Get the medicine immediately!'

Janardhan howled in despair.

'Where shall I get the money to pay for the medicine? We don't even have food for tomorrow.'

'Ah, what misery!' Dr Ghose muttered desperately. 'All right, all right,' he sympathised. 'Here's some money. Take it and go back home quickly.'

Janardhan touched Dr Ghose's feet in veneration.

'If such poor patients keep calling constantly,' Dr Ghose resumed, strangely echoing Harimohan's thoughts, 'what will happen to my own children studying in England? But how can I watch this godforsaken race die miserably before my eyes while these Britishers busily carry everything out of the country to get richer? I sincerely hope that Beno, Mano and Auro think rightly of me …!'

'Sir,' Harimohan interrupted Dr Ghose, 'you have the fullest support of your worthy sons in your mission to uplift the poor. To them you're nothing less than a demigod. How many times I've heard Mano repeat that with pride.'

'My God! I always feared, you know, that they would misunderstand me. Ah, I'm a happy man now,' said Dr Ghose and brightening up considerably.

Harimohan then narrated to him the comical event that ultimately led to old Mrs Drewett giving up their charge, fearing blasphemy and sacrilege. Amused by the incident, Dr Ghose laughed aloud delightedly. Just then the valet came to announce that the zamindar's mother's condition had deteriorated and that his carriage was waiting to take the doctor to his mansion.

'Harimohan, would you like to come with me?' Dr Ghose asked. 'You'll be bored here.'

As Harimohan passed through the town with Dr Ghose, he got to know about the latter's immense popularity. On both sides of the road, people bowed graciously as soon as they recognised him. And, in turn, the doctor lovingly responded by repeatedly taking off his hat. Dr Ghose completed his professional duty within a matter of half-an-hour. The old lady was suffering from acute asthma and fell blissfully asleep. The grateful zamindar himself came to the door to see them off.

The weather had changed by evening. A cool moist breeze was blowing, carrying the smell of humid earth. After dinner, when the children had retired to sleep, the valet came in hurriedly to announce that Rahim *gowala* wished to meet the doctor. A frenzied man ran in yelling that a snake had bitten his child.

'Did anyone see the snake?' asked Dr Ghose. 'No? All right let's go,' he said firmly, asking for his umbrella.

As the two men stepped out into the rain, it began pouring very hard. But unmindful of the physical discomfort, Dr Ghose thoughtfully pulled in the milkman under his umbrella, while Rahim took charge of his kit.

As the two figures disappeared into the darkness, Harimohan realised how Dr Ghose's reputation lived on.

9

A Theft and an Abduction

Dhonu had some shocking news to give Harimohan on his return to Calcutta.

'Horey, Saraju has disappeared!' he said lowering his voice discreetly. 'Please pardon me for any mistake that I may have unknowingly made. But the fact is that Jetha Babu called me one day and asked why you were refusing to marry. I feel ashamed of myself. I shouldn't have told him that you loved Saraju.'

'Oh! You told him that? And when did Saraju disappear?'

'Immediately after you left for Jessore. There was a big hue and cry in Seiya about the deity's crown and throne being stolen. Everybody knew that both these items were made of solid gold. Well, it seems that Mashima was given charge of the puja room, as she was a Brahmin. And the key was in her possession all the while between evening and morning. Actually it was in the early hours of the morning that she noticed that the golden crown and throne were missing. Now she's in jail.'

'What? How can there be conviction without proof?'

'What proof? Isn't it enough that the key was in her possession?' Dhonu continued with difficulty, 'Apparently, Saraju was carried off at night. No one knows who her abductors were. Later, after a long search, one of her silver anklets was found in the fields in the direction of Chinsura.'

Harimohan knew the consequences of such atrocities. Not only would her society reject and banish her forever, there would be no other alternative for her but to spend her life in a brothel. Why did he not have the courage to run away and marry her in a temple? But then something else struck him. Was it not a strange coincidence that both the abduction and the theft took place simultaneously? And, how is it that they took place precisely during his absence?

On his way to his village with Indraneel, Harimohan stopped over at Chinsura Court and moved a bail application for the release of Subodhbala who was imprisoned in the Polba Jail. The English magistrate was furious to know that an elderly lady had been detained for more than a week without his knowledge.

'Ask the officer in charge of Polba Thana to report personally at this court tomorrow,' he thundered angrily. 'I want an explanation how such high-handedness is perpetrated within my jurisdiction!'

The next morning, a visibly shaken officer came to court as summoned, bringing along Subodhbala.

'There's no need for bail, Mr Datta,' the magistrate said emphatically. 'As there has been a serious deviation of law, the prisoner is freed by this court with full apology. As for you, Mr Officer, you'll forgo a week's salary for your high-handedness and departure from legal norms.'

But the mystery of the missing crown and throne still remained. Where did they vanish? Harimohan knew that his father was in Seiya. Soon he left for his village, taking with him Subodhbala, who probably due to the presence of her grandchild in the court room was extraordinarily silent and poised throughout the proceedings. But the real commotion started as soon as she heard that her daughter had not yet been found.

'There,' she shouted, 'it's that youngest son of the Mukherjees who got her lifted. It's he who tried to molest her on numerous occasions after she was widowed!'

Harimohan instinctively knew that was impossible. His father was now the undisputed landlord of the area, feared and venerated by everyone. The Mukherjees would not dare even to lift their little finger against Gourmohan's workers. No, this was a well-organised crime perpetrated by a gang from outside Seiya.

As Harimohan's carriage entered the open square in the middle of his village, he could not help remembering his first visit there, exactly twelve years ago, in the midst of his people. Some of the old members who had received him then were present even now.

'Oh, how are you, Horey,' his father's old friend Manik Dolui enquired with affectionate care and solicitude. 'Ah! the evil that has befallen your father! How sad that Sri Lakkhinarayan's crown and throne are lost!' he exclaimed, wiping a non-existent tear from his eyes.

While walking down to his house, Harimohan slowed down near the dilapidated hut of Kedarnath. Subodhbala broke down and started sobbing uncontrollably.

'Please come in for a while, Hari,' she said dignifiedly, 'your Meshomoshay will be very pleased to see you.'

Seeing his wife and grandson, Kedarnath reacted positively.

'Dadubhai!' he mumbled with joy. 'Thank God, you're all right,' he continued speaking to his wife. 'Do you have information about Saraju?'

'Wherever she is,' Harimohan affirmed, 'I'll surely find her, Meshomoshay. That's a vow.'

Contrary to all expectations, there was no confrontation between Gourmohan and Harimohan. In fact, the father openly hailed his son's decision to get Subodhbala out of the prison.

'Yes,' he said courteously, 'in the absence of any evidence that's what the police should have done.'

Then after repeatedly scratching his belly and belching, Gourmohan pondered aloud, 'But who on earth would have the guts to steal the deity's crown and throne from my house?'

'Well, whoever that may be, I think you owe Mashima an apology. It would only be fair if you paid a just compensation.'

'How can one not suspect her when all the evidence pointed at her?'

'I want compensation for giving your tacit approval for detaining her even when no evidence was found against her! I could file a defamation case against you, you know, and subtract damages of, say, ten thousand rupees! But I think it would be best if you agreed to pay a monthly amount to the old couple, of fifteen rupees throughout their lifetime instead of such a big amount.'

'What? But that's preposterous! If they live for twenty years that would amount to three thousand six hundred rupees!'

'That's appreciably lesser than ten thousand rupees. And, besides suffering an imminent loss of prestige of having your own son fighting against you, such news would definitely make very attractive headlines in the Calcutta dailies.'

'But that's blackmail! I have already been wronged by the theft of the deity's costly crown and throne. You know how much money their replacement would cost?'

'Baba, isn't it necessary here to make a difference between a common thief and a respectable person? Kedar Banujje's wife is a person of dignity and virtue. Otherwise, why did you place the charge of the puja room in her hands? I would, therefore, suggest an additional one-time payment of twenty-five rupees for urgent repair of their hut where they must henceforth live and a month's dole in advance.'

Evidently, it was the fear of his son that drove him to accept the deal. But the seasoned businessman tried to make a gain even in defeat.

'I shall accept all that you want only on one condition that you marry before the month of *Ashar*.'

'I promise nothing. And don't change the subject. I want your solemn oath about the maintenance of the old couple. Good, I assume then from your silence that you agree on this. There's still another aspect of the unfortunate affair that we haven't touched,' said Harimohan evenly, looking at his father straight in his eyes. 'I personally don't know who the abductors of Saraju are, nor do you, I suppose?'

'My dear Horey, are you implying …? No. I don't have the vaguest idea. I can't think of anybody who would dare to abduct such a graceful young lady from my house.'

'Thanks for filing the FIR in reference to her disappearance. I shall personally take up the case and follow it up till the end at all levels. But I warn you, I shall not spare anyone, big or small, found guilty of having a hand in the affair—even if it turns out to be one of your intimate associates.'

'Calm down, my son. I assure you that the girl will be found. I've a queer feeling that wherever she is, she's all right,' Gourmohan replied firmly.

10

Saraju's Escape

Gourmohan sent for Birju Kahar, under whose custody Saraju was kept on the outskirts of Chinsura. Birju, a giant of a man with a powerful and muscular physique, was a professional tough who accepted money from the rich to do their odd jobs. The abduction of Saraju was the first evil deed that he had performed in his career. In fact, Gourmohan had chosen Birju for the job deliberately, knowing that his honesty would safeguard Saraju's dignity. He had instructed him that no harm must befall the girl.

'Birju,' Gourmohan said after carefully shutting the door and taking him inside his bedroom, 'here's your full due in advance, but you would have to do something big this time. You must get rid of that girl you abducted!'

'What are you saying? I'm extremely sorry. I refuse to do such an evil thing.'

'Look, Birju,' Gourmohan said angrily, thrusting the bag in his hand containing the money, making a loud jingle, 'if you can't do the job, then ask your deputy to do it.'

Birju knew that he had no choice but to obey Gourmohan. The landlord had once saved him from a compromising murder case in which he had been falsely implicated by a smaller landlord of Puinan with whom Birju had had a disagreement. Gourmohan had then provided the vital alibi which had saved Birju from certain conviction. Out of gratitude he owed his master whatever he was asked to do. He unwillingly gave in.

'All right, this time I shall do as you say. And as soon as I finish the job I must go to my ancestral village. I have just received a message that my old mother is unwell.'

'Do as you wish, Birju. That money will then come as a great help,' Gourmohan said with happy relief. 'Go, and don't let me down. No one must ever know about this.'

It was well past midnight when Birju returned to his desolate house where Saraju was confined. He spoke about his discussion with Gourmohan to his assistant, Dehora and showed him the money he had received. Birju decided to face Saraju alone after Dehora gave his consent to proceed along with his plan. But Saraju was in a state of shock. In fact, she had practically not slept through the past week out of fear and anxiety. And as soon as Birju opened the door she sat up with a jerk, screaming at the top of her voice in apprehension.

'Calm down, Bitiya. I've come to discuss an urgent matter,' Birju began.

He placed a lantern in the middle of the small room and sat down facing her. Somehow, Saraju found this man to be a little more reliable of the two who kept guard over her. She tried to remain calm as the man began speaking.

'I know you're an intelligent girl. Please don't be afraid and try to understand the situation.' Just then, his eyes fell on the untouched platter of food. 'Come on, didn't I assure you that you're under no threat? Then why don't you eat?'

'I'm not hungry and I want to be let out at once.'

'Listen, Bitiya, what you're asking is impossible. Someone wants you permanently out of his way, and look,' he said holding out the bag containing silver coins, 'he has given me this money to kill you.'

Saraju wanted to scream but held herself instinctively. There was something very gentle in the man's manners that seemed to reassure her.

'However, I have a different proposition to make if you want to listen and cooperate,' Birju continued. 'If you go back home as you suggested, you'll be slaughtered instantly. So don't even dream of it! The best thing for you would be to lie low until everything becomes normal again. You would have to escape to a far-off place where you wouldn't run the risk of being recognised.'

'Who wants to kill me?' Saraju asked cautiously.

'I don't have the slightest idea why this person wants you dead. All I know is that he is desperate, greedy and unscrupulous. He has no conscience at all. Right now, the best thing would be to forget the past and look only into the future.'

'And what will happen to my son?'

'He's definitely not in danger. Anyway, I can guarantee this much—nothing will happen to your son unless you make an error. Please understand that time is running out, so can we discuss the plan of escape right away?'

Saraju nodded in consent.

'Good. I have a brother who is a woodcutter and works in the forests of Assam. He stays with his family. According to my judgement, the best thing for us would be to go away to that remote jungle and lie low. See, this money,' he added, jingling it, 'can be used for your own good and to finance our journey, which is a long and arduous one. So think fast and give me your reply. We must get out of here under cover of the darkness to avoid being recognised. Your life will be threatened further with the passing of each hour.'

'All right, but what's the guarantee that I won't be harmed? And why should you do all this good to me? I mean,' she said, pointing to the pouch containing the money, 'all that could be yours without any extra trouble!'

'Can anyone ever prosper through evil? If I had wanted to gain through dishonesty and fraud, I would have been one of the richest men of the region by now. Unfortunately, there's no bigger guarantee of my honesty than my word. But has any harm come to you during the last eight days?'

'Tell me,' Saraju said brightening up visibly, 'where do we go from here?'

'We must hire a boat and sail northward to Berhampore. Then we catch a steamer and go upstream through the Ganges and the Brahmaputra to Gauhati. All that may take as long as a month. Let me give you a small piece of advice. For the sake of your own life, forget all those you love dearly. Leave them to the care of the Almighty. For, you're not likely to see them again before very long.'

'All right,' Saraju said, after deliberating carefully. 'Let's go.'

'Good, then eat your dinner fast. We may not have anything to eat for a long time. Meanwhile, I must make preparations for our journey.'

Walking through the dark and deserted fields, Birju and Saraju reached the banks of the Ganges at about three in the morning. Then they set off by boat for Berhampore, the first leg of their journey to Gauhati.

The next day Gourmohan sent for Birju but it was Dehora who answered the call.

'Birju has left for Lohardaga,' he curtly explained, squatting on the floor near the door, holding erect a long stick that he always carried. 'Your work has been done, Kartamoshay. Here's something that Birju asked me to deliver to you.'

Dehora took out a pair of gold bangles with designs in *meenay* etched on its surface that belonged to Saraju and gave them to Gourmohan.

The landlord exhaled a deep sigh while placing the ornaments unmindfully on the table beside his large bed. This was definitely not how he would have liked to settle the affair but his son's adamant attitude had forced him to take this extreme step.

'All right, you may go,' he said and Dehora left with a courteous namaskar. Gourmohan began to ponder hard. Now that the girl was out of his way, he would have to convince Harimohan to marry soon. Or else the offer from the Ghoses of Jorabagan would be lost. And with it his last chance of repaying his debt. At this point one of his servants unexpectedly came in to announce that the fisherman had brought a live carp weighing six seers from one of Gourmohan's ponds. Gourmohan rushed out excitedly to see it on the veranda.

Just then Harimohan entered his father's room. Unable to find him, Harimohan stood absent-mindedly for a while. Suddenly his eyes fell on the pair of gleaming objects on the small side table that seemed strangely familiar. As he picked up the bangles, he realised that they were Saraju's. His heart missed a beat. There was something sinister about the presence of the ornaments there. Slipping them in his pocket, Harimohan walked out of his father's room with tears gleaming in his eyes.

That night at around ten, father and son sat down for dinner. Gourmohan felt a strange tension in Harimohan and instinctively knew that something had upset him.

'By the way,' he said affectionately, 'can I see you a little later in my room?'

'Certainly, let's go right away.'

After settling in his favourite reclining chair and contentedly inhaling the aromatic smoke from his hookah Gourmohan began, 'I say, Horey, why are you so obstinate about not marrying? Are you thinking of remaining a bachelor? Give marriage a chance. Why are you so pessimistic in your outlook? Haven't you taken charge of Kedarnath's grandson? Doesn't he need a mother's love and care?'

Strangely, this was precisely the conclusion that Harimohan himself had reached the night before while tossing helplessly in his bed. What Indraneel needed was a mother, and at the time of his greatest need, Saraju had disappeared!

'Look, Horey,' his father went on smugly, 'I let you be adopted by Cockerell sahib because you were assured of the love of an alternate mother and you needed emotional support to begin a new life. Now think of this kid. He's bound to remain forever starved of his mother's love. Aren't you ignoring the boy's basic need? Aren't you being selfish when the kid's future is threatened?'

Harimohan was stunned at his father's contention. If truly Saraju was untraceable, there was no use dreaming of spending his life with her. But before he gave in he had to get to the root of the matter.

'Yes, I admit of not having seen the situation in this light,' Harimohan said, getting up and walking towards the window. He stared out at the soothing moonlit nature that seemed to comfort him.

'All right,' he said at last, 'but I need time to think it over before before giving you a final answer.'

Gourmohan was overjoyed. Without wasting any more time in Seiya, Gourmohan left the next day for Calcutta to communicate the good news to his son's would-be-in-laws.

Harimohan had to see Indraneel at Kedarnath's hut. Harimohan took Subodhbala aside and told her about the arrangements he had made for them with his father. 'Now, please don't refuse the dole. I strongly believe that Father was not behind any attempt to victimise you, yet he needs to be taught a lesson for his arrogance. Besides,' he continued calmly, 'he will pay you a sum of twenty-five rupees for the urgent repair of the hut and will send you a month's subsistence in advance.'

After thanking him for his concern, Subodhbala patted his head with affection.

'Do me one last favour, my son,' she said sobbing openly. 'I have a conviction within my heart that Saraju is all right wherever she is.' Then noticing that Harimohan was subtly moving his head in disbelief, she emphatically said, 'Believe me, she's alive. As a mother, I can feel it very strongly here,' she said pointing to her heart. 'Please find her.'

When Harimohan returned to Rawdon Street, an unexpected letter bearing the postmark of London altered the situation.

'My dear Hurry,' Horace's letter began as usual, 'I have something to announce that is at once sad for me to say and difficult for you to bear. Your mother is critically ill and has very little time to live. I know what her last desire is, even though she hasn't mentioned it even once. Knowing you as I do, I doubt if you will err in choosing what is best for both of you.'

Till then, Harimohan was unaware that he could be so emotional. Big tears rolled down his cheeks, as he stood petrified, looking out of the window towards the Park Street graveyard. Strangely, till then he had not even shed tears for Saraju realising that she might have died.

He quickly ran down to the drawing room and took up *The Statesman*. Within a few seconds his eyes fell on an advertisement that announced the departure of a mail steamer for London in three days. Harimohan immediately instructed the coachman to make the carriage ready. First, he went to his office and dictated special petitions to all the concerned judges for the respective cases to be postponed for six months. He also sent his assistant to the office of the agents of the British India Steam Navigation Company to book a first class cabin for a six-month package to London and back. Next, he arranged that Dhonu may stay the night in his house and look after Indraneel till his return from England. Harimohan had no other choice but to leave Indraneel alone at this sensitive stage for sending him back to the village was sure to ruin an entire year's education. Finally, he headed north to Baghbazar to break the news of his immediate departure to his father.

'Come dear Horey, come,' Gourmohan happily welcomed his favourite son. 'You'll no doubt live more than a hundred years! I was about to send for you. Indeed, I have excellent news! Your marriage is fixed for the next month.'

'Baba, I am sorry I can't marry. I am rushing to England.'

'What?' Gourmohan asked incredulously. 'I've already fixed the date of your marriage. Get married and go wherever you wish.'

'Baba, I've no time to argue. Don't you understand that it's a question of life and death? I couldn't meet my own mother before her death. At least allow me to be near my foster mother before her time runs out. I definitely owe her that much!'

'Wait, I'll consult the priest just now and find out if there's a good date before ...'

'My steamer is leaving in less than seventy-two hours. Now, try to be reasonable. It's just not possible for me to think about marriage now!'

Gourmohan was stupefied. He could not believe that it was finally happening to him. The fact was that he had given an irrevocable undertaking to the bank that the repayment of his loan would be made within the last day of *Sravan*. Therefore, without Harimohan's lucrative dowry, on which he had pinned his last hopes to settle his dues, the bank would automatically appropriate his Bhowanipore house.

Eventually, by the time Harimohan reached the shores of England, his unscrupulous father suffered his first major financial setback triggered entirely by his own deeds. Unfortunately, reversing the decade-long trend of prosperity and expansion, the trigger of the first spark of a family feud threatened the peace of Gourmohan's home. Angered by the duplication of his signature and sale of his house without his consent, Gopimohan unceremoniously walked out of *Datta Kuthi* with his wife and two sons. And as there existed a strong bond of love and affinity between the grandfather and the grandchildren, the departure of Gopi's two sons Durgaprasad and Debiprasad also created an oppressive void in his home. He could have swallowed every insult, every accusation hurled at him but the separation from his grandchildren was a punishment he could not stand.

In glaring contrast to his earlier self, Gourmohan tamely succumbed to the curse that suddenly befell him. Soon he began drinking heavily, remaining in a constant state of inebriation. He seldom came out of his mistress' house in Bowbazar and the administration of his main sweet shop at Baghbazar was left to Panchanan Barat. However, Gourmohan silently thanked God for bestowing him one last favour—the fact that he had bought a house for his mistress had remained a secret.

11

Aurobindo's Vision

In faraway England, the prospect of Julia Cockerell's recovery looked bright after her reunion with Harimohan. But the old family doctor shook his head pessimistically on the chances of her recovery as the dreaded disease had advanced far too much. Julia had contracted bronchitis which would inevitably lead to emphysema, a disorder that damages the lungs, reducing the absorption of oxygen into the bloodstream.

Harimohan tried to spend as much time as possible with her. He, however, took half a day off to pay a quick visit to Cambridge, where Aurobindo was preparing for the ICS. The short train journey was a welcome one as it allowed him to relax and think about more positive things than the grim death that stared his mother in the face. After alighting at the station, he asked for directions. A short while later, he reached the ornate, imposing main gate of King's College.

Once inside, he called at the reception office and waited until Aurobindo could be contacted. Harimohan had come at the end of the day on a Friday purposely in order not to upset Aurobindo's routine. After about fifteen minutes, Aurobindo emerged, wearing the usual cap and gown of King's College scholars. Although he had grown considerably taller, his frail frame had not changed much except for his hair that touched his shoulders. Aurobindo expressed surprise and contentment upon seeing Harimohan. After consulting his pocket watch, Harimohan proposed that Aurobindo accompany him back to London where he could spend the weekend. He formally extended an invitation to him for staying at Beaufort Gardens. As the evening train to the capital was due to leave in about half-an-hour, Aurobindo quickly went back to his boarding house to collect his change and few essential items. After reaching Beaufort Gardens, Harimohan presented his young friend proudly to his parents. 'Mother and Father, here's Aurobindo,' he said 'of whom you've heard so much already.'

'Welcome, Aurobindo,' Horace said warmly, extending his hand. 'We are delighted to meet an old friend's son.'

'Thanks,' Aurobindo replied. 'The honour is entirely mine.'

Harimohan quickly explained that his mother was unwell and escorted her back to bed as fits of coughing and wheezing seized her again. After dinner, Horace took his young guest to his study. A few moments later, Harimohan also joined them.

'What are your plans Aurobindo after you return to India?' Horace asked him.

'Well, it was my father's desire that I study for the ICS exam,' Aurobindo replied softly. 'But, you'll please pardon my frankness, I find the prospects of serving under the British Government rather revolting, although I realise that there aren't any better prospects for jobs.'

'What is your vision of modern India?' Horace enquired.

Aurobindo looked a little surprised.

'I feel that a strong and vibrant India must emerge out of the clutches of darkness. I know that a great change is coming but I'm still a little unclear about its exact time and nature.'

Horace and Harimohan exchanged glances. Harimohan had never heard him speak so frankly before.

'By that, I suppose, you foresee a resurgent India?'

'Undoubtedly, India must first acquire independence for itself by any means at its disposal. Nothing worthwhile can be achieved unless it is free to determine its own destiny. Only then can India's virtue and knowledge overflow into the whole world. Whichever country, race or creed may feel the urge for true knowledge must inevitably turn to India. But it is this dark and heavy demon of inertia that is keeping India decayed, bloodless and lifeless. The truth is beyond anyone's grasp. India is eternal, ever-nascent and young and from it knowledge must pour out. If India is to survive the onslaught of the Empire, it must be made young again. Rushing and billowing streams of energy must pour into India. Its soul must become, as it was in the old times, like the surges, vast and puissant, an ocean of action and force.'

Horace and Harimohan were deeply struck by Aurobindo's profound mysticism.

'When you speak of inner strength, don't you equate it with religion?' Horace asked.

'Not at all. Self-purification transcends religion, dogma or fanaticism. There are so many powerful men in every religion. For India, we need thousands of such souls to hold aloft the force of virtue. It is strength of character, righteousness and morality that I am talking about.'

12

Laying the Foundation

As predicted, Julia's bronchitis slowly gave way to the dreaded emphysema. By now she had understood that death was near. Horace and Harimohan took turns to be at her side along with the trained nurses who took care of her needs. One autumnal morning she looked unexpectedly bright and cheerful. She beckoned Harimohan and embracing him ardently, kissed him on the cheeks. As Horace came in, she extended her arm and the next instant she became very emotional. Never before had Harimohan seen his father cry, but at this point he broke down completely. As Horace went on talking fondly to her, he did not realise that Julia was not listening any more. Her soul had quietly left her body in the lingering sweetness of her husband's embrace.

After his mother's demise, Harimohan proposed that Horace accompany him back to India.

'Thank you, Hurry, but my days are over. Now India needs young people like you and Aurobindo. Whatever time is left for me, I would like to devote to the spirit.'

'And what do you think of Aurobindo?' Do you indeed see any future for him in the reawakening of his motherland?'

'Yes.' Horace continued with a pleasant smile, 'There's a light in that boy that will one day outshine the mighty sun! I suppose it's a premonition. Today, I know that the one who will lead India to its ultimate fulfilment is present among us. He's the chosen priest for the worship of Mother India. Like all incarnations of the Supreme, he has come to struggle and prepare the path and lay the foundation on which the temple shall solidly stand. I have never seen before so much light and inner beauty! But I can't rest until he consciously puts on the heavy mantle of the Deliverer. I shall not find true peace until that hour.'

Following this conversation, Harimohan's interest in Aurobindo increased even more. Now that he had one full month in hand before sailing back to India, he made it a point to visit Aurobindo more often.

Aurobindo admitted that he foresaw a great revolution in his motherland. He revealed that when he was eleven he had indeed received a strong indication that a period of great general upheaval and revolutionary changes was coming into the world and that he knew that he had a part to play in it. Already, Aurobindo was a member of the *Indian Majlis* at Cambridge and was soon to become its temporary secretary. Other than playing an important role in the social life of Indian students in England, the *Majlis* also moulded their political outlook. Being an active advocate of free India, Aurobindo was deeply involved in the political agenda of the society and had made numerous fiery speeches at its sittings. However, what Aurobindo did not know was the bearing these speeches were having on the minds of the authorities.

13

In the Name of God

It was early morning in a remote state in north-eastern India. The atmosphere was one of joy and festivity. Sitting around a bonfire, about a hundred Bihari labourers were chanting the name of God in a state of intoxication. Suddenly two figures emerged out of the darkness and walked up to the place of worship.

'Chhenu bhai?' the voice of one of the dark figures boomed from the distance. 'Won't you welcome your older brother?'

'Birju bhaiya?' Chhenu responded ecstatically, running up to him. 'What brings you here so suddenly in the middle of the night? Who is this?'

Chhenu Kahar suspiciously asked pointing at Saraju.

'Oh! This is Saraju Bitiya. I've brought her with me.'

A few women and acquaintances had assembled by then and hugged Birju to greet him. As Saraju was standing shyly away from the scene, the ladies quickly took her to Chhenu's hut. After the meal, Birju took his brother and sister-in-law aside and told them the entire story of Saraju's planned murder. He also explained that he had brought her to these jungles around Gauhati for her security. He suggested that after lying low for a considerable period, she could be allowed to work and earn her livelihood in a society of her own choice. He promised to pay Chhenu well on behalf of Saraju for her stay and also extracted a word of honour that even after his departure they would look after her properly. Birju lived with his brother for a week and after being satisfied that Saraju had settled herself well in the village, he decided to leave.

He handed her the pouch containing the remaining money that Gourmohan had given him and said, 'I've spent whatever was necessary from the money that I'd received. Please give me something to return home and keep the rest with you.'

At this point, Saraju broke down and wept. She could not imagine that such nobility still existed. Here was a hired thug begging her for money that he believed belonged to her. Instead of taking any undue advantage of her pitiable state, he had called her his own daughter and cared for her like a real father.

Saraju opened the pouch and poured the contents at the end of her sari. She counted a hundred rupees and gave them to Birju.

'Ah, this will largely suffice for fulfilling my wildest dreams,' Birju said ecstatically. 'And Bitiya, don't forget to pay Chhenu ten rupees every month.'

As Saraju stooped down to touch Birju's feet, he took several steps backward as he was not supposed to accept reverence from the member of a higher caste as was prevalent in those days.

'I may belong to a higher social hierarchy, but you belong to a much nobler humanity,' Saraju remarked.

'Bitiya what have you done? I'm a Shudra, people consider us untouchables.' Then he continued emotionally, 'I've a small piece of advice for you before departing. You must on no account try to contact your son or the Babu with whom he stays. Remember, there are spies everywhere and you will end up putting your son's life in danger along with your own. Besides,' Birju hesitated a little, 'my life also will be threatened if my employer ever finds out that you are alive. Do you understand?'

The forest where Chhenu Kahar worked overlooked the mighty Brahmaputra River midway between Gauhati and Palasbari. Saraju heard from Birju's sister-in-law, Behula, that there was an 'awakened' deity not too far from the Brahmaputra, known as Kamakshya. This Devi is said to grant whatever boon one asks of her. As soon as she heard about Kamakshya, Saraju pleaded with Behula to take her there. Taking pity on the widow as she had recently lost all contact with her only son, Behula agreed to take her to the temple.

Situated on the small Nilachal Hill, the temple of Kamakshya is among the fifty-two holy *pitha*s of the Hindus. A descending flight of steps leads into a natural cave with a spring where the relic of Goddess Sati is enshrined within a shallow pool of water.

On the day of the journey, Saraju put on a new white sari that widows traditionally wear. She had let her long hair hang loose down her back. She was looking radiant and had entered into a trance-like state even before going into the cave. As she moved in, she knelt down on the edge of the pool and became deeply immersed in meditation and ardently prayed for her reunification with Indraneel.

Meanwhile, a young couple had entered the cave behind her and on beholding her resplendent beauty, remained mesmerised in admiration. To them she looked like a reincarnation of the saint Mirabai. As the unknown lady would not leave until she had met this uncommon widow, the couple waited until Saraju finished her prayer. And as she stepped out of the cave, she heard someone call from behind.

'My name is Golapkamini, and this is my husband,' the unknown lady said amiably. 'We live in Shillong. I feel curious to know who you are. Is there anything we can do for you?'

'I am Sujata from Burdwan,' Saraju lied. 'I have no home but only a few friends here.'

'My name's Bhupal Chandra and I am a government servant,' remarked Gopalkamini's husband affably. 'Can we not take you to Shillong with us since you say you have no home? You can live with us as a member of the family. You see I have to go out on official tours very often and am home only for a few days in a month. My wife has to look after the children and manage the household all by herself. We shall be delighted if you agree to live with us and take charge of our children, of whom the oldest is four.'

The couple's warmth and friendship appealed to Saraju. They were not only sociable and amicable but also respectable and dignified.

'All right,' she said. 'Please tell me where to contact you.'

The couple looked pleased and readily provided the information. The next day, Saraju met them at the appointed place and accompanied them to Shillong.

14

A Meeting with Birju

Upon his return to India, Harimohan resumed his work with earnestness. However, although he was sad to learn about his father's misdeeds leading to the final disposal of the Bhowanipore property, he could not understand the motive behind it.

One afternoon, Harilal, the office peon, announced that Barat sahib had come.

'Your father is very depressed ever since you left, Chhoto Babu,' Barat informed worriedly. 'Besides, things are getting out of hand. The entire chain of sweet shops presently hinges around one man—Baidhar. He has assumed full control of the production of sweets. Now I have a queer feeling that he is planning to set up his own shop. When Baidhar approached a moneylender for an advance of two thousand rupees, he immediately came to see me. Although Baidhar hasn't disclosed the purpose of obtaining this loan, I have very little doubt that it's for hiring a new premise for setting up an independent business. Now, other than your father, only Baidhar knows how to make some of our special sweets. And if he leaves, we are doomed.'

'Well, now, tell me what exactly is ailing Baba?'

'I know only one thing. He needed money for some purpose so he discreetly hypothecated his Bhowanipore property, which he had acquired through the bank in your elder brother's name to evade taxation. He faked Gopi's signature and obtained a loan of seventy-five thousand rupees from his own bank in my name. In other words, Gopi was made to stand guarantor for the loan by pledging his property. This way, no one could know that your father had obtained the loan. However, somewhere along the line his calculations misfired and he had to sacrifice his house.'

'What were the modalities of the loan? I mean, can you tell me what was the ceiling of accumulated interest or cut-off date for paying back the amount?'

'I suppose the cut-off date was the first of *Bhadra*.'

'How interesting! So it had to be cleared within the month of *Sravan?*' Harimohan said leaning back in his swivel chair.

'And how much was the dowry that Baba was expecting to get for my marriage?' Harimohan enquired.

'Ah, so that was it! That's where your father was pinning his last hope!' Panchanan Barat's face lit up in sincere admiration of Harimohan's genius.

That's the confirmation of what the old man was up to, Harimohan reflected quietly. Wasn't it for that reason that he got Saraju out of his way?

'Now, Barat Moshay,' he asked, 'you must give me some important information. Tell me the name of the *goonda,* whom Baba hires for his dirty jobs in and around the village.'

'I have often heard him mention a big guy called Birju. Yes, Birju something. I can't tell you more. But what's the solution regarding Baidhar?'

'Let's see. What if we offer Baidhar a partnership? Say, we give him the equivalent of a three per cent cut over his salary for a period of ten years? Well, good luck. Contact Baba and give him my regards.'

Harimohan remained motionless after Barat left. He had learnt much more than he had asked for. For the first time since Saraju's abduction, Harimohan knew where to start looking for her. He went at once to the Bar Association Library and met one of his colleagues who was from Chinsura. Advocate Natobar Bhattacharya spent the weekends with his family in Chinsura. The elderly lawyer was sure to know everyone of the area, thought Harimohan.

'Oh yes! I've heard of him. Birju is a dreaded man who takes up special assignments for a premium,' Advocate Bhattacharya confirmed. 'He lives in the outskirts of Chinsura and I've reasons to believe that your father is one of his chief patrons. I think he had saved Birju from a serious prosecution by providing the all-important alibi that he needed. Since then, Birju is his slave.'

'I would like to contact him discreetly without letting him know who I am.'

'All right, but where would you like to meet him?'

'Please ask him to come to my house in Calcutta. Here's my address. He should come on Sunday week. Naturally, I'll pay his expenses. Just tell him the owner of this house wants to meet him, say, at noon.'

As expected, the undoubting Birju reported at Harimohan's house on Sunday week. He had returned from Lohardaga a month earlier, and had come expecting a big assignment. Birju was a massive man, three hundred pounds and over six feet tall. But it was his thick jutting moustache and long sideburns that gave him his fearful look.

Harimohan had sent away Indraneel with his coachman to keep him out of the way, with instructions not to return home before two o'clock. As Harimohan entered the drawing room, Birju quickly bowed his head and touched his joined palms to his forehead. Harimohan returned the namaskar and motioned him to sit down.

'Are you Birju?' he enquired casually. 'Well, Birju, I must first inform you that my name is Harimohan Datta and I am Gourmohan Datta's son.'

'But I didn't know that …' Birju tried to explain, betraying his astonishment.

'I have a big reward to offer you if you can find me someone who has disappeared some months ago without leaving a trace.'

Birju grew alarmed and got up from the sofa.

'The one I want you to find,' Harimohan went on unperturbed, 'has disappeared from Seiya, near where you live. Now, here's your fee,' he added, putting three big hundred rupee notes on the table. 'I'm giving you this money in advance and shall be happy to pay you more if you bring back the person alive and unharmed.'

Birju's expression underwent a change. He was trapped in a piquant situation. On one side, he had to safeguard the prestige of Gourmohan Datta and by the same token, could not afford to vex his favourite son. He thought best to remain calm and listen to whatever Harimohan had to say.

Harimohan surveyed Birju attentively and seemed to understand what was going on in his mind.

'By the way Birju,' he said calmly, 'I have gone through the old records of your case with the zamindar of Puinan in which you escaped indictment narrowly, thanks to an alibi offered by my father. However, in it he lied that you were with him in Calcutta on the day of the murder. Well, I can prove before any court that that was a fabricated piece of evidence. At the exact time of the alleged murder he was actually celebrating the gala opening of our new house in Seiya. Here's the evidence,' he said laying down an invitation card in Bengali, showing that the housewarming ceremony was held to coincide with the auspicious occasion of Sri Panchami of the Bengali year 1288 B.S., the precise date when the murder took place!

Birju balked under pressure and beads of perspiration appeared on his forehead.

'I am begging you, Chhoto Babu, have mercy on me!' he pleaded. 'The zamindar of Puinan falsely implicated me in that case although I admit being there when the murder supposedly took place. Please believe me I haven't killed anyone in my life.'

'And what about these? Do you recognise these?' Harimohan asked curtly, placing Saraju's bangles on the small table beside the bank notes.

'Where did you get those?' Birju asked in astonishment.

He fell silent and closed his eyes to take stock of all the negative things piling up against him. He had never before faced such a tight situation where, to save someone, his own security was put at stake. Then he made up his mind to help the honest son, who, in stark contrast to his deceitful and coercive father, was genuinely asking for help.

'Chhoto Babu, do I have your word that you will not drag anyone to court? Your Saraju is safe. But no one else knows it. Not even the person who ordered her murder.'

Harimohan's eyes lit up as he ran his hand tiredly through his hair and picked up the notes and held them within Birju's reach. He shut his eyes in deep gratitude to God for protecting Saraju.

'No, that will not be necessary,' Birju said, handing back the notes. 'I believe I've already performed a good deed by saving my Bitiya. I don't want to insult her by accepting a bribe that may give her away.'

'But what's the guarantee that you are not lying? Doesn't the presence of those bangles prove the contrary? Remember, a person like me who could get you here so effortlessly, could also put you behind bars without any problem.'

Birju weighed all the pros and cons of a full confession. Then he slowly began his narration.

'One day, your father summoned me to his house. He wanted me to abduct a young lady from his outhouse and carry her away to where I live on the suburbs of Chinsura. You understand Chhoto Babu that I had no choice but to accept. I owe your father my life. With the help of Tarapada, the servant, one of my men slipped into Saraju's room under the cover of darkness while she was not there. Then as soon as she retired to her room for the night and bolted the door unsuspectingly from inside, my man made her unconscious by holding a piece of cloth sprinkled with chloroform over her face. That is why she didn't make any noise or awaken the inmates of the house.'

'Will you now explain where the throne and the crown of the deity are?'

'Which throne and crown are you talking about? I know nothing about them.'

'All right, please continue with your narration.'

'A week later, your father sent for me again and unexpectedly ordered me to kill her. Naturally, I refused. He thrust a pouch containing some money in my hand and insisted vehemently. Then I understood two things. First, that if I didn't do the job, someone else would gladly do it for so much money. Second, as I knew what he was planning to do, he would naturally eliminate me to safeguard his misdeed, to avoid having irksome witnesses. I hatched a plan even while he was offering me those five hundred rupees. I told him that I would leave for Lohardaga as soon as I finished the job, because, I said, my old mother was very ill. Of course, this was a ruse. What I actually planned to do was to take Saraju somewhere to a faraway place where nobody knew her. It wasn't too difficult to convince her that escaping with me was the only option.'

'Now hold it. There are a few things that you must explain. First, who else knows about Saraju's escape other than you? And second, how is it that her bangles were with my father?'

'I was coming to that,' Birju said with a nod of approval. 'You see, as there was only my assistant, I had no problem taking him into confidence. As for the bangles, I knew that your father would have to be convinced about the girl's death and some personal belonging would have to be produced. So I convinced Saraju to part with her bangles. We then left. We reached Gauhati a month later and immediately started for the forest near Palasbari where my brother Chhenu works. I think my idea was good and Saraju seemed happy to live in the forest with my Bihari associates. I have asked my sister-in-law to personally look after her so there should be no problem now.'

'Oh, yes, there is still one,' Harimohan said. 'How is she earning her livelihood?

'Well, she doesn't have to,' Birju replied, with a touch of pride. 'You see, we only spent about two hundred rupees for our entire journey. That meant we had three hundred rupees left from what your father had given me. So I gave it all to her.'

Just then, Indraneel came in running.

'Mama, Mama,' he shouted excitedly, but the words froze on his lips as soon as he saw Birju's massive frame.

'Neel, this is Birju uncle,' Harimohan said happily, taking him in his arms. 'Please ask him to stay for lunch.'

Although Harimohan's heart was filled with joy on learning that Saraju was alive, the sudden mention of her name had the opposite effect on Indraneel. He grew morose and slowly lost his appetite. Being the only child, the boy was extremely attached to Saraju but with love and patience, Harimohan had succeeded in making him forget her temporarily.

Suddenly an idea struck Harimohan. How about getting in touch with Dr Ghose's children, Sarojini and Barin? He knew that Dr Ghose's youngest children had been brought from Deogarh and now lived in the city. It was during one of their trips to Khulna, where Krishna Dhone had settled after serving in Rangpur, that Harimohan had met them for the first time. Barin and Indraneel were almost of the same age and could probably get along well. So the next Sunday, Harimohan and Indraneel went to Gome's Lane. The half-circular single-storied bungalow was situated beyond a small courtyard. Soon Barin and Sarojini came to receive them.

'I hope you recognise me? We met in Khulna.'

'Oh yes,' Sarojini said shyly. 'Please come in. And who is this boy with you?'

'This is my nephew, Indraneel.'

'Welcome Indraneel,' she said with unusual warmth. 'Do you like sweets?'

Soon Sarojini returned with a platter of sweets and invited Indraneel to share them with Barin. Within a matter of seconds Sarojini had taken charge of Indraneel. She made the two boys sit on either side and eat alternately, while she talked to both of them affectionately.

'When will your father come?'

'Next weekend perhaps, as he usually comes twice a month from Khulna.'

'Didi,' Barin asked eagerly, 'may I tell him some of the ghost stories I know?'

'In our village, there's a lady ghost near the bamboo grove,' Indraneel said. 'That's why everyone avoids the place at night. Once, Ma saw it and ...' Indraneel could not finish the sentence as his voice choked and seconds later, to everyone's astonishment, big drops of tears began rolling down his cheeks.

'What's the matter?' Sarojini asked with serious concern, holding Indraneel to her bosom. By now he was sobbing frenziedly and let Sarojini take him in her arms and coax and cajole him.

With the increasing frequency of Indraneel's visit to Gome's Lane a strong bond of friendship developed between the two boys. Also, having been deprived of his mother's love, Sarojini's tender presence brought about a positive change to his personality.

15

Motimala

Unfortunately, things continued to be bleak at Gourmohan's home. After Gopimohan's exit, Madanmohan had also quit *Datta Kuthi* with his wife and daughter. Earlier, the grandchildren held his heart, but now in their absence, his big dwelling seemed to be a cursed house.

Gourmohan's passion for Motimala was now showing signs of decline. He felt that she was trying to get rid of him after acquiring the Bowbazar house. Unable to come to terms with her misbehaviour, Gourmohan turned up one evening in Harimohan's office accompanied by Panchanan Barat.

'Chhoto Babu,' Panchanan began, 'I suppose you know that your father gifted a house to someone in Bowbazar? Well, he now feels that he should have the right to keep the house for himself even if he terminates his relationship.'

'I'm sorry,' Harimohan said haughtily, 'I refuse to discuss the matter. However, you are welcome to consult me about anything else that you may want.'

An uneasy silence followed while Gourmohan and Panchanan exchanged looks.

'But how can a relationship be equivalent to the price of a house? Chhoto Babu, please help him to recover the house.'

'Why, have the lady murdered!' Harimohan spoke with his eyes fixed on Panchanan. 'I'm sure your master knows the rules of the game better than I! Aren't his hands stained with the blood of a young lady already?'

'What do you mean?' Gourmohan said lamely, pretending ignorance. 'What are you implying?'

Harimohan then got up abruptly and bringing out a bag, poured out its contents.

'Tell me, do you recognise these items?' he enquired rudely. 'These bracelets and this,' he said, shaking a piece of paper before his father's face, 'is the sworn affidavit of your hired assassin, confessing your edict and his complicity.'

'Birju Kahar!' Gourmohan clenched his fist and hissed angrily, 'That deceitful scoundrel!'

'And, as a witness,' Harimohan went on unperturbed, 'here is his assistant Dehora's separate affidavit. Also, I have here another sworn document by your ever-dependable Tarapada, who acted as the contact between the assassin and yourself. May be you are wondering what prompted Tarapada to betray you? Well, for one thing,' Harimohan said, putting the documents and the bracelets back into the pouch and neatly tucking it into his drawer, 'Tarapada has also made his separate written confession about stealing the deity's throne and crown on the day of Saraju's abduction and then putting the blame on Mashima. The cunning rascal thought that he could get away with his act in the general turmoil.' Then turning towards Panchanan Barat he continued, 'So here we are Barat Babu with plenty of explosive material against your employer.'

'Tarapada, that double-headed, despicable vermin!' Gourmohan passionately swore again. 'I'll have him publicly flogged for daring to steal my sacred artefacts! But how to catch him now, the rascal has left my service!'

'Now, calm down. If you do anything rash I shall not hesitate to place this evidence before a magisterial court and obtain a sentence against you. I owe you that much for betraying my mother and murdering my beloved Saraju!'

Gourmohan sat with his head bowed in shame, stupefied at his son's ability to rake up the past and sift out the truth.

'Now that you know the truth about Birju,' Harimohan proceeded defiantly, 'you must also know that my Saraju is alive. However, I also would like you to understand something clearly. If anything further happens to her or Birju, you'll leave me with no choice but to go to court against you. So just drop the matter and let bygones be bygones.'

Harimohan had aroused fear and alarm within old Gourmohan's heart and he seemed on the verge of tears.

'Believe me, Horey, I couldn't sleep for at least a month after ordering the girl's execution,' Gourmohan sincerely admitted while wiping his tears. 'I know I'm not worthy of your forgiveness. I had no choice but to hide one mistake with another for fear of losing you. You're my most worthy possession and I didn't want to lose you a second time. Besides, I badly needed that dowry.'

'How can you go to such lengths just to satisfy your ends?' Harimohan remonstrated curtly. 'Do you equate yourself with God that you can play about with the fate of others? Are you aware that without Birju's goodness, someone would have lost her life unnecessarily because all you were interested in was collecting the dowry that a conscientious father was going to offer you for assuring your son's hand in marriage?'

'By the way Horey,' Gourmohan asked suddenly, changing the subject, 'how could Tarapada steal the crown and the throne when even Kedar's wife admitted that the key had been always in her possession?'

'Your trusted servant used a fishing rod and a hook. The lamp that burned on the rack of Mashima's room helped him locate the keys without difficulty even in the darkness and he lifted it from there and put it back through the open window. He did this in the dead of the night. Mashima told me that she was surprised to see Tarapada hanging around the gate of the courtyard that morning and following her to the puja room. And no sooner had Mashima entered the puja room that the scoundrel pointed out that the gold items were missing. It was as if he had foreknowledge. So I straightaway told him that I would not file an accusation against him if he signed the prepared document that I had taken with me admitting his complicity in Saraju's disappearance. I also said that he could keep the gold items. I was not much interested in catching a small fry but the bigger rogue who organised the whole crime,' Harimohan said looking straight in his father's eyes.

'Horey, I'm ready to fall at your feet, please pardon me,' Gourmohan blurted between sobs. 'You told me Saraju is still alive. Just bring her to me and I shall pray for her forgiveness too. I also undertake to get her married to you as you wish. You are my only son now. I want to do a final good act to atone for my past errors.'

There was something genuine about Gourmohan's confession. He seemed to be truly willing to turn over a new leaf. Panchanan, who sat baffled throughout the conversation between father and son, also shed tears silently when Gourmohan finally broke down and wept.

'Baba,' Harimohan addressed him by that name for the first time that evening, 'I'm willing to help you in whatever new project you take up only if you give me your word that you'll never again do anything immoral and unethical. Now tell me what would you like me to do?'

Gourmohan looked happy again. He quickly wiped his face and brightened up visibly.

'The thing uppermost in my mind is the recovery of the Bowbazar house. In the beginning I used to pay her dues but since I bought her the house, I have naturally not given her any money but paid for all my food and drinks. I don't think I owe her anything above a small fraction of what the property is worth.'

'Have you brought the original deed of conveyance?'

'No, she won't part with it. But here's a copy that I've kept.'

It took the seasoned barrister just five minutes to read the deed closely.

'I see that the house was bought from Kailashnath Karmakar for seventy-five thousand rupees by Motimala Dassi. But my question is—if we challenge the deal before the court, would this Motimala Dassi be able to show the source of the money? I mean did she ever possess so much money at any time during her life? No? Then I suppose, Panchanan Babu, you still have some documentary evidence to prove that you borrowed that big sum from the bank preceding the execution of the deed? Good, then I have a plan.'

The following day, Harimohan summoned his assistant Amulya Ratan Burman to his chamber and instructed to have the Bowbazar conveyance deed verified word for word with the original document kept at the government registration office. He then asked him to send word to Shakuni Chakladar to meet him at 1 p.m. Shakuni, who arrived on time, was known by his pet name, meaning vulture. A dangerous outlaw of Bowbazar who rendered service for a fee, he was the city counterpart of Birju, though considerably slimmer and smaller but perceptibly deadlier.

'Shakuni,' Harimohan began, 'I suppose you have heard of Motimala Dassi?'

'Who hasn't, Datta Moshay?' Shakuni grinned, baring his red, betel-stained teeth.

'Now I want you to lead my assistant to her. All I'm asking you is to wait till the end of the discussion and affirm clearly that you are serving her with an ultimatum to quit her house exactly in a month's time and that upon the termination of the deadline you will come to take possession of it. You'll get your cut of two per cent on the twenty thousand rupees that my man will pay her. How much does that make?

'Four hundred rupees, Datta Moshay,' Shakuni answered with alacrity.

'Amulya, I have already told you what to say to the lady. Is there still any point you want to clarify? Then here's Shakuni Chakladar, a local man, who'll accompany you.'

Burman and Shakuni were shown into a large sitting room in Motimala's house. A little later, Motimala came out in a plain sari. Her sight took both men's breath away. While Shakuni eyed her as a lion his meal, Burman began talking straight away like a seasoned professional, avoiding any clumsy silence.

'Namaskar,' he said coldly with a frown. 'I've come from the High Court. My name is Amulya Burman and this is my friend, Shakuni Chakladar.'

The lady recoiled visibly hearing the name of Shakuni and looked apprehensively at him while he touched his forehead in a form of a crude salaam.

'May I know the reason for your sudden visit?' Motimala asked with dignity.

'My client, Panchanan Barat, has served you notice to vacate this house. Here it is,' Burman said, handing over the single sheet of typed paper to her.

'But who is Panchanan Barat? How can I be ordered to leave my own house?'

'Your own house? Here is the title deed of this property, look,' Amulya said unemotionally, handing over a thick bunch of papers.

'Wait a minute,' Motimala said, getting up like a nimble-footed gazelle. 'Let me show you my papers.'

She returned a couple of minutes later with a document of a similar nature. 'Look carefully. The house is in my name.'

Pretending then to read the document with a frown, Burman remarked haughtily, 'But you are totally mistaken. This document clearly states that *my* client is the undisputed owner of this mansion. There is no ambiguity whatsoever.'

'You are a bunch of liars!' the lady exploded suddenly. 'Give me back my papers!'

Burman did so and got up to leave.

'Remember, you are given thirty days to vacate, failing which, we shall be back with a court order and the police.'

A little later, Burman stood proudly smiling before his senior advocate, Harimohan.

'I've got it, Sir! Everything worked according to your scheme. She noticed nothing.'

'Thanks a lot, Amulya,' Harimohan said gratefully accepting the papers.

The next day Burman and Shakuni went back to Bowbazar.

'My client has changed his mind,' he said calmly. 'He offers you twenty thousand rupees for quitting his house with your entourage. That is, if you quit his house quietly within this week.'

And before the lady could shout he took out two fat bundles of hundred rupee notes and showed them to her.

'So you think you can buy me off with money? This property is worth a lot more! And I shall produce my document to prove my ownership!'

'If you look carefully, Madam, the document you possess is an unsigned and unregistered deed between Panchanan Barat and yourself stating that you've sold this property to him for twenty thousand rupees. But unless you sign and give it to me now you won't get even your twenty thousand rupees! You handed me your original title deed yesterday for safekeeping. Meanwhile I left with you the unsigned document.'

Motimala screamed in panic and desperation. She was not smart enough to know that a 'certified to be true copy' of her lost document could be easily brought out from the Registrar's office. Harimohan's ploy had worked.

'Except God no one can help you now,' Burman reassured her gently. 'Now Madam, please go and get the document while we wait here.'

Motimala returned a little while later thoroughly chastised and with a remarkably changed countenance. Having verified the document she realised that Amulya Burman had not been lying to her. In her excitement and hurry she had forgotten to verify it the previous day and handed back the original.

'My client is an honest man,' Amulya added, while paying her the promised cash after she put her signatures in Bengali on every page of the document. 'He has already found a new tenement for you down the same road. The rent will be fifty rupees a month with three months' advance rent to be deposited as security money. And as a special gesture of goodwill for displacing you, he has sent these hundred and fifty rupees extra for depositing the security money before entering into a lease agreement for ten years. Of course, it's up to you to accept or reject the offer.'

Earlier, Shakuni had caught furtive glances when Motimala came to the window. He knew that her fee was unaffordable for an ordinary man like him. She was the prized jewel of the affluent. Secretly, he had grown alarmed at the news of her displacement during the discussion between the barrister and himself but felt reassured by Harimohan's nobility in asking him to find an alternative house for her within the same locality. The task would not have been easy had Shakuni not stepped in with his clout and influence. Afterwards, Shakuni and his men had involved themselves in Motimala's relocation and earned her sympathy. Following this rapprochement, Shakuni's visits to Motimala's domain increased until a friendship based on mutual trust grew between the two.

The last phase of the deal was the shortest and also the easiest. Panchanan signed another deed of conveyance in favour of Gourmohan Datta for a consideration of twenty-five thousand rupees, which was duly registered. Gourmohan won possession of his Bowbazar property, marking a memorable victory for himself. However, it was Harimohan's idea that the property first be transferred to Panchanan and through him to his father in order to avoid making a direct deal between the courtesan and Gourmohan.

But the whole story ended on a satisfactory note that pleased everyone, except of course Gourmohan's ex-mistress.

'You owe Panchanan Babu this extra sum of five thousand rupees for using his name. Baba, I hope you don't mind paying it to him?'

'Certainly not, my son. Evidently, you think of every little detail don't you?'

'I've also sent the lady an extra amount of one hundred and fifty rupees for paying the security deposit for entering into a long-term lease agreement of tenancy in the same locality. I didn't wish to displace her—thereby throwing her out of business. Besides, I had to hire an agent of the area to get the new tenancy for her and to make her accept the deal. To him I paid four hundred rupees. So in all you owe me five hundred and fifty rupees more.'

'Done, and what do I owe you for all this good work?'

'Your support for improving the living conditions of the people of Seiya.'

16

A Favourite Son

Sometimes people do strange things in a fit of depression. Harimohan had lately been dreaming of his foster-mother calling him to be by her side. Ultimately, the vividness of her memory and the urge to lay a floral wreath at her tomb became so strong that he reserved his passage back to England to mark her first death anniversary.

As Indraneel had behaved well during his previous trip, leaving him under Dhonu's care was no longer a problem. In order not to shelve Saraju's case, Harimohan engaged a retired detective for three months to go to Palasbari and trace Saraju, so that he could bring her back to Calcutta on his return from England.

After arriving at the Royal Albert Docks forty-five days later, Harimohan was surprised to see his foster father with a flowing beard. But although he seemed older, his eyes shone with a strange glow of strength that added a peculiar charisma to his personality. The two men warmly hugged each other before climbing into the family carriage.

At home, they sat facing the hearth. Harimohan told his father about the sad disappearance of Saraju. His heart felt a lot lighter after sharing his anxiety with his father. On his part, Horace informed him that he had become engaged in exploring the origins of Sanskrit and, more specifically, the origins of the Indian civilisation.

'By the way, Father, do you have any news of Aurobindo's ICS exams?'

'No. But why don't you run down and meet him?'

'The trouble is I don't know where he lives. By now he must have quit his lodgings at Cambridge. But wait,' Harimohan said suddenly as an idea struck him. 'There's Mr James Cotton at the South Kensington Liberal Club. He should be able to inform me of Aurobindo's whereabouts.'

But Harimohan had a more urgent mission on hand. The next morning, he and his father passed an hour at his mother's grave in communion with her. And as Harimohan broke down and sobbed like a child, the reassuring hand of his father gently grabbed his shoulder, helping him to regain his composure.

The next day, Harimohan set out for Cromwell Road, where the office of the South Kensington Club was located. He was informed that the club had shifted to another premise on Hogarth Road, which he found easily. Cotton knew the three sons of Dr Krishna Dhone Ghose well as his elder brother Henry Cotton was a good friend of the doctor.

'Yes, I remember you,' said Cotton, after greeting Harimohan. 'You used to come to meet the boys during Mrs Drewett's time.'

'Sir, I came to enquire about Aurobindo. I shall be happy to meet him during my short stay. By the way, could you please tell me the result of his ICS exam?'

'As far as Aurobindo's present address is concerned, you've come to the right place,' Cotton informed happily. 'He and Benoy are staying right here in this building. But you'll be disappointed to know how gloomy Aurobindo's state of affairs is. Faced with his lack of concern for the compulsory horse-riding test, I was determined to push the young man to take it because passing the ICS would admittedly assure him a future that even Englishmen dream of. Earlier, Aurobindo had deliberately failed to appear for the riding test. He also wilfully ignored numerous reminders that were sent to him. But this oddity was in glaring contrast with his success in the other written exams. Ultimately, irked by his repeated failure to appear for the riding test, the Commission had notified the India Office that they rejected Aurobindo's candidature!

'He finally admitted that lack of money was the cause behind his inability to prepare for the test. So I proposed to provide the expenses of the riding lessons if he was willing to take the test. After that, Aurobindo wrote a petition addressing the Secretary of State for India requesting him to grant him a last chance to appear, but this application is now pending before Lord Kimberley for his consideration.'

Harimohan wondered whether a sudden fit of insanity had not struck Aurobindo. This peculiar behaviour did not match his friend's rationality. After the inevitable exchange of civilities, he brought up the sore topic during the hour-long meeting he had with Aurobindo later in the evening.

'What's all this I hear about your refusal to take the riding test?' he enquired.

'I hope you will understand me at least,' Aurobindo replied earnestly. 'I tried my best to explain it to Benoy but he does not seem to care for my feelings.'

'I shall try my very best to understand you,' Harimohan assured him.

'I chose the ICS only because my father wanted it. But later, I found out what sort of work it is and I hate an administrator's life. So I devised some way of getting myself disqualified without rejecting the service myself, which my father would not allow me to do. He has already made arrangements through Mr Henry Cotton, for my posting as the district collector of Arrah, which is regarded as a very fine place.' Then Aurobindo seemed to hesitate a little. 'To tell you the truth, only two activities interest me—writing poetry and taking part in the *Indian Majli*s.'

Harimohan appreciated Aurobindo's logic even though he did not like the idea of getting himself disqualified.

'But by God!' Harimohan mused silently, 'it requires guts to willingly sacrifice the emolument and prestige of an ICS officer!'

'I think you're wasting your time,' Harimohan dryly informed James Cotton the following day. 'Aurobindo has made up his mind to get himself disqualified from the ICS. That's why he's behaving so oddly.'

'Mr Datta,' the Englishman interrupted excitedly as an idea struck him. 'Tell me, do you or do you not agree that your friend should appear for his riding test?'

'Of course, I agree. But Auro is very stubborn. Once he makes up his mind ...'

'Never mind about that, let's go to Cambridge and get some attestations made about his abilities and character from his tutors. And they will certainly reinforce his case if borne out with his petition. Will you accompany me to Cambridge?'

Willing to leave no stone unturned to help their young friend, Cotton and Harimohan took the next train to Cambridge. And to their happy surprise, the praelector of the King's College turned out to be one of Aurobindo's ardent admirers.

'Good morning,' the gentleman said, shaking their hands, 'I am G W Prothero and I'm a historian. How I can help you?'

'Good morning, Sir,' Cotton greeted him back jovially. 'My name's James Sutherland Cotton. I'm the younger brother of Henry Steadman Cotton who is currently the chief secretary of the government of Bengal. I'm also an editor of *Academy*. And here is my friend Barrister Datta of Calcutta who is a friend of someone in this college. I wonder if you know a young man named Aravinda Acroyd Ghose.'

'Of course,' Prothero replied warmly. 'Although I have never taught Ghose, I can tell you on authority that he's one of our brightest scholars in the classics. But why do you ask? Is anything wrong with him?'

'Well, yes, he was made to fail in his ICS exams. You see, he did not appear for the horse-riding test.'

'Now, that's very odd!' Prothero said ruefully. 'To my knowledge, no candidate has ever been disqualified for that insignificant riding test. Besides, the written examinations ended four months ago and the riding tests should have been over by the middle of August too. How the can the issue remain open up to the end of November?'

'You're right,' Cotton sighed in desperation. 'Ghose was given four chances between August and November to appear for his test. But feigning one thing or another he deliberately abstained from taking it. Sadly, the real reason for not appearing was a lack of money to pay for lessons.'

'Oh! What a pity! You rarely come across such fine talent. I've got it from the contemporary writer and university lecturer in history, Oscar Browning, that he has never seen such excellent classical papers as those of Ghose's entrance exam, to qualify for his scholarship!'

'I did not know that!' Cotton cried happily. 'That sounds really interesting!'

'Honestly, Ghose's conduct has been exemplary throughout the last two years. Before passing his ICS examination he obtained a foundation scholarship in the classics. And his financial condition prevented him from turning down the money that the scholarship fetched him. However, the regulations of the scholarship in turn obliged him to devote a great part of his time to classics which must have been of some disadvantage to his ICS studies. But the man performed his part of the bargain most honourably and took a high place in the first class of the Classical Tripos at the end of the second year of his residence. That a man should have been able to do this which alone is enough for most undergraduates, and at the same time to keep up his ICS work, proves very unusual industry and capacity.'

'We couldn't agree with you more on that.'

'Moreover,' Prothero went on, 'that a man of this calibre should be lost to the Indian Government merely because he did not keep an appointment appears to me a piece of official short-sightedness which would be hard to beat. Besides, the man has not only ability but character. Remittance from home had almost entirely failed and yet his courage and perseverance have never failed. Several times I wrote to his father on his behalf, but unsuccessfully. It is only lately that I managed to extract from him enough to pay some tradesmen who would otherwise have put his son into the County Court.

'However, these pecuniary difficulties were not due to any extravagance on Ghose's part. His whole way of life was simple in the extreme. And I can fully believe that his inability to keep his appointment at Woolwich was entirely due to the want of cash.'

'Sir,' Cotton appealed fervently, 'will you please put all these points down in writing? I'm sure your contentions will persuade Lord Kimberley to allow Aurobindo one last chance to appear for his riding test.'

A couple of days later, James Cotton called at the India Office armed with Mr Prothero's letter and an application made out in his own hand. He met the secretary, judicial and public department and personally handed over the two memos. Following this, the long-drawn process of bureaucracy began, the memoranda reaching the office of the Secretary of State for India, thirteen days later.

Lord John Wodehouse, first Earl of Kimberley, was no novice at India Office. As a veteran diplomat whose exalted career spanned forty years, he was serving his third term as the secretary for India. Expectedly, his attitude hardened on reading the last paragraph of Prothero's letter which he found to be rather cheeky. In it Prothero had contended that to reject so able a Hindu just because he cannot ride is likely to give rise to a serious misunderstanding in India and to open the door to a plausible charge of partiality. Lord Kimberley then told his under secretary, George Russell, in no uncertain terms, what he thought of the Indian candidate's case.

'If Prothero or anyone else,' he began sarcastically, 'is under the dubious impression that a candidate ought to have a special exemption from the requirement of riding just because he is a Hindu, then the sooner he is disabused of such an absurd notion the better.'

'Lord Kimberley,' Russell gallantly intervened, 'you know that I fully share your views as to the importance of riding. However, in this case, I would give the candidate another chance to qualify. The candidate seems to me a remarkably deserving man, and I can quite believe that poverty was the actual cause of his failure to appear.'

'My dear George,' Lord Kimberley replied, looking at his under secretary straight in the eye, 'I am sorry that I cannot take a compassionate view of this case as you suggest. In the light of those reports of inflammatory speeches from the podium of the *Indian Majli*s, I should much doubt whether Mr Ghose would be a desirable addition to the service. How can you expect such an avid British-hater to administer well a large country such as India? I refuse to intervene in the case.'

But in a final act of chivalry, in spite of rejecting Aurobindo for horse riding, the Indian Civil Service Commission granted him the stipend of one hundred and fifty pounds that was awarded to all bona fide candidates of the ICS. This substantial amount enabled Aurobindo to pay all his debts before sailing back to India.

Not to be outdone by such an unexpected turn of events, Cotton managed to secure Aurobindo's employment in the royal service of the Gaekwad in Baroda. To Harimohan however, the appointment appeared far too submissive and hasty. Aurobindo's salary was fixed at a tenth of what it should have been to engage a civilian. And the Gaekwad triumphantly went around telling people that he had recruited a civilian for just two hundred rupees a month! Following this episode, Harimohan returned to India with the hope of meeting Aurobindo again in Baroda.

Meanwhile in India, Dr Ghose was anxiously waiting for his favourite son as he came to know of Aurobindo's plans to return home after the ICS exams. As Aurobindo had initially anticipated boarding the *Roumania* sailing from England towards the end of October, Dr Ghose went to Bombay to receive him in a fit of excitement. But when Aurobindo did not come, Dr Ghose returned to Khulna in a depressed frame of mind. Somehow, he was still under the impression that all was well and that Aurobindo was admitted into the ICS in spite of the delay.

But one afternoon an unexpected telegram from his bankers informed Dr Ghose that although Aurobindo's name did not figure on the list of the *Roumania,* the vessel had met with heavy weather and was wrecked off the coast of Portugal, with 113 people on board.

Coincidentally, an ICS officer of Khulna had invited Dr Ghose and the local superintendent of police to dinner on the same evening. But when Dr Ghose failed to show up, the officer sent his orderly to remind Dr Ghose about the appointment. He returned minutes later with the news that Dr Ghose was unwell. The officer rushed to the doctor's bungalow and found him unconscious. Dr Ghose passed away a couple of days later, just as lonely in death as he had always been in life, without meeting his dear son but with his name on his lips.

PART TWO

Search Within

It is possible that when the forces are ready, a man of destiny comes forth embodying the times appearing to make the nation. But, in reality, it is the nation that has to make itself. Nations, like all other living entities, must grow by themselves. No one can actually make them. And if a greater India is to arise it should be in the image of the Truth. Actually, India has the greatest chance because of its past and because a spiritual force is accumulated here.

Blank page

17

The Spiritual and the Mundane

A large number of passengers rushed to the deck as soon as the Indian coastline became visible. After a long journey of thirty-four days the *Carthage* was approaching Bombay, her ultimate destination.

Amongst the travellers on the deck was Aurobindo Ghose. The young man of twenty was returning to his land of birth after living for fourteen years in England. Something in that hazy landmass was stirring Aurobindo. He wondered whether the breeze blowing from the ancient land of spirituality was bringing this sense of uplift. Then he remembered an old experience that he had had when he was five. One day, a huge cloud of darkness entered into him and also covered the whole world. Today, for the first time in many years, the gloom of that experience was weighing less.

Aurobindo purposely let the heavy crowd of passengers, porters and sailors leave the ship before debarking. He helped to put his steel trunk on a porter's head and led him down the sloping ramp, gazing at the Apollo Bunder that stretched along the picturesque coast of the Arabian Sea.

Suddenly, the world around Aurobindo seemed to blur. He realised the significance of the extraordinary moment when his thoughts began to vanish. And no sooner did he tread on Indian soil than a stupendous calm engulfed him. Stepping aside from the crowded entry, Aurobindo became in-drawn, letting the vast downpour of peace rush into him. It was an unusual, concrete spiritual experience that carried a clear feeling of the Infinite pervading material space and the Immanent inhabiting material objects and bodies. Within moments, this downpour of peace vanquished the darkness dwelling within him. It was as if an invincible force from above was reclaiming Aurobindo's inner being without any opposition from the alien usurper.

But a gentle tap from the porter soon brought him back to earth. Although the peace that had descended was to remain within him for months, the buzz of the surrounding crowd came back to the fore as soon as the effect of the spontaneous spiritual experience began to fade away. The din raised by the tonga drivers trying to catch his attention as he emerged from the customs office was in glaring contrast to the peace he had just experienced. Forcing his way through the obstructing men, the porter pushed Aurobindo's baggage into the rear of a single horse-drawn tonga. Since the rear was blocked by his big metallic trunk, Aurobindo climbed in beside the coachman as the tonga drove off.

He mechanically directed the coachman to take him to a hotel where he could spend the day before catching the next train to Baroda. Avoiding the midday traffic of the main thoroughfares, the coachman deliberately wound his way through smaller streets offering Aurobindo a glimpse of the poverty of the great city of Bombay. Men were bathing in open spaces around municipal taps and women were washing clothes. However, not everything about the city offended his senses. The myriad saris hanging from the balconies on both sides of the road appealed to him. They seemed to add a vivid touch of artistry on the bare, colourless walls of the city. And just as the bright attire of the citizens stirred him, he was impressed by the elegance of Indian women.

But Aurobindo was totally unprepared for what was to follow. As soon as a vegetable cart overturned on hitting a pothole a European sergeant appeared on the scene and soundly beat up the cart-puller for holding up the traffic. What surprised Aurobindo was the meekness of the crowd that had assembled to watch the event. However, he felt reassured when people rushed to comfort the cart-puller as soon as the sergeant departed.

Something revolted within Aurobindo. There must be hundreds of such incidents occurring daily, he mused. He remembered his father's letters in which he used to highlight the alarming rise of racial atrocities all over India. In fact, the late Dr Krishna Dhone Ghose used to send Aurobindo cuttings from *Bengalee* to illustrate his point.

~

From Bombay, Aurobindo proceeded to Baroda, a sovereign state in West India, ruled by the young, charismatic Sayajirao Gaekwad. Earlier, through some friends, Aurobindo had met the Maharaja in England during the latter's tour of Europe. Being satisfied with Aurobindo's credentials, the monarch had immediately appointed him as a junior administrative officer and asked him to report at Baroda.

Although the coaches of the Indian Railways were less comfortable than those in Europe, Aurobindo's train journey from Bombay to Baroda was rendered lively by the warmth of his fellow travellers. They were neither too shy to ask the purpose of his visit to Baroda nor too tired to offer him food.

The next morning, Aurobindo's tonga took the wide boulevard, lined on both sides with brick-red buildings, leading from the railway station towards the city of Baroda. The Baroda College stood out conspicuously on the left, displaying its architectural oddities: pillared verandas and huge domes. The tonga crossed the narrow stretch of the Vishwamitri River and after a two- or three-minute drive further down from the hospitals he reached the Secretariat, or the *kothi*, from where the dewan ruled the state.

Aurobindo was soon directed to join the survey settlement department as an attaché. The Maharaja also urged the newcomer to learn Gujarati, the official language of the state.

Aurobindo was shifted by turns to the revenue department and to the state secretariat. But the job entrusted to Aurobindo was mostly dull, requiring only mechanical skill in doing research. Once he was even asked to consult the railway timetables of Europe! Clearly, his interest lay in areas other than administrative work.

Simultaneously, unwilling to relax or rest, Aurobindo swung into action. His close association with such radical groups as the *Indian Majlis* and the *Lotus and Dagger* in England had sharpened his interest in Indian politics so that his knowledge was quite deep and complete. Soon, he got in touch with Keshav Ganesh Deshpande, another fellow-student of Cambridge. Deshpande was a practising barrister in Bombay and was also a part-time editor of an English magazine named *Induprakash*. Knowing his strong nationalistic views in Cambridge, Deshpande requested Aurobindo to write a series of articles about the affairs of the Indian National Congress, the largest political body of the time.

Soon, through a series of articles named 'New Lamps for Old', Aurobindo applied himself to exposing the wrong policies and the defects plaguing the eight-year-old Congress. He began publishing his articles within six months of his return to India in 1893. Understandably, the publication of the first two articles created a furore in the political circles of Bombay, and Justice Mahadev Govind Ranade, the eminent Maratha leader who was connected with *Induprakash*, sent a warning to the editor that he might be prosecuted for sedition. Deshpande was in a fix. He requested Aurobindo to tone down his criticism. But feeling unable to air his views sincerely, Aurobindo lost all enthusiasm for writing the series and even though he somehow finished it, he took a long time. He despised the Congress' mendicant policy and had openly aimed at finding a remedy.

As an interesting sequel, Justice Ranade sent for the intelligent, young writer who had mounted the maiden attack on the 'blind' leaders of the Congress. When Aurobindo turned up for the half-hour interview in Bombay, not only did Justice Ranade extract a promise from him not to attack the Congress leaders but he also insisted that Aurobindo should turn his energies to some constructive work such as jail reform.

18

Re-establishing the Family Links

A year after returning from England, Aurobindo travelled to Deogarh to re-establish his links with his only sister, youngest brother and the other members of his maternal family.

The beautiful Hindi-speaking Santhal belt of Bengal, rugged, undulating and red, is interspersed with hillocks and craggy boulders strewn over fertile fields. Clusters of mud huts punctuate the vast fields, surrounded by the shade of bamboo groves. Small rivers such as the Darowa, Yamunajor and Oosri criss-cross the region, their sandy beds lying exposed during the greater part of the year.

Several small towns had sprung up in these parts during the nineteenth century and because of their nearness to the Bengali-speaking region, they had attracted the gentry to invest in diverse businesses. Many well-to-do Bengalis had also migrated to this region in search of peace and tranquillity. But more than its fame as a holiday resort, the quiet little town of Deogarh is famous for the temple erected in praise of Lord Baidyanath, earning the township its second name—Baidyanath Dham.

One summer afternoon, in the year 1894, a tonga halted in front of Rajnarayan Basu's house in the Purandaha locality of

Deogarh. Soon Rajnarayan's eldest son, Jogendranath, came out to receive the guest, whom he was expecting.

'*Arey* Auro, *aye*,' he said affably, embracing his nephew fondly. 'Do you remember me, Auro? I'm your Borho Mama, Jogen.'

Soon they were joined by a slightly younger but avowedly tougher man resembling Jogendra. This was Aurobindo's Chhoto Mama, Monindra. Aurobindo bent down and touched his uncles' feet. By then Aurobindo's grandfather, the venerable Rajnarayan Basu and his wife, Nistarini, had also arrived at the gate.

This was Aurobindo's first visit to Deogarh since his return to India. Soon a girl of about sixteen stepped forward and sought Aurobindo's blessings. This was his only sister, Sarojini, who was a two-year-old toddler the last time he had seen her.

After a refreshing bath, Aurobindo put on a dhoti and a tight-fitting shirt. Then as he was opening his trunks, he noticed that four children were curiously waiting to see what was inside. As they had expected to find expensive clothes and perfumes among the belongings of their Europe-returned cousin, the children were quite baffled by the presence of dozens of books underneath a few essential clothes. 'Does Aurodada read all these books?' they seemed to ask one another in awe.

Later, a teenager ran into the big courtyard behind the house and requested his grandmother to serve him lunch. His upper body was bare and he only wore a dirty dhoti below his waist.

'Bari,' his grandmother admonished, 'first wash your hands and meet your brother. Didn't I ask you to return home early?'

This was Aurobindo's first meeting with his youngest brother since he was three months old. Aurobindo was amused at the sudden thought that his brother had been christened Emmanuel Matthew at birth. However, he was later renamed Barindra Kumar, meaning son of the ocean, because of his birth in Norwood, close to the Atlantic Ocean.

Later in the afternoon, Sarojini brought Aurobindo a cup of tea and sat down beside him. She was fascinated by her brother's quiet personality and looks—a very delicate face, long hair cut in English fashion, and a very shy person.

'Why don't you stay with us in Baidyanath instead of living alone in Baroda?' she asked sweetly.

'I would be delighted to settle here,' her brother assured. 'But mustn't I work and earn? Who'll look after mother, Barin and you if I don't earn? By the way,' Aurobindo said, changing the topic, 'who are the kids that were here a while ago?'

'Oh, the three good-looking ones are our Nau Mashi Lilavati's children—Kumudini, Sukumar and Basanti. They are from Calcutta. The other one is another aunt's son Abinash or Hoopo, as he is called. However, why don't you join us for our evening excursion down the Darowa River? I'll introduce you to them.'

Half-an-hour later, Barin, Sarojini and the four children led Aurobindo towards the river. It was an enchanting evening with the soil rendered redder with the slanting rays of the sun. The excursion began in a relaxed mood under the boundless, effulgent sky and amidst the heady aroma of the *mahua*. Soon the children dispersed into the woods. But deeply drawn by his Sejda's quiet personality, Barin lingered on beside Aurobindo who spoke to him after what seemed an eternity.

'Bari,' he asked softly, 'has this beautiful display of nature ever stirred you? Have you ever thought that this river, these hills, the woods actually represent the body of Mother India?'

Barin was taken aback. 'No I have never thought about them that way,' he confessed.

'Have you heard of a book called *Ananda Math* by Bankim Chandra Chatterjee?'

'I have heard of Bankim Babu of course, but no, I haven't heard of the book.'

'In it there is a wonderful song that contains these exact thoughts and describes the country as the Mother. Read it and tell me what you think of it.'

During his stay at Deogarh, Aurobindo also paid a visit to his mentally-deranged mother.

'My Aurobindo was not so big,' Swarnalata argued, 'he was very small.'

When it was explained to her that he had come back from England after completing his studies she suddenly had a flash of memory and said, 'My Aurobindo had a cut on his finger.' He indeed bore the mark of a cut received from a broken bottle and Swarnalata recognised him instantly after the mark was shown to her.

Having taken a fancy on Sejda, Barin gave up his bohemian life and pored over *Ananda Math*.

'Sejda, the song is wonderful,' Barin professed after a week. 'But isn't it strange that half of it is in Bengali and the other half in Sanskrit? I must confess that I could understand only the parts written in Bengali.'

'You see,' Aurobindo explained patiently, 'some verses contain a strange power which, incanted aloud, creates the magical effect of a mantra. And that song by Rishi Bankim goes beyond just glorifying our Motherland. It is indeed a mantra!'

Admittedly, Dr K D Ghose's fourth son was quite different from the other three. While Benoybhushan, Manomohan and Aurobindo were born in India and educated in England, Barin was born in England and brought up in India. Eight years younger than his third brother, Aurobindo, Barin grew up to be an independent lad, endowed with a strong mind. Secretly, he respected intellectual and clever people. For this reason, Aurobindo was the subject of his immense admiration and worship.

Possessing a natural flair for managing youth, Barin was ideally cut out to be Aurobindo's lieutenant. Living near the legendary Rajnarayan Basu had also given him a natural penchant for patriotism. Another event that marked an important turn in Barin's formative years occurred when he came in contact with Sakharam Ganesh Deuskar, a Marathi living in Bengal. Barin came under Deuskar's tutelage while studying at Deogarh High School. A little after this, a small club for body building was started on the bank of the Darowa and Barin became one of its active members.

One afternoon, Barin and his two friends went on an excursion to the Nandan Hills. Satyaranjan Guha Thakurata and Suresh Ghose were Barin's classmates who had often come together to this place with Deuskar. The view from the summit was captivating. Being aware of Aurobindo's second visit to Deogarh, Satyaranjan asked Barin to say something about his Sejda.

'Oh, Sejda is the most fascinating person on earth,' Barin bragged proudly. 'And among the first things he asked me to read is Bankim Chandra's *Ananda Math*. The book contains a unique song written in praise of Mother India known as *Vande Mataram*. Sejda says it's a poem whose meaning will slowly be revealed with time. He says that Mother India is waiting to be delivered from the shackles of the alien rulers. We should give up luxuries and pool in our extra resources to help the needy who are also the children of Mother India.'

The words of Aurobindo seemed to have struck a deep chord within Satyaranjan's heart. He requested Barin to tell more.

'Sejda has a clear vision of the future. He advocates that young men build strong bodies, strong minds and strong characters. These men should form small armies of dedicated soldiers who will readily lay down their lives for the liberation of the Mother! Sejda also envisages a spiritual awakening in the country before the work of nation building can begin. And this process of re-awakening has begun for all to see.'

By then, evening had descended on the countryside. And the boys dashed down the slopes of the Nandan Hills like dark nimble-footed gazelles against the crimson backdrop of the western sky.

In a remarkably contrasted situation thirteen years later, destiny would bring back Barin and Suresh together again. But this time, Barin the patriot, would have to face the brunt of a criminal investigation led by the law-enforcer Suresh.

19

Distant Rumblings

Sayajirao Gaekwad had ascended the throne of the state of Baroda at the tender age of thirteen and his history reads like a fairy tale. Twelve years later, coinciding dubiously with Aurobindo's arrival at Baroda, the monarch was facing one of the most formidable political challenges of his lifetime. There was a keen battle for supremacy between four leading personalities of his state—John Biddulph, the agent of the governor general (AGG), Manibhai Jassabhai, the dewan, FAH Elliot, an ICS officer and the administrator of the Barkhali department and Vasudev Sadashiv Bapat, an officer working under Elliot. It was Bapat who suddenly found himself suspended from service by the dewan under pressure from the AGG.

Two years later, the Maharaja was still in a deep predicament as the case had been over-publicised and blown out of proportion, bringing the entire focus squarely on him. He knew that whatever decision he made was sure to irk either of the two parties—the Gujaratis or the Marathis. While, on one hand, he was assured of Bapat's continued honesty and integrity, he also knew that he would have to skilfully play his cards in order not to vex the

Residency. On the other hand, showing injustice to a meritorious officer would demoralise his cadre and inevitably send the wrong signal of servility and submissiveness to the British. Yet he must also be careful not to drive a bigger wedge between him and the Gujarati majority of the state. The predicament weighed so heavily on Sayajirao's mind that he lost sleep.

It was at this point that the Maharaja had a chance meeting with an officer of the Bengal cadre who suggested that he should consult an upcoming young barrister from Calcutta, of whom the Maharajas of Burdwan and Darbhanga were the illustrious clients. Harimohan Dutt was known for his adroitness and was sure to give good advice to His Majesty. The Maharaja wondered whether anyone could actually find a solution to the problem plaguing him. Yet something about the name did stir him and he asked his private secretary to send an urgent telegram to his agent in Calcutta asking him to contact Barrister Dutt immediately and send him to Baroda.

To Harimohan, the gap of over two years since his last meeting with Aurobindo seemed enormous, and he thought of him constantly. But when a Marathi gentleman dropped in at his office and announced that he was the representative of the Maharaja of Baroda and showed him the monarch's telegram soliciting the barrister to come to Baroda immediately, Harimohan was extremely thrilled at the thought of meeting Aurobindo again. He set off within two days of the invitation and reached Baroda on the fourth day. To his astonishment, it was Aurobindo who had been deputed by the Maharaja to receive him at the station. At twenty-three, Aurobindo now looked a lot more mature and wore his suit and *pugri* with an informal dignity and elegance.

His cane added a peculiar touch of gentility accentuated by the imposing moustache and his shoulder-length hair.

Harimohan could not hide his smile.

'What a pleasant surprise,' he said holding out his hand. 'I had no idea that *you* would come to the station.'

'Well, well, fancy Hurry Mohun Dutt, bar-at-law and legal advisor to India's entire monarchy!' Aurobindo remarked jokingly. 'The next call may come from the viceroy himself!'

'Yes, in that case my advice to him would be to pack up and leave the country!'

The two men laughed heartily while the coachman was putting the visitor's baggage onto the carriage.

'The Maharaja expects to speak to you tonight after dinner,' Aurobindo said. 'He seemed to be in an awful hurry to meet you. But then not finding any free time, he asked you to join him for dinner. So present yourself at the gate of the Luxmi Vilas Palace on the dot of 7.55. Dinner is served at eight.'

'Now, wait a minute! Don't wriggle out of the situation so easily. I'm not going anywhere without you. Besides, I don't even know where this palace is. Are you telling me that the Maharaja has not invited you?'

Aurobindo's diplomatic silence said it all.

Harimohan looked perplexed.

'I can't believe this! There are thousands of men waiting for a brief meeting with His Majesty, and you refuse the honour of an invitation to dine with him?'

That evening, Harimohan was waiting in the hall for a quarter-of-an hour when Aurobindo came down unhurriedly. He was appalled to see Aurobindo in the same casual clothes that he wore in the morning.

'Aren't you going to offend His Highness with such plain clothes?' Harimohan asked sceptically.

'I don't think he'll even notice,' Aurobindo replied, looking admiringly at Harimohan in his black evening suit and stylish bow tie. 'The Maharaja's guest of honour looks so elegant that he himself may feel under-dressed.'

Soon they mounted the open phaeton that was waiting under the portico. There was something about the carriage's old, neglected look that instantly suggested that it belonged to Aurobindo. And even though the horse was big and stout, it moved at an alarmingly unhurried pace that matched its master's sense of smug informality.

As the silhouette of the Luxmi Vilas Palace stood out against the glow of the moonlit sky, it reassured Harimohan that they were not too far away from their destination. He now understood that the reason for Aurobindo's aplomb was because of the trivial distance that separated Dandia Bazar from the palace.

'By the way, Auro,' Harimohan asked, 'do you have any idea why the Maharaja has sent for me?'

'I suppose it is in connection with the ongoing Bapat case in which the land officer has been charged with allegations of corruption and extortion.'

'But surely, the dewan or any local legal expert would be better instructed than me to guide the Maharaja to a conclusion.'

'That's where the complications begin. The dewan himself is a party to the whole affair and is acting in connivance with the British Resident. Besides, the matter has degenerated into a local political feud—the Gujarati dewan against the Marathi land officer. And the whole entanglement arose during the Maharaja's tour of Europe so that he now finds himself in the unenviable position of an adjudicator! Whichever side he takes, he is bound to hurt the sentiment of the other.'

By then the phaeton was in front of the royal gate and the two friends alighted. The palace was a massive structure of many domes and minarets, surrounded by seven hundred and twenty acres of lawns and artificial pools which took ten years to build at the astronomical cost of six million rupees.

Aurobindo led Harimohan through an elaborately carved *porte cochère* and a wide corridor. He showed him the famous Durbar Hall. As the two visitors climbed up the grand marble staircase, Harimohan's attention was drawn to the huge Italian classical paintings and statues of the same style adorning the corners and niches of the staircase.

At the top of the staircase they met two uniformed guards who immediately stood to attention and saluted Aurobindo and the Maharaja's distinguished guest. A pageboy took the visitors to the Maharaja's drawing room. The Maharaja sauntered to the door to welcome them.

'Thanks, Mr Dutt, for answering my call and coming so soon,' he said, warmly holding out his hands. 'I am truly grateful for your solicitude.'

'Your wish is a command, Your Majesty,' Harimohan replied, shaking the Maharaja's hand. 'Pray, what can I do for you?' he asked courteously.

'There's no hurry. We can discuss the matter leisurely after dinner. I know Mr Ghose is a nocturnal bird, so it would not be a problem for him but would you mind if we discuss something after dinner, till as late as, say, eleven o'clock?

'Not at all, I'm totally at your disposal,' replied Harimohan.

'Good then, let's finish dinner first. Please come.'

The Maharaja was short and stout but had a charismatic presence. The dinner was a simple European repast, cooked by a French chef and served by a portly English butler. After dinner Sayajirao invited Harimohan into his drawing room. Harimohan noticed that he was alone with the monarch and understood that Aurobindo had discreetly withdrawn.

'Please take your seat, Mr Dutt. I hope you are comfortable here?' the Maharaja enquired graciously. 'I put you up with your friend thinking you would be happy in his company.'

'I'm very satisfied, Your Majesty. I couldn't possibly be happier anywhere else in your beautiful city except near Aurobindo.'

'I entirely understand your feeling. It is difficult not to be swayed by Mr Ghose's simplicity and intellectual abilities. He has the potential to be of much greater help to my administration, if only he was a little more regular and punctual. But somehow he isn't interested in administrative work. Yet I have a tremendous soft corner for him and for his uncommon command over English. I won't hide it from you, but I use him freely for writing most of my important speeches. And believe it or not,' the Maharaja added with a laugh, 'Mr Ghose has the impudence to refuse my invitations! I don't think you'll find a single employee or subject in my kingdom who has the guts to decline such solicitations.'

'I suppose, Your Majesty, Aurobindo wouldn't be as likeable as he is if he became more conforming and punctual,' Harimohan replied cautiously.

The Maharaja laughed out merrily again.

'Well said, my friend. The only reproach I have against Mr Ghose is his stubbornness. When he decides not to do something I feel even my royal edict will not be able to make him budge.

For instance, I had instructed him to learn Gujarati within six months of his appointment. Yet, even after two years, Mr Ghose refuses to appear for the vernacular language examination. And so far,' the monarch added with a chuckle, 'even indirect threats of cutting his pay have yielded no result. So I suppose the matter has to be dropped.'

The short silence that followed was soon broken by the Maharaja himself.

'Now, then, Mr Dutt,' he said growing suddenly serious, 'I suppose you are aware of the basics of the Bapat case? It is not a solvable predicament.'

The Maharaja showed Harimohan a précis of the case prepared by none other than Aurobindo. For its preparation, Aurobindo had had to visit the monarch at the quiet South Indian hill resort of Ooty where he was spending his summer holidays. It covered all aspects of the case from the beginning to the setting up of the Bapat Commission, whose verdict was due shortly.

'However,' the Maharaja added, 'I've gathered from dependable sources that they've found a way to wriggle out by leaving the final decision on me!'

'Your Majesty, I would like you to clarify some points. Please pardon me for being so blunt, but I suppose dismissing Bapat summarily would affect the morale of your cadre and also bring a great blow to your personal pride.'

Harimohan noted satisfactorily that this brought a significant smile of appreciation on the Maharaja's face.

'I have a suggestion instead. Suppose you dismiss the mischief-maker himself? In Bengali there's a proverb: "An empty stable is preferable to owning a naughty cow." Why not get rid of the tormentor, Manibhai Jassabhai?'

'But Manibhai is Biddulph's man. So wouldn't it amount to supplying the Resident with more grist to depose me like one of my ancestors?'

'Then Your Majesty, acquit Bapat, but dismiss both! That way you're sure to kill the snake without breaking the stick!'

The Maharaja remained thunderstruck for a couple of seconds but recovered fast.

'Yes,' he said triumphantly, with an oblique smile playing across his mouth. 'That is indeed the solution that has been eluding me all this time!'

Then as if glossing over his sudden victory, he kept twisting his short moustache absent-mindedly.

Sayajirao was so impressed by Harimohan's sharpness of intellect and his friendly assistance that besides paying him his requisite fees of forty gold *mohur*s, he generously gave away one of his magnificent pearl rings as a special token of gratitude. But Harimohan was totally unprepared for the next surprise. With appreciation written in his eyes, the ruler then made the enviable proposition to the barrister to become his next dewan.

Khaserao Jadhav, one of the Maharaja's favourite employees, was a distant relative of the monarch. He was posted as the collector at Navsari and returned to Baroda occasionally. The day after the appointment with the Gaekwad, Harimohan and Aurobindo met their host over tea, where his brother, Madhavrao, was also present. After the cool westerly breeze had set in, the master of the house ordered four armchairs to be installed under the big neem tree. From where Khaserao, Madhavrao, Aurobindo and Harimohan now sat, nothing but the Luxmi Vilas palace's central tower could be seen. It seemed to reach high in the sky longing, as it were, to capture the dying rays of the setting sun.

'That's a beautiful sunset,' Madhavrao said. 'But will the sun ever set on the British Empire?' he wondered metaphorically.

'No, I am afraid the axiom is very true,' Harimohan replied. 'I see no possibility of the British supremacy declining over its vast empire.'

'What is needed,' Aurobindo asserted quietly, 'is the organisation of the national will to counter the Raj's vice-like grip over us. What we should do is to organise local committees of action throughout the country to carry out any mandate of the central organisation. These local leaders must stay among the people.'

'But this will require a lot of time and a lot of preparation!' Khaserao exclaimed.

'Its preparation and action may indeed take thirty years before fruition. In fact, there are three sides to these political ideas and activities. First, a secret revolutionary organisation must be founded and its central objective would be an armed insurrection. Second, there must be a propaganda intended to convert the whole nation to the ideal of independence. And third, there must be an organisation of the people to carry on a public opposition to foreign rule.'

The others listened to him stupefied.

After a pause, Aurobindo continued, 'It is true that India is disarmed; but with proper organisation and help from outside, this difficulty might be overcome. India is a vast country and given the smallness of the regular British armies, even guerrilla warfare might be effective here. However, what would make it even more practical is a general resistance and revolt. Besides, I don't rule out the possibility of a general revolt in the Indian army.'

The Jadhavs and Harimohan did not realise how prophetic Aurobindo's utterances were. But his far-off visions had a power of conviction, particularly, his plan for a three-pronged attack against the government seemed very well-conceived.

'First and foremost,' Aurobindo emphasised, 'lies the task of establishing the idea of independence in the minds of the people. At the same time, first we need to push a party and then the whole nation into an organised political activity. The Congress must be captured and made an instrument for revolutionary action. And after this, voluntary forces must be created all over the country. These will have to form the nucleus of an army of open revolt in the future.'

There was something captivating about Aurobindo's speech that held the listeners spellbound.

As there were a couple of days left before his departure, Harimohan kept a close watch on Aurobindo's routine. He was not only intrigued by the Gaekwad's appraisal of Aurobindo's intellectual abilities, but also by his comments on his irregularity and lack of punctuality at the office. He found that Aurobindo read far into the night and rose late. After the morning tea, he would sit down to write poetry up to ten o'clock. He took his bath between ten and eleven when lunch would be served. A cigar and the journals that he liked to read would be by his side while eating.

'Would you like me to look for a job for you in Calcutta?' Harimohan asked on the eve of his departure. 'I have contacts with some big business houses and quite a few royal and aristocratic families too. I can try.'

'No, not yet,' Aurobindo replied frankly. 'There's a clear anti-British feeling building up in western India which I feel will soon crystallise into a viable movement. I earnestly feel that this discontent needs to be exploited so that its rumblings may be transported some day to Bengal. However, right now, it is inconceivable to start anything directly in Bengal where the ground is unprepared. I'm trying to contact the leaders in Maharashtra who can help me in this regard.'

20

Aurobindo at Home

Five years after his return to his homeland, Aurobindo felt the urge to learn his mother tongue properly as he could not write or speak it well. So he decided to find a tutor who would assist him in conversational Bengali. With the help of Rabindranath Tagore, Aurobindo's uncle Jogendra Nath Basu found for him, within a short time, a tutor with an interest for literature. So on his way back to Baroda, Aurobindo was accompanied by Dinendra Kumar Roy.

At first, Dinendra was a bit unnerved by his pupil's exceptional intellectual credentials. When he heard that Aurobindo's marks in Greek and Latin in the Classical Tripos were unrivalled even by the best of European students, he imagined him as a spectacled youth of big stature, attired in European clothes, complete with hat, coat and boots.

Quite unexpectedly, Dinendra received a jolt on meeting his pupil face to face. He was struck by Aurobindo's Indianness. His long, thin, undulating hair, parted in the middle, lent him a somewhat mystic air. And while his face bore some marks owing to chicken pox and his eyes had a soft, dreamy expression, Aurobindo's dark complexion was more that of the middle-class Bengali rather than a Europe-returned aristocrat.

However very soon, Dinendra was to discover Aurobindo's uncommonness. One day, Dinendra asked him, a trifle perplexed, 'Why don't your two brothers ever send money to their mother and sister?'

After a thoughtful pause, Aurobindo replied, 'My eldest brother is a moody bachelor and never seems to have enough money to cover even his own expenses. My second brother has just got married and has discovered marriage to be an expensive luxury!'

Another simple incident brought forth before Dinendra a taste of Aurobindo's profound love and compassion. He noticed him filling a money order form. He also wanted to send some money to his family but was hesitating to ask for his dues. But now, he brought up the topic. Aurobindo smiled, took out his bag and poured out everything that was there.

'This is all that is left,' he said. 'Send it to your family.'

Dinendra was embarrassed. But Aurobindo would not listen to his protests. He insisted that Dinendra's need was greater and therefore he must send that money home.

At the height of winter which is quite severe in Gujarat, Dinendra never saw Aurobindo use more than a simple blue shawl. To Dinendra, Aurobindo was a *brahmachari* sanyasi, to whom acquiring knowledge was the sole mission in life. Ignoring the ubiquitous mosquitoes, Aurobindo would sit motionless for hours beside his lamp immersed in the study of books.

Aurobindo liked to eat his food cooked simply. He had a preference for Bengali cuisine and hence a Bengali cook was engaged and brought to Baroda. But within a few days, it became evident that the man knew nothing about cooking. The reason for his accepting this job was his inability at getting one at home. But Aurobindo would eat without a murmur, which only emboldened the cook in his ignorance. However, for Dinendra, the cooking was usually so bad that he could not get it down his throat.

Once, Aurobindo wanted to invite guests for dinner and asked the cook if he could prepare a four-or-five-course meal. Ghee and spices were bought in huge quantities. The cook managed to mess up the dishes and the food was quite inedible. But Aurobindo's magnanimity and sense of humour did not allow him to be upset. On the contrary, he had a hearty laugh at the amusing incident.

Krishna, the local servant, once bought two tiny lemons for a pice. Suspecting dishonesty, Dinendra went to the market and bought three bigger ones for the same price and showed him. But Krishna had his own peculiar logic that baffled Dinendra.

'Didn't you notice how extraordinarily small my lemons were? How can you get more than two such lemons for a pice?'

Instead of getting upset, Aurobindo found such incidents amusing and laughed like a child.

Barring Khaserao's mansion, all the houses in which Aurobindo lived were queer. He could have got much better accommodation for the same rent even in a big city like Calcutta. But at Baroda 'Mr Ghose' was known to all. He was as much respected by the poor as the elite of Baroda. The love and respect he got from his college students bordered on reverence for a God. Almost from the beginning, Aurobindo lent his services to the Baroda College as a lecturer in French. Slowly over the years, other work of the college was added and this culminated in his obtaining the post of professor of English. Many students belonging to other colleges availed themselves of his lectures, which were given at the close of the term. But more than his college lectures, Aurobindo drew huge crowds whenever he presided over the meetings of the College Debating Society. For, it was a treat to hear him on the platform. On such occasions, the large College Central Hall would overflow with audience, which not only consisted of college students but also many educated persons from outside. Aurobindo was always at his best when the subject matter pertained to religion or philosophy.

Often, a well-decorated horseman would carry a message from the Maharaja's secretary. 'The Maharaja will be very pleased if you join him for dinner tonight.' or 'Can you please meet the Maharaja at such and such hour?'

But what was astounding was that Aurobindo would sometimes refuse such invitations. The Maharaja fully understood Aurobindo's worth and relied on him more than his highly paid administrative staff who were earning ten times his salary.

The famous Bengali artist, Shashi Kumar Hesh, once visited Baroda during Dinendra's stay and became acquainted with Aurobindo. He painted an oil portrait of Aurobindo in the Gaekwad's state guest house where the artist had stayed as an invitee of the Maharaja.

Another thing that puzzled Dinendra was Aurobindo's simple living style. He openly wondered how the glamour, opulence and other attractions of European society had not affected Aurobindo at all. Dinendra noticed that praise, even from people of eminence, meant little to Aurobindo. One interesting incident highlights this. Ramesh Chandra Dutt, an ICS officer, was once invited to Baroda by Sayajirao Gaekwad. Dutt's fame had already spread as the translator of the Ramayana and the Mahabharata, which had been published from abroad. Dutt had heard that Aurobindo was translating portions of these two epics. Naturally, he was curious and asked Aurobindo to show him his work.

On reading Aurobindo's translations, Dutt was so moved that he exclaimed, 'I feel sad to have wasted my time in translating these epics. I would never have published my own had I read your verses earlier.'

But even such praise failed to stir Aurobindo. He remained as quiet as ever. In fact, Dinendra felt that Aurobindo's calm was equally stoical before joy and sorrow, loss and gain, as well as praise and criticism.

21

Gunshots

During Harimohan's short stay in Baroda, a small news item in the *Kesari* had drawn his attention. Among its varied syllabus, Fergusson College of Poona was offering a degree course for undergraduates in botany. Knowing Indraneel's interest in the subject, the barrister made a mental note of it and informed Indraneel about the course on his completion of the First Arts. This eventually led Indraneel to western India.

Indraneel had no difficulty adapting to the new environment or in striking new friendships but a sudden outburst of plague in the region became a source of worry.

It all began innocuously with the virulent plague afflicting the districts of Bombay and then rapidly transforming the region into a playground of the scourge. Soon the government promulgated the Epidemic Diseases Act of 1897, the measures of which seemed by and large fair to the native leaders. But when the government posted the assistant collector of Satara in Poona to enforce the provisions of the Act, it unknowingly unleashed a far bigger terror among the natives than the dreadful plague itself. It was Assistant Collector Rand's dictatorial attitude that offended the public the most. Unexpectedly, the moment had arrived when peace-loving Indians in western India began to talk freely about self-defence, resistance and reprisal.

In the midst of this public anger, the British administration was gearing up for a rare event—the sixtieth anniversary of the coronation of Her Majesty the Empress Victoria. The state banquet at the Government House that was arranged in honour of the Queen was expected to host the entire who's who of Poona's high society.

On the evening of the Diamond Jubilee day, three boys were wandering through the streets to enjoy the lights and the celebrations. They were Sampatrao Fanse, Ganeshrao Dashputre and Indraneel Gupta, students of Fergusson College. It was quite late but none of them was willing to go back to the hostel even though the rules specified that they return before ten o'clock. At this point, Sampatrao got the idea of watching the official celebrations. The three friends sauntered towards Modibagh and turned left to reach Ganehkhind, where the Government House was located. As they approached the area, the dazzling lights took their breath away.

Since the celebrations were confined to the impregnable walls of the Government House, all that they could hear from the road were loud rounds of cheers and applauses. This went on till late evening. When the party broke, the policemen urged them to move along, explaining that the stretch of the road was reserved for the passage of the sahibs.

By then, the boys had had enough of the celebrations and decided to go back to their hostel. No sooner had they walked a quarter of a mile and reached the yellow mansion of Jamsetjee Jeejebhoy that they were startled by an animated cry. Their attention immediately fell on a man running along the opposite footpath. Another man who was simultaneously sprinting behind the hooded phaeton of an Englishman now jumped onto its rear stand. Then a gunshot rang out shattering the silence of the night. Instantly, the plucky man jumped down from the carriage and with his accomplice, dashed off into the open fields on the side of the road. Having carried out their attack, they quickly disappeared into the darkness.

All hell broke loose following the sound of a second gunshot. Even before the three boys realised what was happening, they were surrounded by gun-totting policemen and whisked away to a police station. They had a hard time proving their innocence. The boys vainly explained to the inspector conducting the enquiry that they were out on the streets solely to enjoy the lights and the celebrations. Expectedly, their pleas fell on deaf ears. Their presence at the site of the crime was far too incriminating, considering that they should have been in their hostels at that unearthly hour.

Fortunately, the real story behind the twin murders began to emerge soon after the arrest of Damodar Hari Chapekar, the chief perpetrator of the crime. But this was not devoid of controversy as it turned out that Damodar was a dropout of Fergusson College! Besides being witnesses of the crime, disproving their link with Damodar became another contentious issue for Indraneel and his friends in the court.

Finally, the presence of Barrister Harimohan Datta swung the case in their favour. Arguing the case through a local criminal lawyer, the dextrous barrister proved with relative ease that Indraneel and the two other boys had in fact enrolled after Damodar had dropped out of the college. But heightened by its prolonged hearing and a sensational final act of retribution, the Chapekar lawsuit was destined to gain immense popularity.

Damodar, Balkrishna and Wasudev Chapekar were three brothers living in Poona. Damodar was aggrieved by the excesses committed by Rand in handling the plague victims and took it upon himself to avenge his people by killing the tyrant. Just as he and his associates began to plan the assassination, the programme of the Jubilee Day celebration was published in the local dailies. Consequently, Damodar and Balkrishna planted themselves near the main gate of Government House while Mahadev Vinayak Ranade, another accomplice, hid himself elsewhere. Damodar allowed Rand's carriage to move ahead and ran behind it. He was aware that an officer named Ayerst was following close behind. He let Rand's carriage advance and jumped noiselessly onto its back. After undoing the flap, Damodar put in his pistol and fired at point-blank range at Rand. Mrs Ayerst saw a man jump down from the carriage in front and even as she was mentioning this to her husband, Ranade's gun rang out and Ayerst lay dead in her arms. Damodar was caught after a vigorous search was launched and he admitted to killing Rand. Ultimately, following a well-publicised trial, he was sentenced to death.

Earlier, a reward of twenty thousand rupees was announced for Damodar's associates. But the third Chapekar brother, Wasudev, swore vengeance when he learnt that two informers had given away Damodar to the police and determined to do something drastic. Eventually, Ranade and Wasudev assassinated the two informers, Ganpatrao and Ramchandra Dravid, in a sensational climax.

Indraneel and his friends were acquitted due to the absence of evidence, but they were unlikely to forget this episode.

22

Destiny's Hand

Through cautious efforts, Aurobindo got in touch with the revolutionary organisations of western India. He was also able to meet the legendary Thakur sahib sometime during the late 1890s. Prince of a small province, but the undisputed leader of a vast organisation of secret societies, Thakur sahib remained largely invisible to the rank and file of the organisation because his interaction was limited to his lieutenants only. He had captivated the minds of a large section of armymen who in principle had accepted his invitation to mutiny whenever the call would come.

Aurobindo was made the leader of the Gujarat circle soon after his meeting with Thakur sahib. These secret societies did extensive work and were able to influence many men. Aurobindo also met many other Rajput Thakurs who had revolutionary ideas, and they worked secretly remaining unsuspected by the government. One such leader, Thakur Ramsingh, was the president of a secret society in Maharashtra, the Bombay branch of which was managed by a council of five members. Aurobindo contacted this group and became a member. Eventually, Ramsingh was caught and put in jail. Later, he suddenly died there, possibly poisoned by the police.

But all these secret activities in Maharashtra could not possibly have paved the way for the revolution to reach Bengal. This was made possible by a tall and well-built youth who arrived in Baroda, carrying a *lota* and a lathi in the style of a touring sanyasi. His name was Jatindranath Banerjee. To Aurobindo and his friends, Jatindranath's arrival represented destiny's seal of approval on their plans. Jatindranath may not have been an intellectual, but he had a sharp tongue and large sparkling eyes. When Aurobindo learnt that Jatindranath's real intention for coming to Baroda was to learn the art of warfare, he contacted his friends lieutenant Madhavrao Jadhav, Khaserao Jadhav and K G Deshpande, who had little difficulty in arranging for his admission into the Gaekwad's army.

Earlier, with the aim of achieving total freedom, Jatindranath had set out to visit one princely state after another for joining their private armies. But no one was ready to employ a Bengali. His aim to master military skills remained a faraway dream. However, following Aurobindo's advice for circumspection Jatindranath posed as an up-country Brahmin, forsaking his Bengali antecedents and took on a *dehati* Hindi which he had learnt sometime earlier. Thus, he was able to get over what had earlier seemed an insurmountable hurdle. Jatindranath could have become an officer straightaway but chose to be a common soldier instead, judging that mastering the techniques of warfare would be easier at the lower level. His keen physical and mental abilities enabled him to get rapid promotions. He rose swiftly to the grade of the elite royal bodyguard.

The British resident of Baroda was supposedly asked by the government of Bengal on two occasions to look into the illegal induction of a Bengali youth into Baroda's royal army. But the charge could not be proved.

Coinciding with Dinendra Kumar Roy's stay in Baroda, K G Deshpande, the editor of *Induprakash*, joined the service of the Maharaja. Here, he and Aurobindo shared common lodgings in Khaserao Jadhav's bungalow. One evening, after returning from work, Deshpande and Aurobindo went out for a stroll, taking Dinendra along. While walking through Dandia Bazar, the three men stopped on the edge of the beautiful Sur Sagar, a vast pond on the outskirts of Baroda's old township. Leaning lightly against the railing that surrounded the mini-lake, they watched the large flock of birds.

'Don't these wild ducks remind you of the water birds of England?' asked Deshpande.

'Yes,' Aurobindo replied pensively. 'When my brothers and I went on vacation to Keswick, we saw plenty of them. After that excursion when we came to stay in London, Mrs Drewett came to stay with us. Soon we moved to rooms at the top of the building on Cromwell Road where the office of the South Kensington Liberal Club was located. These three years were perhaps the most trying of all in England for us. We were all so hard pressed that my elder brother, Benoy, had to agree to be an assistant to James Cotton, the secretary of the club, for five shillings a week. We used to get a slice or two of bread and butter and a cup of tea in the morning and in the evening only a penny saveloy, a kind of sausage. For nearly two years we had to go practically without dinner at that young age. We had no overcoats to protect ourselves from the awful winters of London, nor did we have proper bedrooms to sleep in. Besides, there was no heating arrangement within the club premises. There was also the confounded railway behind this place. Coincidentally, it was the same James Cotton who arranged my employment with the Gaekwad. And recently, he even came and met me here at Baroda College.'

'There's also some confusion surrounding your rejection in the ICS exams. What happened, couldn't you actually sit straight on the horse for a quarter of an hour?'

'My father did not send money and riding lessons at Cambridge were expensive,' Aurobindo admitted sincerely. 'However, my brothers took the rejection quite sportingly. After wandering in the streets of London when I should have been at Woolwich for my horse-riding test, I returned home and casually informed Benoy with an almost derisive smile: "I'm chucked!" My older brother took it rather philosophically and offered to play cards. After some time Manomohan dropped in and on learning about the rejection he set up a howl as if the heavens had fallen. After that all three of us sat down to smoke and played cards.'

'I also heard that you once met Oscar Browning,' Deshpande said excitedly.

'Yes,' Aurobindo replied, 'that was one night, when I was invited to coffee with one of the Dons, and in his rooms I met the great OB who was the feature par excellence of King's College. And while discussing the lively subject of a cotillion with the people who were gathered there, Browning passed to that of scholarships. He told me, "I suppose you know you passed an extraordinarily high examination. I have examined papers at thirteen examinations and I have never during that time seen such excellent papers as yours," meaning my Classical papers, at the scholarship examination.

'The great OB afterwards asked me where my rooms were,' Aurobindo humorously added. 'And when I answered, he said, "That wretched hole". Then turning to Robert Mahaffy, one of my later contemporaries at Cambridge, he added, "Look, how rude we are to our scholars! We get great minds to come down here and then shut them up in that box! I suppose it is to keep their pride down."'

The three men laughed aloud, causing a mild flutter among the migratory birds on the banks of the Sur Sagar.

~

Rajnarayan Basu had passed away by the time Dinendra Kumar Roy came to Deogarh in 1899. He met Jogendranath accidentally on the banks of the Darowa where Rajnarayan was cremated and conveyed his condolences.

'By the way,' Dinendra said, 'your nephew wrote a touching sonnet on his grandfather's passing.'

'Ah, yes,' Jogendranath acknowledged. 'I've been reciting it to all the people who have been calling on us ever since Auro's sonnet reached us.' Then Jogendranath enquired about the spread of plague in the western parts of the country.

'When plague broke out in Baroda,' Dinendra said, 'Aurobindo Babu had to shift to a bungalow on the outskirts of the town. But his new quarters are quite unfit for living and its roof is made of tiles. Frankly, cowsheds are better suited for human habitation than this dingy old place.'

'I've been wondering,' Jogendranath said, 'You know we feel concerned about Auro's future. Can't you convince him to get married and lead a family life?'

'And why don't *you* make the proposal? I don't think he can ignore your suggestion.'

'Whenever I tell him, he just smiles evasively. He doesn't even comment or reply.'

'Well, when I spoke to him about a *tantrik* whom I know, he eagerly wished to have his horoscope cast by him. Recently, on meeting me the astrologer confided, "Your pupil is a cut above other ordinary men and is very close to the monarch." But he also warned that he would face great hardship and deprivation in the future. He further said, "Although he earns well and would marry soon, his domestic life would bring him little or practically no happiness." So there you have your answer.'

'What? Auro will marry soon?' Jogendranath was aghast. 'Why, I must immediately run home and give this good news to my mother and Saro!'

23

Aurobindo's Marriage

Despite his considerable success, Harimohan was feeling frustrated as he had failed to bring back Saraju even after the stiffest psychological barrier had been cleared for her return. Although this mission had been uppermost in his mind during the ten long years that had passed since Saraju had been abducted, his fame and prosperity had fully bound him to Calcutta, turning him into a virtual prisoner of the city. However, the former CID officer whom Harimohan had deputed to trace Saraju had been successful in meeting Chhenu Kahar. From him he learned of Saraju's departure for Shillong with a couple named Bose. But even though the detective was able to track down the Boses in Shillong, there was no one in their house called Saraju. Nevertheless, the sleuth did find enough evidence to corroborate Birju's story. All he could say on his return to Calcutta was that there was indeed a widow living with the Boses but her name was Sujata and not Saraju, hailing from Burdwan and not from Seiya. Unfortunately, due to Sujata's refusal to appear before the officer, the detective was unable to give her physical description.

One nagging thought hounded Harimohan constantly. Was Saraju still interested in him after all these years? He tried to convince himself that whatever the consequence of their long separation may have been, he was duty-bound to bring her back at least for the sake of re-uniting her with her child.

Was it because she did not wish to come back to him that she did not meet the retired sleuth from Calcutta whom he had sent to investigate?

Among Bhupal Chandra Bose's eight children, Mrinalini or Menu, was the oldest. The beautiful fourteen-year-old girl was hardly four when Saraju, renamed Sujata, had taken charge of her and her siblings. Very soon, the Boses had ceased to look upon Sujata as an employee and treated her as a member of the family. Over the years, Mrinalini had grown extremely attached to her 'Sujudi'.

By thc cnd of thc third year at the Brahmo Girls' College, destiny had brought Mrinalini to the zenith of her life when her fate was about to get tied up with one of the most remarkable and forceful personalities of the age. The event occurred when her father's friend, Girish Chandra Bose, came across an advertisement in a leading newspaper. Realising that a professor would be a good match for Mrinalini, he contacted the advertiser.

Aurobindo met Mrinalini at the house of Girish Chandra and chose her at first sight as his destined wife. And while Aurobindo was then almost twenty-nine years old, Mrinalini was only fourteen. As it was unthinkable in those days of making the maiden visit to a prospective in-laws' house alone, Aurobindo had sought Harimohan's company and counsel to help him choose his future wife. While Girish Chandra was negotiating the marriage proposals for Mrinalini, Sujata had been given full charge to accept or reject any offer for Mrinalini on behalf of Bhupal Bose and Golapkamini who were not in Calcutta.

Asking Aurobindo and Harimohan to wait, Girish Bose's wife disappeared in the inner rooms where Sujata was busy preparing sweets and snacks for the two visitors. While Mrs Bose took one main plate and a smaller side plate in her hands, she asked Sujata to bring the other two. Sujata had not yet seen the prospective son-in-law. Keeping her eyes down, Sujata accompanied her hostess to the main hall where all the members of Girish Chandra's family were gathered to admire the prospective groom. As soon as they entered, the murmurs stopped. Mrs Bose bent forward to put the plates down before Aurobindo and made a gesture indicating Sujata to place her dishes before the other visitor. As Sujata stooped forward, keeping her eyes fixed on the bridegroom, she was amazed to hear her name being softly called by the man sitting before her. She had not noticed him at all.

'Saraju, is that you?' he said.

It was a name that she had not heard for a very long time. She looked up in wonder while her heart began to beat faster. Her eyes met those of Harimohan for the first time in a decade. A joyous expression of recognition was written all over her face just as it was on Harimohan's. But remembering that the room was full of known onlookers, she checked herself with dignity and quietly left the hall. Somehow in the buzz of excitement none except Aurobindo noticed the little drama that was enacted.

As it had fallen on Harimohan to supervise and co-ordinate everything on behalf of the groom, he was constantly in touch with the Bose family. Although Harimohan met Saraju whenever he called on Girish Chandra to settle small details such as the names of the invitees or to fix the time of the wedding, the first opportunity he got to speak to her was only the day before his friend's wedding.

Saraju eagerly asked a lot of questions about Indraneel and made Harimohan promise to bring him to the wedding feast. Commendably, Saraju kept up a dignified and brave front, not betraying her pent-up emotions even for an instant. When she finally saw Indraneel from behind a pillar she could not believe her eyes. How handsome and tall he looked! He was now twenty.

As Aurobindo's decision to marry in Hindu style had irked his Brahmo relatives, they had excused themselves from taking part in the ceremonies. This had created a void, but only momentarily. Meanwhile, Harimohan introduced his friend to Saraju one day when they dropped in to inspect the preparations. At first, Aurobindo was a little surprised by their fondness for each other but remembered the little exchange during the engagement.

Aurobindo's marriage took place on the last day of April 1901 in a rented house belonging to the Hatkhola Datta family on Baithakkhana Road in Calcutta's Sealdah area.

By a happy accident both Aurobindo and Mrinalini meant the lotus in Sanskrit. There may have been more to their relationship than met the eye for the similarities did not end just with their names. If an explanation given by Aurobindo is to be believed, both of them were born earlier as husband and wife at least in one past life. Elucidating how he had incarnated as Lord Krishna's grandson Aniruddha, Aurobindo highlighted the fact that Mrinalini had been his wife Usha. Therefore, it may not have been a coincidence that he had chosen her as his bride at first glance.

Mrinalini was an accomplished singer and would often play the table organ presented to her on the occasion of her wedding. Mrinalini's fair complexion glowed with a roseate hue. In fact, her soft hands and feet were forever tinged with that pinkish radiance of a baby's skin.

Expectedly, Aurobindo's lifestyle changed with the arrival of his wife. The relatives, who had boycotted the marriage, now showered blessings on their favourite nephew. As a result, the couple was reinstated in their midst and received with a huge show of affection.

And, with many others, they also received a call for dinner from the Tagores of Jorasanko. Dinendra Kumar Roy was a regular correspondent of Rabindranath Tagore even before his emigration to Baroda. It was through letters written by him from Gujarat that Tagore had learned much about Aurobindo. Being impressed by whatever Dinendra wrote to him about his uncommon employer, the poet sincerely regretted not knowing Aurobindo personally. As the ancestral family abode of the Tagores was a meeting place of leading intellectuals of the time, Rabindranath felt that Aurobindo's visit there was largely overdue. And on the appointed evening, the poet himself received the Ghoses.

'I formally welcome the two bloomed lotuses on behalf of all the members of my family,' he said affectionately, with an obvious reference to their names.

He led the visitors to the first floor of a section of the palatial mansion where other guests were assembled. Among them, scientist Jagadish Chandra Bose and his wife Abala were the most prominent. Another lady who instantly captivated their attention was Sarala Ghosal, a niece of Rabindranath.

At this point, Rabindranath brought up an old issue that he had kept in mind for a long time.

'Aurobindo Babu,' he began, 'your book of poems *Songs to Myrtilla* is really wonderful. I sent you word through your elder brother Manomohan.'

'Yes, I do remember Mano mentioning it to me,' Aurobindo replied shyly. 'Thanks.'

'I chanced upon some of your recent poems too. I find a clear undercurrent of mysticism in them. Could you define in a nutshell what the true connection between spirituality and art is?'

'Well, spirituality is the basis of art. Art tries to express the soul of things – the divine element in them. In a sense, spirituality is the highest form of art – the art of life itself. For it aims at creating a life of beauty pure in line, faultless in rhythm, replete with strength, illumined with light and vibrant with delight.'

The poet was ecstatic.

'You summarised it so beautifully!' he said with a touch of admiration. 'But now, please allow me to introduce you to the other guests.' Jagadish Chandra and his wife were already known to Aurobindo and had attended his wedding. And among the other guests were other luminaries of the Brahmo Samaj.

But it was Sarala Ghosal who began speaking to them. At twenty-nine, Sarala Devi was still unmarried—something that was unheard of in early-twentieth-century Bengal. Besides, she had independently taken up teaching in a school in remote Mysore and had become its secretary. She had also attained notoriety for freely mixing with men from all walks of life, treating them as her equals.

'Mr Ghose,' she said pleasantly, 'your friend Barrister Datta has apprised me of your nation building efforts in West India.'

At this point, Mrs Abala Bose called Mrinalini to introduce her to some friends who had just arrived. Aurobindo turned to Sarala Devi and nodded his head in approval.

'It seems you are in touch with such great leaders as Thakur sahib and Thakur Ramsingh,' Sarala Devi added, lowering her voice discreetly. 'I've also tried to organise things here so that youth power can be used for the benefit of the country. Young men are encouraged to imbibe the patriotic spirit at the gymnasium that I've set up in Ballygunge. But sadly, it is the true military spirit that is lacking in their training. I think it is essential to simultaneously develop the disciplines of the mind, body and character to become a worthy soldier.'

'You're right Miss Ghosal,' Aurobindo assented. 'And let me congratulate you for your commendable work among the youth. The surest way of achieving our goal is through the formation of small armies at the village level. Nothing worthwhile will come of the movement unless a true military grounding is given.'

Sarala Devi's eyes glowed brighter with excitement. Here was someone at last who supported her initiative to train the youth. So far, all others had criticised her.

'But can we really achieve anything without the use of arms?' she wondered.

'You'll find some oddities in the Indian Army. Given the smallness in the number of English officers, another mutiny could effectively be engineered within the army. Besides, guerrilla warfare could successfully be used against such an insignificant number of Europeans. And you'll be happy to know that there is someone who is actually undergoing training in the Baroda Army and hopefully, might soon be able to take up the task of instructing others.'

'Why, that's wonderful! How soon can he come?'

'I can't say that for sure but I'll send him to you with a note as early as possible.'

Then noticing that Mrs Abala Bose and Mrinalini were coming towards them, Sarala Devi quickly added, 'My address is 26 Ballygunge Circular Road.'

At that point, the scientist's wife sought Aurobindo's permission to let Mrinalini sing before the gathering. After Aurobindo consulted his wife and gave his approval, the older lady led the teenager to the organ. Mrinalini sat down and sought the poet's permission to sing one of his popular songs.

Then timidly at first, but gradually picking up confidence, Mrinalini sang the evergreen number: '*Aamaaro pauraano jaahaa chaay, tumi taai tumi taai go*,' to the delight of the audience. The first line of the song meant, 'You are that for which my heart yearns.' Even Aurobindo looked pleased to hear his wife sing so freely before the elite audience. As the presentation ended, the poet walked up to the singer and congratulated her for such a soulful rendition.

Then he looked at the listeners and said, 'I have a small confession to make.' He paused and continued with a glint of mischief in his eyes. 'When I composed this song for my musical play *Maayaar Khelaa*, I wrote it precisely with someone as timorous as Mrinalini in my mind to be sung to her beloved … but,' he added, subtly moderating his voice, followed by a pregnant break, 'in a far more romantic setting than this!'

The audience burst into laughter, followed by a thunderous round of applause. And Mrinalini swiftly covered her face with the end of her sari to hide her embarrassment.

24

Another Marriage

Once Mrinalini's wedding was over and the Boses were preparing to go back to Shillong, Harimohan met Bhupal Bose privately and explained to him the circumstances that led to Sujata's disappearance from their village. Moreover, his disclosure about sending an investigator to their house in Shillong brought about a sense of credibility.

Bhupal Chandra called his wife and told her everything. She seemed as bewildered at first as her husband. Ultimately, the couple sent for Sujata and asked her what she intended to do. Realising that she was feeling shy to reveal what was in her mind, Harimohan came to her rescue.

'Saraju,' he said calmly, 'I have told them the whole story about your abduction. Bhupal Babu and his wife have acted as your guardians for the past ten years and have provided you shelter and the most decent home you could expect. You are now a member of their family. So now I am asking for your hand from them. Will you please marry me?'

Everyone was aghast. Even Saraju was not prepared for such a rapid development.

'I have waited for you for over twenty-five years,' Harimohan continued sincerely. 'Do you realise that today we are nearing forty? If not now, when?'

'And how do you think Indraneel is going to react?' Saraju asked cautiously.

'I think, the best thing would be to tell him everything frankly. Besides, I've already acted as a father to him through all these years since your disappearance and will always remain one.'

'And the people of the village? Have you given thought to their reaction?'

'Look, I am sure the villagers won't dare say anything since my father has already given his blessings. Suffice it to say that there's going to be less trouble if we marry now than if we don't marry at all. You must understand that you will find neither shelter in the village nor in my house unless you become my legal wife.'

'I think Harimohan Babu is right,' Bhupal Bose said with authority. 'If he marries you first and then takes you to the village, no one can ever oppose it in consideration of his and the family's social status.'

'Now that Menu has gone, there's very little left to cheer me in Shillong,' said Saraju after a long struggle with herself. 'I knew even before my first marriage how much Harimohan loved me, but my superior caste stood in the way of our union. Now, on realising that he still loves me just as before, I don't dare refuse him any longer. He has turned down dozens of proposals from rich families for *my* sake. Besides, I want to be near my son.'

'Definitely,' Bhupal Bose replied with a broad smile. 'But before you leave, Sujata, we must first settle your wage. You have looked after the children and our household for so long. We have never discussed payments!'

'That you two have looked after Saraju and given her your affection is her greatest reward,' Harimohan intervened. 'It's indeed her good fortune that she found such wonderful hosts under the terrible circumstances of her life.'

'And see, what a wonderful ending it has brought to her story,' Golapkamini said with an air of pride. 'Who could have thought that by looking for a match for Menu we would stumble across such a noble suitor for Sujata!'

After marriage, Harimohan began spending entire weekends at home. Saraju was not only efficient but also knew her responsibilities well. Her decade-long exile from rural life had transformed her into a refined city girl, though she retained some of the rustic simplicity and sensibility. Her disarming smile contained a warmth that was alien to her urban sophisticated counterparts.

25

The Cause

After Jatindranath Banerjee was enlisted as a soldier under the pseudonym of Yatindra Upadhyay, a real Upadhyay discovered him and under the threat of being exposed he had to give up his cherished service in the Baroda army. Happily by then his training was over and he felt sufficiently disciplined to train others. With Aurobindo's blessings, he then set off on his journey back home carrying with him a letter and the colourful attire of the Maharaja's mounted bodyguard to establish the first-ever school for training young revolutionaries in Bengal.

Jatin called upon Sarala Ghosal and gave her Aurobindo's sealed letter, explaining that he had come from the far-away state of Baroda. Sarala Devi's large eyes instantly lit up and a smile appeared on her comely face.

'We've been waiting,' she said, 'for someone like you to teach the art of warfare, proper military temperament, discipline and moral character to the youth of Calcutta. I must immediately give the good news of your arrival to my associates.'

By virtue of her birth at Jorasanko, Sarala Devi had developed natural talents for music, literature and arts while imbibing the elements of patriotism from her father. She had attained considerable fame as a singer and had sung *Vande Mataram* from the platform of the Indian National Congress.

Another person who became associated with the movement was an Irish woman named Margaret Noble, a disciple of Swami Vivekananda. The Swami arranged for a house for Margaret, later renamed Nivedita, who established a Hindu girls' school. Slowly, Nivedita became convinced that India's troubles awaited political solutions and thereby got in touch with men of more advanced political views such as the Japanese Kakuzo Okakura, who came to Calcutta and spoke about British dominion of India.

In this climate of 'revolution', a barrister named Pramathanath Mitra was unanimously selected as the commander-in-chief of the newly-founded organisation called the Anushilan Samiti. Under the scheme, Jatindranath took up the overall charge of training the boys with Pramathanath Mitra as president, Barrister Chittaranjan Das and Aurobindo as vice presidents, and Surendranath Tagore as treasurer. With Sarala Devi's help, Jatindranath was able to influence a fairly large section of the anglicised *nouveau riche* society of Ballygunge. He selected an ideal spot for his club at 108 Upper Circular Road.

When Swami Vivekananda abruptly passed away, it predictably left a big vacuum in the life of Nivedita. She soon drew up her political agenda and resolved to visit West India, ostensibly to deliver speeches. But at the back of her mind there seemed to be the secret desire to win over the Gaekwad for the cause. Therefore, it was imperative that she should pay an urgent visit to Baroda.

When Nivedita arrived in Baroda in late 1902, Aurobindo and Khaserao received her at the railway station. Before that, however, Aurobindo only knew her as the writer of the book *Kali the Mother*, which he found very inspiring. After Khaserao left, Nivedita and Aurobindo walked to the vast garden adjoining the house where she stayed.

With disarming candour she enquired, 'I hear, Mr Ghose, you are a worshipper of Shakti?'

'You're right,' he agreed.

This was a direct hint that Nivedita knew him already as a committed revolutionary.

'And your book *Kali the Mother* is revolutionary as well as not non-violent.'

'Yes, I was commissioned by Swamiji, you know, to awaken the nation.'

'Why don't you tell me something about him?'

'Oh sure, to speak about him is a privilege. There's so much to tell about him to the world.'

The two sat down on a wooden bench beside a gigantic neem tree. Then Nivedita, tall and fair, with deep blue eyes and brown hair, turned her gaze on Aurobindo. She looked the very image of purity and austerity in her simple white gown, with a rosary of *rudrakṣha* round her neck.

'The time was a cold Sunday afternoon in November, seven years ago,' she began, 'and the place—a West-End drawing room of London. Swamiji was seated, facing a half-circle of listeners, with the fire in the hearth behind him, as he answered question after question. There was an element of unexpectedness in Swamiji's teaching, which surprised me. His intention was clearly to call the world to enter into the kingdom of God. I was, therefore, much struck by the strangeness as well as the dignity of some of the Indian conceptions, which I was hearing for the first time.' Here Nivedita paused for a moment as if lost in a reverie.

'Yes, Vivekananda preached something for which our hearts yearn,' suggested Aurobindo, 'which is the impulse towards brotherhood whose object of existence is to help the poor and nurse the sick.'

After a short pause, Aurobindo began again as if musing to himself.

'Vivekananda, drawn by the Absolute, also felt the call of the disguised Godhead in humanity and above all the call of the fallen and the suffering. This, it could be said, is the call of the self to the self in the obscure body of the universe. Don't you agree that it was in religion first that the soul of India awoke and triumphed? There have always been indications and forerunners. Vivekananda's going to the West was the first visible sign to the world that India was awake not only to survive but also to conquer. We must show ourselves to the nations as a people with a great past and ancient civilisation who still possess something of the genius and the character of our forefathers. We must prove to them that we still have something more to give to the world and therefore deserve freedom—by proof of manliness and fitness, not by mendicancy!'

Nivedita was touched by Aurobindo's depth of thought. She was so moved that her eyes were glistening with unshed tears.

To know more about his uncanny qualities, she asked his views about India's freedom and how he planned to bring it about. Then in rapt attention, she listened as he explained point by point the dual needs for an armed insurrection and a passive resistance at the national level.

'Mr Ghose,' she pleaded, 'it is imperative that you come over and settle down in Calcutta. I have met many great men and leaders but none posessing such extreme polarities in character. While you are dreamy and childlike yet unfathomably deep, you are also a man whose strength can be gauged through the undercurrent of fire in his speech. After meeting you my worries about India have vanished and the future looks bright. It is time now for the real struggle to begin!'

26

The Mantra

From Deogarh, Barin left for Dacca where his second brother Manomohan had been appointed professor of English. Here he read up to the First Arts standard. Then moving over to his oldest brother Binoybhushan in Patna, he set up his 'B Ghose's Tea Stall' at the gate of the Patna College for earning his livelihood. But here too, his stay was cut short. The unexpected scourge of plague dealt a nasty blow and sealed the fate of his tea stall. So, confronted with unemployment and starvation, its unlucky, teen-aged owner, had no other option left but to catch the next train to Baroda for seeking his Sejda's hospitality. He took a rikshaw at Baroda railway station and with his cheap canvas valise and in travel-stained clothes, appeared before the red brick-built two-storied house of Khaserao. The butler met him at the door and dubiously ushered him into the fine drawing room near the portico. Almost immediately, Aurobindo came down the grand staircase and spirited him away to a bathroom. After a refreshing bath, the shy callow youth met Khaserao.

Coinciding with Barin's stopover at Baroda, Mrinalini was enjoying a year's stay with her husband. Following Sarojini's brief marriage to the superintendent of post offices in Bankipore, she was also spending her widowhood under her brother's care. A year later, Aurobindo brought back both Mrinalini and Sarojini and left them in Deogarh.

Soon after Barin's arrival, Aurobindo was administered the oath of secrecy by a Marathi man named Mandavale. This ceremony was considered important at that time. The well-built man, dressed in battle uniform with a long sword dangling from his waist, alighted from his horse at Khaserao's house. Aurobindo welcomed the visitor whom he was expecting, and took him indoors in hurried steps. Half-an-hour passed before the two men emerged. Aurobindo's oath-taking had been completed.

In December 1902, Aurobindo accompanied Sayajirao Gaekwad to the Ahmedabad Congress. The inaugural speech of the Maharaja at the Ahmedabad Congress was written by Aurobindo. As Aurobindo sat through the session of the Congress, he heard the proceedings take on the same old aspect of a process of futile petition and protest.

During the course of the session, Aurobindo came in contact with another like-minded politician, Bal Gangadhar Tilak, whom he termed as a possible leader of a revolutionary party. Tilak expressed his contempt for the reformist movement and explained his own line of action in Maharashtra. For a long time, Tilak had wanted to know Aurobindo personally and their brief meeting had only whetted his desire to know him better.

During a subsequent visit to Baroda, he easily found Khaserao's newly-built, two-storied, red brick building, but felt a bit disheartened when a servant informed that Aurobindo was not at home.

'Would you like to meet Ghose sahib's younger brother?' the servant asked.

Tilak agreed, knowing well that his friend Deshpande would not be at home either at this hour. Soon, a young lad of about twenty appeared. He was wearing glasses, and had a tuft of hair on his chin.

'May I know your name, please?' Barin asked politely.

'Bal Gangadhar Tilak.'

Barin turned pink with embarrassment. He could not believe that such an important man could call on his brother.

'Please come in, Sir. Pardon me for not recognising you. I'm Barindra Kumar Ghose. My brother will return in an hour. Can I serve you some tea?'

Tilak gave his consent and asked, 'So my young friend, what have you been learning from your brother?'

Barin looked surprised, but before he could answer, the older man continued, 'Have you been imbibing some of your brother's courage and patriotism or are you just whiling away your time doing nothing?'

'My brother has in fact been urging me to go to Calcutta and help his representative organise a committed core group of devoted young soldiers.'

'How much older is your brother than you?' Tilak enquired casually. 'About eight years? Which means that in 1893 he was about the same age that you are at present? Yet he did begin a revolution of sorts at such a young age. Have you heard of a series of writings that he contributed to *Induprakash* named "New Lamps for Old"? Well, this series undoubtedly was the first organised endeavour to expose the limitations and narrowness of the policy of constitutional agitation pursued by the Congress.'

Barin then invited the visitor to Aurobindo's living room and Tilak accepted the request with pleasure. At first Tilak was shocked by the room's apparent disorderliness. Books were heaped or strewn practically everywhere. He noticed a couple of half-open wooden chests through the lids of which more books were peeping out. It took Tilak very little time to realise what an amazing reader Aurobindo was.

'This is extraordinary!' he exclaimed. 'I have not known a more voracious reader.'

'And see books of how many types and different languages exist in his library. To my knowledge there are French, German, Greek, Latin and even Russian books besides English. And they cover such subjects as poetry, literature, history and philosophy.'

Tilak's attention then fell on Aurobindo's ordinary metallic bed. It had no mattress. Even an office clerk would have declined to use it, he thought.

The two men grew quiet on hearing the noise of an approaching carriage. And as Aurobindo climbed the stairs, Barin informed him that Tilak was waiting for him.

'When we met in Ahmedabad I didn't know that you were the author of the series "New Lamps for Old",' explained Tilak warmly holding Aurobindo's hands. 'Ever since I read it, I have wanted to meet its courageous author. Finally, it was Deshpande who gave me the information as well as your address.' After a brief pause Tilak continued, 'Mr Ghose, what according to you is India's future?'

'It is possible that when the forces are ready, a man of destiny comes forth embodying the spirit of the times appearing to make the nation. But, in reality, it is the nation that has to make itself. Nations, like other living entities, must grow by themselves. No one can actually make them. And if a greater India is to arise, it should be in the image of the Truth. Actually, India has the greatest chance because of its past and because a spiritual force is accumulated here. But if India remains indifferent and sticks to old worn out forms and refuses to move forward, or listen to the call of its soul, the Truth may recede somewhere else. But there is very little chance of it succeeding elsewhere if it fails in India.'

Tilak experienced a strange thrill of exhilaration as Aurobindo's mysticism unfolded. However, Tilak, the patriot, was surprised at the fact that the manifestation of the Truth was more important to Aurobindo than India's freedom! He had never visualised it that way. How extraordinarily noble Aurobindo's perceptions were, he reflected silently.

27

Anushilan Samiti

Ever since his arrival at Baroda and thanks entirely to his Sejda's generosity, Barin could enjoy an idyllic life for the first time in his twenty-two years. He read and wrote poetry, played the *esraj*, did some fanciful gardening and passionately participated in bird hunting. Among the serious stuff that he read were some stimulating history books.

Before sending Barin back to Bengal in early 1903 for helping Jatindranath recruit volunteers, Aurobindo initiated him into the secret society. Making Barin hold the Bhagavad Gita in one hand and a sword in another, Sejda made him recite a Sanskrit verse and pledge to fight for India's freedom as long as there was life in his body.

When Barin arrived at 108 Upper Circular Road he found to his dismay that Jatindranath had left on a recruiting mission. However, he was warmly received by Jatindranath's wife and invited to stay in the house.

Having left a couple of weeks before Barin's arrival, Jatindranath was in Arbelia, a village not too far from Calcutta. Among the boys who came to see him was a young Brahmin named Abinash

Bhattacharya. Jatindranath had asked the lad to report at his *akhara* in Calcutta. Abinash had kept his word and arrived on the appointed day but Jatindranath was not yet back. It was four in the afternoon and having travelled such a distance from home Abinash was wondering what to do.

Barin had just arrived the day before from Baroda and was reading a book lying on a campcot. There was a feeling of vulnerability on Abinash's quiet face which instantly moved Barin's gentle heart. Barin threw his shawl and book aside, and greeted Abinash. It was friendship at first sight.

'When we met,' Abinash explained, 'Jatin Babu spoke about some volunteers that he needed for the country's work. So here I am.'

Barin was stunned. He clearly felt small in the presence of this unusual man whose readiness of mind in responding to Jatindranath's call was extraordinary!

'For myself,' he thought 'did Sejda not have to repeat for seven long years to make me take up action? But here was a villager who had heard the call once and obeyed it without the slightest hesitation.'

'Come, my friend,' Barin said. 'If what you desire is the country's liberation, then plunge into the work at once. Join us in this work today, this very moment!'

Abinash had never imagined that he would have to start immediately. But he clasped Barin's hand without hesitation.

'Right, brother!' he exclaimed. 'From now on I am always with you!'

That evening, Abinash waited for Jatindranath in vain and left. But when he called the next morning, Jatindranath was back and he welcomed Abinash with open arms.

Aurobindo himself followed Barin to Bengal after taking leave for a month. One day when Barin brought in Abinash, Aurobindo and Jatindranath were seated on a mat spread on the floor. And no sooner had Abinash paid obeisance to his mentors and sat down before Aurobindo than Barin proudly introduced him. 'Sejda, his name is Abinash, Bengal's first volunteer!'

Abinash felt completely thrown off balance as Aurobindo looked at him closely.

'Your first recruit is quite fine,' Aurobindo finally concluded. 'He is a determined, faithful and silent worker.'

A few days later, Aurobindo, Jatindranath and Barin went to Midnapore where Rajnarayan Basu used to reside before migrating to Deogarh. But his brother Abhaycharan had continued to live there with his family. Satyen Bose was his son.

Younger than Aurobindo and Barin, Satyen was actually their uncle twice removed. Satyen had already begun an *akhara* where quite a few young men had come together. Notable among them were Hemchandra Das and Khudiram Bose. It was resolved to form six more such centres in Bengal.

Admittedly, this was one of Aurobindo's most hectic visits to Bengal. P Mitra also took the oath of joining the revolution from Aurobindo. Aurobindo and Jatindranath thereafter met magistrate Jogendranath Vidyabhushan at his residence in Shyampukur. It was Vidyabhushan who had earlier initiated Jatindranath into politics. During this meeting, a young man of twenty-four named Jyotindra Nath Mukherjee was also present.

Powerfully built, Jyotin was well known for his strength and rare courage. While Jyotin was instantly captivated by Aurobindo's magnetism, the latter was impressed by his personality, uprightness and intelligence. Later, enthralled by Aurobindo's revolutionary work, Jyotin would regularly visit Jatindranath, and finally accepted him as his mentor.

After some formal conversation, Jyotin asked Vidyabhushan to narrate the incident relating to Bankim Chandra Chatterjee's composition of *Vande Mataram*. No sooner had the question been asked than silence descended.

'The event took place nearly twenty-eight years ago,' said Vidyabhushan. 'Every evening a group of intellectuals used to gather at Bankim Babu's residence in Naihati. I too was an occasional visitor. Soon, Bankim Babu was in our midst singing something softly. He said he had received a song that day. It was not his composition; it had "arrived" from above. At someone's request he sang the entire song for us. At the conclusion of this memorable experience, however, some of the eminent writers protested at the strange combination of Sanskrit and Bengali in the poem. But Bankim Babu ignored these protests and reiterated that he had no right to change anything as it was not his composition. Bankim Babu prophesied that this song would become the harbinger of the religion of patriotism, the inspiration for thousands of young revolutionaries. He also predicted that, in about three decades' time the song would cause a big revolution.'

'But one thing is clear,' Aurobindo agreed. 'The poet certainly referred to a mass awakening. And our duty lies in revealing to the countrymen the "mother" of Bankim's vision, so that it may convert the entire nation to the cause of the "Religion of Patriotism".'

'You mean start a new religion?' asked Vidyabhushan.

'No, not quite,' Aurobindo reassured him. 'Ours is the eternal land, eternal people and eternal religion, whose greatness, strength and holiness may be overclouded but never utterly cease. Only a vivifying mantra is needed to create a new India. And God chose

Bankim to shape the message. It will now impel his countrymen to do things, which would have been impossible to them in their ordinary moments. *Vande Mataram* is the mantra that Rishi Bankim was born to reveal.'

No one stirred. Through his usual quiet way, Aurobindo had once again cast a spell over everyone.

After what seemed a long silence, Vidyabhushan asked, 'But how can a mere song written in praise of one's country bring about a revolution? Why must this one succeed while the others before failed?'

'Ah, but there's only one *Vande Mataram*!' reiterated Aurobindo. 'All songs are not mantras. Have you ever tried uttering the words *Vande Mataram* aloud?'

Vidyabhushan suddenly sat up with a jerk. He was overcome with emotion as he softly muttered the mantra again and again.

'Oh, what a fool I was,' he said in a choked voice. 'I was among the handful of people who had the rare privilege of being baptised, so to say, by Bankim Babu himself, and never realised it till this moment.'

'Perhaps it was necessary to let the thirty years expire as he had predicted,' explained Aurobindo. 'It may not yet be too late to try.'

Barin wanted to meet Indraneel and revive his old relationship. He had not met him for almost ten years ever since he had shifted to Deogarh, before being shunted from Calcutta to Dacca, then Patna and finally Baroda. Now, on reaching Park Street, he easily found the house on Rawdon Street. When Barin gave his identity as Aurobindo's younger brother, Saraju happily exclaimed, 'So you're youngest Thakurpo.'

She sent word to Indraneel to come down at once. When Indraneel met Barin face-to-face, he looked blankly at him.

'I'm your friend, Barin,' he said with a throaty laughter.

'Barin!' Indraneel exclaimed happily. 'Where were you all these years?'

'In Deogarh, Dacca, Patna, Baroda! I have come here on a special mission.'

Barin briefed Indraneel about Aurobindo's scheme for setting up an army of volunteers. Then turning around abruptly, Barin enquired, 'Neel, will you join us?'

Indraneel was caught completely off-guard. He looked at Barin in utter bewilderment.

'You can find me at 108 Circular Road. In any case, drop in to see me. You needn't get involved if you don't want to.'

Keen to meet Barin, Indraneel dropped by at the Anushilan Samiti club a week later. Established by stalwarts like P Mitra and Satish Bose and run by Jatindranath, the aim of this association was to prepare young soldiers with a solid physical, moral and mental background, devoted to the liberation of the motherland. On reaching the club, Indraneel was surprised to see a young man of his age riding a horse in the open field adjoining the house. As soon as Barin saw Indraneel from a distance, he came out to welcome him accompanied by another man. Barin introduced Indraneel to Debabrata Bose who stood nearly six foot tall and wore glasses which gave him an unmistakably intellectual air. A little later, Nalin Mitra, the rider of the horse also joined them.

'Welcome to the Anushilan Samiti,' Barin theatrically invited him on behalf of all the others. 'You've already met the second and third recruits of the Samiti. And here comes Abinash, the first member of the society.'

And as Barin spoke these words, a man brought tea and a snack. 'Thanks, Abinash,' Barin said. 'My friends, let me introduce you to Indraneel Gupta. Well Neel, would you like to come along with me? I need to go out.'

'Sure, I'm in no hurry,' Indraneel replied.

'All right, Debabrata,' Barin said assertively, 'Continue your reading of Digby's *Prosperous British India*. You, Nalin, carry on with the autobiography of Mazzini, and Abinash, read up the next chapter of the Gita! I'm off to Hedua with Indraneel.'

On their way, Barin explained the purpose behind his going to the park. 'You see,' he said, 'young boys come to play and chat at the park after school. And that's the place to catch them.'

'I suppose you'll try and get them interested in your ideology. Would the reading of a few books achieve the lofty goal of building an army of dedicated men? Do you propose to raise a force of not less than three hundred thousand men to counter the Indian army militarily, man for man?'

'Well, you have to make a beginning somewhere. Sejda's aim is to have an army in every block, every village of the country, an army that could strike as one force, with or without arms to cripple the British forces. Sejda feels that given the nature and composition of the British army, guerrilla warfare could be very effective in the rural areas. Besides, he doesn't rule out the possibility of another mutiny. But basically, the need of the hour is to have strong men physically, mentally and psychologically prepared to lay down their lives for the liberation of our country.'

Indraneel experienced a peculiar sense of uplift. Barin's oratory carried a curious stamp of conviction and credibility.

Cutting through Beadon Street and moving up to the junction of Cornwallis Street, the two friends entered the park. There were groups of people scattered all over the public garden surrounding the vast pond, called Hedua. While many young men were playing water polo on one end of the pond, there were many swimmers, bathers and revellers in the other parts. He carefully hunted out a group of youngsters to start a conversation or possibly a debate with. The three boys that he picked were hardly fifteen. Barin began the conversation with a sense of smug confidence.

'Are you students of the Scottish Church College?' he asked.

'Yes, we are studying history with honours.'

'Oh, that's interesting. Now let's see who can tell me the name of the famous secret society dedicated to Italian self-rule of which the great Risorgimento leader, Giuseppe Mazzini, was a member?'

The boys scratched their heads but no one could find the right answer.

'Come, come,' Barin chided mischievously. 'How can students of history with honours be pardoned for a lack of such contemporary knowledge? The right answer is of course the Carbonari. Now, my next question: who were the foreign rulers that the Carbonari were secretly plotting to overthrow?'

'The Austrians,' one of the students said.

'Right! Ten out of ten!' Barin declared, shaking his hand. Then feeling satisfied about winning their trust, he brought his head close to theirs and whispered, 'Are you aware that secret societies exist in India, here even within the heart of Calcutta, seeking to overthrow the British?'

The boys exchanged glances.

'How else can the foreigners be expected to leave the country unless there's a big public opposition to their rule?'

Emboldened by the silence of the boys, Barin went on confidently. 'I tell you, without revolution there's no future for us. One must dare in order to win. If your aim is to live forever with your heads bowed, hands tied and mouths gagged, then I have nothing to say. But if you wish to liberate your motherland then raise your heads to be heard. As a first step, shout at the top of your voice—aliens, leave our country, stop looting and plundering our wealth, look elsewhere to satisfy your greed!'

Indraneel was admiring his friend's oratory. Here was someone who could impressively lead young men, cleverly mixing logic with rhetoric. He was discovering a new Barin. The blood was racing swiftly in his veins and he suspected the three younger listeners were feeling the same thrill.

'Now, brothers,' Barin resumed with dignity, 'if you're convinced that the time has come to take up cudgels and shape a new nation, and only if you decide to dedicate yourselves to the cause, meet me here tomorrow at the same time.' Thereafter, he abruptly said goodbye to the boys and led Indraneel away by the arm.

On their way back, Barin briefly explained, 'You see, the ones who talk the least are interested in our cause.' Then he impulsively added, 'By the same token, I think you'd be a very good recruit.'

That night, all that Barin had told the youngsters seemed to churn in Indraneel's mind. But one particular phrase kept echoing in his memory. 'One must dare in order to win!' And why on earth did Barin say in the end that he, Indraneel, would make a good recruit?

28

Secret Activities

Thirteen years before Harimohan, P Mitra was called to the bar. During his stay in England he had been strongly influenced by the ideals of secret societies. When he returned to India, he brought with him a strong urge to found a revolutionary society on the lines of the Carbonari. He later shared with Harimohan his dream of founding a secret society which would mould the minds of the youth and give them physical training to prepare an army of volunteers. Harimohan vaguely mentioned a friend harbouring similar ideas in West India, but the conversation never went further than that.

One day P Mitra unexpectedly invited Harimohan to accompany him after the high court closed for the day. He said that the place they would visit was a secret location where some very interesting activities were conducted. Ignoring where he was being taken, Harimohan sat pensively, looking out of his private carriage. After they had crossed the Sealdah Railway Station and rolled on northward down Upper Circular Road, they stopped half a mile short of the Maniktala Junction. Located adjacent to the Sukeas Street Thana, the premises number 108 had a two-storied house overlooking an open field and a pond. After being warmly greeted at the gate, P Mitra proudly presented Jatindranath Banerjee to Harimohan, saying that he was a real military man trained in Baroda. 'See how tough he is!'

'If you are from Baroda, then you surely know my friend,' Harimohan said excitedly. 'His name is Aurobindo Ghose.'

'Oh, Aurobindo!' Jatin said proudly. 'Who doesn't know him in Baroda?'

'But you never told me that you knew Aurobindo!' P Mitra interrupted. 'I would have been glad to know that our Aurobindo was your friend.'

That evening P Mitra introduced Harimohan to a charismatic lady, Nivedita. Upon learning that Harimohan was Aurobindo's friend, she invited him to her school at Bose Para Lane. A little later, about a dozen young men assembled, among whom was Barin. Harimohan had not met him since he had shifted to Deogarh. Barin eagerly greeted Harimohan and introduced his friends to him.

Addressing the gathering, P Mitra delivered a lecture on the political and military history of the Sikh Khalsa and Nivedita briefly spoke about the greatness of ancient India, seeking to arouse patriotic feelings amongst the young. The meeting broke after about an hour. But behind the impressive appearance, things were not shaping up according to expectation in the newly-opened *akhara*. Sadly, there seemed to have appeared an open rivalry between Jatindranath and Barin.

But commendably, by the time of his settling down in Garpar, Jatindranath had already established his sway over the barristers of Bhawanipore and Ballygunge, receiving as much as two hundred rupees a month from them. Another big achievement was his acquisition of about 200 books on nationalism. This was

Nivedita's gift to Anushilan Samiti. In accordance with her wishes, Jatindranath had also started a school of politics and a study-circle in which world history, great biographies, economics, religion, society, the uprising and fall of races was being taught and discussed to prepare workers. And all this was no mean achievement for a lone man in a matter of just six months!

Around this time, Sakharam Ganesh Deuskar, Barin's history teacher at the Deogarh High School, came to Calcutta. As the Marathi's lectures on economics were very instructive, full of comparisons and statistics pointing to the systematic drain on the nation's coffers, almost everyone connected with the club attended the evening sessions. P Mitra had advised Harimohan to keep his evening free to listen to Deuskar's speech. Accordingly, he accompanied his more successful junior colleague to Garpar.

Harimohan was amazed to meet his other professional colleagues such as B C Chatterjee and Chittaranjan Das among the audience who received him with great respect and warmth as soon as he entered the premises. Nivedita was there too. She once again reminded him of visiting her school at Baghbazar. Finally, Jatindranath introduced him to Deuskar. As the enlightening sitting began, Barin and some other boys crept in at the last minute and sat down on the front row. Harimohan was stunned to see his son among them. Harimohan kept wondering since how long Indraneel had been associated with the *akhara*. Saraju had complained to him about Indraneel's asking for ten rupees.

'My God,' Harimohan pondered to himself, 'the lad must have asked for the money to donate it to the *akhara*!' He had a lot more character than he thought.

Deuskar's speech was well illustrated by current news items and analysis. Later, encouraged by Aurobindo, he would write on the subject and have it published under the name of *Desher Katha* which would achieve instant success. In fact, the book's success would eventually force the authorities to outlaw it.

At the end of the session Harimohan quietly walked up to where Barin and the young boys were talking. He politely said hello to Barin and took his stupefied son aside. Indraneel was terrified to be caught red-handed in a place where it was dangerous for any young man to be present without the knowledge his family, particularly, as the head of his family happened to be the legal representative of the Crown.

'You never mentioned about your association with Barin's group,' Harimohan accused deliberately. 'Finish whatever work is left and come to the carriage. You can return home with me. By the way,' he added, astonishing his son by handing out a ten-rupee banknote, 'your mother told me about this. But I forgot to give it to you earlier.'

Following Nivedita's second invitation on the day of Deuskar's speech, Harimohan called at her school. Nivedita received him with warmth. She held Harimohan in great esteem not only because of his reputation as a leading barrister, but also because of his nearness to Aurobindo. From their first meeting at Garpar, on the day she delivered the lecture on the greatness of ancient India, she had seen honesty and nobility written across his handsome features and he had somehow reminded her of their common friend.

'What a pleasant surprise,' Nivedita said with feeling. 'Please come in. But what's all this sad news about Barin's dispute with Jatin Babu?'

'Barin is an impulsive young man. Through my son, Indraneel, I tried to advise moderation but he won't listen to anybody so long as he finds support for his brashness. Unfortunately, the future of the entire movement is at stake. It is very hard to believe that Barin is the younger brother of one of the noblest men I've ever met.'

'Yes, indeed. But has Mr Ghose any plans to settle down in the city? Such unfortunate developments would never have arisen if he were here now instead of living in Baroda. I've tried to make him see the good that his presence could bring to the movement.'

Although Barin's immature tirade to oust Jatindranath succeeded, it ultimately boomeranged on the club itself, destroying it completely.

29

The Master

Soon after Sayajirao Gaekwad's coronation, the adolescent monarch made the acquaintance of another boy of identical age—Maharaja Chamarajendra Wadiar of Mysore. A friendship based on mutual respect blossomed between the two Maharajas. But Chamarajendra died prematurely and his eighteen-year-old son Krishnaraja Wadiar assumed his princely duties.

The new dynamic Maharaja of Mysore instantly took over the development work of his state from where his illustrious father had left it. As the young monarch looked upon Sayajirao, his father's friend, as a dependable benefactor and statesman, he asked his advice for a particular project he had in mind during their first meeting. Sayajirao heard with admiration the young prince's ambitious plan to introduce a legislative council by restructuring the present representative assembly in his state. Krishnaraja then enquired if the Gaekwad knew anyone who could guide him in drafting the necessary document for the introduction of such a council. As this was an unusual project, Sayajirao wondered if anyone in India was worthy of such an exalted engagement. Suddenly he remembered someone who had come to his aid during a particularly difficult moment of his life. Although this work was very different in nature, he readily recommended the name of Barrister Hurry Mohun Dutt of Calcutta to his young friend, adding effusively, 'If indeed anybody can, it is this man!'

Within a fortnight, Krishnaraja's representative called on Harimohan with the Maharaja's invitation to visit Mysore as a royal guest. Harimohan was quick to see the merits that the invitation offered and agreed to take up the assignment.

'Please inform the Maharaja,' Harimohan said with authority, 'that I shall be extremely glad to be of service to His Highness, particularly since my name has been recommended by the Maharaja Gaekwad himself.'

When Harimohan broke the news to Saraju, she grew as excited as he at the prospect of visiting the southernmost state of India. Since their marriage, almost two years earlier, Harimohan had been waiting for such an opportunity to break away from the drudgeries of his job and go on for a well-deserved journey. So on a pleasant afternoon in early 1903, they left for Mysore.

The hospitality of the teenaged Maharaja charmed Harimohan and Saraju during their stay in Mysore. Harimohan was able to complete his official duties within a week, working concertedly with the state's principal law officer and the solicitors to the Maharaja.

Harimohan and Saraju's expedition took off thereafter through the vast Madras Presidency. As planned, they toured Madurai, Rameshwaram, Cape Comorin, Trichinapolly and reached Tanjore at the end of the third week. The couple visited the nine hundred-year-old Brihadishwara Temple, a two hundred-feet edifice dedicated to Lord Shiva. The temple was so grand and impressive that they looked at it from all sides in order to admire its near life-size sculptures.

'Excuse me,' someone called out in English, in a thick South Indian accent. 'I suppose you are visitors from far away?'

'Yes,' Harimohan said after a brief namaskar. 'We are coming from Calcutta.'

'Ah! Bengalis! But my friends, it is *amangalam* to go round the temple from right to left. You must always go clockwise, from left to right.'

Suddenly Harimohan and Saraju were surrounded by six identical girls and one more in their mother's arms. Like their mother, they were all fair, slim and elegant with enchanting, angelic smiles. They also noticed the two boys who were standing slightly apart.

'Come with me, my friends, let me show you the temple,' the middle-aged gentleman said enthusiastically. 'But wait, let's first introduce ourselves. We are from Kodiyalam, a village from a nearby *taluk*. I am Zamindar Kodiyalam Vasudeva Iyengar. This is my wife, and these are our nine children.'

'My name's Harimohan Datta and this is my wife Saraju. I'm a barrister.'

'Ah, such distinguished people! But tell me first, where are you staying? You must stay in my house. It's our privilege to welcome you and madam as our guests.'

When Harimohan turned around to ask Saraju what she thought about staying with the Iyengars, he found her conversing through signs and broken Hindi with the zamindar's wife. Saraju was proudly displaying her white *shankha*s and the red *pala*s that married Bengali women wear on both wrists. It was a picture of total harmony.

The following day, Harimohan had a further opportunity of discovering how kind but insistent the zamindar could be.

Having heard that Harimohan and Saraju had been the royal guests of the Maharaja of Mysore, the zamindar insisted that they accompany him to Kodiyalam to spend an entire week at their ancestral house. All that Harimohan could gain through some polite bargaining was a reduction of the length of their stay. The zamindar promised to send them back with his man to Tanjore to resume their return journey.

The tiny village of Kodiyalam belonged to the the Iyengar family entirely, and consisted of acres of cultivated land and gardens, situated about nine miles south-west of the big town of Mannargudi, off Pattukottai Road. The sublime greenery of the area and the narrow rivulet Kannanaar serving as a natural barrier between Kodiyalam and a large scattered village called Vadaseri, were extremely pleasant to the eye.

During their stay at Kodiyalam, the zamindar took Harimohan and his wife on a bullock cart excursion through the six-and-a-half miles stretch that separated the deserted village of Nagai from Kodiyalam. He explained that thirty-three years earlier, a saint called Vasudeva had made the momentous prediction of the advent of the Uttara Yogi, who would cross over to the South from the North. Iyengar further explained that he was anxiously waiting for the arrival of the Uttara Yogi but also lamented that although the predicted period was over, there was still no sign of him. Slowly he unravelled, how after the demise of the spiritual Guru, the Nagai Japata community had disintegrated during the intervening years.

Iyengar led Harimohan and Saraju through the ruins of the village of Nagai.

'Today, it's hard to believe that barely a generation earlier the surrounding barren countryside used to be so lush and fertile,' he said ruefully. 'And look at the pathetic state of this pond Mandakini which used to welcome visitors with its milk-white water, now choked beyond recognition with algae. A visitor like you would find it hard to imagine that this was once the centre of a thriving spiritual community. Yet look, there can be no doubt that collective meditations were once held here. This *Kusumakaram,*' he added pointing at the *yantra*-shaped one-storeyed structure, around which those collective meditations were conducted, 'stands intact among the ruins of the community, forlorn, desolate and forgotten.'

After remaining with eyes closed and in complete silence, the zamindar bent down and touched his head to the floor of the auspicious *Kusumakaram*.

'My friend,' he told Harimohan with emotion, pointing at a spot about ten yards from the covered structure, 'this is where the Master is said to have stood while foretelling the advent of the Avatar.'

Harimohan experienced a peculiar sense of déjà vu. A tingling sensation ran down his spine as he was unable to connect with something that appeared to him very familiar. He was so moved by the tale of the Uttara Yogi that he could think of nothing else for a long time.

~

Happily, in spite of the dissolution of the Nagai Japata, its traditions were well preserved in the Kodiyalam Iyengar family. Zamindar Vasudeva Iyengar, who was born about three years before the Nagai Swami's demise, became a devotee of the saint after marrying his younger sister-in-law. At thirty-six, the zamindar was a worried man. He had an uncanny feeling that his time was running out and that his long cherished dream of beholding the Uttara Yogi with his own eyes and receiving his blessings would remain unfulfilled. He was afraid that after him there would be no other known member of the Japata who could be relied on to take interest in the predicted arrival. How could such an important event be left unattended?

One evening, following his visit to Nagai with the Dattas and after having dreamt of his Guru, the zamindar wanted to share his joy with his children and visitors by telling them about the Swami's miraculous deeds. The eagerness on the faces of his children as he narrated incident after incident, brought him great satisfaction. Just then, the servant came in.

'I beg your pardon, Master,' he interrupted. 'But there is a stranger who is seeking shelter. Will you please talk to him?'

Soon, the servant came back with the stranger. The visitor bowed respectfully. His white hair suggested that he was about seventy-five years old but the man held himself remarkably erect despite his age. He exuded nobility and purity and a strange glow of self-confidence in his bearing marked him out as a leader.

'My name's Ayanar Gounder,' the stranger announced in a tired voice. 'I'm from Ariyalur, a village near Tirutturaippundi on the Adappar River. I'm on my way to Valaiyakadu, the little village near here, but I am very tired and night has fallen. Will you be kind enough, Sir, to offer me shelter?'

'Of course,' the zamindar replied with warmth and respect. 'Be our guest.'

'Thanks. May God bless you and grant all your wishes,' said the visitor. Then as he turned to follow the servant out, his eyes fell on the painting of a godman in the classical cross-legged seated pose.

'Isn't it a representation of Swami Vasudeva of the Nagai Japata?' he eagerly enquired.

Everyone was surprised.

'Yes,' the zamindar replied. 'Did you know him?'

'Well, not exactly. But once I led a party from my village to the fortified township of Nagai to meet the Swami. That was thirty-three years ago.'

'But that was the year the Swami made the prediction about the Uttara Yogi's arrival!' the zamindar exclaimed.

'Yes indeed,' Gounder firmly replied, 'I was witness to that great revelation!'

As Gounder spoke a strange eeriness, similar to that which he had experienced on the night during the prayer in the Nagai village, crept into the big room. The lights flickered and steadied again. The silence became so profound that each one could hear his own breathing, and the zamindar's heart was pounding with a strange excitement.

'It was like a bolt out of the blue to his disciples. And quite understandably, too, for the Swami looked hardly forty. I later heard that he had in fact married a few years before that.'

'What you've heard is right. My wife is the younger sister of the Swami's wife.'

Gounder's eyes lit up with reverence and admiration.

'Then I'm privileged indeed to spend the night with such honourable hosts as you.'

'On the contrary,' the zamindar iterated enthusiastically, 'we are proud to have amongst us someone who has had the sacred darshan of our guru.'

At this point the zamindar realised that he had not asked his tired guest to sit. He quickly requested him to take his seat and asked, 'But what happened after that?'

Ayanar Gounder sat contemplating on the Swami's portrait, trying to recall the events of that day.

'Oh, what a magnificent sight it was to behold the saffron-clad saint against the backdrop of that colourful dawn! It was indeed a sight for the gods. It was the Master's voice again that broke the disciples' stupor. "A Uttara Yogi will come soon from the North," he said. "He will lead you in the future." The Swami then rose and looked at the play of colours in the eastern sky and said, "I can now read the writing of God. A saviour is coming. He will not only deliver India from the bondage of colonialism but also free the world from the darkness of the Kaliyuga."'

'And did he mention any specific time for his advent?'

'In three decades, I think he said. Yes, I'm sure that's what he said. Well, I never realised that the predicted three decades had passed.'

'But, have you ever thought about it?' Iyengar interrupted excitedly as a new idea struck him. 'What is predicted is that he will cross over to our land from the North. That means he's perhaps living unnoticed and undiscovered somewhere up there or has just recently settled here. God! Isn't there a way to find him in his present state?'

'Ah!' exclaimed Gounder. 'I'd almost forgotten! The Uttara Yogi is to be identified by three utterances!'

'Oh, yes! I too had completely forgotten about that. So now there's a definite clue! We must be on the lookout for someone who has made three utterances.'

'How often I've wondered what happened to the Swami's famous predictions.' Gounder remarked. 'Well, one of them seemed to come true almost immediately afterwards with his withdrawal from the body. This was reported to me within a month. But where indeed is the Uttara Yogi? I can't believe the Swami's prediction has failed.'

'No, certainly not, if he has announced it, it's bound to happen,' asserted the zamindar. 'But what an unusual coincidence! Only last night I dreamt of the Master whom I've never physically met and today following a visit to Nagai and while speaking about him to my children, you arrived as if out of thin air to tell us about your own experience. Aren't these events too well-timed and orchestrated to be mere coincidences?' Then he seemed to hesitate a little. 'But strangely in my dream,' he resumed softly, 'the Master was clad in a white dress and not in his usual saffron. And although his eyes smouldered with the fire of power, his face bore an expression of limitless compassion. What was surprising is that he was standing by the sea. But, strangest of all, the Swami hardly resembled his own portrait!'

The pregnant silence that ensued was finally broken by Gounder. 'You're the luckiest man I've ever met! For not only did you experience a divine vision, you actually lived part of the future! You beheld the Uttara Yogi himself!'

This conversation left a deep impression in the minds of his two sons, Rangaswami and Srinivasa, both teenagers. The coincidental arrival of Ayanar Gounder on the very night that their father was describing the Nagai Swami's yogic feats to them was not only significant but also deeply symbolic and premonitory.

30

Country First

Following the dissolution of the *akhara* that had taken a year, Aurobindo had concluded somewhat despondently that even the worthiest of men were undependable so long as they let their lower natures override their sincerity. And when a tangible alternative had to be found to the dependence on others, a path slowly revealed itself before him.

Ever since his landing in India, Aurobindo had undergone very significant spiritual experiences. His contact with India's sacred soil had instantly brought about a feeling of God inhabiting material objects and bodies. Sometime later, while approaching the city through Baroda's Camp Road, an incident involving his carriage had triggered off another occult experience. With the will to prevent it, there appeared a Being of Light in him who was as it were the master of the situation and was able to control the details. Later, Aurobindo further explained the experience through his mystic poem 'Godhead'. Without any effort, he once felt the vacant Infinite in a very tangible way while visiting the Takht-i-Suleman or the hill of Shankaracharya in Kashmir. The experience no doubt served as inspiration for his sonnet titled 'Adwaita'.

During the earlier part of his stay in Baroda, Aurobindo had another personal but indirect experience of the powers of occult knowledge when an astrologer named Narayana Jyotishi made some remarkable predictions. Without any reference to the horoscope, he foretold Aurobindo's three political trials and also his subsequent release by mentioning that he would come to trouble while fighting against white enemies. The interesting thing was that Aurobindo had not even taken up politics at the time.

Aurobindo became interested in yoga when he learnt that the same penance that one does to get away from the world can be turned to action. He decided to take the plunge as it became increasingly evident that now the country came first, humanity afterwards and the rest nowhere.

He consulted Engineer Devdhar of Baroda, who was a disciple of Swami Brahmananda of Chandod, for details about pranayama. After practising pranayama, Aurobindo's experience was his brain and mind worked with greater illumination and power. At that time he used to write poetry and his powers of writing revived with great vigour. His health improved and he grew stronger. His skin became smooth and fair and he felt a flow of sweetness in his saliva. He used to feel a certain aura round the head and saw luminous patterns and figures, mostly in the awakened state.

During this time, Barin's obsession with the planchette continued. Although the séances of planchette had not much value from the point of view of yoga, they nonetheless revealed that the physical world was not the only reality. In fact, their importance to Aurobindo lay in the fact that they showed him the clear existence of supra-physical agencies and planes of consciousness, and the possibility of attaining them.

His initial spiritual experiences got more strongly rooted with a particular incident. Geared up by his new scheme of establishing the Bhavani Mandir, Barin set off to the Vindhya Mountains with the aim of finding a suitable place for erecting the temple. He trekked for days but ultimately returned to the plains after contracting a persistent mountain fever. Even after being treated by physicians, he showed no signs of recovery. Finally, a Naga sanyasi came to Barin's rescue, and from him Aurobindo got direct proof of the utility of yoga on the material plane as well. Making light of his spiritual achievements, Aurobindo would humorously explain that his was a side-door entry into the spiritual life.

31

Many Surprises

On the day of the artist Shashi Kumar Hesh's departure from Baroda, Aurobindo made the accidental acquaintance with Charu Chandra Dutt, a Bengali ICS officer. Aurobindo and Dutt did not meet each other again until four years later in 1904 when Aurobindo paid him a visit following Dutt's posting in Thana.

At his residence Dutt was practising shooting with a small rifle on a rainy day. His wife, Lilavati, urged Aurobindo also to shoot the targets floating in the courtyard. At first Aurobindo objected because he had never held a gun before. The targets were the black heads of matchsticks thrown into the stagnant water ten to twelve feet away. And Aurobindo calmly hit the bull's eye with each shot!

Another incident occurred when Dutt's cousin-in-law, Subodh Mullick, was present at Thana. As the four sat down to play a hand of whist, Lilavati and her unusual partner beat Dutt and Mullick over and over again. This prompted Dutt to give up playing and fondly charge Aurobindo of using some extrasensory power for picking the best cards and seeing through their hands.

That same day, Lilavati was preparing frozen watermelon juice for her guests. When Aurobindo asked if there was time to finish his meditation, she urged him to conclude as the juice would take a little while to freeze. When everything was ready they realised that Aurobindo was still meditating. Dutt and Mullick decided to call him. At first, they politely knocked at his door a few times. Then in the absence of a heavy pole, they rammed the door throwing their combined body weights together with a loud thud. After this, they let fall all the metallic utensils that were available in the house. But even when this ear-splitting din failed to arouse Aurobindo, the others finished their share of the delicacy, leaving his share to melt. When Aurobindo eventually came, Dutt enquired if he had not heard any noise. Aurobindo answered sincerely that for a fraction of a second he did in fact hear something but immediately became indrawn again.

Aurobindo's familiarity with Mullick grew stronger during his stay at Thana. They discussed politics and seemed to agree on each and every point regarding the launching of the movement in Bengal. As a result, the two struck a deep friendship. A couple of years later, this time in Mullick's palatial mansion in Wellington Square, Calcutta, Aurobindo's host had the pleasure of testing another of his extraordinary abilities. Aurobindo found a stray book and became instantly engrossed in reading it. When he put it down after half-an-hour, Mullick deprecatingly enquired if Aurobindo had finished reading the entire hundred pages of the book.

'Yes,' Aurobindo replied amusedly.

Then turning to his brother-in-law who was on a visit to Calcutta, Mullick added, 'Here, take the book and test him.'

Dutt read out a short passage at random and asked him to recite the rest. To the astonishment of everyone present, Aurobindo repeated all that was written on the rest of that page.

During his stay in Bengal, Dutt paid a visit to P Mitra who took him to Harimohan's office.

'My dear distinguished colleague,' P Mitra began theatrically, 'I have the special honour of presenting to you Judge C C Dutt of Bombay. More than anything else, he may be introduced as a close friend of our Aurobindo.'

'My friendship with Auro began in England, roughly twenty years ago,' Harimohan observed with a touch of nostalgia. 'But please tell me what are his plans?'

'Well, after reading a book on spiritualism, Barin began experimenting with planchette. Mr Ghose also joined him in the evenings. It was during one such séance that they called Sri Ramakrishna who said, "*Mandir karo* [erect a temple]." This advice was taken literally as the Saint's consent to Barin's scheme for the erection of the Bhavani Mandir, a temple of the Mother, where a spiritual fraternity in line with Bankim's *Ananda Math* is supposed to come up. So the latest phase is the Bhavani Mandir,' remarked Charu Dutt.

'Sounds odd to me,' P Mitra said softly. 'I'm not denying its merit, but the addition of another temple in the country can't change the face of the revolution. Initially, it was Aurobindo's scheme to open revolutionary centres in every village. And so, I've been meticulously following his instructions and going ahead in right earnest.'

'Anyway,' Dutt intervened quickly, 'with all this talk about the partitioning of Bengal, it is high time that a common agenda is set up to oppose it.'

Soon after P Mitra and Dutt left, Harimohan was in for another surprise.

'Greetings, Datta Moshay!' Shakuni Chakladar said entering his office, followed by a lady whose face was hidden by the end of her sari. 'We have just come back from Kalighat,' Shakuni explained. 'After performing the sacred ceremony we thought of asking for your blessings as you are the only man I respect after God. But wouldn't you like to see my bride's face?'

The woman slowly bared her face but did not look up. Although dark, she was definitely the most beautiful girl that Harimohan had set his eyes on.

'You have a very beautiful wife, Shakuni,' he said waiving his visitors into chairs. Then as an afterthought, he quickly drew out his wallet and handed over a couple of ten-rupee notes and added, 'Please buy her a sari on my behalf.'

'Datta Moshay,' Shakuni said evasively, turning to his wife, 'she is Motimala Dassi.'

Harimohan was stunned. This was the woman who had caused his father's downfall!

Ultimately, Motimala saved him further unease and said, 'Babu, please be rest assured; I have not come to cause you any trouble. I need your help. I am infinitely grateful to you for letting me have the twenty thousand rupees that I know you arranged for and also for the new house that you hired for me. I think these are the only selfless acts of genuine charity ever shown by any man to me. I shall never forget your nobility.'

Motimala smiled for the first time.

'I would like you to help me invest the money you offered somewhere safe, so that the cash lying idle is not spent uselessly. I don't need it right now. What we need is a regular income.'

Harimohan thought for a moment.

'Before I give you any suggestion, may I ask you about your future plans?' he asked Shakuni.

But Motimala amazed him by replying instead.

'I have given up my profession,' she assured him. 'Now that I am his wife, I have at last earned the self-respect that I always longed for. I've made up my mind to leave Bowbazar forever. He has also agreed to change his line and give up living dangerously. He has promised to find a decent job. Will you help us, Babu?'

'Of course, I will,' Harimohan replied with satisfaction. 'Good, you gave me all the answers I needed. Now give me some time to think. Please come back on Monday.'

When Motimala and Shakuni returned on Monday, there was another middle-aged, distinguished gentleman sitting in Harimohan's office.

'Please come in,' Harimohan said warmly to the couple. 'Meet my friend Dr Pradyumno Sarkar. He is looking for a house in central Calcutta to set up a nursing home. Your house, I think, will suit him perfectly. Besides with an investment of twenty thousand rupees, all materials including beds, equipment for the operating theatre and a general clinic can be taken care of without approaching any bank or financing agency. What remains to be worked out between him and you are the modalities. I think both parties are ready to abide by a lending bank's common rate of interest?'

'I have no objection,' Dr Sarkar affirmed enthusiastically.

'I leave the negotiation entirely to you, Babu,' Motimala told Harimohan graciously.

'Good. Dr Sarkar, I suppose you've no objection in mortgaging all your equipment and movable properties in the name of your lender until the payment of the entire principal amount of twenty thousand rupees with interest is completed? In the absence of any collateral, I would also request you to pay her simultaneously a simple fee of five per cent over your net annual income after all statutory deductions, including income tax. This last provision will remain effective until such time that the nursing home ceases to exist, or Motimala Dassi dies—whichever is first—even after full payment of the principal amount of the loan and interest is complete.'

'Done,' Dr Sarkar assured solemnly. 'For all the benefits that your client is offering, it is the least I can do. But I don't wish to be a sub-tenant. Please ask her to transfer the right of tenancy directly in the name of the nursing home.'

'All right,' Motimala consented readily.

'Another thing, Doctor,' Harimohan intervened. 'May I ask you the favour of employing my friend Shakuni in your nursing home? I can assure you that he'll be very useful as a local man.'

'Very well,' Dr Sarkar rose happily. He enquired when the deed of agreement would be ready for signing and left.

'Thank you Datta Moshay,' Shakuni said ecstatically, baring his stained teeth.

'So, may I enquire,' Harimohan asked, 'where you two will live now?'

'I've a small house in Hartukibagan,' Motimala answered.

'But won't Shakuni contribute anything to your married life?' Harimohan asked.

'He already has, Datta Moshay,' Motimala replied gratefully. 'It takes a lot of character to marry a concubine!'

PART THREE

A Special Destiny

India cannot perish, our race cannot become extinct, because it is to India that is reserved the highest and the most splendid destiny, the most essential to the future of the human race. It is she who must send forth from herself the future religion of the entire world, the Eternal Religion which is to harmonise all religion, science and philosophies and make mankind one soul.

32

Lord Curzon

In 1904, Lord Curzon temporarily laid down his viceroyalty to return to England. In Britain, he led a fairly busy life taking part in engagements such as attending a number of dinners, some of which were hosted in his honour by retired civilians and friends of India. Herbert John Reynolds, a one-time distinguished member of the governor general's legislative council and former president of Calcutta's Asiatic Society, as well as an acquaintance of the Cockerells happened to meet Curzon in a routine soirée. They talked at length and Curzon asked him some very pertinent questions about the roots of Indian culture. Reynolds' depth of knowledge impressed Curzon. As the evening drew to a close and the guests began leaving, both men realised that their conversation was far from over. So Curzon proposed another meeting and Reynolds willingly accepted the offer.

Three days later, they met again at Curzon's palatial mansion in London's stylish Carlton House Terrace. Reynolds had brought an old friend whose magnetic personality drew Curzon's attention and he could hardly keep his eyes off him. Unable to hide his eagerness, Reynolds promptly sought to introduce his friend to Curzon.

'Horace, I accidentally discovered that Lord Curzon loved India as much as we do and was sure he would be glad to discuss the roots of Indian culture with you.'

Curzon seemed a little uncomfortable to face the short man's strange eyes.

'And this, Your Excellency, is my illustrious friend, Horace Abel Cockerell, the one-time acting governor of Bengal.'

'My Lord,' Horace began calmly, 'India's greatness has been reflected by the everlasting tenure of one mighty religion throughout its civilisation. Indian science, law and philosophy have served as models to the Egyptians, Greeks and, broadly speaking, to the entire world. India has welcomed foreigners and it is by assimilating all the good elements of other cultures that Hinduism has grown richer and wider. Do you know what is so unique about this religion? Whereas all other major religions of the world were founded by an individual, Hinduism was born out of the spiritual achievements of innumerable saints who devoted their energies to higher pursuits and *tapasya*. That is why it has lasted fifty centuries and has the potential to last fifty more.'

'But I thought wisdom was brought to India by the Aryans from a region called Indo-Europe,' suggested Curzon.

'My Lord, as Western thinkers pursued their studies, research on Sanskrit revealed that there were striking similarities between it and Latin and Greek. Now, it would naturally be disgraceful for Europeans to accept Sanskrit as the root of its two most ancient languages. Hence, the greatest myth and lie of all times was born and the baseless theory of an Aryan invasion was formulated. Anyone who has studied the origins of Sanskrit will vouch for its timelessness. The Vedas are the earliest among the sacred writings that were written in an even older form of the language known as Vedic Sanskrit. I can assure you that not a single European language can be traced so far back. It is beyond doubt, therefore, that Hinduism, just as its principal language and texts, was born in India and the proverbial Aryans were the Indians themselves. And if at all there has been an exchange, it is far more likely that the Indians took their language to Europe, rather than the other way around. The Aryan invasion, a malicious theory, was essentially hatched to suppress any notion of superiority that the Indians might feel over the British.'

'Your Excellency,' Reynolds confirmed, 'Mr Cockerell's views on the subject are quite extraordinary. I feel he has presented India's case in its true light, as vividly and lucidly as can be expected.'

'Well, gentlemen, I am truly overwhelmed,' Curzon said at last. 'Your arguments seem convincing and are quite final indeed. How wonderful it would be if I could also find time for such exciting research.'

And as he got up to bid goodbye, Horace asked politely, while shaking hands, 'My Lord, what's this rumour about the partition of Bengal?'

The viceroy tightened his grip around his hand. 'As head of state I am obliged to carry out mandates that are beneficial only to the empire,' he replied with dignity. 'And these may appear to harm the sentiments of the nation over which I rule. Will you promise me to look beyond all outward appearances when the time comes? I love India just as you do, but I am a loyal servant of His Majesty above everything else. And that's final!'

33

No Compromise

Ultimately, the cult of extremism was ushered into Indian politics by Lord Curzon himself. And eventually, it was the viceroy's partitioning of Bengal that fuelled discontent, and brought about the much-awaited revolution. The government had expected some kind of opposition from the natives but its vehemence surprised everyone.

As the sentiment against the Partition became stronger, it did not take much time for Aurobindo to realise that it could be used to give birth to the revolution that he had so long nurtured in his heart. Abinash received a note from Aurobindo showing how rightly his political instinct had led him.

'This is a golden opportunity,' Aurobindo predicted. 'We will get many workers from this movement.'

And true to his word Aurobindo ushered in the resistance to the Partition by writing a pamphlet titled *No Compromise*.

About three months before the Partition was actually made effective, the fifty-seven-year-old Surendranath Banerjea was busy writing an editorial for *Bengalee,* of which he was the proprietor and editor. Surendranath was almost halfway through his editorial, when his peon abruptly announced the arrival of two visitors. The office of *Bengalee* at Colootollah Street had of late become an important landmark for young men enthused with the patriotic zeal. The two young visitors were Barin and Abinash. They had brought an article to show the venerable leader.

'Sir, we would like you to read this small pamphlet and get your views,' said Barin, handing it over to Surendranath.

Reluctantly, the old man picked up the pamphlet and glanced at it. Belying his fears at the very onset, Surendranath was struck by the article's excellence of style and fluency of expression. Besides, he found its title, *No Compromise,* very bold and revealing. As he read on, the author's intellectual prowess began to emerge with each line.

'This can't be the writing of an Indian,' he said at last. 'No Indian could muster such a command of English. In fact, I can't think of any Indian who could present all the facts so cogently.'

'Well, I am proud to say that its author is my dear Sejda Aurobindo Ghose.'

'Ah! Do you mean Anushilan Samiti's Aurobindo?' the old man asked incredulously.

Barin nodded proudly.

'Yes!' the old man said after a long pause. 'He's the only person who could write in this way. I fully support his view that the right moment has truly arrived to launch a full-scale war against the British. But tell me something. What is Aurobindo's next plan of action?'

Barin was only too happy to explain the details about the Bhavani Mandir project, underlining its philosophy and concept. He also mentioned how Aurobindo foresaw a mass armed uprising to rid the country of the British.

Surendranath was at first stunned by the revelation. Then he grew visibly excited.

'Listen, my children,' he said with feeling. 'You must take up the work immediately. My support and blessings shall forever be with you. I'm an old man now. But I promise to help you with funds whenever I can. You just go ahead and do it!'

34

Swadeshi and Boycott

On returning home after a long day's work, Krishna Kumar Mitra learnt from his wife that Aurobindo had arrived. The welcome news instantly melted away the day's fatigue and his face beamed.

'Lila, do send some tea and snacks,' he told his wife and stepped into the drawing room to greet his favourite nephew.

'How are you Nau Mesho?' Aurobindo said cheerfully, standing up. 'I arrived in the afternoon.'

'Not bad, not bad. Actually, you could not have come at a better moment.'

'Yes, indeed. This nefarious scheme to divide Bengal seems to be gaining momentum each day. But are we adequately prepared to face it? Why not do something drastic and effective? How about declaring open war on the British?'

The old man opened his mouth to say something but the words froze on his lips.

'Aren't we weary of the economic conditions of the British rule in India? Aren't we dissatisfied with the continual bleeding of its resources, the chronic famines and the rapid impoverishment that result? I suggest, therefore, that we refuse to help this process of exploitation. The steps that I foresee can at least restore some of our lost honour by striking hard at the roots of our rulers' economic exploitation. And that alone can undo the ignoble scheme of partitioning Bengal.'

Aurobindo slowly elaborated his plan as Krishna Kumar listened silently.

'Actually, what I have in mind is the age-old device of Boycott. In my opinion, Boycott is a rediscovery of national self-respect and a declaration of national separateness. In fact, in most of the national uprisings of modern times, it has been the forerunner of the struggle for independence. You may recall how in the American struggle with England an enthusiastic and determined boycott of British goods was enforced by a stringent and effective organisation. The Italian uprising was heralded by the boycott of Austrian cigarettes and the tobacco riots of Milan.'

'My dear fellow,' Krishna Kumar said with a chuckle, 'If you were asked to give up your cigars and tobacco ...'

'Actually, I have all along recommended the Indian Swadeshi brands,' Aurobindo rebutted jovially, 'they're excellent,' and the two men laughed aloud good-heartedly. Then Aurobindo grew serious again. 'My proposal, therefore, is that we should henceforth refuse to purchase British goods or to condone their purchase by others. Nobody blames the Americans for throwing British tea into Boston harbour, nor can anybody blame a similar action in India on moral grounds. Another necessity of Boycott is to aid our nascent energies in the field of self-help. The boycott of foreign goods is a necessary condition for the encouragement of indigenous industries.'

'You seem to have a well-laid plan in your head,' Krishna Kumar said after a brief silence. 'Yes, I fully endorse your proposals and shall definitely inform Suren Babu during our next meeting. By the way, have you worked out a formula for awakening the nation?' Krishna Kumar added with a mild touch of deprecation.

Aurobindo smiled, as his mind raced back to the day when Vidyabhushan had narrated the story of Bankim speaking to them about his immortal creation. 'By a mighty mantra,' he affirmed. 'Have you read *Ananda Math*?'

'Of course,' Krishna Kumar replied, 'who hasn't? But I don't see your point.'

Just then Lilavati walked in, followed by her two daughters, Kumudini and Basanti, with tea and snacks. In the meantime, Sukumar had also returned home and on learning that Aurobindo had arrived, came into the hall eagerly to join his family.

Aurobindo smiled as his eyes fell on Sukumar. He looked pleased to see all his cousins together.

'Will you three do me a favour?' he suddenly asked. Then beckoning them closer he explained what they had to do. At his signal they raised their voices and uttered: '*Vande Mataram! Vande Mataram! Vande Mataram!*'

Its effect was electrifying! Krishna Kumar and Lilavati exchanged glances and looked at Aurobindo, seeking an explanation.

'Yes! This is how I propose to awaken the nation,' Aurobindo said triumphantly.

Accordingly, the older leaders promptly fell in line and adopted Boycott as their principal weapon against imperialism. Soon the protest day was fixed for 7 August 1905. As was to be expected, the day was marked by a solemn sentiment of mourning. Business houses were closed in the predominantly commercial areas of Calcutta and the movement was so unanimously supported that even a bottle of lemonade could not be obtained after noon. The delegates from distant districts of Bengal, besides the well-represented student community, marched from College Square to the Town Hall. They wore blue pennons inscribed in Bengali with the words 'United Bengal', 'Unity is Strength', 'No Partition' and '*Vande Mataram*'. Not less than five thousand students from all major colleges of the capital took part in the demonstration, crying aloud *Vande Mataram* and holding aloft black flags. The happy inclusion of the slogan *Vande Mataram* on the banners was notable. There was no record to suggest that Bankim's mantra was ever used publicly before.

On their arrival at the Town Hall, the students sat in wide circles and sang solemnly. Others gathered round their orators, while enthusiasts distributed literature and handbills. Here also cries of *Vande Mataram* filled the air. As an estimated twelve thousand protestors had assembled spontaneously, two separate additional meetings had to be held, besides the main meeting on the first floor of the Town Hall. The leaders described the proposal of Partition as a political blunder of the gravest magnitude.

The news of the protest meeting triggered a debate in the British Parliament the next day. A notable member of the Parliament presented a petition from Bengal for the withdrawal of the orders for the Partition. The secretary of state for India was quick to reassure the member that the British Government had no intention of settling the subject with undue haste. He emphatically promised to present all the information as soon as possible, only to break his vow and get the Bill for Partition passed slyly. Thus, the way was paved for the final division to be effected in mid-October.

Ultimately, the long-awaited Partition papers were published in Simla with just two days left for the division of Bengal to take effect. The despatch dealt at length with the debatable advantages of such a separation. Gloom hung over Bengal on the eve of Partition. Never before in the history of a subject nation had its rulers so autocratically disregarded the people's wishes.

The Statesman professed that following the division of the administration, the government's expenditure had roughly increased to over a million rupees, and the initial cost of government buildings at Dacca by another million—the original projected cost of the South African Boer War. And, in a postscript, it sarcastically added that there would probably be other expenses of which no estimate could, at present, be given.

35

Partition of Bengal

On the day of Partition, there was neither any sign of violence nor unpleasantness anywhere. According to the injunction issued by the leaders, the day should have been kept with the Indian equivalents of sackcloth and ashes—in fasting and lamentation, in prayer and humiliation. But in effect, the sight suggested anything but lamentation and mourning. From much before dawn large crowds could be seen moving towards the Ganges for a holy bath. The riverside was alive with a mammoth crowd and the ghats swarmed with bathers. The road by the river was a moving mass of humanity, and from the crowd came a loud hum, above which rose at regular intervals the cry of *Vande Mataram*. The police were out in force, but they had very little work to do.

North Calcutta, which was predominantly native, was the hub of the city. It was, therefore, natural that it revealed the full extent of the popular demonstration. It seemed as though the whole Bengali population had turned out. Horse-carriages stood in interminable lines. Men and boys in processions greeted the stray European with loud and good humoured shouts. In Baghbazar the scene was indescribable. A wide facade of an immense Indian house belonging to Rai Pashupati Nath Bose faced a quadrangle as large as a football field. Its entire space was filled with a sea of humanity. Here and there a speaker stood in the midst of a circle of seated figures, around whom stood hundreds of others. A continuous stream of people made its way to the house, each paying his mite to the National Fund. In Chitpore Road the noise was deafening. The ear wearied of the din.

One of the biggest events of the day was the laying of the foundation for the Federation Hall, a monument meant to represent the permanent bond of unity between the two Bengals. The spare open space of land selected for the site was the scene of the most remarkable demonstrations witnessed in Calcutta for many years. No meeting held in Calcutta for a very long time could have equalled the attendance on that occasion. The crowd waited patiently for the arrival of the leaders. Organised cries of *Vande Mataram* and other patriotic songs helped them to while away the time. Immediately at the conclusion of the stone-laying ceremony, the people started moving in an orderly procession towards Baghbazar. But by ten o'clock the people had dispersed and gone home. The proceedings had ended without disturbance and no trouble of any kind was reported anywhere.

Like all devout Hindu women, Saraju had decided to go to bathe in the Ganges on Partition day. Taking her son and Haripriya, Saraju set off in their carriage for the Burrabazar ghat. Chitpore Road was literally overflowing with a sea of humanity.

The crowds had been increasing ever since their carriage crossed the Esplanade Square. Indraneel realised that it would be much faster to walk through the throng than to helplessly sit in a motionless carriage. Dozens of trams were sharing the fate of the private carriages. Since parking anywhere on the road was unthinkable, Indraneel instructed the coachman to return home whenever he could manage to disengage his vehicle from the line. Parked carriages stood in rows of two on each side of the road, making it difficult even for the pedestrians to move along. Finally, the two ladies got down near the Nakhoda Masjid and began walking the remaining distance behind Indraneel.

Never before had the city witnessed such a grand event of peaceful but dynamic protest. Everyone, including the children was barefooted. The men wore only a dhoti with one end flung over their upper bodies as during bereavement, and the women were clad in white saris and white blouses, the customary dress of widows. After nearly three-quarters-of-an-hour, the three emerged from behind the Mint onto the Strand near Posta. From there, they could now see the river. Swarms of men, women and children covered every inch and the omnipresent whiteness of the dresses was spectacular and unforgettable. Impulsively, Saraju clutched at Indraneel's arm as a young Muslim surged forward to tie a *rakhi* on his wrist. Indraneel hugged him with feeling.

'Bhai,' he said apologetically, 'I am sorry that I don't have one to tie around your wrist. But tell me where I could buy some.'

After showing him where he could purchase *rakhi*s, the stranger melted away into the crowd. As they were crossing to the other side of the Strand to reach the river, a group of singers accosted them. They were singing the new song that Tagore had especially composed for the Partition day.

'O Lord,' they sang, 'Render the soil, the water, the air, the fruits of Bengal sacred! Let the heart and mind of all the brothers and sisters of Bengal unite.'

Near the river the exchange of *rakhi*s between Hindus and Muslims was taking place on a larger scale with sincerity and fervour. Indraneel also exchanged *rakhi*s with nearly a dozen unknown Muslims.

After making their way laboriously through the milling crowd, the three finally emerged at the head of the stairs that led down to the river. They began to descend the large, slippery steps carefully. The water instantly rejuvenated them. Just as Saraju closed her eyes to pray to the Goddess Ganga for the reunification of the divided nation and let the water drip through the tips of her joined palms, she heard her name being called by a very familiar voice.

'Sujudi,' it cried in delight, 'I haven't seen you for so long!'

'Menu,' Saraju yelled back, 'I had no idea you were in Calcutta.' By then Mrinalini had happily flung herself on her Didi after wading as fast as she could through waist-deep water. Saraju held her tightly.

'How are you?' she asked. 'It is more than four years since we last met. But here, meet my son, Indraneel,' Saraju said proudly signalling him to come closer. Indraneel made a namaskar and stood awkwardly. Then Saraju turned to Mrinalini and asked about Aurobindo, 'Where is he now?'

'As usual in Baroda,' Mrinalini replied. 'He seems to have grown even more distant ever since he has taken up yoga. I have lived with him only for a year.'

Saraju signalled to Indraneel and Haripriya to wait at a distance. Then leading Mrinalini to the side of the large step on which they stood, Saraju made her sit down on the raised edge of the stairs.

Saraju lovingly slipped her hand around Mrinalini's waist and whispered, 'I didn't know that he has taken up asceticism.'

'No, it's not asceticism,' Mrinalini explained. 'Any spirituality that gives up life is not meant for him. At the same time, a life of pleasure, comfort or worldly happiness is not acceptable to him either. He has taken up spirituality to uplift his country and his own countrymen.'

After an uneasy silence, Mrinalini continued. 'Recently, he wrote to me a long letter in which he refers to his three madnesses.'

'What madnesses?' Saraju asked in alarm.

Obviously, Mrinalini could not have confided even in her own mother about such an intimate problem.

'In this letter,' she resumed, 'he wrote that a madman will not make his wife happy, he can only make her miserable. His first madness is his belief that his accomplishments, genius, learning and wealth given to him by God are His. That he has the right to spend only whatever is needed for his family and himself but the rest must be returned to God. His second madness is to have a direct vision of God by whatever means at his disposal. If God exists, there must be some way of meeting Him face-to-face. He has also invited me to be his companion on this path. And his third madness is that while others look upon their country as an inert piece of matter, he looks upon his country as the Mother whom he worships. Then he earnestly asks, "What would a son do if a demon sat on his mother's breast and started sucking her blood? Would he quietly sit down to his dinner, amuse himself with his wife and children, or would he rush out to deliver his mother?" God sent him to earth to accomplish this great mission of deliverance of the motherland.'

For a long time Saraju remained speechless. She had no previous knowledge of Aurobindo's deep spirituality. Saraju did not know how to console Mrinalini. But through simple instinct she understood that only an inner opening could allow Mrinalini to recognise Aurobindo's greatness. After comforting Menu, Saraju made her promise to visit her at her residence whenever she could. Mrinalini went back to her family.

Harimohan grew worried by the delay of his wife and son and felt concerned about their health as they had fasted throughout the day. That night he sensed that a strange change had occurred in his wife following her bath in the river.

The Boycott movement began to gather momentum as a spontaneous reaction to the Partition, and the student community, in particular, responded ardently to the call of nationalism. Soon students began to drop out of government institutions. The rulers realised that the movement started as a result of an administrative measure threatened to bring about an economic, cultural and political revolution in the country.

Sir Bamfylde Fuller, the lieutenant governor of the new state of East Bengal and Assam, unwittingly added fuel to the fire of the existing discontent by attempting to drive a wedge between the people of the two most populous communities of his state. And the public soon learned the hard realities of the government's newest policy of divide and rule.

Ashwini Kumar Dutt was the undisputed leader of Barisal, an important district in the lieutenant governor's domain. As Ashwini Kumar lent full support to Boycott, the people of the district strongly rallied behind him. The result was a sharp fall in the sale of British goods, a success not yet seen anywhere else in the country at the time. During the Puja season, dealers in foreign goods became shaky and literally lost their peace of mind. Meetings were being held all over the district and shouts of *Vande Mataram* filled the air.

Meanwhile, the situation was slowly getting out of hand. The police began reporting that Hindus were using force to prevent Muslims from purchasing foreign goods and misbehaving with Europeans. Soon, punitive police action covered the far ends of the district, unleashing a reign of terror. The Gurkhas were given a free hand to loot, rape and plunder, making it difficult for the citizens to come out of their houses even in broad daylight. A large number of respectable people had been ordered to leave Barisal within fifteen days for having participated in a movement against Partition. Adding insult to injury, Sir Bamfylde ordered that cries of *Vande Mataram* be banned and passed a series of orders banning meetings in public places. If a student or any other person shouted *Vande Mataram* on the street he would be arrested as an ordinary criminal. The gentlemen of Rangpur were forcibly appointed as special constables. They had to take part in drills like ordinary constables, belted and armed with a baton and were required to submit daily reports of subversive activities in the town. There was no provision in law for the humiliation that was heaped on them. When news of such barbarity reached England, it drew a sharp reaction from *Manchester Guardian*: 'It is doubtful if such pettifogging tyranny exists even in Russia,' it curtly observed.

36

National Council of Education

The concept of national education in the field of learning was born in an atmosphere charged with intense political activities. This development brought to the common Indian what he needed most: the development of technical skills and the blossoming of his Indian spirit. So far the rulers were feeding him with an alien education that was irrelevant in his milieu.

The National Council of Education (NCE) was born at a public meeting held in Calcutta in less than a couple of weeks after the Partition of Bengal. Four days later, Subodh Mullick pledged a hundred thousand rupees to promote national education, for which he was spontaneously honoured with the title of 'Raja'. The next day, few other zamindars of Bengal promised to contribute five hundred thousand rupees for setting up the Council. The intellectuals of Bengal met to determine the nature of the national education that was needed. Accordingly, they took some crucial decisions for setting up the National College.

While these sweeping reforms were taking shape in Bengal, an incident occurred in the Presidency College that catapulted Ullaskar Datta, one of the most dynamic members of the student circle, to the forefront. The Presidency College fracas, a sequel to a report filed eighteen months earlier, was unprecedented in a British institution of that period. Charles Russell, a professor at the Presidency College, had earlier prepared a confidential report on some local institutions, casting aspersions on the moral conditions at the hostels and messes. The disclosure of the findings in the report was like a spark in a powder dump in the volatile atmosphere of schools and colleges. The students began asking why this could not be avenged. Should the white man be let off the hook?

Ullaskar Datta, a student of the second year, came to college with a slipper wrapped in a newspaper. With an élan of fearless self-sacrifice, he severely thrashed Professor Russell with it. Ullaskar had thus, on his own, avenged the student community, but at the cost of his own academic career.

Following the formal request of the school authorities to the Maharaja, Aurobindo was transferred to the Baroda College where he assumed full-time duty as a teacher. Soon he was promoted to the post of the vice principal and a couple of months later, became its acting principal.

Meanwhile, having taken note of the significant creation of the NCE, Aurobindo considered it a step forward towards the moulding of the youth for the liberation of the motherland. But this implied that he must first settle down in Calcutta. Therefore, he decided to pay a visit to the capital towards the end of the year. As the yearly session of the Congress was to be held in Benaras, Aurobindo chose to travel back to Baroda through the holy city.

In Calcutta, he met his friend Subodh Mullick and discussed with him some details about the launching of the National College. Thereafter, he cautiously brought up the topic of administering the institution.

'In fact,' Mullick reassured him, 'judging by the past experience of running a big institution, I have in mind only your name for the post of the principal.' However, Mullick was quick to sound a note of caution. 'But do you really want the job?' he asked sincerely. 'Have you given proper thought to all the aspects involved?' And strangely, even after Aurobindo gave his assurance, Mullick looked unconvinced.

Harimohan met his friend in Subodh Mullick's house and took him home. Aurobindo told him about his desire to assume the post of the principal of the National College.

'So you want to fill this insignificant post by relinquishing the job at the Baroda College?' Harimohan was aghast. 'Do you imagine that your salary at the National College will be at par with what you're earning in Baroda? How then do you propose to run your family?'

'Well, not only my own family,' Aurobindo said with a wry smile, 'I have to look after my mother, my sister and Barin too.'

'Precisely, how then will you run the show? There's no doubt in my mind that the NCE would rather employ retired men who will happily accept a token salary. I shall be surprised if an institution depending on the munificence of donors could afford to pay you a wage of, say, more than a couple of hundred rupees a month!'

'I've been promised a hundred and fifty rupees,' Aurobindo corrected calmly.

'What? And you're willing to accept it? Now, wait a minute, aren't you earning seven hundred and odd rupees at present?

How can you readjust your lifestyle to less than a fifth of your present income?'

'All I can say is that my presence here is essential.'

'Are you suggesting that your presence here was less necessary at the time when the *akhara* was breaking up due to Barin's infantile feud?

'That was an entirely different issue. Being inspired by idealism and enthusiasm, young men come forward to join the movement. But these elements do not last long. It becomes very difficult to observe and exact discipline. Small groups begin to form within the organisation and rivalries between groups and even between individuals grow. There is competition for leadership. Sometimes they sink so low as to quarrel over money.'

'Then what was the point of getting Jatin trained in the army if his services could not be utilised?'

Aurobindo smiled disarmingly. He knew that arguing with the seasoned barrister would be futile. However, he had to make a point.

'Don't you agree that a new political awakening has occurred among the Bengalis following the Partition of Bengal? This phenomenon needs to be exploited in order to give shape to the new Bengal. The rulers have thrown out the challenge and there is every sign that it will be taken up. Nevertheless, to leap at once from an overpowering *tamasic* condition of the mind into a *rajasic* one is not easy for a nation. But national education is by no means impracticable or difficult. It needs a resolute enthusiasm and the courage to take a leap into the unknown.'

Harimohan was absolutely amazed. He looked at Aurobindo and wondered whether he belonged to this world or to a much higher sphere of consciousness.

'You are right, Auro,' he said dejectedly, realising the hardships that his friend would have to face in his new environment. 'Yes, it's imperative that you should shift to Calcutta. But I have a piece of advice for you. Take a year's leave without pay instead of entirely giving up His Majesty's service. That way, if you're not satisfied with your work here, you can go back to Baroda at the end of the year. You may rest assured that the Maharaja will take you back with open arms.'

Mrinalini and Saraju met again in early 1906 following their chance meeting on the day of Partition. This time Mrinalini came prepared to spend the whole day with her older friend. After greeting Mrinalini briefly, Harimohan left for the high court with Indraneel, who he had engaged as an administrator to run his office.

Taking off her expensive *jamdani* sari, Mrinalini slipped into an ordinary one that Saraju offered her. Then the two ladies ate lunch and went to the terrace to sit in the pleasant wintry sun. Here, Mrinalini began talking earnestly to Saraju.

'I think he is coming to stay in Calcutta,' she said excitedly using the third pronoun rather than utter her husband's name. 'Well, nothing's definite. Now we can stay together, can't we?'

'Of course,' Saraju said reassuring Mrinalini. 'When my husband went to Baroda, he found Thakurpo homesick. And now with such a pretty wife here, there is so much more reason to feel homesick. Isn't it?'

Mrinalini hid her face on her friend's shoulder and Saraju broke into a peal of laughter, hugging her fondly.

'Menu, will you listen to me?' Saraju said, suddenly growing serious. 'If your husband has taken a vow of austerity, I think it is your duty not to interfere. I discussed the matter of his three madnesses with my husband. And his immediate reaction was, "Yes, I had been expecting something similar. Aurobindo has come for something very big. As his wife, Mrinalini surely must understand more than anyone else that he is not an ordinary being."'

Thereafter, a long silence followed and both ladies withdrew into their shells.

'All right,' Mrinalini said at last, 'I'm indeed convinced that he isn't a common being like us. Yet Sujudi, can an ordinary person like me be satisfied with someone so distant and aloof?'

'*Door boka* (you little fool),' Saraju admonished her fondly. 'Do you realise how lucky you are to have such a husband? Don't you realise he's one in a million? Maybe he's unlike us but that doesn't mean he's cold or indifferent to you.'

'I never said that but how to bridge the immense gap? I've never heard him talk about mundane things like us. Speaking for myself, I know that I would grow insane if I had no one to talk to or be with throughout the day. And yet there's so much compassion in those mesmerising eyes.'

Mrinalini fell silent, fighting with her emotions.

'I have only one sorrow,' she complained. 'I know that I am too plain to be worthy of him. I wish I could be more deserving of being his rightful companion.'

After returning from Calcutta, Aurobindo applied for an extended leave to the Maharaja of Baroda. Though it took a fairly long time to be granted, Aurobindo reached Calcutta just in time to attend the meetings of the executive committee of the NCE. At about the same time, Barin also came to Bengal from Baroda where he had been staying following the dissolution of the Anushilan Samiti. He brought with him a copy of *Bhavani Mandir,* which he had printed in Calcutta secretly. This was clearly the period for seditious pamphlets. Several others were being distributed throughout the province.

At a time when Surendranath Banerjea's *Bengalee*, Bipin Pal's *New India* and Brahma Bandhab Upadhyay's *Sandhya* were being openly anti-establishment, Barin decided to launch his own radical paper in collaboration with Debabrata, Abinash and Bhupendranath Dutt. Upon learning about the scheme, Aurobindo readily supported it and even found adequate funds to launch it. It was decided to call the paper *Jugantar,* The New Age. Later, Aurobindo contributed an article called 'Our Political Ideal' in which he set forth the paper's credo. As its rhetoric became visibly sharper and bolder, *Jugantar* professed that the fundamental need for India was independence. Ultimately, *Jugantar*'s aim became that of preaching open revolt.

With the arrival of Barin in Calcutta, Indraneel renewed his association with the boys and became a regular visitor at the *Jugantar* office at Kanailal Dhar Lane in Bowbazar. His involvement with the paper began to increase with the frequency of his visits. One night he felt inspired and wrote a short article, sitting up half the night. He called it 'Motibhram'—a lapse of judgement.

'The time has come now,' he suggested, 'for rising en masse and throwing a challenge to the foreigners' ruthless and selfish policies.' Then in a vein of rising rhetoric, he boldly asked his readers, 'Would it not be a thousand times better to drown oneself in the Ganges than to remain a shameful eunuch, insensitive to such debasing abuse?'

Not too sure about his ability to write, Indraneel showed it to his father.

'Baba,' he called for the first time, 'would you mind giving me your frank opinion on this article?' The transition from 'Mama' to 'Baba' had required a lot of effort. Harimohan also noted the change with satisfaction although he did not show it.

Finally, Harimohan looked up, disbelief written on his face.

'Have you written this?' he wondered aloud. 'It's fully worthy of being published in *Jugantar*.'

That evening, Indraneel walked down to Kanailal Dhar Lane after work. There he met Narendranath Gossain and Abinash's brother, Upendra. Indraneel showed his writing to Barin.

'Oh, what a pity!' he regretted sincerely. 'We have just begun printing our next issue and now it's too late to include your article. But Indraneel, I promise to publish your article in next week's edition. Till then, please bear with me.'

True to his word, Barin published Indraneel's 'Motibhram' in the following issue of *Jugantar*. At a time when funds were short, it was unthinkable of depending on the talent of established writers. Besides, it was doubtful that any senior writer would risk ruining his career by publishing seditious articles. As the silence of the government emboldened the editors, they began dropping hints of a secret conspiracy and veiled assassinations of *Firinghees*.

Meanwhile, the Anushilan Samiti had shifted its base from Calcutta to East Bengal, gradually spreading its activities owing to the untiring efforts of P Mitra. Dacca had become the hub of all secret activities. During a visit by P Mitra and Bipin Pal, the latter asked a large gathering of youngsters to obey the call of the hour and join the movement against the alien government. At the end of his discourse, eighty fiery young men stepped forward in response to the invitation. One of them was Pulin Behari Das, a dextrous wielder of the lathi and sword and a natural leader of men. With the enrolment of Das, a powerful 'captain-general' was now installed at the head of a revolutionary machine that P Mitra had visualised in vain through Jatindranath Banerjee.

The Samiti spread like wildfire and within a short time as many as five hundred centres had sprung up all over East Bengal. These comprised many organisations bound firmly together by one central authority, just as Aurobindo had foreseen. The tough, ruthless and dedicated young men of East Bengal recruited day after day were just what Jatindranath had sought but failed to assemble in Calcutta. Legally, there was very little reason for the government to try and discourage their formation, as these *samitis* bore the facade of body building and community service. Nonetheless, the administration took no chances and had their secret agents infiltrate the new organisations.

The cause for the rapid spread of the movement was the unpopular measures adopted by the Lieutenant Governor Sir Bampfylde Fuller himself. Realising that it was impossible to rule the province by law, Fuller resorted to draconian tactics such as issuing the infamous *Vande Mataram* circular, prohibiting public utterance of the 'war cry'. He also issued the outrageous Carlyle circular that forbade students from taking part in any anti-government movement.

Finally, on the occasion of the Bengali New Year, the anti-Partition movement exploded with all its fury. The annual Bengal Provincial Congress was held on this day at Barisal. These routine conferences generally attracted only a couple of hundred delegates and visitors. But at a time of intense political activity, it drew an unforeseen ten thousand men, including emminent nationalist leaders from Calcutta. Aurobindo and his associate Subodh Mullick were also present. Held under the shadow of the anti-*Vande Mataram* circular and an express order prohibiting processions, the popular mood of the Calcutta delegates was for testing their validity. They spontaneously formed columns and began marching through the streets, shouting *Vande Mataram*. But the police also had a well-laid-out plan. They let the leaders pass by and pounced upon the younger men with lathis and beat them up severely. The most notable among the injured was Manoranjan Guha Thakurata's son Chittaranjan. After relentlessly chanting *Vande Mataram*, even as he was thrown into a pond with serious head injuries, Chittaranjan miraculously survived and his popularity vied with that of Surendranath Banerjea during the older leader's later clash with the police. But after a rapid arrest, trial and imposition of a fine for contempt of court, Surendranath became the greatest hero, securing more strongly his position as the uncontested leader of the Bengal Congress.

37

National Schools

Ananda Chakravarty, a member of the local school committee, brought Bipin Pal, Aurobindo and Subodh Mullick to Dacca at the conclusion of the Barisal Conference. Significantly, they were put up in a house that was later to become a national school. For four or five days they attended many meetings and Pal delivered scores of speeches. As a result of their visit a new enthusiasm awakened in the hearts of the local youth.

Later, the headmaster of the Kishoregunj School was so impressed by Aurobindo's views that he readily converted his teaching centre into a national school, setting a new trend in the field of education. The three leaders left for Mymensingh, making a brief stopover at Golakpur where a national school was founded. After their introduction to Hemendra Kishore Acharya Chaudhury, the founding of the Sadhana Samiti followed soon. And such was the enthusiasm among the local people that within a couple of days the number of adherents crossed the one hundred mark.

From Mymensingh, Aurobindo and his companions travelled to Comilla, where advocate Ananda Mohan Naha received them. Here, too, a popular national school was started and a novel way for collecting funds for this project was introduced. Two pairs of boys and girls dressed in the orange robe of sanyasis were made to sing their way from door-to-door. The collection soared to an unexpected sixteen hundred rupees by nightfall! Trying to fix their range of national duties in the presence of their honourable guests, the people of Comilla would enter into heated exchanges. At such uneasy moments, Aurobindo's advice would invariably be sought. This quiet and reserved spectator would then magically soothe all differences with just a few words and a sweet smile.

As many as eight to ten thousand people reportedly congregated twice daily to listen to Bipin Pal's addresses. In an era when microphones were non-existent, Pal's powerful oratory not only carried through to the farthest corners of the ground, but also penetrated deep into the hearts of the listeners, awakening a new patriotic fervour. And while Pal openly hinted at bullets and cannons in his speeches, Aurobindo and Mullick held discreet closed-door discussions with local leaders, because of their inability to address large crowds in their mother tongue.

In Brahmanberia, the three leaders came in contact with the firebrand Ullaskar Datta, who had escaped there after beating up Professor Russell. After this, the group left for a little village called Kalikachchha where the three men met Dr Mahendra Nandi, whose son, Ashok, would shortly come to know Aurobindo. After returning from the tour of the interior areas, the three men resumed their tour of East Bengal.

During the hectic expedition, not only was Pal impressed by Aurobindo's depth of knowledge and personality but also felt helplessly drawn by his unassuming, selfless nature. He had rarely come across someone who had sacrificed so much for so little. Indeed, Aurobindo's decision to relinquish the highly honoured office at the Baroda College to fill up the post of the principal of the National College at one-fifth of the emolument received earlier would soon create ripples and become an inspiration for the country's youth to forgo a life of pleasure and join the anti-British movement.

Bipin Pal had all along wished to start a nationalist paper and approached a few wealthy men for donations. Five hundred rupees was pledged to him. Evidently, the amount was not big, but it set the ball rolling. Since his acquaintance with Aurobindo, Pal had been secretly wishing to rope him in as one of the paper's editors. The opportunity presented itself unexpectedly during their journey from Comilla, when they were left on their own by the local youth.

'Have you ever tried your hand at writing articles?' Pal asked Aurobindo eagerly.

'I've written some articles in the past,' Aurobindo admitted. 'Probably you've heard of the series named "New Lamps for Old" in *Induprakash*?'

'You don't mean you were the author of that remarkable series?' Pal asked in disbelief. 'And does journalism interest you? You see, I'm soon launching a paper called *Bande Mataram*. I wish to make it a nationalistic paper. Would you like to join the board of editors? Let us work together to assure *Bande Mataram*'s success!'

'So be it,' Aurobindo asserted calmly, 'Let Bankim's dream be fulfilled.'

Calling at the *Jugantar* office, Upendra learnt that his brother Abinash and Barin had gone to receive Aurobindo in Howrah.

Since long Upendra had wished to meet Aurobindo and now this unexpected prospect thrilled the teenager no end. He thought Aurobindo would be overbearing and eager to win people over with his oration, but he was baffled when a seemingly unassuming man of disproportionate leanness alighted from a second class hackney accompanied by Abinash and Barin. His youthful face bore a strange mixture of poise and contentment. None could escape the sparkling effulgence of his large smouldering eyes.

The same evening, Aurobindo went to stay with Subodh Mullick in his mansion at Wellington Square. While Abinash was arranging Aurobindo's belongings with loving care, Upendra felt a strong urge to take home Aurobindo's discarded clothes. He managed to get Barin's permission and returned to Arbelia the same night with Aurobindo's suit, headgear, boots and socks. Later, he displayed these proudly before his Swadeshi friends and narrated the exciting episode of Aurobindo's coming. The arrival of Aurobindo's clothing miraculously rekindled the old spirit and bound the whole group together with a new ardour. Everyone vowed to liberate the motherland by touching the sacred headgear.

Upendra's involvement with Swadeshi had begun taking its toll on his studies. One day in a fit of patriotism, he went to school wearing Aurobindo's suit and pugree. He also carried a walking stick to match the outfit. As soon as he entered the classroom his teacher began shouting at the top of his voice: 'Get out you idiot! Your way of dressing is unsuited to a school!'

However, imbued in deep sentimentality, Upendra remained adamant and refused to budge, provoking the teacher to try and remove him forcibly. Upendra began wielding his stick dangerously. As soon as the teacher came within reach, he was hit on the head. The two grappled with each other for some time while everyone in the classroom looked on with an air of stupefaction. Finally, on hearing the thuds and the cries emanating from the neighbouring classroom, other teachers intervened and brought the situation under control.

Abinash heard the whole story with an expression of disbelief and reported it to Barin. In his short and prompt message Barin urged the spirited youngster to come to Calcutta. 'You needn't continue your studies in Arbelia,' he wrote affectionately. 'Come at once to Calcutta.' Thus, although Upendra was thrown out of the village school, he was propelled straight into the National College in the capital.

Born in a reputed upper-caste Hindu family, Bhavani Charan Bandopadhyay who later adopted the name of Brahma Bandhab Upadhyay was well known for his quick wit. His articles in *Sandhya* were famous for their hard-hitting satire and humorous tenor.

Once, Brahma Bandhab requested Surendranath Banerjea, his former professor of English, to preside over a public meeting. The old man, piqued at being openly scorned by a former pupil, asked jokingly, 'Tell me, Bhavani, is it consistent with your sense of etiquette to invite me to preside over your meetings while maligning me through your writings?' To which Brahma Bandhab politely shot back, 'Sir, is there anyone greater than you worth abusing and better qualified for presiding?'

Admittedly, Brahma Bandhab's life did not lack change. His close association with Keshav Sen, the Brahmo apostle, brought about his initiation into the Naba Bidhan cult. A few years later, he became a Protestant and later converted to Roman Catholicism.

Afterwards, Brahma Bandhab joined Shantiniketan, the abode of peace, at Tagore's invitation, but soon his restlessness led him back to Calcutta. By then Brahma Bandhab had become a full-fledged Vedantist.

A few months before he left for Bolpur, Brahma Bandhab had a chance meeting with Noren, an old friend from his school days, who later blossomed into the famous Vivekananda. Strangely, being preoccupied, Vivekananda did not appear to be his usual self.

'My dear Bhavani, I've undertaken to build a *math* in honour of my Guru Sri Ramakrishna,' Vivekananda affirmed, 'Work is now going on in full swing and I want to finish that. Actually, I have very little time left to live. You don't believe me, do you?' The urgency in the Swami's voice numbed Brahma Bandhab. The undercurrent of pathos was unmistakable. 'When the time comes, you'll know your duty.'

Coincidentally, a few months later, on his return from Bolpur, when Brahma Bandhab came to know on the platform of the Howrah Station about Vivekananda's sudden passing away, he felt as if a knife had pierced his heart. Then a message flashed in his mind 'You must go to England to preach Vedanta.' Brahma Bandhab was overwhelmed with love and admiration for his departed friend. This was the moment when he understood who Vivekananda really was. Brahma Bandhab was soon on his way to England. He delivered lectures at such august institutions as the Oxford and Cambridge University, where the greatest intellectuals of the time came to listen to his speeches, giving him warm and memorable ovations. But with the unleashing of Lord Curzon's tyranny, it had now become imperative that Brahma Bandhab take up his pen again.

As soon as the news of Aurobindo's return from East Bengal spread, Brahma Bandhab Upadhyay, Congress leader Shyamsundar Chakravarty, his meshomoshay Krishna Kumar Mitra and his cousin Sukumar came to see him. A little later, Subodh Mullick and Charu Dutt also called on him. Aurobindo began a discussion with them.

'The first principle of true teaching is that nothing can be taught. The teacher is not an instructor or taskmaster—he is a helper and guide. He only shows the student how to acquire knowledge for himself.' Aurobindo was responding to Brahma Bandhab's query on national education.

'All that is ennobling and lofty,' Brahma Bandhab commented. 'Isn't it the parents' duty to help a child pursue a professional career? And for that a degree is of paramount importance for getting employment.'

'The idea of hammering the child into the shape desired by the parent or teacher is a barbarous and ignorant superstition,' Aurobindo responded calmly. 'It is the child himself who must be induced to expand in accordance with his own nature. A degree is necessary for service and, therefore, people try to get a degree. Good! Let it remain so. But in order to enable a student to get a degree let's give him a good education. The mother tongue is the proper medium of education and the first energies of the child should be directed to the thorough mastering of the medium. When the mental instruments are sufficiently developed to acquire a language easily and swiftly, that is the time to introduce him to many other languages.'

'Then should other subjects such as history, science, art and philosophy be taught simultaneously?' Dutt wondered.

'A foundation should be laid for the study of history, science, philosophy, art, but not in an obtrusive and formal manner. Every child is a lover of interesting narrative, a hero-worshipper and a patriot. Appeal to these qualities in him and let him master the living and the human parts of his nation's history. Every child is an inquirer, investigator, analyser, a merciless anatomist. Appeal to these qualities in him and let him acquire the right temper of the scientist. Every child has an insatiable intellectual curiosity and turn for metaphysical enquiry. Use it to draw him on slowly to an understanding of the world and himself. Every child has the gift of imitation and a touch of imaginative power. Use it to give him the ground work of the faculty of the artist.'

'Don't you believe that moral training should be given through national education?' Brahma Bandhab asked.

'While it is easy to arrange some kind of curriculum or syllabus for the training of the mind, it has not yet been found possible to provide a suitable moral training for the school and college. On the other hand, to neglect moral and religious education altogether is to corrupt the race.'

By now complete silence had descended in the room. As Aurobindo's explanation continued, the others were all ears.

'Once the taste is created, the boy can be trusted to follow it up with all the enthusiasm of youth in his leisure hours. This will prevent the necessity at a later age of teaching him everything in class.

'Apart from the training of the faculty of direct logical reasoning and of the senses like sight, hearing, smell, touch and taste, the one faculty I have omitted is imagination. This is the most important and indispensable instrument. It should be developed informally, drawing on curiosity and interest, avoiding set teaching and the memorising of rules.'

Aurobindo's arguments seemed so novel, impressive and overwhelming that for a long time no one spoke.

It was Brahma Bandhab again who broke the silence.

'Well, Aurobindo, you seem to have devoted a great deal of thought to the matter,' he said in appreciation.

'The lucidity of your thinking is also commendable. I wish you success in the principal's post. May you produce brilliant souls for the country's future!'

Then he got up to leave and added from the door, 'While initially, all of you gentlemen were talking, I was mentally composing an article to launch your *Bande Mataram* through the columns of *Sandhya*.'

Following his discussion with Aurobindo, Brahma Bandhab sat down to write the promotional article he had promised for *Bande Mataram,* to be launched shortly. But the more he gave thought to it the more his imagination turned towards the soft-spoken, firm-minded Aurobindo. He began writing with feeling.

'*Maanoshwarobaurer Aurobindo,*' he wrote, giving a double meaning to both the words. While on the one hand it meant, 'The lotus of the heavenly lake Manoswarovar', poetically it also signified 'Aurobindo of the lake of inward mental splendour'.

'Have you seen Aurobindo, the immaculate white lotus—the full-bloomed, hundred-petal flower on India's lake of inward mental splendour? He is not the rose or dahlia ...' he pondered and decided against it.

The names were not foreign enough and did not carry the magic he sought. He struck off the sentence and began writing it again.

'He is not the lily or daffodil from far-off, obscure regions of the heathen foreigners' land. Those flowers are unscented and offer only splashes of colour. They are unworthy for use in God's worship or on altars of religion. They simply symbolise the foreigner's pomp and show. There is no one like Aurobindo in the whole world. Through him emanates a divine beauty of snow-white purity. Boundless like the oceans are his heart and mind. The inner incandescent world conquered by great Hindus expresses itself through him in its glory. While on the one hand he exudes the light and heat of a thunder-puissant fire, his lotus-leaf-like soft endearing nature vibrates with founts of knowledge. A true and complete man like him, deeply engrossed in meditation, is rare in heaven or on earth.'

After this personal introduction, Upadhyay thought it fit to bring in matters related to *Bande Mataram*.

'Aurobindo has forsaken allurements of the heathen culture,' he wrote, 'and has undertaken to edit the paper *Bande Mataram* in accordance with his vow to liberate the motherland. He has also put aside the comforts of daily life.

'Aurobindo is not a gentleman puppet made from the refuse of the heathens. A worthy son of his motherland, he has succeeded in erecting the Bhavani Mandir for her. Chant then the *Vande Mataram* mantra and offer your obeisance at this temple. The country's independence is imminent.'

Brahma Bandhab Upadhyay finally published this magnificent piece of writing in *Sandhya*, shortly preceding the launching of *Bande Mataram*.

38

Dare to Dream

Eager to utilise his holiday on account of Janmastami, Indraneel walked a long distance to shake off the boredom of sitting at his desk all day long. But suddenly, he began to regret his decision. For, it was *Sravan*, the worst month of monsoon and the sky was threatening ominously. Soon the first big drops began to fall and everyone rushed to look for shelter. Noticing a big portico down the road close to the junction of Cornwallis Street and Maniktala Spur, Indraneel sprinted towards it.

It was a heavy downpour. Within minutes, water started accumulating on the road and Indraneel grew alarmed when the level reached his knees. How could he wade his way home through the city? Just then a carriage halted in front of the portico, creating a small wave. A middle-aged gentleman alighted from the coach and began plodding through the dirty water. Inevitably, his eyes fell on Indraneel clutching at his dhoti.

'Please come in, young man, till the rain stops,' the gentleman requested amiably.

'Thanks, I'm quite all right,' Indraneel answered, 'I think the rain will stop soon.'

The gentleman did not insist much but soon sent a servant to fetch Indraneel. Deeming it improper to ignore this second invitation, Indraneel followed the servant into the house. Although it was mid-afternoon, the shadows were dominating and the lanterns were shining brightly. Indraneel was led into a neatly laid-out drawing room. Soon the servant brought tea, which was served to him by a young woman in her late teens.

'My father is changing his clothes and will join you shortly,' she said charmingly. Indraneel was impressed by the girl's elegance. But why was she dressed as a widow? He shuddered to think that this angel was married and already widowed at such a tender age.

'I don't mind drinking tea,' he said smilingly, 'but please take away the rest.'

'Oh, it's very little really,' her father said leisurely ambling into the salon in dry clothes. 'By the way, let me make the introductions: I'm Advocate Madhusudan Dasgupta and this is my daughter Kusum Kumari.'

'I'm Barrister Harimohan Datta's son,' Indraneel replied with folded hands, rising to his feet. 'Thanks for inviting me in.'

'Please sit down and drink your tea. Who hasn't heard the name of your illustrious father? And may I know what your profession is?'

'I work at my father's office at Temple Chambers.'

'Oh, I see. And I'm a member of the Bar Council of the City Civil Court.'

Then noticing that Indraneel's eyes were following his departing daughter, Madhusudan sadly added as if reading his thoughts, 'What a curse that the girl is widowed so early in life!'

'And where is the rest of your family?' Indraneel enquired, trying to change the topic.

'My wife and my younger daughter are away in Puri. They are not likely to return before Durga Puja. Kusum stayed back to look after me.'

At this point, he excused himself and left the room. Soon Kusum joined Indraneel. 'Where were you when it started to rain?' she asked casually.

'I was at Hedua. I go there sometimes.'

'I too go there with my sister in the evenings. And where do you live?'

'I live on Rawdon Street, off the Park Street cemetery. And, my parents will be awfully worried if I don't return.'

'Please stay here tonight. I'm sure they'll understand that you're held up because of this excessive rain. We have a spare room. There won't be any problem.'

Indraneel was touched by Kusum's earnestness. Even then, he kept hoping that the rain would stop and he would be able to return home later in the evening, but the rain continued to lash the city till well into the night. Expectedly, Indraneel's hosts heaved a sigh of relief when he announced his decision to stay. After dinner, the hosts invited Indraneel to sleep in a hall on the ground floor, the only dry place in the entire house. Although he felt embarrassed at the prospect of sharing the room with his hosts, the unusual situation prompted him to gracefully accept it. Feeling hot and suffocated, Indraneel sat up after tossing about for an hour.

'Aren't you able to sleep?' a sweet voice enquired, surprising Indraneel in his state of half slumber.

'Oh it's you,' he replied, realising it was Kusum. 'Well, I've never shared a room with a young lady,' Indraneel admitted candidly and smiled.

'But look how unaffected my father is. He's snoring as always. Even our conversation doesn't seem to disturb him although he's lying right in the middle.'

'Kusum, may I ask you a personal question? How long did your marriage last?'

'Just one night.'

'You mean that your husband died on the very night of your wedding?'

'My husband was so drunk on that day that he was snoring and falling asleep even during the ceremony but somehow was propped up by the members of his family. And he promptly fell asleep as soon as he lay down in the decorated bed to mark our first conjugal night. I reckon he did not even realise then that he was married.'

Kusum struggled to recall that horrifying experience.

'Then in the wee hours of the next day he hastily got up from the bed,' she resumed. 'But because of his bulk and unsteady legs he tripped over a low table in the middle of the room and seriously injured his head on one of its sharp edges. The next instant, he started bleeding profusely. My terrified shriek alerted the entire household. He died on the way to the hospital and a police investigation began in earnest. I was mercilessly interrogated because of the suspicious circumstances of his death. This created a lot of bad blood between the two families. My in-laws openly accused me of murdering their son, and branded me a witch!'

The tale was so absurd that Indraneel could not utter a single word of comfort. 'Do you also believe it was my fault that he died so suddenly?' she asked.

'Of course not,' Indraneel pacified, 'don't believe everything that people say. Tell me, Kusum, don't you ever dream of starting a new life?'

'You mean, dare I dream of such an improbability?'

'But what is so improbable? Don't widow marriages take place these days?'

'Yes, they do for ordinary widows—but not for witches accused of consuming their husbands! Such accursed creatures are condemned to hell even before they die.'

39

On the Move

Quite typically, Barin was growing restless as the novelty of journalism that *Jugantar* had offered him was wearing off. Although the paper was beginning to attract some public attention, Barin and his enthusiasts were far off their target. People still preferred *Sandhya*, *Hitavadi* or *Sanjivani* to their amateurish journal. So when Nirode Mullick, cousin of Subodh Mullick, offered him a thousand rupees to liquidate the despotic Bamfylde Fuller, the lieutenant governor of East Bengal and Assam, Barin took up the assignment with alacrity. Collecting a couple of revolvers and a crude bomb, he dashed off to Shillong, the summer capital of the new province, where the lieutenant governor was camping. Before leaving, he agreed with Hem Das, a fellow revolutionary from Midnapore, to send him a wire as soon as the arrangements would be complete.

But Barin's style of functioning shocked Hem. When Hem set off for Shillong after receiving Barin's telegram, he met him on his way back to the plains. Barin, the commander-in-chief of an unnamed organisation that would eventually be involved in gathering arms and conducting a violent movement, looked worried and felt that the attempt would be easier in Gauhati. In Gauhati, he suggested that Barisal would definitely be a better place to try it. Wherever the two went, Barin was quick to take the local people into confidence and share with them openly the whole plan to kill the lieutenant governor. But while they openly sympathised with the boldness of their plan, none actually came forward to help.

Having failed to assassinate the lieutenant governor in Shillong, Gauhati and Barisal, the two desperados next went to Rangpur and awaited his arrival. By this time, Barin had already spent so much money that he was forced to send Hem back to Calcutta to procure some more. Aurobindo was only able to spare twenty-five rupees. Apparently he suggested to Hem that they rob someone to raise the funds. At this juncture, Aurobindo sent Narendranath Gossain to Rangpur to assist Barin and Hem.

At Rangpur, Gossain was able to lay contact with them. Guided by Paresh Mullick and Prafulla Chaki, the men left Rangpur an hour after sunset. So desperate was the society for funds that they decided to rob the house of a widow who lived alone in a village, seven or eight miles away! As the members were all from decent families, no one felt right about taking part in such an immoral expedition. However as the local sub-inspector of police had visited the place that morning, it was deemed imprudent to make any attempt that night. Secretly everyone heaved a big sigh of relief. But unknown to them, this scheme to rob would be a precursor of several hundreds of successful political dacoities to take place over the following years.

On the other hand, when it became clear that the lieutenant governor was not coming to Rangpur, Hem and Prafulla went to Naihati Junction, a station north of Calcutta, determined to assassinate the lieutenant governor there. Fortunately for the governor, his train did not take the expected route and the whole attempt failed yet again. At the end, Hem and Prafulla went to see Aurobindo in Calcutta and told him the entire story. After listening to them calmly, Aurobindo asked them to go home.

Hem Das was so disgusted with Barin's amateurish methods that he resolved to find out firsthand how to run a secret society. He bought a ticket to Marseilles and quietly left the country. In France, he contacted the prominent French anarchist, Libertad and also another Russian revolutionary named Nicolas Safranski. By the time the British detectives took up their assignment of tracing him in Paris, Hem had slipped out of France on his way back to India after acquiring the basics of bomb-making!

During the entire length of Hem's absence from India, Calcutta was buzzing with excitement and political activity in view of the forthcoming annual session of the National Congress to be held in the city in December 1906. Left seriously handicapped by the absence of an adequate publicity organ, Bipin Pal promptly launched his *Bande Mataram* in July. He left on a lecture tour of East Bengal after the publication of the first issue of the new daily. However, he left with relative peace of mind after extracting a promise from Aurobindo for contributing one article each day to his paper.

For a month after his return to Calcutta, Aurobindo had been participating in the prenatal supervision of the Bengal National College, which significantly saw the light of day, just a day before Aurobindo's thirty-fourth birthday. Sadly, Aurobindo became disillusioned by the moderate stand of the NCE. Even then, he became engrossed in teaching and in administering the college, hoping that things would slowly change and that good sense would prevail in the minds of its members.

Aurobindo's involvement with the journal was proving more successful than his association with the college. His blend of patriotic spiritualism with eloquent but restrained rhetoric, did not fail to stir the hearts of thousands of nationalists all over the country. But a struggle for power between the supporters of Pal and Aurobindo soon erupted, throwing a shadow of doubt over the management of *Bande Mataram*. Eventually, it was not until October, when Aurobindo was taken seriously ill, that Pal's detractors declared Aurobindo as the editor. As he was opposed to having his name mentioned officially, Aurobindo soon wrote a strong letter to the secretary and to Mullick and thereafter had the insertion discontinued.

Bande Mataram earned the admiration of many British citizens living in the country. Aurobindo Ghose became known to many Englishmen living in Calcutta as a revolutionary nationalist and editor of a revolutionary newspaper that struck a new note in Indian journalism. They became enamoured of the paper, which was full of articles written in English with a brilliance and pungency not hitherto attained in the Indian press. They also felt that it was the most effective voice of what then became known as nationalist extremism.

Unbelievable as it might seem, *Bande Mataram* was not only stirring the imagination of young India but its fame was spreading very far. For, even President Theodore Roosevelt of America wrote to Viceroy Minto requesting him to send a copy of *Bande Mataram*. And after Lord Minto obliged, an indebted Roosevelt gratefully acknowledged that it was indeed an interesting paper.

Aurobindo recast the editorial policy and financial structure of the paper following which the paper became a joint stock company with the appointment of a board of directors. Although

Aurobindo remained the editor, the responsibility now belonged to the entire board, enabling him, as the brain behind the enterprise, to function even in the eventuality of the government cracking down and prosecuting it for publishing objectionable material. The articles were so cleverly written that they remained theoretically within the ambit of law in spite of violating its spirit. But in spite of the respect of the public that *Bande Mataram* enjoyed, financial difficulties persisted throughout the paper's publication. Although the incurring expenses mounted to a staggering three thousand rupees a month, only about half of it came from its sale. So Mullick was forced to advance fifteen thousand rupees to cover the loss.

At a period when demand for the paper was growing, its managerial board met to chalk out its future course of action. This was done principally by cashing in on the approaching colossal event that the city was going to host—the twenty-second session of the National Congress. Later, a crucial decision was taken to publish a morning and an evening edition of *Bande Mataram* through the entire session of the Congress.

40

Prospective In-Laws

Looking from his familiar corner of Hedua Park, Indraneel was admiring the eight-columned, single-storeyed building that housed the Bethune College across the road. This was the first education centre for girls in the country set up twenty-eight years earlier by John Elliot Drinkwater Bethune.

Suddenly, a familiar figure dressed in white caught his attention right in front of the college. With four days left for Kali Puja, she was obviously buying fireworks from one of the small traders who had opened stalls all along Cornwallis Street. Indraneel left his favourite bench and walked up to her. Nearly three months had passed since he had made acquaintance with Kusum and its warmth had remained fresh in his memory.

'Namaskar,' he greeted her. 'Do you recognise me?'

'Oh! How are you?' she enquired readjusting the end of the sari over her head on recognising Indraneel. 'Have you also come to buy fireworks?'

'No, I was sitting in my usual corner at Hedua and watching the crowd from there,' he said indicating the spot. 'That's when my eyes accidentally fell on you.'

'By the way, here's my sister, Sushama.'

'Hello, Sushama,' Indraneel greeted her fondly. 'Which fireworks do you like the most?'

'The flower pots,' Sushama replied without batting an eye. Indraneel bought an assortment of fireworks and presented it to the girl.

'Please, let me pay for them,' Kusum insisted, 'Baba will scold us for accepting such expensive gifts. Or else, give them to Sushi in Baba's presence. He'll be very happy to see you again. Besides, you'll also be able to meet Ma.'

A quarter-of-an-hour later, Indraneel once again found himself in the familiar drawing room. After greeting Kusum's parents, Indraneel offered them the packet of sweets that he had bought from Simla Street, on his way to their house. Kusum brought up the topic of the fireworks that he had given to Sushama. Madhusudan and Jaya Dasgupta politely refused to accept them on the ground that the sweets were enough.

'It's nothing compared to the hospitality I enjoyed the other night,' Indraneel countered politely. 'I spoke highly of you to my parents and they asked me to thank you for your generosity.' That sealed the matter and the discussions veered to other topics.

'By the way,' Madhusudan enquired, 'I didn't even ask your name the other night. All I know is you are Barrister Harimohan Datta's son.'

'My name is Indraneel Gupta. And, Barrister Datta is my stepfather.'

Madhusudan and Jaya quickly exchanged glances.

'I see,' he said contentedly, 'then you belong to our own Baidya caste. And how many children do you have?'

Indraneel was taken aback.

'None,' he answered, 'I'm unmarried.'

At this point, Jaya got up and quickly went into the kitchen to prepare a collation for the guest and called her husband through the servant.

'*Ogo shunchho* [listen],' she said excitedly, 'the boy is handsome and unmarried. Besides, he belongs to our own caste and comes from an impeccable background. I know he's genuinely interested in Kushi. A mother's instinct can't be wrong.'

'Do you imagine the boy's parents would consent after learning the dubious circumstances of her husband's death?'

'Consider this—his mother has also remarried.'

'I understand, but let the boy formally propose to Kushi.'

'What if his marriage has been fixed elsewhere?' Jaya replied, her eyes filling with tears.

'I agree. But you're ignoring that such a rare jewel will attract a fat dowry from his prospective parents-in-law and I'm virtually a pauper. So have patience. This is just his second visit to our house. Don't dream of bringing up the topic now or he may never return.' Then after hesitating a while, Madhusudan added, 'Besides, more than the boy I'm scared of Kushi. Surely, she will disapprove of the whole scheme if she gets wind of our selfish motive! Don't you know how ruthless she is? Let's wait and watch the developments and say nothing to her.'

The trees looked bare and colourless because winter was around the corner. Taking an early hour off at the office, Indraneel had lately been coming to Hedua even on weekdays. But it was all in vain. Despite her earlier assurance that she often came here in the evenings, the person whom he so desperately wanted to meet remained out of bound. Was something wrong with Kusum? Yet Indraneel could not bring himself to visit her house to enquire. Inexplicably, Kusum had vanished!

After sitting for an hour, Indraneel dejectedly got up to return home. A little later, he stood in front of the Scottish Church College to catch a tram bound for Esplanade Square. As he waited, he suddenly noticed a private carriage travelling at high speed, trying to overtake an approaching tram. Clearly, the carriage was on the wrong side of the tramcar and he quickly mounted the pavement to avoid being knocked down. Just then he noticed that a passenger was getting ready to alight from the slowing tram, quite unaware of the danger lurking behind. Indraneel raised an alarm to warn him. But the passenger could not hear him and fell under the hooves of the speeding horses.

Indraneel rushed to the man as soon as the carriage came to a halt. But the victim's tattered clothes and blood-stained body made him feel nauseous. Unbelievably, the man was still conscious and was groaning in pain. And as Indraneel and another man lifted him up, they heard him feebly say, 'My name is Shakuni Chakladar. I live nearby at Hartukibagan. Please carry me home.'

By then the apologetic owner of the carriage had come down and gallantly offered to transport the injured victim to his house. Helping to put the poor man in Indraneel climbed into the carriage and explained where the injured man lived. Within minutes they arrived at Hartukibagan and its inhabitants showed them Shakuni Chakladar's house.

The victim was a tough man. He then requested Indraneel to call a doctor named Pradyomno Sarkar from his nursing home at Bowbazar. After examining the wounded man Dr Sarkar removed him to his nursing home. Indraneel was impressed by Mrs Chakladar's dignity. Not only did she not breakdown or cry, but also requested Indraneel to come in and change his dress which was full of blood. Indraneel could hardly wait for a refreshing bath.

So he promised her to come back the next day and left. The next evening, Indraneel took Mrs Chakladar to Dr Sarkar's nursing home and spent half-an-hour with Shakuni. He was amazed to see how much the victim's condition had improved in spite of a fractured leg and a broken rib. Shakuni thanked Indraneel for helping him during his distress and also for bringing his wife to see him.

On returning home, Mrs Chakladar offered Indraneel some light refreshments. She enquired what he did for his living and casually asked who his father was. She heard him quietly without uttering any comment. There was something very noble in her that made him spontaneously address her as 'Mashima'. Indraneel happily told her about his involvement in his father's law firm.

During a later meeting, Indraneel also informed her of his association with the Anushilan Samiti and about the role it played in promoting awareness among the masses of foreign misrule. Speaking at length, he also revealed to her the society's true aim of producing worthy soldiers to overthrow the British and liberate the motherland. Mrs Chakladar then went to an inner room and returned with a pouch, and neatly placed it beside him. Indraneel was totally unprepared for what the small bag revealed.

~

When Indraneel met Barin again at Goabagan Lane, he looked exceptionally morose.

'I've failed miserably in my mission,' he said ruefully. Although he displayed his usual appetite while eating the *alur chop* that Indraneel had brought, the tasty potato snack failed to pep up his spirit.

'I wasted the thousand rupees that Nirode Babu gave me,' he said repentantly, ' and yet that despotic Fuller lives on! I suppose we bungled because of our lack of experience. But that's not all. We failed in our bid to acquire some money by force from those who had too much. I suppose you realise that our success at detonating even the crudest bomb requires considerable spending?'

Then Indraneel changed the topic.

'One evening, I had the horrible experience of witnessing a man being trampled under the hooves of horses and then run over by a carriage arriving at great speed. This man—Shakuni Chakladar—is recovering well. I called on his wife who now lives alone with no one to look after her. I've been visiting the lady and something in her made me tell her that I was involved with an association that had pledged to bring about the independence of our country. Her interest seemed to grow as I spoke. Then she returned with a small pouch and asked me to take it.'

'And what did that small pouch contain?' Barin asked genuinely intrigued.

'These,' Indraneel said, placing two heavy gold bracelets beside Barin. 'She specifically said that it was for our noble cause of liberating India. I had no previous knowledge that my father knew both this man and his wife. However, it was his suggestion that I hand over these bracelets to your Sejda on her behalf.'

'Please wait till I get dressed,' Barin said excitedly.

Then he whisked Indraneel out of his house and led him onto an Esplanade-bound tram. The two friends waited in the big hall on the second floor of the Mullick mansion. Indraneel had never met Aurobindo and was visibly nervous. Barin jumped up as soon as he saw a man in a dhoti enter.

'Sejda,' he said, 'this is my friend, Indraneel. He's the son of Barrister Datta.'

Indraneel quickly bent down to touch Aurobindo's feet. But he could not utter a single word. Indraneel's voice choked with emotion and his eyes grew moist as Aurobindo smiled and placed his soft hand over his head.

'What can I do for you?' Aurobindo whispered.

Indraneel silently produced a pouch from which he took out the two bracelets and held them out in his joint palms as if making an offering to a deity.

'Whose are these?' Aurobindo enquired, a little surprised.

'One Mrs Chakladar's,' Indraneel replied, at last finding back his speech. 'I shall be happy if you accept them on her behalf.'

Aurobindo held the ornaments for sometime without uttering a word. His eyes seemed to be focussed beyond the horizon.

'It is very difficult to find the right words to thank the lady. Please tell her that this is the first ever unselfish gift made to Mother India. I accept this invaluable present with gratefulness and appreciation.'

Around this period, Subodh Mullick learnt that his wife was fatally ill. Other than emptying out his resources, this was something that caused him considerable mental and physical strain. Besides, Aurobindo, the primary moving spirit behind *Bande Mataram*, was so ill that the editorial that he contributed daily had to stop temporarily. As the pressure mounted, Aurobindo soon found himself with no time to practice pranayama. For a yogi used to doing this exercise regularly, total discontinuation brought about very severe consequences. Thus, having contracted malaria, Aurobindo was forced to live at his in-laws' house at Serpentine Lane under Mrinalini's care.

By now Aurobindo was fully confined to bed and his high fever persisted despite care and medicine. It was a time of great anxiety for Mrinalini as she had never before faced such an emergency relating to her husband's health. As his condition vacillated constantly between bad and precarious, Mrinalini requested Harimohan to send Saraju to assist her. Harimohan complied and from the next day, the two ladies took turns looking after Aurobindo. Earlier, Mrinalini had remained by Aurobindo's bedside without a break, tirelessly fanning and applying water-soaked cloth on his forehead.

One night, towards the end of November, noticing that Mrinalini was leaning over drowsily, Saraju carefully put her on the mat that was spread on the floor, without waking her. Saraju knew that there was no harm letting her take the night off since the most critical part of Aurobindo's sickness seemed over.

Late at night, Aurobindo woke up and asked for Mrinalini. Saraju whispered that she was asleep on the floor beside his bed. Aurobindo looked at his wife with infinite compassion and appreciation, and then smiled.

'She is an unfailing worker,' he said gratefully, 'it is rare to come across such devotion and dedication.'

'May I ask you something?' Saraju enquired, taking a fleeting look at Mrinalini, 'I fully understand that you have a lot of work and that you're engaged in serving the country. But why do you insist upon living separately? After all, while you men have your activities, we women have nothing to occupy us.'

Aurobindo smiled.

'Bouthan,' he began gently, 'The fact is dedication to a simple lifestyle is the most important part of a *brahmachari*'s oath. Indulging in any form of gratification is against this form of renunciation. Do you think it would be right to force her into sharing such a dry life? Besides, there's a far more significant thing waiting for me, which I had written to her about.'

'And do you have the strength to single-handedly liberate the country?'

'I think I can awaken the nation. I definitely have a role to play, a mission to fulfil!'

'May I ask you for a small gift? Please give me an article that you have used for safe-keep so that I may effortlessly enter into communion with you,' she said.

Aurobindo asked her to rummage through his belongings. He specifically asked her to look for a worn-out dhoti.

Saraju readjusted the cover over him and urged him to go back to sleep. As the room became quiet again, she touched Aurobindo's gift to her forehead in deep reverence. Her eyes filled with tears in recognition of the uniqueness of the moment. She realised how concrete was the aura of peace that surrounded Aurobindo. Even the air that he breathed had a different quality. As she leaned her head against Aurobindo's bed, and as she gradually drifted into sleep, the magnificent image of a golden being appeared in her mind's eye. He began walking away after looking at her intensely and she spontaneously followed him. The journey through light and space continued endlessly. What remained with her was light, more and more light until her entire being became suffused with it. Finally, the golden being stood on the shores of a vast sea and blended into the ethereal glare of the surrounding.

Saraju woke up with a shudder and looked around the room in disbelief. A pre-winter breeze was blowing through the window. She quickly shut it.

As her eyes fell on the sleeping form on the bed, she suddenly recognised the golden being of her dream.

'So you are the Uttara Yogi who is so eagerly awaited in South India!' she thought, as tears of joy filled her eyes. Then remembering the deep devotion of old Ayanar Gounder and Vasudeva Iyengar, she sincerely asked, 'Oh! How long will you make those faithful people wait?'

Then, leaning forward, she lightly touched her forehead to Aurobindo's extended feet. The insight that she had so unexpectedly been given was to transform her life.

Harimohan became a regular caller at Subodh Mullick's mansion where Aurobindo was staying. He was overwhelmed when his wife mentioned to him about Aurobindo's three madnesses. Now he felt assured that the big change that was coming in Aurobindo's life corroborated the prediction about his mission.

Meanwhile, true to his self-imposed obligation for the uplift of his village folks, Harimohan had started work through Gourmohan. Already a school for primary and secondary education had come up at Seiya. Three teachers and an experienced headmaster were brought from Chinsura to instruct a hundred students. A medical centre was also set up where doctors from the Chinsura Hospital offered their services once a week. The small hospital, which was named after Kattayani, included a pathological lab that saved villagers a walk of ten miles to Chinsura for their tests. Predictably, the medical centre became the British Block Development Officer's pride as no other block in the entire district of Hooghly could boast of such modern facilities.

The most prestigious scheme that had been mooted by Gourmohan was one free-meal-a-day programme. It was meant for all inhabitants of Seiya, irrespective of caste or religion. However, this scheme was for the members of the village and no visitor was allowed to share the simple night meal. Arranging to provide drinking water, Gourmohan had had wells and large ponds dug to store rain water in every surrounding village where he owned property. These welfare schemes put together created an additional benefit for the villagers by generating employment. For the first time, there was a semblance of prosperity in Seiya. Now virtually in the autumn of his life, Gourmohan was enjoying an upsurge of goodwill from his people who began to regard him as a demigod. Gourmohan was being looked upon as the central authority for all major disputes. His advice was sought by Hindus as well as Muslims and he was universally addressed as 'Kartamoshay'.

Apart from Gourmohan's direct contributions, these donations cost Harimohan huge sums of money. Harimohan also had other obligations to fulfil. He had promised a yearly contribution of a thousand rupees to the NCE and a monthly gift of two hundred rupees to P Mitra for the Anushilan fund. Though Harimohan was earning more than before, nevertheless his finances did not permit any extravagance.

With Harimohan's reputation reaching new heights, the government offered him briefs for some of their prestigious cases and even those clients who did not employ him directly paid a retainer's fee to ensure that he did not appear for the opposition.

Paradoxically, Gourmohan's downfall was caused by the national insurrection that he supported wholeheartedly. At first, the Swadeshis mounted political pressure on the elites amongst the natives, the principal patrons of the Bengal Urban Bank Limited in which Gourmohan had a nineteen per cent stake, to boycott the foreign-controlled financial establishment.

Initially, the bank's bad debts did not directly affect Gourmohan's personal assets as the company's liabilities were limited. Although he lost a big income and substantial investment, his loss was largely offset by the generous profits earned through the past quarter of a century. Simultaneously, a group of Swadeshi activists began picketing before all the three outlets of Sri Tarakeshwar Mistanna Bhandar. This was because Gourmohan's delicacies were made out of imported sugar. In fact, every sweet vendor within the city was facing the same fate as Gourmohan. But while the smaller sweet manufacturers quickly switched over to making cheap sweets with natural, impure sugar, the bigger shops were forced to pull down their shutters since no quality products could be made from non-purified sugar. Thus, in one swift stroke, Gourmohan's paradise crumbled to dust! The last straw was the forced selling of his much-vaunted *Datta Kuthi* at Baghbazar. Gourmohan was forced to take this extreme step to settle the dues of those ordinary people who, at his instance, had put their entire savings in his bank.

At this point, Harimohan stepped in and took his father to his Rawdon Street residence to stay with his family. Deplorably, with the dissolution of his wealth, Gourmohan's ambitious one-meal-a-day scheme in Seiya also came under a cloud due to lack of funds. Meanwhile, moving through the right channels, Harimohan was able to hand over the administrations of both the school and the dispensary to the government, ensuring that these facilities would keep benefiting the villagers.

One fine morning, Gourmohan gave Harimohan the title deed of the Bowbazar house.

'I don't want this last possession to fall into wrong hands after I die. Besides, gather all the papers corresponding to the various tenements, ponds and agricultural lands in Hooghly and have them transferred to your own name.' Then Gourmohan resumed after a short pause. 'Look, Horey, I have learnt it the hard way who is who. Besides, your brothers would ruin whatever property, goodwill and respect I have amassed over the years in Seiya. That's all that is left now. I therefore suggest that you quickly take over charge of the Bowbazar house and then by pooling in the earnings from the various properties in Seiya and combining them with the handsome rent earned from this city dwelling, I have no doubt that you will be able to keep up the meal scheme that we started.'

'All right,' Harimohan replied after deliberation. 'I shall take it up on one condition—that I be given free hand to organise the affairs of the estate in my own way.'

'Done,' Gourmohan said with a happy sigh of relief. 'I knew I could trust you.'

Harimohan became very busy during this time. Apart from his usual workload, he was seriously involved in floating a Trust in which the ownership and management of Gourmohan's properties in Seiya would be vested. Out of the board of five trustees to be nominated, Gourmohan and his three sons were to be the logical members. The trouble was with the choice of the fifth member. Realising that Indraneel was his stepson and not directly related by blood to Gourmohan, Harimohan hesitated to nominate him to the trustees' post. Gourmohan surprised Harimohan pleasantly by asking about it himself. Gourmohan ordered that Saraju's name be included as the fifth trustee.

'But Baba,' Harimohan protested mildly, 'do you want a woman, and that too Saraju, to be nominated to that post? 'Of course,' the old man answered confidently, 'isn't it logical to include a native of Seiya? Besides, I shall be very happy to have Indraneel appointed as secretary to look after the functioning of the society.'

Harimohan was stunned. His father was far more farsighted than he had imagined him to be. Involving Indraneel in the Trust's activities was a clever ploy as being a local boy and knowing the geography of the land, he would be able to manage the work with an advantage. Besides, Indraneel was the only one in his family's next generation to truly love Seiya.

Earlier, Gourmohan's business acumen had warned him against liquidating his vast property to repay his debts in Calcutta. For, even if the value of all his colossal rural assets were put together, it could not have matched the value of his few city estates. That is what prompted Gourmohan to close a whole chapter and sacrifice almost his entire assets in the city, while clinging on to his village resources passionately.

Quite appropriately, the Banseiye Gramodyog Samiti came into existence on the holy day of Jagaddhatri Puja when Gourmohan signed a deed of investment of all his immovable properties within the district of Hooghly to the trust. The primary aim of the society was to improve and uplift life in the village by initiating new activities, enterprises and social work. The society could acquire and enlarge in the interest of its beneficiaries, but could not dispose or sell its assets as was incumbent on such welfare boards. It was principally this last point that Harimohan wanted to safeguard.

41

Deogarh, 1907

The Congress session began soon after Christmas with an unprecedented number of delegates and thousands of visitors. But unexpectedly, Dadabhai Naoroji, the president, surprised everyone by setting Swaraj or self-rule, as the objective of Indian politics. This set in motion an endless debate on the actual meaning of the term. While the extremists thought it meant full independence, the moderates desperately stuck to their own interpretation of self-rule of the colonial type. The writing on the wall was clear. Even though the extremists were not entirely successful in carrying away the Congress, they were on the rise and the moderate force was on the wane.

Although Aurobindo had left for Deogarh to recuperate from his prolonged illness, he came back in time to attend the Congress. His poor health, however, did not allow him to work for long. As a result, in the first week of January, Aurobindo returned to Deogarh. Meanwhile, fate had dealt a heavy blow to Mullick, snatching away his wife in her early twenties.

In spite of its smallness, Rajnarayan's house conveyed a feeling of cosiness. Here, Aurobindo happily spent four months. He had taken with him Mrinalini, Sarojini, a cook and the indomitable Sudhir Sarkar, a seventeen-year-old lad from Khulna, suffering from malarial fever.

One day, things worsened and Sudhir's fever shot up very high. At this time Aurobindo was translating the Mahabharata into English and his typed sheets were kept where Sudhir was lying. In his state of semi-consciousness, Sudhir threw up on these manuscripts. Sudhir felt mortified at the damage he had caused. But Aurobindo's serene face did not bear any sign of dismay, nor did he hurry to save his manuscripts.

Another day, Sarojini reported to Aurobindo that the cook had refused to prepare a bucket of hot water for her. Upset first by the cook's misbehaviour and then feeling peeved by Sejda's indifference, Sarojini exclaimed loudly, 'If you don't say anything he will become more and more insolent!'

Aurobindo looked surprised, as if only now he could understand its seriousness. Then he said in an even tone to the cook: 'You don't listen to Didi? This is very bad indeed! You must never be disobedient—never!'

But the incident that surpassed all others concerned a prank only Sudhir was capable of. One of Rajnarayan's sons, reportedly insane, lived within four walls with the doors and windows forever shut to the outside world. Apparently, the poor lunatic enjoyed sitting on a thick pile of old newspapers! All this tickled Sudhir's imagination and a tremendous urge grew in him to see the face of this recluse.

So one morning, as he went out for his usual target practice with his revolver, an idea struck him. Stealthily, he approached a window and fired in the air. A horrible howl came from inside the room as if Sudhir had fired right at him. As the long and sustained groan grew louder, the teenager realised suddenly that the situation had slipped out of control and there was no escape from being caught.

At midday, Sarojini came in search of Sudhir and merely kept repeating, 'It's getting late, Sejda is waiting for you for lunch.'

As he followed her back, feeling like an apprehended outlaw, Aurobindo took in his sorry plight with a single glance and said nothing. Ultimately, Sudhir admitted his fault to Aurobindo.

Aurobindo explained to him, 'Human beings are weak. It is not good to make them weaker by dwelling on their weaknesses. Rather one should think only of that which brings strength to their minds.'

Indraneel paid a surprise visit to Deogarh during Aurobindo's stay there. Unable to meet Sejda, Indraneel handed over the packet of medicines to Sejo Bouthan. As the remedies for Aurobindo's recovery from the weakness caused by his recent malarial fever were not available in Deogarh, Barin had bought them in Calcutta and entrusted them to Indraneel to deliver in Baidyanath.

Knowing it to be the auspicious day of Makar Sankranti, the occasion for the Gauri Shankar Puja, Indraneel went to the temple of Lord Baidyanath. But he was shocked by the presence of an overflowing crowd at the spacious complex of the temple. He was also surprised to find as many as twenty-two temples surrounding the sprawling courtyard, among which, Baba Baidyanath's seventy-two-feet edifice was the tallest.

Just as he was contemplating of leaving the premises, a sturdy priest firmly grabbed his forearm and dragged him towards Baba's temple. 'I shall take you to Baba,' he grinned, 'but you must tip me generously. What's five rupees to a Babu like you when all your sins will be washed away?'

'This is robbery! I refuse to pay so much. Please let me go.'

But the priest's hold was too strong to break away. A sudden panic gripped Indraneel on noticing that two other *panda*s were closing in from the sides to trap him.

'Let me go!' Indraneel yelled in desperation but it was the disdainful laughter of the priests that greeted him.

Just then, a female voice rang out sharply.

'Release him!' it commanded with authority. The small distraction that it caused in the mind of the tormentor allowed the lady to snatch Indraneel's hand and disappear in the crowd. She swiftly led Indraneel between the Kal Bhairav and the Ma Sandhya temples and Indraneel followed her without a murmur. The unknown lady kept tugging him till they reached a banyan tree outside the complex and there she turned around and smiled for the first time.

'Kusum!' Indraneel exclaimed in astonishment, 'what on earth are you doing here? Thanks for helping me,' Indraneel said turning pink with shame. 'You see, I came in all bhakti, but they were trying to extort five rupees out of me. But what about the puja I came to offer to Baba Baidyanath?'

'Follow me. I shall arrange it through our family priest.'

Half-an-hour later, they sat facing each other again under the same banyan tree. 'By the way, you haven't yet answered my first question,' Indraneel said.

'Well, I live here now with my widowed aunt who needs to be looked after. I wanted to inform you but didn't know where to contact you. Let me return home now before Pishima gets worried. How about meeting here at four o'clock this afternoon?'

Kusum turned up an hour after the agreed time and suggested going for a walk down the Darowa instead of hanging around the crowded temple.

'Won't you tell me why you came to Deogarh?' she asked casually on the way.

'I think I ought to explain something about my association with a special group of people. My friend Barin Ghose is one of the co-founders of a secret society run by his Sejda, Aurobindo Ghose. Therefore, I need your solemn vow that whatever I'm going to tell you will remain a secret.'

Kusum took Indraneel's hand into hers, leaving it gently intertwined with his. 'Having roped in some dedicated young men,' Indraneel continued, 'Barin has taken a vow of liberating the country from the alien rulers. He has also started collecting firearms. You'll be surprised to know that Barin actually attempted to assassinate Lieutenant Governor Fuller.'

'Have you come to Deogarh to liquidate somebody? Is Sejda also a terrorist?'

'Far from it, he is as detached as I am from the nitty gritty of the society. Nevertheless, Sejda is the indisputable commander of the organisation that Barin runs.'

'Doesn't issuing orders for murder make the commander as culpable as the subordinates who carry out his mandate?'

'Listen, it was Barin's idea, not Sejda's. Sejda is a brilliant intellectual and a master of English, French, German, Greek and Latin. Besides, Sejda is also my father's friend. Recently, I had the chance to meet him and talk to him. I don't think there's anyone in the world who I respect more than Sejda. Sejda and Barin are the grandsons of the legendary Rajnarayan Basu. Following an attack of malaria, Sejda is staying here to recover his health. Barin sent some medicines for him through me because they weren't available here. Unfortunately, I couldn't meet Sejda when I arrived this morning and had to hand over the packet of medicines to Sejo Bouthan.'

By now they had reached the rivulet and sat down on a low, flat boulder.

'Oh, the sunset looks wonderful from here,' Kusum exclaimed excitedly. 'I wish I could come here more often. But how can I come here alone? This place is so deserted.'

Just then, a gentleman passed by. He wore a full-sleeved shirt over his dhoti and sauntered leisurely along the Darowa with his eyes fixed on the setting sun.

'There goes Sejda,' Indraneel whispered, staring at him longingly. 'I wish that you too would someday have the pleasure of knowing him.'

Although Shakuni had shown early signs of recovery, his health began to deteriorate following his discharge from the nursing home. The reason was the damage caused to one of his kidneys, which remained undetected due to the seriousness of his outer wounds. As the inflammation of the kidney prevented him from resuming work even after a gap of ten months, Dr Sarkar resolved to perform surgery to remove the affected kidney. For this, Shakuni had to be readmitted at the nursing home.

While filling the form for Shakuni's admission, Indraneel realised that it was necessary to affix Mrs Chakladar's signature. So he decided to return to Hartukibagan and absently stepped out onto Bowbazar Street. It was a rainy afternoon and he mechanically opened his umbrella to protect himself from the light drizzle.

Just then, a hand reposed on his shoulder. As he turned back, the smiling face that greeted him set his heart racing.

'Kusum!' he exclaimed, 'is it really you?'

'Yes. Pishima is in the nursing home. Indiscriminate fasting has aggravated her stomach ulcers. She won't listen to anybody and abstains from eating on *ekadasi* days. So Baba brought her back to the city for treatment. But is something wrong with you? Why are you here?'

'I've come to admit a friend for an operation,' Indraneel reassured her. Realising that she was unprotected against the rain he suggested accompanying her and gently pulled her under his umbrella.

'It's wonderful meeting you so unexpectedly!' he said by way of resuming conversation. 'There hasn't been a single day that I've not thought of you since we met in Deogarh.'

'Thanks for reassuring me. I was wondering if my friendship meant anything to you. You know, I don't have a single friend in my small world. Sometimes I wonder how my life would have been had my husband lived. Would I have been happier in that drunkard's company or am I better off enjoying the freedom I've earned following his death? But now, in spite of being a widow, I'm my own master. Take for instance, my decision to live in Deogarh. My widowed aunt wanted to be near Baba Baidyanath during the last phase of her life. So I decided to live with her as she needed to be looked after. True, life is quite boring in that little town but knowing that her days are numbered my little sacrifice can go a long way in bringing her some happiness.'

Indraneel was amazed at Kusum's sense of sacrifice.

'Yes, I admire you for living in Deogarh despite the odds of boredom,' he said. 'But wouldn't you have been happier to start your own family?'

'I concluded long ago that conjugal life wasn't meant for me. I have no right to imagine, or worse, dream of marital bliss. It will only bring me more sorrow.'

By then they had crossed College Street and arrived in the vicinity of Thanthania Kali Bari. Kusum stopped abruptly. 'Will you buy me a garland of hibiscus and sweets for offering to the Mother?' she asked. 'I forgot to bring my purse.'

'Of course,' Indraneel replied happily, 'follow me.'

A quarter-of-an-hour later, they emerged out of the temple, surrounded by an aura of fulfilment. After ringing the sacred bell, Indraneel casually asked, 'Kusum, what did you ask from the Mother?'

Kusum naughtily stared into Indraneel's eyes before answering the question.

'I prayed that She might grant someone as nice as you a perfect wife who is noble, beautiful and intelligent. And may this companion breathe happiness into your life!'

'I sincerely wish that the Mother grants your prayer, Kusum. For I think I've found such a girl!'

42

Growing Insurgency

When Upendra Nath Banerjee called at the *Jugantar* office he found a few boys sitting on a torn mat, deeply engrossed in salvaging India. At first he felt a little upset by the absence of firearms, but only momentarily. For the strong rhetoric in use easily made up for the lack of actual ammunition. That the British could be defeated and driven out with comparable ease was a matter of complete unanimity with them. No one even remotely doubted that the *Jugantar* office would shortly shift to the Government House.

A few visits allowed Upen to get acquainted with *Jugantar*'s oligarchy. Soon he realised that these gypsies were closely bonded by a common nomadic spirit. Debabrata had done his graduation and was busy studying law, but when he heard that the country was on the verge of gaining independence, he promptly took up the editorship of *Jugantar*. Swami Vivekananda's youngest brother, Bhupen, also was an editor. But the unostentatious housewife in this madman's family was Abinash. Just one look allowed Upen to recognise the principal qualification of Barin. His lean skin-and-bone body, wide forehead and a broad nose clearly revealed that he belonged to a special class of men who can turn impossibility into reality. For Barin it was his strong imagination and the tremendous flow of emotion that achieved it. In fact, he managed to convince Upen in merely three sentences that India would be free within ten years.

This rare privilege of rescuing his country was too tempting to let go. And soon, Upen also settled in the *Jugantar* office. Upen was a revolutionary from Chandernagore who later, during his degree course in the Duff College, met his two life-long friends—Hrishikesh Kanjilal and Amarendra Nath Chatterjee. Ramkrishna's gospel cast a binding spell on Hrishikesh and Upen, and after giving up the comforts and luxuries of home, the two set out in quest of a saintly life. But monastic life was not for them; they soon became disillusioned and returned home.

It was at this time that a stray copy of *Bande Mataram* unexpectedly came into Upen's hands. He found its tone and language to be astonishingly bold; one sentence that caught his attention was to remould his entire life—'We want absolute autonomy free from British control'. Its far-reaching implication resonated deep inside his heart. When he came to know that a group of revolutionaries was said to be editing *Jugantar* he was so thrilled that he sought a meeting with the intrepid editors. Upen became acquainted with Aurobindo when he joined the *Bande Mataram* staff as an assistant editor. This association left a lasting impression on his mind for it was only upon assuming the joint editorship of *Jugantar* that he blossomed into a mature journalist.

With the Partition of Bengal, Hrishikesh also gave up his sanyas. One day his eyes fell on some copies of *Jugantar* that Upen had brought. After reading them, he was deeply moved. Upen took Hrishikesh to meet Aurobindo and he also introduced Hrishi to

Barin. Soon the portly, fun-loving teacher was to become one of the close members of the society and earn the fond nickname of Pundit Hrishikesh!

The quality of articles improved appreciably with the arrival of Upen in the *Jugantar* circle. Now with the duo of Debabrata and Upen writing the leaders and Barin assisting them, sales soared to unthinkable heights. *Jugantar* began to publish a bold and stimulating series called 'Principles of Revolution'.

In East Bengal and Assam, the majority Muslim community of the new state was now waking up to some major advantages of Partition. Urged to oppose the rise of Swadeshi and Boycott in their domain, the Muslims became openly hostile to buying coarser apparel at a higher price. Thus the ranks supporting Partition began to swell. The Hindu and Muslim communities had lived amicably together for centuries without the slightest disorder. But now instigated to adopt the path of confrontation, tension was brewing within the Muslim community in the district of Mymensingh.

When riots broke out in Jamalpur, Aurobindo sent Indra Nandi, a young revolutionary from Barin's society, to East Bengal for helping the victims of communal unrest. He gave him two hundred rupees towards travelling expenses. Among the boys who accompanied Indra to Jamalpur were the intrepid Sudhir Sarkar, Sisir Ghose, Bipin Behari Ganguly and two others.

When this group of Hindus dressed as Muslims was found wandering about the streets of Jamalpur armed with revolvers, they were challenged by the Muslims and asked to report at the local police outpost. But instead of listening, they turned into the side lane and fired upon their followers, wounding Gendu Sheikh in the leg. The youths then ran into a nearby temple, which had been barricaded in advance. Unfortunately, Gendu had recognised the shooter, Prakash Datta, a local lad. Soon the superintendent of police accompanied by the sub-divisional officer tried to induce the occupants of the temple to surrender. Instead, four shots rang out, narrowly missing the superintendent.

The same evening Prakash was arrested. Although the youths from Calcutta were apprehended, no one was armed at the time of their arrest. Ultimately, Prakash was unanimously found not guilty by a jury and discharged. Even though the detainees from Calcutta were initially kept under arrest, the case did not stand against them because identification proved impossible. And eventually, they were set free.

Interestingly, it was Sudhir who took away with him the firearms of his companions and gave the slip to the police. Mingling in the crowd with ingenuity he was far away by nightfall. The only thought that gnawed at his heart was that he had escaped alone, leaving his colleagues behind. Back home in Calcutta, the leaders consoled him by saying: 'How can the work go on if everyone gets caught? You have done well to return among us. Moreover, you gave the slip to the British.' As a result, Sudhir received a priceless gift from Barin for his bravery and valour. He was given charge of looking after Aurobindo and asked to stay with him after his return from Deogarh.

Gifted with rare intelligence and loyalty, Charles Augustus Tegart was reputed to be the perfect police officer for the capital. But to Tegart himself, the personal trust that Sir Andrew Fraser reposed in him was most important. The lieutenant governor often invited him for a friendly chat.

Sir Andrew liked having breakfast in his sprawling garden. When he caught sight of Tegart, he began to fold his newspaper smiling happily. Tegart greeted him politely and sat down facing the governor. Sir Andrew assumed charge of the beleaguered government of Bengal in November 1903 and merely eight days later, he had discovered the formula to check the Bengalis' growing strength. At once he had written to Lord Curzon advocating the division of Bengal!

'May I know why Your Excellency wished to see me?' Tegart enquired earnestly.

'Well, it's to try and find an answer to the growing problem of insurgency.'

'Here I've brought some newspapers. I'm sure these would interest you.'

'All right, but be very quick. I am expecting Chief Secretary Macphearson at nine.'

Tegart promptly took out a bundle of newspapers and gave a short introduction.

'Over the past few months the local press has been pretty active in criticising His Majesty's administration. And in my opinion here is the best native English daily. It's called *Bande Mataram.* I shall now read out certain passages from *Bande Mataram*. This exceptionally well-written article is a sequel to two earlier ones named: 'The Doctrine of Passive Resistance'. This part is called: 'Its Necessity'. And I quote: "We have defined, so far, the occasion and the ultimate object of the passive resistance we preach. It is the only effective means, except actual armed revolt, by which the organised strength of the nation, gathering to a powerful central authority and guided by the principle of self-development and self-help, can wrest the control of our national life from the grip of an alien bureaucracy, and thus, developing into a free popular government, naturally replace the bureaucracy it extrudes until the process culminates in a self-governed India, liberated from foreign control ..."'

The governor sat up with a jerk.

Tegart read from a later section: 'This is the spectacle we have all watched with such eager interest in Russia. We have seen the most absolute autocrat and the most powerful bureaucracy in the world still in unimpaired possession of all the most effective means of repression, yet beaten to the knees by the determined resistance of an unarmed nation ...'

'Enough Charles, this writer's pen is far more dangerous than a madman's gun!'

'And I have here some copies of *Jugantar*. It's openly spreading the seeds of armed rebellion. This article is called: 'Principles of Revolution', part 3, sub-titled as 'Collection of arms'. I quote: "We have shown before this that the preparation for a revolution has two stages—forming public opinion and brute force or collection of arms. We have shown last time, how to form public opinion. We shall show now how arms are collected for bringing about a revolution. First means: To manufacture arms silently in some secret place. The work of manufacturing arms is not such a wonderful affair as will be beyond the intelligence of a subject nation. Second means: Import of arms and weapons from foreign countries. Third means: Help of the native soldiers ..."'

'Good Gracious! May I know who the editors of these two papers are?'

'That, Your Excellency, is a big mystery. But our informers feel that both papers are run by the same de facto editor whom very few people know. His name is Aurobindo Ghose, Sir, a disqualified civilian. He was educated in England and served until recently under the Maharaja of Baroda. Now, he has settled in Calcutta and currently holds the post of the principal of the National College.'

'I see. My instinct says that we have a formidable adversary here. My word, he has a strong pen! Charles, I need every bit of information that can be gathered on this Ghose. Will you personally look into it? And please do me one more favour. Give me the copies of *Bande Mataram*. I would like to read them at leisure.'

In early June 1907, simultaneous warning notices reached the editors of *Jugantar*, *Sandhya* and *Bande Mataram*. Expectedly, none of the papers paid heed to the caution and continued to maintain their usual pitch.

Earlier, Inspector Purna Chandra Lahiri of the Calcutta Police had paid a visit to the *Jugantar* office to make an on-the-spot investigation; and through a fit of bravado, Bhupen Dutt had come forward and owned full responsibility. When the inspector returned, he brought a warrant of arrest for Bhupen, charging him with sedition. Bhupen was taken into police custody and later produced before Magistrate Douglas Hollinshead Kingsford. Following Bhupen's sentence of one year's rigorous imprisonment, the nationalist editors wrote laudable editorials. Even some loyalist newspapers could not suppress their secret acclamation for Bhupen's patriotism. All this adulation caught the government on the wrong foot and it sighed in desperation.

The *Bande Mataram* office was searched on the last day of July and many files were seized. A complaint against Aurobindo was lodged and a warrant of arrest was served in mid-August at the *Bande Mataram* office during his absence. The same evening, Aurobindo surrendered at the detective office where he was arrested and produced at the Puddo Pukur Thana. The next day, Aurobindo's bail was ratified after he appeared before the police commissioner, as was required by law. After Aurobindo's release, he returned to 12 Wellington Square and continued his daily routine with his usual composure and equanimity.

No material or circumstantial evidence was found to implicate Aurobindo as the editor. Neither was the police able to pinpoint clearly any seditious writing among the big pile of papers that they had confiscated. Indeed, a former editor of *The Statesman* had laudably written: 'The paper reeked with sedition patently visible between every line, but it was so skilfully written that no legal action could be taken.' When Aurobindo's role seemed impossible to prove, the court subpoenaed Bipin Chandra Pal to depose against him. They argued that even if Pal did not implicate Aurobindo, he could at least be sentenced for contempt. Predictably, Pal refused to take oath and was sentenced to six months' imprisonment.

Aurobindo, the kingpin, who the government sought to prosecute, escaped indictment and continued to edit his paper. Following the *Bande Mataram* trial, he submitted his resignation as the principal of the National College. The students and teachers of the Bengal National College met to express their appreciation of the qualities of Aurobindo as a teacher and recorded their deep regret at his resignation from the office. The next day Aurobindo was invited to go to the college premises to be photographed. The boys of the college came up to their principal and bowed at his feet and garlanded him. In response to the desire of the boys, he delivered a short and simple address. 'What we want here is to build up sons for the motherland to work and suffer for her: work that she may prosper; suffer, that she may rejoice. All is contained in that advice.'

~

When there seemed no possibility of implementing the *Bhavani Mandir* project anywhere among the hills, Barin decided to erect it in the extremity of Calcutta's urban limits. The late Krishna Dhone Ghose owned a two-acre plot on the eastern fringe of the city in a place called Muraripukur, a little under a mile from Maniktala. It was an abandoned garden house, almost in ruins, surrounded by big trees. The place was also covered by heavy undergrowth, making it inaccessible to outsiders. At the centre of this huge tract of land a lone, one-storied house stood desolately, with a big central room, two verandas and an adjacent shed.

The frequent police harassment of *Jugantar,* coupled with Barin's systematic boredom at the wearing off of the novelty of each enterprise, bid him to abandon mere propaganda for ushering in terrorism through the columns of his newspaper and concentrate on action by promoting a real armed revolution. A few months earlier, the *Chhatrabhandar*, Students' Store, was established by Aurobindo and some others like Subodh Mullick and Nirode Mullick who had founded *Bande Mataram*. Meant to promote wholesale and retail commerce to fund philanthropic work, the *Chhatrabhandar* became the meeting point of the revolutionaries and a fund-raising machinery for buying arms for the society.

However, the success story of *Jugantar* reads like a fairytale. In a matter of months, the sale of *Jugantar* had picked up from a mere two hundred to seven thousand and ultimately soared to a national high of twenty thousand copies! Therefore, Aurobindo instructed the members of *Chhatrabhandar* to continue the profitable publication of *Jugantar* while Barin was advised to chart a new direction for his group.

In August, Barin and his companions began to frequent the garden, nurturing the idea of establishing an ashram as envisaged in Bankim's *Ananda Math*. Soon Upen and Prafulla Chaki joined them. A student of the National College named Bibhuti Bhushan Sarkar also arrived. Besides Abinash, who paid an occasional visit, Gossain, Kanjilal and Bhababhushan Mitra also visited the place, although infrequently. Finally, when Bejoy Nag, a fifteen-year-old boy from Khulna, became an inmate of the garden, it was certain that the ranks of the society would soon swell.

By the time the Pujas arrived, several new members had joined the society, among whom were Paresh, Sachin and four others. While these lads came mostly from the adjoining areas in West Bengal, Prafulla Chakravarty, Nolini and Sushil Sen were from East Bengal. There was no regularity in the lifestyle at the garden. The society's only fixed activity was the daily reading of the Bhagavad Gita, conducted by Upen.

Nolini soon received an unexpected but happy assignment from Barin. He was asked to go to Subodh Mullick's house and bring Aurobindo to the garden. It was four in the afternoon when he arrived at Wellington Square and Nolini would forever cherish this moment.

A short while after he sent a message, Aurobindo came down and looked questioningly at Nolini.

'Barinda has sent me to take you to the garden,' he explained in Bengali, 'will you come now?'

Slowly, measuring each syllable, Aurobindo replied, in Bengali. 'Tell Barin that I've not yet had lunch. I can't possibly go now.'

This short conversation was enough to remould Nolini's life by dedicating its remaining seventy-seven years to his future mentor's cause.

Wild enthusiasm swept over the entire province and the student community openly resented when Bipin Chandra Pal was sentenced to six months' imprisonment for refusing to depose against Aurobindo. They lustily cheered him for his principled stance. Sporadic shouts of *Vande Mataram* rent the air.

In those days, the police courts were located within the police headquarters at Lalbazar. As had become the procedure, Kingsford passed an order to teach students a lesson in good behaviour and vacate the court's compound of unwanted, noisy elements. As a result, the police swiftly beat up innocent men, including some uninterested passers-by.

On that fateful day, the fifteen-year-old Sushil Sen was also present at Lalbazar with two of his college friends. Sushil had joined the National College a couple of months earlier. Sergeant E B Huey, in-charge of the proceedings, began using his powerful fists to clear the footpath outside the police headquarters and struck Probhash Deb, one of Sushil's fellow students. Sushil spiritedly struck back the sergeant on the neck and a scuffle ensued. Then Sushil used his umbrella as a weapon to hit him. Sushil's companions fled, leaving behind their friend to be overpowered by constables. However, Huey intervened and did not allow the constables to hit Sushil.

As expected, a criminal case was started against Sushil for obstructing a public servant in the discharge of his duties. Kingsford awarded fifteen stripes by way of student discipline, which perversely accounted the number of years of Sushil's life. The action unleashed extreme reactions among the countrymen and its echoes received due mention in the columns of *The Nation*. The daily disapprovingly wrote that the flogging of an educated man for a political offence was rare even in Russia.

As was to be expected in that volatile atmosphere, the flogging catapulted Sushil to instant glory. Reportedly, Aurobindo wanted to see the martyr boy and Surendranath wanted to felicitate him in a public meeting. The following day, Sushil was duly congratulated in a big public rally and awarded a gold medal. After the meeting, Sushil was taken around the city in a hackney and the National College was said to have kept its doors closed for a day.

These were hard times for the local press. After *Jugantar* and *Bande Mataram*, it was now the turn of *Sandhya*. And simultaneously with Aurobindo's prosecution, another big drama was getting ready to be unfolded in the city. Like *Jugantar*, the tenor of *Sandhya* had been rising steadily, veering close to sedition. Known for his catchy, sarcastic, rhyming headlines, which often served as catch-phrases to describe a situation, Brahma Bandhab Upadhyay had been excelling himself. As a result, his printing press was searched and the editor himself was arrested and released on bail.

Tragically, no one knew at the time of his arrest that Brahma Bandhab was suffering from hernia. His ailment began to aggravate fast as he was made to stand for hours while the case was being heard before Kingsford. One day, when the case was called for hearing, the court was informed that the accused had to be admitted to the Campbell Hospital. Suspecting foul play, the British public prosecutor demanded that the surgeon declare his opinion before the court. Fortunately, in one of his rare acts of clemency, Kingsford overruled this contention. Desperate to get quick results, the government brought a second charge of sedition against Upadhyay. This resulted in his bail bond being cancelled and the threat of being hurried into jail on his release from the hospital. Meanwhile, Upadhyay lay convalescing at the hospital, having been operated for strangulated hernia. When he heard about the second charge having been brought against him, he boldly declared that he would never go to the *Firinghee*'s jail, as he had never before obeyed anyone's command.

Uncannily, within a few hours after his prediction, Upadhyay developed sudden signs of tetanus. Till then, his condition had been stable and he was convalescing well. And just as he was forever prone to living recklessly, he bewildered everyone by leaving his body the next day. The impact of Upadhyay's death was so strong that nearly ten thousand people accompanied his hearse to Nimtala Ghat.

In faraway England, a similar sad development had become the cause of worry for some former Indian civil servants. The news of Horace Cockerell's illness plunged Herbert John Reynolds into a depression. At this point, Reynolds was reminded by his wife that Horace's birthday was hardly a week away. Reynolds thought that it would be the right occasion to commemorate a friendship spanning over five decades, and swung into action. A simple but sentimental party was quickly organised to mark his seventy-fourth, which probably would be his last birthday. Horace arrived on the appointed date at the Travellers' Club.

Everyone eagerly rushed out to welcome the one they all wanted to meet, but Horace's vitality and charisma were clearly missing. A suppressed cry of anxiety escaped involuntarily from everyone's lips as it became clear that his end was much nearer than they had expected. The gathering had quite unexpectedly assumed the unmistakable air of a funeral congregation. Standing beside the chair, which seated his inseparable friend of the last fifty-two years, Reynolds spoke briefly but convincingly.

'Ladies and gentlemen,' he began nostalgically, 'I welcome you in the name of one of the noblest sons of England and friends of India. Horace and I began our careers almost simultaneously. Right from the beginning he had endeared himself to the people of India and his popularity had to be seen to be believed. When he retired from service, all the leading dailies of Calcutta were full of praise and openly lamented the country's and the government's loss.

'Horace was decorated with the prestigious Companion of the Order of the Star of India. Earlier he married the sweet and lovely Julia in India and the couple spent the best part of their conjugal life in that exotic land. But unfortunately, four years after their return to England, fate took her from him. Yes, the great tragedy had transformed the mortal Horace Abel Cockerell into the immortal Hermit of Beaufort Gardens!'

There was spontaneous applause from the assembly. Reynolds had wonderfully communicated his pent-up grief to his listeners.

'I would now request Horace to speak a few words to us,' he said, turning towards the lonely figure sitting on a chair.

With another round of mild applause everyone stepped closer, expecting Horace's voice to be quite inaudible. In this, however, they were mistaken, for by now he had fully recovered his breath and the usual sparkle of his eyes had returned.

'Not everyone has the privilege to listen to his own obituary,' Horace began, 'but Herbert just did me that honour!'

The twinkle in his eyes was unmistakable and caused an excited flutter, followed by thunderous applause.

He continued with a clear note of consternation.

'My friends, the scheme of dividing Bengal has been hatched and engineered by a small coterie of ignorant men. Let us not dwell on the political turmoil that engulfs India and concentrate more on its future. A few months ago, an interesting pamphlet came into my hands. It is an extremely interesting document inasmuch as it throws light on India's spiritual destiny.

'This pamphlet is called *Bhavani Mandir* or the Temple of the Mother,' Horace said, holding it up for everyone to see. 'The authorities believe that a young man named Aurobindo Ghose is its author. He must be a prophet to make such uncommon predictions. Let me quote a small passage from *Bhavani Mandir*: "India cannot perish, our race cannot become extinct, because it is to India that is reserved the highest and the most splendid destiny, the most essential to the future of the human race. It is she who must send forth from herself the future religion of the entire world, the Eternal Religion which is to harmonise all religion, science and philosophies and make mankind one soul." He is none other than the editor of the English daily, *Bande Mataram*, who presently finds himself in the limelight as a seditionist. Friends, the happy news is that I can die in peace after acquiring the crucial knowledge that the future of my spiritual home rests in worthy hands.'

There was stupefied silence around Horace as two streams of blissful tears flowed down his cheeks. But a sudden draught of cold breeze came in through an open window and shook the big chandelier above his head. Its metallic squeak and moving shadow broke the intensity of Horace's concentration and brought the usual sparkle of love and benevolence back into his eyes as he focussed their gaze back on his audience. 'And let this birthday hold the promise of a newer birth,' he said conclusively. 'Remember me always as the aspiring hermit awaiting rebirth in India.'

43

Messenger of God

Rabindranath Tagore had learnt the sad news of Aurobindo's arrest through the columns of *Bande Mataram*. Overwhelmed and upset, he wrote with deep love and admiration, '*Aurobindo Robindrer lauho namoshkaar*'. This was the opening line of the poet's immortal 'Salutation'. Inspiration flowed as Rabindranath continued with greater intensity.

> Rabindranath, O Aurobindo, bows to thee!
> O friend, my country's friend, O voice incarnate, free,
> Of India's soul! No soft renown doth crown thy lot,
> Nor pelf or careless comfort is for thee; thou'st sought
> No petty bounty, petty dole; the beggar's bowl
> Thou ne'er hast held aloft.

He beheld Aurobindo as the one who has sacrificed his all for the sake of his country, standing with the fateful lamp whose light pierces the gloom that has engulfed the motherland since ages. Can any king ever imprison such a messenger of God? Tagore fittingly composed:

And puts he, with love austere,
In thy right hand, today, the fateful lamp and drear
Of sorrow, whose light doth pierce the country's agelong
gloom,
And in the infinite skies doth steadfast shine and loom,
As doth the Northern Star? O Victory and Hail!
Where is the coward who will shed tears today, or wail
Or quake in fear? And who'll belittle truth to seek
His own small safety? Where's the spineless creature weak
Who will not in thy pain his strength and courage find?
O wipe away those tears, O thou of craven mind!
The fiery messenger that with the lamp of God
Hath come—where is the king who can with chain and
rod
Chastise him? Chains that were to bind salute his feet,
And prisons greet him as their guest with welcome
sweet,
The pall of gloom that wraps the sun in noontide skies
In dim eclipse, within a moment slips and flies
As doth a shadow.

And then, in a vein of rising rhetoric, the poet continued:

Sorrow's naught, however drear,
And pain is naught, and harm is naught, and naught
all fear;
The King's a shadow, punishment is but a breath;
Where is the tyranny of wrong, and where is death?
O fool, O coward, raise thy head that's bowed in fear,
I am, thou art, and everlasting truth is here.

As the government had attempted to convict Aurobindo on the assumption of being the editor of *Bande Mataram*, he had to be acquitted on technical grounds, as he was not the declared editor of the paper. Following this official blunder Aurobindo was firmly established as the leader of the nationalists in Bengal. Thus, the man who preferred to remain and act and even lead from behind the scenes, was forced into public view. His release also generated tremendous jubilation in Calcutta and the districts. When telegraphic news of Aurobindo's release reached Barisal, the local people went about the town on bicycles circulating the news. During the day, notices announcing the acquittal printed by *Barisal Hitaishi* were stuck on lamp posts and walls. In the evening, about two hundred persons assembled in Ashwini Kumar Dutt's house to celebrate the event.

Daccaprakash had remarked during Aurobindo's trial that the patriotism of this great man and his uncommon sacrifice attracted the heart of every son of Bengal. This patriot, who in response to the call of duty, threw away all luxuries of life and was, though a human being, exhibiting divine traits, was sent to jail by the rulers of the land! The editorial lamented that the reckless rulers were unable to understand that as a result of their misdeeds a fire of disgust was burning in the country, which would be beyond their power to extinguish.

At the conclusion of the case, thus Tilak's *Kesari* declared that Aurobindo's learning and patriotism were so profound that the hand of providence could be discerned in his acquittal.

During this time, author and journalist Henry W Nevinson, special correspondent of *The Daily News* of London, met Aurobindo for an interview. Demonstrating unusual perception and deep insight into the human psyche, Nevinson noted his impressions of

Aurobindo's mysticism. According to him, in an age of supernatural religion, Aurobindo would have become what the irreligious mean by a fanatic. Like a horse in blinkers he ran straight, regardless of everything except the narrow bit of road in front. But at the end of the road he saw a vision more inspiring and spiritual than any fanatic saw, who rushed on death with paradise in sight. Nevinson further remarked that nationalism to Aurobindo was surrounded by a mist of glory, the halo of the medieval saints beheld gleaming around the head of martyrs. Grave with intensity, careless of fate or opinion, he was of the stuff that dreamers were made of, but such dreamers who act their dreams, indifferent to the means.

A couple of days after Aurobindo's release, his elder brother Manomohan Ghose came to see him at Wellington Square. As expected, there was great jubilation following Aurobindo's unexpected release.

Subodh Mullick, Nirode Mullick, Charu Dutt and Manomohan were all sitting around Aurobindo when the gatekeeper came up to announce that 'Robi Babu' had come. Naturally, the poet's arrival created a stir and everyone rose to his feet. Tagore was very moved to see Aurobindo free and hugged him emotionally. 'You have deceived me!' he said with mock seriousness. The poet was obviously alluding to his poem that he had penned in expectation of Aurobindo's wrongful detention. 'Not for too long,' Aurobindo assured prophetically, knowing well that the British were now conspiring to prosecute him.

It was now the turn of Aurobindo's father-in-law to visit 12 Wellington Square. Aurobindo had not yet returned from college, which he had rejoined as a professor following his acquittal. However, Bhupal Bose requested the Mullicks to convey an invitation to Aurobindo to dine at their house the same evening. He also said that his daughter had come to Calcutta hoping to meet her husband and that Aurobindo should spend the night with the Bose family. The sudden prospect of Aurobindo's spending the night with his wife brought unexpected cheer to his hosts.

With eagerness and great excitement, written over their faces, everyone gathered around Aurobindo as soon as he returned home at five. With a straight face Subodh Mullick conveyed to him Bhupal Bose's invitation and urged him to spend the night at his in-laws' house.

And no sooner had Aurobindo said, 'Yes, I understand,' than Lilavati quickly added, 'We've made all arrangements to crease your dhoti. Now hurry up.'

Later, Aurobindo's hosts held their breath as he emerged looking prim and aristocratic. No one could miss his shy smile. Stepping up, Lilavati handed him two garlands.

'Remember,' she instructed, 'one is for you and the other one is for your wife. You must put them around each other's neck.'

'All right,' Aurobindo assured, 'I shall do as you say.'

'Now, for heaven's sake, don't return home before daybreak!' Mullick added as Aurobindo was stepping onto the carriage.

As the coach rolled out, Mullick issued instructions to the gatekeeper to lock the gate at ten o'clock. But the next morning Mullick was surprised when a servant enquired on behalf of Aurobindo whether they would come down for tea.

'How could Ghose sahib return so early?' Mullick asked in utter disbelief.

'But he returned last night,' the servant informed.

Everyone rushed down to meet Aurobindo as he sat smiling gently. 'I returned at eleven,' he explained calmly. 'And by the way, Lilavati, I obeyed your instructions in letter and in spirit.'

When pressed to explain the reason behind hurrying back so soon, Aurobindo clarified, 'I told my wife everything. And I returned only after she gave me her permission.'

44

The Bomb

Happily, through a mixture of stern training and commitment, Barin, the mentor, was able to imbue a sense of sacrifice in the boys who resided in his garden house. Upen's reading of the scriptures further instilled a deep sense of morality in the young minds. Strangely, in spite of lacking Jatin's military background, Barin succeeded in forming a closely-knit group of soldiers. Slowly a pattern emerged. The students had to rise at four o'clock in the morning and do their daily exercises, wash clothes, bathe and be ready for their first lesson at six. After that cooking was done by turns while the majority practised shooting with a gun. Although the food was kept purely vegetarian because of their strict adherence to the principles of *Brahmacharya*, it was inconceivable that fish or meat be served in the current financial state. Before bedtime at ten, everyone assembled for a lively conversation or for collective singing. Their favourite topic of discussion—the assassination of the viceroy and other dignitaries—would then become the main issue which always excited everyone.

'I'm sure you'll all agree with me,' Barin said to his young recruits one evening, 'that our best bet would be to assassinate the lieutenant governor of Bengal rather than the viceroy or the new governor of East Bengal. After all, Fraser is one of the principal proponents of the division of Bengal.'

'All right,' Upen observed, 'but let's not forget that that notorious scoundrel Kingsford lives on. And his existence is a mockery of our readiness.'

'Yes, but how do you kill someone enjoying police protection round the clock? Besides, you know that he has recently been shifted to 2 Kyd Street where bigwigs like the commissioner and the deputy commissioner also live. No, I am not in favour of risking our boys' lives because escape would be impossible after committing the act. We have to bide our time for a more opportune moment to mount an attack.'

Everyone agreed with Barin's point of view. For the moment, it would indeed be preferable to wait and watch.

But Indraneel, who regularly visited the garden after work, had a different idea.

'Ullaskar informed me,' he interrupted, 'that his first bomb would be ready shortly. Then, why not make an attempt on Fraser's train?'

Everyone was delighted. Although they had been engaged in heated discussions to annihilate the governor, no one had thought that its possibility was so close at hand.

'Yes,' Barin yelled in delight, 'let's do it!'

The desire to develop a viable bomb, which could render considerable damage, had prompted Ullaskar Datta to return to Calcutta. Like Upen, his longing to liberate the country was so strong that he could not resist the temptation of joining secret societies, whose existence was covertly announced in the issues of *Jugantar*. Ullaskar's father was a professor at the Shibpur Civil

Engineering College in Howrah. And to his delight, he discovered that his father's chemistry laboratory was sufficiently equipped for conducting his experiments in manufacturing bombs. After his primary success, he got in touch with Barin who took him in with open arms.

Ullaskar became the favourite amongst the revolutionaries. He could cook well, sing well and was so boisterous and high-spirited that he could laugh and make others merry in any situation. The new bomb-manufacturing wing was inaugurated with his arrival and a small forge was installed in the garden. As a result, explosives such as picric acid and dynamite began to appear. Efforts to procure arms and ammunitions were going on persistently. By now, some guns, rifles and a dozen revolvers had been acquired.

Ullaskar proudly announced that he was now ready with a viable mine to blow up Sir Andrew Fraser's train. The resourceful Barin acquired a detailed schedule of Fraser's special train upon learning that the governor was coming to Calcutta from Darjeeling to spend the first weekend of November touring Bihar.

Barin, Ullaskar, Upen, Gossain and Kanjilal took a train to Chandernagore. From there, Ullaskar walked back to a station named Mankundu, searching for a suitable spot to plant his mine. But Ullaskar was unable to set the mine on time. And as the Governor's Special approached, he desperately threw on the track a couple of dynamite sticks. But as was only to be expected, the train passed over them, merely creating some fire-cracker-like noises. Refusing to accept defeat, Barin once again resolved to make another attempt when, ten days later, the governor returned to Calcutta. Carrying along one of Ullaskar's lethal mines, he went back to Mankundu with Prafulla Chaki and Bibhuti. Then choosing a quiet spot where Bibhuti dug a hole, they waited for Sir Andrew Fraser's train to come. Unfortunately, it never did.

When Charu Dutt paid a surprise visit to Harimohan at Rawdon Street, Indraneel was also present.

'Charu Babu, this is my son, Indraneel,' Harimohan said, introducing him. 'Charu Babu is a judge from Thana in the Bombay Presidency,' he briefly explained to Indraneel.

The three men sat down to exchange the usual civilities.

'I've heard about you from Barin,' Indraneel said proudly. 'I think he paid you numerous visits at Thana.'

'Ah, so you are quite intimate with Barin!' Dutt exclaimed. 'Well, young man, you can help me sort things out. Harimohan Babu, I'm shortly going to join my father in Coochbehar and from there, I plan to proceed to Darjeeling for a short holiday. Now, look at this item,' he said enthusiastically, pointing to a small encircled news report of *Empire*. 'Our friend Sir Andrew plans to be there too. What a coincidence!'

Harimohan and Indraneel read together the short note and looked up with a questioning look in their eyes.

'Let me explain,' Dutt said. 'Since the failure of Barin's attempt on Fuller's life in East Bengal, I've been harbouring a secret desire to involve myself in the affairs of the secret society.' Noticing Harimohan's expression of alarm and apprehension, Dutt quickly added, 'A judicious involvement only. What I plan to do is to take one of Barin's boys with me to Darjeeling, the quiet, deserted, ideal town, where carrying out an assassination would be as easy and effortless as performing a social call.'

'Do you plan to use a bomb?' Indraneel asked with suppressed delight. 'My ideal choice would be Prafulla Chaki, a boy from Rangpur. He's quiet and totally trustworthy. You can ask for the boy by name. Barin is scheduled to meet Sejda at three this afternoon. You can discuss the matter with them both.'

After elaborately studying Sir Andrew's movements in Darjeeling, Dutt decided that the bomb attack must be carried out while the lieutenant governor was walking to the church. It would be fairly easy for Prafulla to hurl the bomb and disappear in the following confusion.

But providence saved the governor. For some unknown reason he went to church that Sunday accompanied by an entourage of bodyguards which upset Dutt's plan.

Then when the two Bengalis learnt about an approaching cricket tournament, they were sure that the governor would go to watch it. Accordingly, they waited at the stadium, but Sir Andrew failed to show up.

One day, Barin called Indraneel aside as soon as he arrived at the garden.

'Neel, my brother,' he said concernedly, 'I'm in a dilemma. I promised Hem Sen of Srihatta to send him Ullaskar's formula for manufacturing bombs as soon as it was ready. But both his brothers, Biren and Sushil, are studying at the National College and can't possibly go to Srihatta now. Would you please do me the favour of delivering it yourself?' And Barin quickly added as soon as Indraneel opened his mouth to protest, 'You understand there's no one else I can trust for such a sensitive mission?'

So Indraneel took a few days off for paying a visit to Beniachong, one of the largest towns in the province of Srihatta in East Bengal. The eight-square-mile historic town of Beniachong had a protective wall on all sides, reinforced further by a surrounding moat to repel possible invaders. It had an imposing population of around forty thousand people.

Hem graciously received Indraneel when he called at Kailash Chandra Sen's house in Senpara. Hem straightaway took him to their South House among the three that his family owned where he made arrangements for his stay.

'I hope you will spend an entire week with us,' he said. Although Hem and Indraneel had met at Muraripukur they had never spoken to each other.

'I've promised my father to return before the end of the week,' Indraneel replied awkwardly. 'By the way, Hem, here's the formula that Barin sent you. He also asked me to tell you that your brothers are studying hard.'

Hem introduced Indraneel to his sister Induprabha who had come to spend a few days with them from her in-laws' house.

'And what about you?' Induprabha asked addressing Hem, 'Are you enjoying your course at the Art College?'

'Oh, yes, I'm thoroughly enjoying my art classes,' Hem replied with a chuckle. 'But right now, art is very far from my consciousness. Ever since I have taken up this special mission, I haven't been able to find time to finish the two paintings I'm working on. I have undertaken the preparation of strong revolutionaries for secret organisations like the Anushilan Samiti of Dacca. And I've recruited as many as twenty-four young men! But what will surprise you is that I've established a club for girls too. And, believe it or not, our eldest sister-in-law, Suprava, has also joined these classes.'

Induprabha looked at Hem with large admiring eyes.

'Well, I hope you succeed in your mission. But please, don't neglect your painting.'

The next day, Hem took Indraneel to his class and introduced him to the boys. Hem distributed a dozen catapults and pellets among his students and asked them to hit an empty tin of Ovaltine from the length of a cricket pitch. Finally, the lessons in Jiu-Jitsu started towards the end of the morning during which Hem demonstrated his awesome skills. The next batch of participants arrived in the afternoon and repeated all that the morning batch had done. Then at six o'clock in the evening, they were joined by the members of the first batch and together they sang patriotic songs for half-an-hour.

At the end of the gruelling day's activities, Hem returned to the South House and had a refreshing bath. He felt a strong urge to complete the painting titled *Doorbhikṣha*. Hem had brought from Calcutta two sheets of cartridge paper and on one of these he had already executed his best creation so far named *Audrishto Bharat*. It showed a poor man in loincloth lying face down in a desert, struggling to ward off death, while a row of five hungry vultures greedily stared at him. The exquisite watercolour had been executed in the wash technique of the Bengal School of Art.

Now, Hem began executing the face of a witch-like woman in a black cloak, commissioning a pack of famished wolves and ravens to scamper across the land. This big painting in rich tones of black and white was obviously meant to accompany his earlier *Audrishto*.

Both pieces were executed in the same style. And, in both cases, the artist had portrayed the desert as a snow-like dazzling surface, reflecting the light of the sun.

As Induprabha and Indraneel tiptoed into the room, Hem's exquisite work took their breath away. They could not help inhaling loudly, betraying their presence.

'You see, Indu,' Hem said fondly addressing his sister without looking up, 'your desire is like an order to me. But I shall definitely be remembered for my contributions to the revolution rather than to the world of art.'

As the high court remained closed for the weekend, Indraneel began visiting Seiya on Saturdays, returning to the city on Sunday evenings. Although the posts of the trustees of the Banseiye Gramodyog Samiti were purely honorary, that of the secretary was remunerative. As a result, Indraneel was drawing a salary of fifty rupees. His work mainly involved having the revenue collected from farmers who grew paddy on their lands and having rent collected for the numerous ponds and orchards hired out to the wealthy Muslims of the area. His duties included paying regular visits to the Polba Thana to keep the police informed about land owners who encroached on the Trust's property.

Indraneel often grew bored in the evening during weekdays. One evening, at the Hedua Park where he went to spend his time, he suddenly remembered Motimala. Indraneel was surprised to see a couple of chappals at her doorstep, indicating that there were visitors. As he hesitated to go in, Motimala's voice rang out in alarm.

'Please go away now,' she entreated, 'I have already explained that I have left that profession. I have no intention of going back to it. My husband may return any minute now. I don't want him to see you.'

By now it was quite clear to Indraneel that the two visitors were trying to force Motimala into a deal which she rejected. Indraneel suddenly became aware that his heart was pounding hard as an insurmountable anger seemed to tighten its grip over him. He vaguely wondered if his presence would ward off the intruders. But just then one of the men raised his voice.

'Come, let's capture her and take her away.'

Indraneel could not bear it any longer. He burst into the hall as swiftly as a panther.

'Khabardaar!' he cautioned. 'Anyone who hurts the lady will surely perish!'

The look of alarm on Motimala's face froze him momentarily. It was puzzling to see her terrified when she should have felt relieved. After the two unknown men left hurriedly, Indraneel went up to Motimala and enquired agitatedly what they had come to seek.

'Men are evil,' she remarked and burst into sobs.

Just then Shakuni walked in.

'What a pleasant surprise!' he said affably. Then noticing his wife crying, he caught and shook her. 'What happened? Why are you upset?' he enquired.

'Those men came back,' she answered between sobs, 'I can't bear it any longer. Please take me away from here.'

Indraneel was unable to make out what had transpired. Who were those men? And what were they seeking from her?

'What's the matter Mashima?' he asked genuinely. 'Why were they threatening you?'

Shakuni tried to pacify him and began to converse aimlessly. Strangely, Motimala did not come out for the rest of the evening, not even when Indraneel announced that he was leaving.

One day, unable to find someone dependable at the garden, Barin told Indraneel about his dilemma. Shrish Ghose had informed him from Chandernagore that the two revolvers that he had reserved with Kishori Mohan Shampui needed to be collected. Barin was apprehensive of losing them unless the revolvers were procured at once for Shampui was a dishonest trader who sold arms to whoever paid more.

'Neel, my brother,' Barin appealed fervently, 'will you do me this small favour? Here's the money to buy the two guns. Now, Shampui will give you a sealed packet. Just bring it as it is.'

As the following day happened to be Saturday, the day when Indraneel usually went to Seiya, he agreed to collect the revolvers on his way to Chinsura. When Indraneel called on Shampui at his residence and gave him Barin's letter, the clerk immediately gave him the packet that he had kept ready.

'I am glad you came today,' he confided. 'Some boys from East Bengal had come yesterday looking for good revolvers. But I sent them back. However, they may return any moment now.' Then bringing down his voice to a whisper, he added, 'They are aware that I still have one left.'

'Will you sell it to me?' Indraneel asked impulsively, surprising even himself. 'I know these sell for only sixty rupees. But here take a hundred,' he said, taking out money meant for payment in Chinsura.

'Here is your prize,' Shampui said offering another smaller sealed packet. 'And here, I also give you two dozen matching cartridges as a special gesture. But take care. You surely know what happens if you're caught with three revolvers in British India!'

Indraneel felt that something within him had changed radically. He was experiencing a strange thrill of self-assurance. Quickly finishing his fieldwork around the village, he took out the single packet from the big iron safe and slid it between his dhoti and his abdomen, covering it well with his shirt. He slipped quietly out of the house. As night was descending on the village, shrill calls of the cricket and the occasional croaking of crows filled the deserted neighbourhood of the zamindar's square pond, which now belonged to Gourmohan.

Indraneel opened the packet bearing the emblem of St. Etienne, revealing a sleek weapon. The six-chamber revolver with a curved butt was so small in size that it weighed less than a quarter of a pound and easily fitted into the palm of his hand. Its rod type safety-catch, striking pin and trigger stood out conspicuously. Indraneel confidently held it up and took aim in the direction of the unseen crows. Then he repeatedly pulled the trigger of the empty gun. This brought him a thrill that he had never experienced. Slowly, an indomitable desire took hold of him while playing with the firearm. He wanted to test the weapon by inserting a bullet.

Meanwhile, following the second fiasco, Barin received the good news that Surendranath Tagore would donate a thousand rupees for a successful attempt on Sir Andrew. Once again enthused by the good news, Barin's desperados eagerly jumped into the fray. Probably due to the earlier failures, the planning for the third bid was more elaborately made, taking into account some other crucial factors.

Accordingly, Prafulla and Bibhuti took the train and got down at a small station named Benapur. After walking about four miles towards Narayangarh they found a suitable spot where they dug a hole for over five hours. Then they filled the hole loosely with earth and strolled back to Kharagpur to catch the train to Calcutta.

On the day the governor was expected to return from Cuttack, Barin, Prafulla and Bibhuti travelled to Narayangarh and lowered the mine into the hole a little before midnight. Barin then took a passenger train to Calcutta, leaving his two trusted lieutenants to accomplish the rest. At exactly 2.30 a.m., Prafulla and Bibhuti placed the fuse on the railway track and, five minutes later, were on their way to Kharagpur.

Earlier, the signal went down promptly at 9.30 p.m. and the Anglo-Indian driver, Wade, sounded the shrill whistle. The next moment the Governor's Special began chugging out of Cuttack, amid a warm, cheerful send-off, on its way to Howrah.

Five hours later, upon entering the Midnapore District, Wade put his engine to full steam and let it gradually reach the flying speed of fifty miles per hour. The engine number 2396 of the Bengal Nagpur Railway weighed 106 tons, with its tender in working order. Everything seemed fine and the Governor's Special was on perfect schedule.

It was 2.50 a.m. and the train was at mileage 83/22 from Calcutta and had crossed a small station called Narayangarh. Suddenly Wade's engine jolted severely and seemed to heave up under him. Simultaneously, the driver heard two or three alarming explosions, the last of which was the loudest. The experienced driver kept calm and shut off steam at once, bringing the train to an ordinary stop. Then he quickly ran down to see what had happened. Surprisingly the engine's cowcatcher and the bogie wheels were quite clear, indicating that he had not run over anything. But on coming to the right, he discovered that the leading and the driving wheels were covered with ballast. This clearly indicated that something must have been wrong with the road. And so the driver went back to examine the line, and discovered to his astonishment that the road had indeed been very badly damaged at about forty yards from the rear of the train.

Wade knew that Superintendent Hayter Duff of the Bengal Nagpur Railway Police was travelling in his train and immediately reported the matter to him. The superintendent found that there was a deep crater on the right side of the permanent way over four feet deep and five feet in diameter. The rail at this spot was hogged or bent upward for a length of five feet to a maximum of about four inches above the horizontal. It was a miracle that the governor's train had not derailed!

The next evening, Major Muspratt-Williams received an urgent communication at his residence in the army headquarters at Fort William. The major was the chief inspector of explosives of the Government of India. Edward Albert Gait, the acting chief secretary of the government of Bengal, had sent him instructions to proceed to Narayangarh where an attempt had been made to derail the lieutenant governor's train. Muspratt-Williams was of the opinion that taking into consideration the size of the crater formed, a high explosive, such as picric acid, had been planted. His finding was quite stunning. Emphasising the degree of professionalism displayed, he stated that a considerable amount of knowledge and ingenuity was displayed by the perpetrators of the deed, who expected the rail to be cut by the explosion. He was convinced that the train would have derailed if the rail had been cut or had bulged outwards instead of hogging upward, and in any case it would have probably been derailed if it had not been for the exceptionally heavy weight of the engine and the pace at which it was travelling. He praised the presence of mind of the driver who did not make an emergency stop, as this would have caused a smash up.

When it became quite certain that a deliberate attempt had been made on the life of the governor, the railway police was given orders to investigate and catch the culprits. But they drew a blank. Following this failure, the case slipped out of the hands of the railway police. This was when the newly-appointed deputy superintendent of the CID, Ramsadoy Mukherjee, stepped in. He was then given a virtual free hand by the deputy inspector general of crime and railways, Cecil Ward Chichele Plowden. Characteristically, Ramsadoy plunged headlong into the enquiry but failed to find a clue. He now had a big problem. His nearly twenty-year-old career was at stake and with it would vanish his lucrative monthly pay of five hundred rupees, of a first grade police officer.

Ramsadoy's worldly cunning came to his immediate rescue. Why not implicate false people, should the actual perpetrators elude? With this crooked and quixotic reasoning, he approached the family who owned most of the land in the neighbourhood of Narayangarh. Through them, he also requisitioned the services of their shrewd manager who knew the local villagers well and together the two produced a remarkable breakthrough. Within less than a week, the much-relieved chief secretary of Bengal could inform the Indian Government that a railway employee had confessed to having taken part in the preparation of the mine and had implicated seven other persons working on the railway, all of whom have been arrested. And even though these stories appeared far-fetched, the officials desperately clung on to them. The coolies were found guilty by a magistrate, then by a sessions judge and later by two high court judges, all of whom gave them sentences. But months later, when these men were independently questioned in jail, they all confessed that what they had said was under police tutoring and pressure.

Ramsadoy's novel style of investigation was self-incriminating, to say the least. It was later found that he had got the statements of these employees recorded before a deputy magistrate who happened to be his son. Besides, when a general enquiry was ordered into the matter by the inspector general (IG) of police, he found that the diaries and the police enquiry files against the accused were missing. The IG further considered these statements of the coolies to be evident concoctions, but served to give plausible explanations of how the police came to be hoodwinked in the case. For these serious lapses, the IG held that the suspicion rested primarily upon Ramsadoy Mukherjee, who had the chief responsibility for the investigation and was afterwards in charge of the office controlling the records.

But while the CID was handling the case to gather information, it was Hayter Duff's assistant Maulvi Mazharul Huq, who got the breakthrough. The information about a 'garden' on the outskirts of the capital was a definite clue, and Huq enlisted the service of Abdur Rahman to conduct a surreptitious enquiry. Within a short while, Rahman was able to obtain information about the functioning of the secret society, including the pivotal role of Aurobindo, which he promptly passed on to Huq. Duff, in turn, reported the facts to his superiors in the city, but the information was considered far too scanty and uncertain to conduct raids to apprehend the miscreants. The authorities rightly feared losing the criminals altogether by showing undue haste in capturing them. Chief Secretary Gait advised caution and urged Commissioner Halliday to lie low for the time being, giving no chance to the conspirators to regroup elsewhere in some secret place.

The members of the society decided to play it safe for the time being, following the partial success of the Narayangarh attempt. Upen, Ullaskar, Prafulla and Bibhuti visited Deogarh, Gaya and Patna, where they became acquainted with a group of sanyasis who were bound for Dhuni Sahib in the sovereign state of Nepal.

Concurrently, a contingent led by Aurobindo reached Midnapore, where the annual district conference of the Bengal Congress Party was to be held for the next three days. The bomb under the Governor's Special had blasted the previous day at a place just twelve miles from the site of the conference, which was attended by both moderates and extremists in large numbers. With Bipin Pal in jail, the leadership of the extremist party had fallen on Aurobindo's shoulders. Carrying lathis and displaying showy turbans and badges, the National Volunteers as the wing of the extremists were so named, headed by Satyen Bose of the Midnapore secret society, was ominously making its presence felt.

The nationalists had to face two adversaries simultaneously: while the government's repression continued unabated, they had also to thwart the reactionary designs of the moderates from within the organisation. Predictably, the moderates clung to their conservative stand, proudly displaying their loyalty. But Aurobindo decided to oppose the moderate creed by replacing it by nationalism. Meanwhile, the reception committee of the district conference had already adopted resolutions on Boycott and national education but had fallen short of declaring absolute Swaraj as their goal.

Thus, the meeting degenerated into a tussle for power. When the president refused to speak out in favour of Swaraj, the National Volunteers created uproar. Quite understandably, Aurobindo did nothing when the moderates appealed to him to restore order. Hence, the following day, the nationalists held a separate meeting instead of attending the conference, marking the beginning of the inevitable split.

Simultaneously, the focal point of extremist politics had shifted to the national scene in Surat, Gujarat, where the next session of the annual National Congress was to be held. As Tilak prevailed on the minds of the Bengalis to make a strong showing at Surat, Aurobindo, became immersed in activities concerning the preparation for the Surat Congress on returning to Calcutta.

Indraneel lay lazily in his grandfather's comfortable reclining chair when the servant informed him that three men from Harit, a neighbouring village, had come to see him. Bhupati, Kailash and Khitin were there to pay their arrears. The three muscular adolescents in their late teens cultivated paddy on Gourmohan's land. After counting the money and writing the receipts, Indraneel sat chatting with them. While the three lads squatted on the courtyard, Indraneel sat a few steps higher. As the courtyard was bathed by the slanting rays of the half moon, Indraneel could clearly see their youthful countenances as they sat facing him.

'What are all these rumours about blowing up the *Lat* Sahib's (lieutenant governor's) train?' Khitin enquired. 'And, yet the *Lat* has survived!'

'But why should anyone want to murder the *Lat* Sahib?' Bhupati asked.

'For taking revenge for looting and plundering the country,' Indraneel explained. 'Now, say you grow paddy on your land and I force you to sell it to me at a throwaway price but sell it outside India for a big amount, wouldn't that amount to robbery?

Mind you, nobody would object if the sahibs gave back something out of their big profits to the farmers or kept sufficient food for distribution within the country. But while famine rages across the land, the rulers go on making big profits!'

'Maybe we are illiterate and backward,' Bhupati asserted agitatedly, 'but why are the educated people of the cities not opposing such *zulum*?'

'There's a terrible lethargy in us that endures every evil and insult. We meekly offer ourselves for further exploitation by the foreigners. I mean why should we allow the *Firinghee* to fatten with our wealth?'

The three boys exchanged looks. They had no knowledge that such things were happening in their country.

'Neelda,' one of the boys said familiarly, 'can't something be done to change the course of things?'

'Of course,' Indraneel replied triumphantly. 'We must love our country from the bottom of our heart and call her our Mother. We must also develop small armies in every village to put up physical resistance whenever it is needed.' Indraneel then closely inspected the faces of the youngsters before proceeding. 'Now, I ask the three of you,' he added impulsively, 'will you join me in this fight? If you are willing, then give me your hand.'

Indraneel symbolically held out his hand like a man moved by his own rhetoric. After a slight hesitation, the silent Kailash got up and extended his hand. And within moments the other two followed. 'Then swear that you will never talk about this discussion to anyone whom you don't trust.'

'We swear,' the three repeated in unison.

The following Saturday, when the boys came again, they brought along Haran and Dolu, two additional members from their village. Indraneel noted with satisfaction that they all belonged to the same age group and, being from the labour class, were naturally muscular and fit. He would now have to provide them with some basic discipline, besides awakening in them the faculty of reasoning.

45

India Awakens

After meeting some extremist leaders such as Chittaranjan Das and Shyamsundar Chakravarty, Aurobindo decided to attend the annual Congress with a large number of delegates from Bengal. Aurobindo held a couple of public meetings, attempting to mobilise whatever force he could. A gathering was held at College Square with Aurobindo in the chair. As the four thousand men that had gathered would not disperse without hearing their chairman speak, Aurobindo had no choice but to make his maiden speech. Another meeting was held at Beadon Square where six thousand people assembled. Aurobindo was once again pressed by the huge crowd to say a few words.

'I have made it a rule not to speak in public,' Aurobindo said reluctantly. 'And I have good reasons for it. I went to England when too young to learn my mother tongue and I cannot speak in it. And rather than address you, my countrymen, in a language which is not mine and which is not yours, I keep silent.' He then briefly went on to explain the stance taken by the nationalists.

Aurobindo and eleven others finally left for Surat a few days before Christmas 1907, leaving the management of the *Bande*

Mataram affairs to Hemendra Prasad Ghose. At Aurobindo's suggestion, Harimohan joined his travel party at the last minute. On the other hand, Barin quickly summoned Indraneel to attend the Surat Congress when his cousin Sukumar Mitra suddenly bought him a ticket on the Bombay Mail. Indraneel boarded the train at the nick of time. At Kharagpur, Barin received a welcome summon from Aurobindo. Taking Indraneel along, he rushed to the third class coach that was carrying Aurobindo, Shyamsundar, Abinash and some others. Harimohan was pleasantly surprised to find Indraneel on board, as he was ignorant of his son's plan to travel to Surat.

The following day, a novel experience occured after the train entered Maharashtra. Wherever the train stopped, curious admirers gathered to get a glimpse of Aurobindo, their beloved leader. They came in thousands with garlands of flowers, food and tea. The loud shouts of *Vande Mataram* reverberated from all sides. Unfortunately, in many stations people had to go back disappointed, after peeping into every first and second class coach where they expected to find an important and foreign-returned leader. Aurobindo's coach became so packed with flowers and garlands that there was no space left for anyone to lie down or sleep! Interestingly, he kept no bedding and used his hands for a pillow while sleeping.

The train started in the midst of deafening cries of *Vande Mataram* and the whole thousand-mile route from Kharagpur to Surat was a triumphal journey of light, crowds, and continued cheering. The wayside stations were lined with keen spectators and cheer after cheer rose and fell as the train rushed into the darkness of the night. Aurobindo alighted at Amraoti and Nagpur. In both places a sea of heads covered the station and the adjoining grounds, and short halts were made in order to let an obliging Aurobindo deliver appropriate speeches.

Aurobindo, the new idol of the nation, was hardly known then by his face. In those days of style, luxury and easy leadership, no one could imagine that Aurobindo, nurtured and educated in England and a high official of His Highness the Maharaja of Baroda would be travelling in third class. The simplicity of Aurobindo was natural and unostentatious. Small in stature and slender in build, this quiet unobtrusive man was very often lost in the crowd of his admirers. When he rose to speak his voice was hardly audible except to those nearest him. It was a thin voice which, in measured cadence, gave vent to truths ringing with strength and beauty. Crowds of thousands materialised as if by magic and were kept spellbound by his personal magnetism.

The two persons who were the happiest by Aurobindo's meteoric rise to fame were Harimohan and Indraneel. They were happy to live this unforgettable experience with Aurobindo, the unmistakable man of the hour. Suddenly, the urge to liberate the country was burning in every heart. The youth felt moved to make sacrifices. And Aurobindo had successfully awakened the nation through the columns of *Bande Mataram* and had taught the power of *tyaga* by his own example. As an enlightened contemporary observed, Aurobindo shone for years as the brightest star on the Indian firmament. His genius shot up like a meteor, flooding the land from the Cape to Mount with the effulgence of his light.

Everyone alighted in Bombay where a meeting was arranged on the sea beach. They could hardly walk to the place through the living streams converging through the streets and lanes towards the chosen spot, automatically stopping all vehicular traffic for a time. It was a sight for the gods: the awakening of the whole nation from its age-long sleep and inertia into conscious life of flaming aspiration.

Later, while Aurobindo was mesmerising the vast crowd on the beaches of Bombay, Harimohan was secretly wrestling with his emotions and fighting back his tears. He could not help remembering the seventeen-year-old Aurobindo's maiden speech at the Pauline Literary Society's session in 1889. More than eighteen long years had passed during which his world and that of Aurobindo's had undergone a sea change, a transformation that had been as weird as it was unexpected. While Aurobindo, who had slowly been pushed by the hand of destiny to lead humanity, was briefly explaining to his public the main features of nationalism, Harimohan was sincerely wondering what his friend would become in the next ten years.

Surat was a magical experience and those images of the newly-awakened India were unforgettable. The moderates were put up in tents near the station adjoining the Congress camp; the extremists were sheltered in temples and houses at the centre of the town. Aurobindo was lodged in a temple where people lay crowding his camp-cot and reclined even under it! Tilak was living in another temple. While he and Aurobindo sat working and deliberating for hours, thousands of people climbed the steps of the temple and went past them to have their darshan till one o'clock in the morning! The doors were always kept open for a meeting with the extremist heads whereas an interview with the moderate leaders was almost impossible.

On the eve of Christmas, the first meeting of the nationalists' conference was held with Aurobindo in the chair. He briefly explained the gospel of nationalism and underlined the need to make sacrifices. Significantly, this meeting was held in camera. The same evening Aurobindo addressed another meeting with Tilak, Ajit Singh and others.

Tilak and Aurobindo both intended to capture the Congress. But a grave danger lurked, and the leaders were aware of it. They feared that if pressed hard, the Congress might break. Although every member in the extremist camp was ready to reconcile for the sake of the unity of the party, they were adamant to uphold the Calcutta resolutions on Swaraj and Boycott. Meanwhile, the moderates made their plans abundantly clear to alter the Calcutta resolutions as soon as the curtain rose. The extremists let the head of the reception committee complete his speech and also let the proposal be made for Rash Behari Ghose to occupy the chair. However, as soon as Surendranath Banerjea rose to second the motion, pandemonium broke loose with shouts from the extremist camp. The sitting had to be suspended after the futile attempts at pacifying the assembly failed.

Pleading for unity, Surendranath invited the Bengal extremists to his tent for deliberation on the same afternoon. He produced an instant written compromise agreement and asked all those present to sign it. But no one was willing to sign after his recent betrayal at the Midnapore provincial conference.

Some hope emerged that the session would go on as scheduled when the chairman began reading his address. Tilak stood up and refused to sit down till his amendment was heard. Within seconds, ten thousand men rose to their feet either in support or in opposition of the proposal. The situation deteriorated as catcalls were heard! A moderate delegate rushed to the podium with a chair held above his head in an attempt to hit Tilak. This instantly sparked off a scuffle with the Marathi delegates rushing to their leader's rescue. Just then an upturned shoe aimed at Tilak missed him and fell on the veteran Surendranath's shoulder, rolling over onto Phirozshah Mehta.

Ultimately, this was the insult that unleashed an unmitigated mob fury, marking the sad end of the Congress. A frantic stampede broke out. Choking with fear, the women delegates were screaming their heads off from the safety of their enclosures. The police took charge and cleared the premises.

In that mad melee, Aurobindo was the epitome of quietude. After the failed session, Barin tried to unite some of the like-minded people and organise a meeting of the revolutionaries. It was obvious that he was itching for action. Unable to get close to Aurobindo for one reason or the other, he wrote a cryptic letter about the need to have bombs distributed throughout the land.

'Dear Brother,' he began, 'Now is the time. Please make them meet for [our] own conference. We must have sweets all over India readymade for imergencies [*sic*]. I wait here for your answer.' Brimming with self-confidence and conceit, he then signed off as 'Barin Kumar Ghose'.

Meanwhile, after the Congress session had ended, both factions held their conventions separately. Under Aurobindo's leadership the nationalists' final refusal to join the new-fangled moderate convention was the second of the two decisive happenings at Surat. After the Congress fiasco, Aurobindo presided over the nationalist meetings twice. A leader who later became one of Aurobindo's associates portentously wrote, 'The wreath of wild olive, the crowning reward of the victor in the Olympian game, was already on his brow and he, who had gone to the fight as the leader of Bengal, came back as the all-India leader of nationalism.'

46

Attaining Nirvana

After the break-up of the Congress, Aurobindo left for his familiar hometown, Baroda, about one hundred and fifty miles north of Surat. Upon reaching Baroda, Aurobindo received the tumultuous welcome that had become customary by now. Crowds with flags and national cries followed him from the station. Meanwhile, the principal of the Baroda College had issued an order to the students to refrain from welcoming Aurobindo. But no sooner had Aurobindo's carriage reached the main entrance of the college, on its way to the town, than every student spontaneously rushed out to greet him with shouts of *Vande Mataram*, in flagrant violation of the order. They even unyoked the horses and pulled his carriage themselves. Later, Aurobindo met the Maharaja at Sayajirao's request.

At Baroda, Aurobindo delivered three lectures on the political situation facing the country. His speeches not only took the audience by storm but entirely changed the course of many lives. A young man named Ambalal Purani was present in one of the meetings. Although at the time the thirteen-year-old lad did not understand everything that Aurobindo said, he had the constant feeling that he was known to him. Ambalal's elder brother Chhotalal Purani called on Aurobindo and met him for a private interview. Aurobindo explained to Chhotalal a scheme for revolutionary work by drawing a pencil sketch on a blank piece of paper. He then instructed Barin to meet Chhotalal and explain all the details concerning their revolutionary organisation. Thus, through the direct inspiration of Aurobindo a revolutionary society was founded in Gujarat, which was to gain fame later. When Barin met Chhotalal for three consecutive days, he also instructed him on preparing bombs passing on the formula given to him by Ullaskar.

Realising that after an initial progress his *sadhana* was becoming more and more irregular due to the heavy and unavoidable compulsions of his political life, Aurobindo asked Barin to arrange a meeting with somebody who could put back his *sadhana* on the right footing. Barin had recently met some prominent spiritual men during his quest for a guru who could lead his proposed fraternity of young sanyasis of the Bhavani Mandir. And the man who had impressed him most was Vishnu Bhaskar Lele, a Marathi who stayed at Gwalior. Consequently, Barin sent a telegram from Surat to Lele to come directly to Baroda. As a result, when the two brothers arrived, Lele was waiting for them at Khaserao Jadhav's house in Baroda. Later, Lele vividly recounted to Ambalal Purani his intuition on receiving Barin's telegram that he would have to give initiation to a very great soul.

Aurobindo spent half-an-hour with Lele. The next day Lele came again and requested Aurobindo to sit with him continuously for seven days. At a time when Aurobindo had become the idol of the nation, nothing was more difficult to arrange than this! But the unexpected happened. The national leader evaporated into thin air, upsetting all programmes and arrangements. Soon a big hunt began for Aurobindo across Baroda, but he was not to be found. This was because Lele suddenly had transported Aurobindo away from the commotion to a lonely old place tucked away in the heart of the city. There, day in and day out, the two of them sat facing each other, wrapped in deep meditation.

Barin had deliberately left Indraneel in charge of managing the big crowd of political activists as they repeatedly mobbed Khaserao's bungalow. Indraneel had come to Baroda at Barin's request, while Harimohan had returned to Calcutta. Indraneel was under tremendous pressure and at one point was even subjected to physical assault and manhandling from the activists.

Three days passed in continuous and silent meditation. When Aurobindo was at last permitted to come out and attend a meeting in the gymnasium, it was clear that a great and abiding peace had descended on him, which from then on formed the basis of all his future *sadhana*.

'Sit down, look and you will see that your thoughts come into you from outside' Lele explained. 'Before they enter, fling them back.'

Aurobindo sat down and saw to his astonishment that it was so. He saw and felt concretely the thought approaching as if to enter through or above the head, and he was able to push it back before it came inside. In three days—really in one—his mind became full of an eternal silence and it remained so forever. The silence clung to his mind like windless air on a high mountain summit. From that moment, the mental being in him became a free intelligence, a universal mind, not limited to the narrow circle of personal thought as a labourer in a thought factory. The sense of ego also disappeared and the movements of the ordinary life as well as speech and action were carried on by some habitual activity of nature alone, which did not seem to belong to him.

Aurobindo lived at his friend Sardar Majumdar's house and sat meditating in one of the upper rooms. In barely a single day, he reached the rare state of the silent Brahman or nirvana as it is prevalently known to the Hindus. Yogis are said to struggle to attain this unique and supreme state of the silent mind through a lifetime, and only an enlightened few can ever reach it.

This condition remained undisturbed in Aurobindo for a long time. At the same time an experience intervened: something other than himself took up his dynamic activity and spoke and acted through him, without any personal thought or initiative. What this was remained unknown until Aurobindo came to realise the dynamic side of the Brahman, the Ishwara, and felt himself moved by that in all his action. What Lele asked him was whether he could surrender himself entirely to the inner guide within him and move as it moved him; if so, he needed no instructions from Lele or anybody else thereafter. Aurobindo accepted to be led by this inner guide and made it his rule of life.

But he faced a dilemma when he had to make a speech before the public. Lele told him that speech would come to him from some other source than the mind. So in fact, the speech came, and from then all speech, writing, thought and outward activity began coming to him from the same source above the brain mind.

At Tilak's request, Aurobindo went from Baroda to Poona. Two days later, he addressed a gathering at Tilak's premises. From Poona, Aurobindo went back to Bombay. Speaking at a meeting arranged by the Bombay National Union at the Mahajan Wadi, Aurobindo asked of his vast audience: 'What is nationalism?' and explained, 'Nationalism is not a mere political programme;

nationalism is a religion that has come from God.' It was thus that Aurobindo got the clue not only to the practicality of yoga but also its dynamism. Not only did he understand it, but he put it to the test throughout his tour from Bombay to Calcutta.

A meeting was fixed for Aurobindo in a hurry and handbills were distributed barely four hours before the meeting was to take place at Halai Lohana Mahajan Wadi in Bombay. Despite such short notice, as many as three thousand people turned up to hear him. However, the main speech that he delivered that day was under the auspices of the Bombay National Union at Mahajanwadi. In all, Aurobindo visited six cities, addressing eleven meetings. From Nagpur he finally returned to Calcutta.

When Aurobindo had gone to Poona, Barin returned directly to Calcutta. Before departing, he requested Indraneel to accompany Aurobindo wherever he was to travel. At that time, Aurobindo had no knowledge that his trip through West India would be so protracted. Hence, Indraneel agreed without a murmur. Also, Shyamsundar Chakravarty stuck on to Aurobindo and remained present at all his meetings. Their journey back to Calcutta from Nagpur remained uneventful and this was probably the first time that Aurobindo was enjoying being by himself on the train.

Indraneel had waited for an opportunity to be alone with Aurobindo and the occasion presented itself after Shyamsundar retired for his afternoon siesta. Indraneel wanted to know about the yogic experience that Aurobindo had undergone with Lele.

'My mind became completely silent,' Aurobindo replied with a sweet smile. 'At first I was in a fix. Being an active political worker, it was out of the question to decline any request to address the public. Divine dynamism was added to my *sadhana,* leading to passivity and inactivity. And then, the final result was a series of tremendously powerful experiences and radical changes of consciousness, which were quite contrary to my own ideas. For, they made me see with a stupendous intensity the world as a cinematic play of vacant forms in the impersonal universality of the Absolute Brahman.'

Aurobindo paused, while Indraneel remained in ecstatic silence and waited patiently for Aurobindo to continue.

'In Bombay the spiritual experience became more intense. The multifarious activities of the city of Bombay, all became unreal against the background of the silent Infinite, which alone seemed real. For instance, I had to go wherever He took me. This time I did not go for my own work; it was on His work that I went. The state of my mind has undergone a change. From now on I no longer am the master of my own will. Like a puppet I must go wherever God takes me. Like a puppet I must do whatever He makes me do. It will be difficult for you to grasp the meaning of these words. From now on all I do depends not on my will but is done at the *adesh* or command of God.'

Indraneel grew conscious that tears were flowing from his eyes. Something in that impersonal speech had touched a deep hidden chord in his heart. After reaching home, Indraneel confided about his experience in the train with Aurobindo to his parents. Saraju listened to the whole episode of his nirvanic experience with an understanding smile and said prophetically:

'Thakurpo will have to leave the land of his ancestors. He will have to settle elsewhere for the salvation of the world.'

PART FOUR

The Man and the Mission

He will be looked upon as the poet of patriotism, as the prophet of nationalism and the lover of humanity. Long after he is dead and gone his words will be echoed and re-echoed not only in India, but across distant seas and lands.

47

Farewell to a Friend

Returning to Calcutta in early 1908, Barin found the prospects looking brighter in the garden. Upen and Ullaskar had come back from Nepal and resumed the process of recruitment. Meanwhile, Hem Das had also returned from Europe after a year and this time, Barin advised him to start his independent establishment in the city. Hem lost no time and got down to serious work. Earlier, the publicity generated by the Narayangarh explosion had compelled the society to choose a new target. And the obvious one was Douglas Kingsford. The magistrate's notoriety had spread wide with the successive prosecutions of Bhupen Dutt, Bipin Pal, Sushil Sen and Brahma Bandhab Upadhyay.

As Kingsford was closely guarded, Hem advised that a bomb be delivered at his doorstep by penetrating through the cordon of security. Using his ingenuity and newly-acquired skills, Hem then prepared a book bomb for the assassination. He disguised the recently arrived Paresh Mallick as a peon and had it delivered at the magistrate's residence. The simple ploy was that Paresh would impersonate the bearer of a European friend who was returning the book to its original owner after consultation. Unfortunately, after taking a cursory look at the package and not even bothering to open it, Kingsford had it put on the shelf! Thus, with the backing of providence, Kingsford survived the first lethal attack.

Around this time, wishing to play it safe, Barin and Ullaskar decided to shift their bomb-making unit to Deogarh. This decision was taken in view of the fact that the bombs needed to be tested once they were manufactured. Obviously, testing them within the heart of the city was out of the question.

One day, Indraneel received an unexpected invitation from his friend Barin, who wanted him to visit Deogarh to take part in the trial of Ullaskar's bomb. Realising that this unforeseen invitation to the 'Abode of the Gods' could bring about more benefits than one, Indraneel accepted it with alacrity. But he made sure that Barin did not get wind of his selfish motive. The last time he had met Kusum was six months earlier when the two of them had offered puja at Thanthania Kali Bari. Two days later, Indraneel was on his way to Deogarh with Barin, Ullaskar, Nolini, Bibhuti and the pensive Prafulla Chakravarty. A couple of days later, the intrepid Bhababhushan Mitra also briefly joined the party.

Situated six miles away from Raidi, the township of Deogarh was not as accessible as Indraneel had thought. Displaying patience, he bided his time till the fifth day when Barin finally gave him a list of supplies and requested him to procure them from the town. Indraneel gladly accepted the assignment and, leaving early the next morning, promised to return before nightfall. He quickly bought the various provisions and handed them over to Mrinalini. Then gulping down the lunch offered by Sarojini Didi, he rushed off to Baba's temple expectantly. Fortunately, he did not have to wait long before the familiar figure of Kusum appeared.

'Neeluda!' she exclaimed, calling him for the first time by that familiar name. 'What a big surprise! When did you come?'

He was very pleased to see the expression of contentment on Kusum's face.

'I came several days ago,' he explained, 'but as I'm living in Raidi, it wasn't possible to see you earlier.'

With the return of winter it was exactly a year since they had met on the banks of the Darowa. As it was pleasant being under the rays of the late afternoon sun, they admired the sublime beauty of nature, sitting on the familiar flat boulder. When Indraneel gently pulled her towards him she leaned over and reposed her head on his shoulder. They sat silently for a long time before Indraneel realised she was weeping.

'I want this moment to become immortal,' she explained. 'I shall feel very lonely after you leave.'

Indraneel had an insurmountable urge to tell Kusum what he had in mind for a long time. But somehow he checked himself at the last moment. What if she spurned his offer? What if she felt hurt and terminated the friendship? Therefore, it would be best to wait until she expresses her own interest, he concluded. There is no need to hurry.

'You need a companion, Kusum,' he said aloud. 'You're still so young. How can you live alone all your life? Your parents won't be around to support you forever.'

'Won't you tell me what you are doing with your companions at Raidi?' she asked, changing the subject.

'Well, our bomb expert is on the verge of a major breakthrough and we're here to try out his first bomb! I reckon it to be just days away.'

'I've been thinking a lot ever since you spoke about the true aim of your society. I am also convinced that our rulers have to be vanquished by the use of force. Today, the majority of Indians prefer foreign rule simply because it spares them the trouble of standing up. And in such a pitiful scenario, the only way to wake up the nation is the bomb!'

Soon, Ullaskar showed the first fruit of his toil which he needed to test physically. A little before sunset, the six young men set out on their way to the less-than-thousand-feet-tall Dighiria Hills, a group of edgeless earthen mounds, where some bare boulders show their faces. The responsibility for carrying the bomb had fallen on Nolini. The group wound its way to the top of one of the hillocks through the thick, dry vegetation and emerged beside a big rock. The spot was ideal. The plan was that Prafulla would hurl the bomb and duck behind the boulder to avoid being hit by splinters and Ullaskar would supervise the act. While Nolini climbed up a tree to survey the entire proceeding from a height, Barin, Indraneel and Bibhuti took shelter behind stray rocks. Sensing that history was about to be made, everyone waited with bated breath.

Suddenly, a flash of blinding light appeared in a cloud of smoke followed by a thunderous burst of sound! The whole sky seemed to shatter to pieces and the unbearable noise of a hundred thunderclaps booming simultaneously seemed to reverberate from one hill to the other.

Shouting 'Successful, successful!' at the top of his voice, a rapturous Nolini climbed down the tree and ran towards the big rock. But what was this ghastly sight? Prafulla's body lay reclined against Ullaskar's and Ullaskar was hugging it helplessly. Slowly everyone helped to lay the body on the ground. Only then did it become visible that one of Prafulla's temples had caved in and a portion of his brain had been blown out! The sight was unbearable. Everyone sat down dumbly surrounding the body. Finally, Barin broke the painful silence and said, 'It is all finished now. There's no hope.'

Slowly, they realised what had happened. Prafulla had not even had a chance to duck. The bomb was so sensitive that the minimal friction of air had made it detonate. Nolini began to understand what a close brush he had had with death while unsuspectingly carrying the bomb in his hands. But then, what was to be done with Prafulla's body? Burying it in a rocky terrain without tools and implements was out of the question. To cremate it atop the hill would draw the villagers' attention—besides starting forest fires in the dry foliage all around.

'Let's leave the body here,' Barin suggested. 'After all, this is our battlefield. And our first soldier has just laid down his life. This is our first casualty.'

Ullaskar was badly wounded. His shirt was perforated in over a hundred places and he was bleeding profusely too.

'Ullas needs immediate medical attention,' Barin said grimly. 'The one who has left us needs no more of our care. Therefore, our primary duty lies in trying to save the wounded. He must be taken to Calcutta immediately.'

The secret society had a special doctor. As it would have been too risky to consult a local physician, an urgent trip to Calcutta became imperative. Then the descent from Dighiria began. The five men struggled to hold back their tears. The passage 'Not a drum was heard, not a funeral note ...' repeatedly crossed Nolini's mind until it became absolutely impossible to bear. Involuntarily, he blurted out: 'Six of us came, but only five are returning now!'

'No sentiments please!' Barin rebuked dryly.

The same night Barin left for Calcutta with Indraneel and Ullaskar but returned the day after with Upen. Upen wanted to see the spot where the fatal explosion had taken place. The good news was that Ullaskar's wounds were quite superficial. On their second visit they were amazed to find the body exactly as it was left two days earlier. And strangely, defying the laws of nature, no stench emanated from the body despite the lapse of time. Once again, the men returned home leaving the body just as before. Fearing police reprisal, the leaders transferred the few trunkloads of bomb material to an acquaintance who was a merchant, and decided to give up the experiment in Deogarh.

Before the final departure, the young men climbed to the top of the now familiar hilltop for a last farewell to their departed friend. But to their stupefaction, they found that the body had disappeared. There was no trace to suggest that an animal had carried it off nor could a shred of the dress be found anywhere. Thus, the chapter closed on a mysterious and enigmatic note. Naturally, the death of one of its members had cast a spell of gloom over the society. After consulting his brother, Barin sent word to Lele to come over to Calcutta to help them tide over their inner agony.

48

A New Energy

After returning to Calcutta, Aurobindo shifted to 23 Scott's Lane. Here Mrinalini and Sarojini once again joined him with Abinash and Sailen. Soon this house was to become a pilgrim centre for the new revolutionaries like Amarendranath Chatterjee a resident of Uttarpara, a town lying to the north of Calcutta. Amar's life reached its apogee when one day Upen took him to meet Aurobindo. The day Amar first met Aurobindo, he saw a very quiet man whose upper body was wrapped simply with a portion of the dhoti that he was wearing. Amar's head bowed in reverence at the sight of this illustrious personality leading such a simple life. Not only was he impressed by that first meeting but he gained strength from him as Aurobindo seemed to have initiated him by merely looking at him. Amar kept watching him in a trance-like state and forgot even the common courtesy of offering his regards with a simple namaskar. Slowly, Aurobindo's radiating expression of peace and restraint opened new vistas in Amar's heart, filling his heart and mind with a totally new feeling. He wondered what it was like coming face to face with God. He had not met such a wonderful man before. Earlier, when Amar had taken the oath dedicating his life for the country by touching Surendranath Banerjea's feet, he had felt nothing special except a tremendous urge to work. But now it was as if Aurobindo was asking him silently, 'Is it too difficult to dedicate your life to the Mother's liberation? Men pass through such extreme tortures for their families; how can any sacrifice be too difficult for the liberation of the motherland? No one can enjoy total freedom until the nation is free.' In this way, Aurobindo had turned the tide of the nation and revitalised the tottering country with a new life force.

At Scott's Lane, Amar had met Shrishchandra Ghose and Kanailal Datta of the French enclave of Chandernagore. Earlier, while studying at Calcutta's Duff College, he had also befriended two colourful personalities—Upendranath Banerjee of Chandernagore and Hrishikesh Kanjilal of Serampore.

The day Amar, Kanailal and Shrish paid their visits to 23 Scott's Lane, Indraneel met them briefly before they left. Just as Amar was leaving, he introduced himself and the two youngsters from Chandernagore to Indraneel and invited him to his ancestral house at Uttarpara for the forthcoming Saraswati Puja. As the next two days were declared public holidays for the occasion, Indraneel had no hesitation in accepting Amar's invitation. An intimacy grew between Amar and Indraneel. Indraneel was surprised to see Upen and Hrishikesh arrive and learned that the two men were old friends of Amar. Indraneel soon discovered Upen's keen sense of humour and Hrishikesh's healthy obsession with food. Although he had known Upen for a long time, he had never had the opportunity to see him in a relaxed mood.

Later, Amar took Indraneel to the nearby Joykrishna Library on the banks of the Ganges. They sat against the picturesque backdrop of the flowing river and discussed India's future.

'Barin seems convinced that India will be free in less than a decade,' Indraneel began, 'but Sejda is actually more pragmatic.'

'I'm very close to Suren Banujje,' Amar explained. 'Although Suren Babu and Aurobindo Babu do not see eye-to-eye on their goals, both respect each other for their sacrifices. Do you know what the old man told me the other day? "I hear that you've recently become Aurobindo's follower," he said, taking me aside. "Why don't you sound a note of caution and ask him to proceed slowly and carefully? At this rate, he's sure to spend the rest of his life in prison. How then will he work for the cause? After all, he's the one tipped to take over the leadership from me. He is going too fast!"

'Well, whether Suren Babu accepts it or not, I feel his days are numbered. Besides, the new generation wants action, not mere promises.'

'Neel, Sejda has given me the responsibility of collecting money for the society. Now, I have an idea. Why not start a shop to promote Swadeshi goods and also earn money for the society? This way, I can do two good things at the same time. The trouble is that Uttarpara is a small and unimportant town and such a venture will never be viable here. Can you please arrange for a place in an important commercial area of Calcutta to establish my shop?'

'I'll try through my father. He knows a lot of people. I'll let you know as soon as I find a place. Your idea appeals to me and I'm sure Sejda also will appreciate it.'

Following this discussion, Amar was shortly to establish the 'Sramajibi Samabay', a shop to promote Swadeshi goods, situated at the junction of College Street and Harrison Road. However, this eventually turned into a popular haven for the revolutionaries and became their central meeting point.

Amar felt energised by meeting Indraneel. The interaction had stirred his profound respect for Aurobindo. Amar could write well in Bengali. That night, after everyone fell asleep, Amar began writing sitting beside his oil lamp. Keeping up the tempo, he finished writing his essay within a week and thought of showing it to Indraneel during his next visit. Eventually, Amar incorporated this composition in his unpublished article, *Bharatey Jatiya Jagoran O Congress Prasanga* [The Congress and the Rise of Nationalism in India].

'Why don't you read aloud some selected portions?' Indraneel suggested happily when the two friends met again on the banks of the Ganges.

'All right,' Amar agreed.

He then began reading briefly from the introduction.

'The leaders who ruled over the Congress till 1904 had largely forsaken their oriental heritage of culture and education and espoused Western values, disregarding India's greatness and inner beauty. While the Parsi leaders were completely Europeanised, the elite circle of Bengali barristers also tried to exercise its control over the Congress as sahibs. But the mighty blow rendered by the Partition of Bengal jolted them back to their Indianness and put them in communion with India's soul.'

'Hmm, you really write well,' Indraneel said sincerely. 'Please go on.'

'With Aurobindo's arrival in Bengal, Bipin Chandra Pal, Brahma Bandhab Upadhyay and Manoranjan Guha Thakurata assumed the state leadership—basing their politics on Indian spirituality. Of them all, it was Aurobindo Ghose who caused the most forceful impact by introducing the powerful mantra, *Vande Mataram*, to the nation. All that had happened since the birth of Sri Ramakrishna until Aurobindo's time assumed a new significance in Bengal and, more broadly, on the centrestage of India, bringing a new enthusiasm to the youth of which the old guard was totally ignorant. At this juncture, the old Bengal receded and gave way to a new India.'

Amar looked up at Indraneel and felt rewarded by the expression of appreciation in his eyes. He read on with feeling.

'Aurobindo, the new sun, within whom *Sanatana Dharma* and nationalism were identified, ascended high in India's firmament. His rays oversaw the foundation of an enlightened India. Within a short period, he was able to cause the dissolution of the past and infuse a new life in national politics. It was at his behest that the policy of prayer and petition died a sudden death. Old Surendranath realised that his exit was imminent. Aurobindo, however, had not entered the field to preach dirty politics. He began his political work under the leadership of Surendranath. Aurobindo breathed a new force and raised high expectations in the path of surrender, sacrifice and dedication to the liberation of Mother India. India's dharma and karma blended into a mighty spiritual quest, which sanctified the whole land from the Gangotri to its delta near the ocean. Indeed, it was in 1905 that the foundation of India's independence was laid.

'It was he, Aurobindo, who transformed *Vande Mataram* into a mighty mantra of power and strength and popularised the song as a symbol of unity for the nation. It became the mantra for the propagation of his revolutionary cult.

'Aurobindo told Krishna Kumar Mitra about his proposal for Boycott. Krishna Kumar then explained Aurobindo's idea of Boycott to Surendranath. Under the leadership of Surendranath, the system mooted by Aurobindo was put into effect in Bengal and India's capital Calcutta, for preventing the partitioning of Bengal. On 7 August 1905, the first protest meeting was called at the Town Hall. During this session, Aurobindo's proposals for passive resistance, boycott of British goods and the implementation of the Swadeshi were adopted. As at the time Aurobindo had not become a public figure, it was Surendranath who lent his leadership to make the new awakening in Bengal effective.

'Aurobindo was then touring through the districts of Bengal and delivering lectures. The headmaster of the Kishoregunj School was so impressed by Aurobindo's views that he readily converted his institution into a national school, setting a new trend in the field of education. Having shown the way, Aurobindo once again returned to Baroda.'

As Amar put down the bundle of papers and looked up questioningly at his friend, he noticed Indraneel's eyes gleaming with unshed tears of ecstasy.

49

Chandernagore

About twenty miles to the north of Calcutta, stretching along the west coast of the Ganges, lies Chandernagore—peaceful, picturesque and serene. This little enclave was governed by an administrator under the direct control of the governor of Pondicherry and formed part of the five separate segments that constituted the French colonies. This notably was the only French settlement outside South India.

Earlier in 1907, some political incidents that had electrified the situation within the sleepy French enclave had also shaken the British. The first call for Swadeshi was heard when Sarala Devi tried to instil in the minds of the Bengali youth a sense of self-reliance. A marked growth of an anti-European attitude was felt in particular among the students of Dupleix College but what worried the British most was that this new tirade aimed at them came from the core of the diplomatically immune French territory of Chandernagore.

Alarmed by rumours of a sudden increase in the entry of arms into Chandernagore which would naturally end up into their own territory, the British authorities sent a special officer to check things out. The findings were indeed highly instructive. While only two guns and six revolvers were imported by natives in Chandernagore in 1906, thirty-four registered parcels, believed to contain revolvers, were received from St. Etienne, the Government Arms Factory in France, during the first half of 1907. And, as many as twenty-two of these parcels were addressed to an individual named Kishori Mohan Shampui.

Among the boys who later joined Barin's revolution was the coy young man named Kanailal Datta of Chandernagore. Although his gentleness was easily mistaken for a sign of weakness, he actually possessed great will power and determination. Together with his studies, Kanailal took up social work to serve his motherland and met Motilal Roy. In those days, small events were enough to make the youth's blood boil for vengeance and freedom from the white man. When a European hotel keeper made an indecent advance to an Indian housewife of a noble lineage, he was given a sound thrashing by the people of the area. Motilal, who was aware of Kanailal's patriotism, seized the opportunity to test his courage. After consulting a close friend named Nonilal Dey, he sent an unsigned letter to Kanailal asking for a daredevil meeting at midnight at the local crematorium. At a time like this the youth were ready to do everything in this cloak-and-dagger manner.

'I'd guessed right,' Kanailal said on meeting Motilal, 'it could be none other than you! So what do you expect of me?'

'There must be some way to deliver justice,' Motilal cried.

'So long as you allow them, that's how they'll treat you,' retorted Kanailal. 'If you want them to respect you, then confront them with courage and determination.'

Just then a strong draught blew away a portion of Kanailal's black wrapper and Motilal and Nonilal were left gaping at a long shiny dagger dangling from his waist. While Motilal's heart filled with pride at Kanailal's display of bravery, Nonilal spontaneously asked for Kanailal's date and time of birth.

'30 August 1888 at 5 a.m.,' he replied casually and left.

As the two men watched Kanailal stroll away unhurriedly, they noticed two shadows creep out of the dilapidated temple in the background and join him. Motilal realised that while he and his friends were happy doing social work and singing patriotic songs, Kanailal had started earnest work for the country.

The next morning Nonilal excitedly came to meet his friend Motilal at Boraichanditala.

'See, Moti,' Nonilal said breathlessly, 'I've cast Kanailal's horoscope. You see, Sun and Saturn together makes him fearless. Also lower Mars in the eighth would make him outshine others in dare devilry. Unfortunately, the presence of Saturn in the second house would make Kanai leave his home and family.'

But as Nonilal fell silent, Motilal knew that his friend was hiding something from him. 'For the moment I find nothing worrying,' Motilal observed evenly.

'What worries me is something else,' Nonilal said with a sigh. 'When Mars and Jupiter are closeted in the same house its implication is fatal! It is clear that Kanai will not live beyond his twentieth year—nor will his death be natural. This is also explained by the Sun, Venus and Saturn being huddled together. However, the position of the Sun in the third house indicates that his name will become immortal. And Kanai is due to complete his twentieth year within just six months!'

~

Barely three months after the Dighiria fiasco, Barin braced up for action again.

'Sejda, I want to kill the mayor of Chandernagore.'

'Why?' Aurobindo enquired a little surprised.

'Because he broke a national meeting there and persecuted the local population.'

'So he ought to be killed? How many people will you kill this way? I can't give my consent to this. Nothing will come of it.'

'No Sejda, if this isn't done, these oppressors will never learn their lesson.'

'Very well,' Aurobindo said indifferently, realising that Barin was seeking his approval and not his advice. Aurobindo had learnt not to try to check him, for he was likely to go off at a tangent and become worse. 'If that's what you think, do it.'

Barin triumphantly told the jubilant boys waiting outside, 'Sejda agrees.'

Almost a year since the first Swadeshi cries were heard, a local aspirant for the mayor's post was trying hard to undermine the influence of the incumbent Léon Tardivel. He was engaged in arranging a Swadeshi meeting to be addressed among others by Bipin Chandra Pal. But as was expected, the mayor vehemently refused to allow the meeting to take place. Discontentment ran high following this oppression, resulting in indignation and anger. The mayor, who had so far not opposed the wishes of the citizens who had elected him, suddenly became the target of their ire.

The plan to assassinate Tardivel was born during consultations in the *Jugantar* office. But when Charu Roy refused to appoint local boys for the job on the plea that their involvement would compromise their safety, Upen managed to extract the promise that Roy would provide at least one volunteer.

It had already been decided beforehand that Barin and Gossain would accompany him to the spot and Indu would hurl the bomb. They would first meet Charu Roy's man at the Strand and from there go to Tardivel's residence on Rue Carnot. However, the first night's failure was caused by the twin absence of Roy's man at Joraghat and of the French mayor's from his home. After waiting for a long time, the group reassembled again the following day at the same place.

To the boys' delight, the mayor and his wife were spotted at the dinner table in a room on the ground floor, on the night of the second attempt. Indu solemnly received the bomb from Barin's hand with some last moment instructions. Next, in typical cloak-and-dagger style, Gossain, local man Nagendra Ghose and Indu walked through the dark, narrow lane carrying the loaded revolvers that were brought from the garden. Barin and the others followed at a great distance. Indu went ahead about fifty yards or so, ran up, and threw the bomb through the window gratings. There was a sound like that of a fire-cracker and the next moment the three of them fled.

After completing his official work at the City Civil Court, Indraneel remembered to meet Advocate Madhusudan Dasgupta at the Bar Council Library. The advocate warmly received him and introduced him to his colleagues as the son of the eminent barrister Harimohan Datta. Then after the usual exchange of civilities, the advocate casually informed him about Kusum's return to the city and invited him to his house for a chat.

'No, wait,' the advocate said suddenly. 'What are your plans for the weekend?'

'Nothing special,' Indraneel replied casually, 'I'm quite free.'

'Then would you like to join my family on a visit to the French town of Chandernagore? We're leaving by boat on Saturday morning and plan to spend the extended weekend of the Bengali New Year at a friend's garden house overlooking the river. The spot is ideally set for holidaying. So how about it, will you come with us?'

Indraneel happily agreed, realising that it would be foolish to miss such a wonderful opportunity of being with Kusum. Besides, there was an issue pending that had to be settled with her. He was keen to apologise for his sudden departure from Deogarh without informing her following the disastrous bomb experiment at Dighiria.

Three days later, impelled by a southerly breeze, a large sail boat was cruising nicely along the Ganges. As Sushama kept everyone animated under the boat's half cylindrical roof, Kusum and Indraneel sat outside under the cool shade of the fluttering sail, enjoying the full extent of the open sky.

'You mean one of your friends had to lay down his life for testing the bomb?' Kusum asked incredulously. 'And what happened to the man who was injured?'

'He survived,' Indraneel explained. 'Finding him bleeding profusely, we had no option but to rush him to Calcutta to consult our society's trusted physician. Luckily, the injured man's wounds turned out to be quite superficial.'

A little later, low tide began to exert its drag, slowing the boat considerably. This meant that they would not be able to reach their destination as scheduled before dusk. Ultimately, the lights of Chandernagore became visible only towards 8.30. The boat slowly approached Telinipara Ghat in that semi-darkness and began the difficult manoeuvre of finding a berth. Suddenly, Indraneel sighted the silhouettes of three young men frantically gesticulating to some others who were approaching from the side of the town.

The familiarity of one of the silhouettes shocked Indraneel. Soon its voice established beyond doubt that it was Barin. So Indraneel spontaneously jumped into the knee-deep water and waded up to the shore.

'Barin!' he exclaimed from behind. 'So what are you doing here?' he asked.

But Barin turned in a flash, dangerously brandishing a revolver at him.

'Now, now, calm down, it's me, Indraneel!'

'Oh, it's you, Brother?' Barin asked tiredly. 'You scared me!' By then, the three other men had also joined them. They were out of breath after sprinting. Soon Indraneel was able to discern the familiar faces of Gossain and Indu. Undoubtedly, there was something sinister about the presence of all those young men wielding guns in that unfamiliar surrounding, making Indraneel wonder what was going on.

'Relax friends,' Barin told the Chandernagore boys, 'Neel is one of us.'

He then led his friend aside and explained that they were out on a mission.

'The French mayor opposed a Swadeshi meeting on the ground that it was seditious. So we decided to teach him a lesson!' Barin chuckled conceitedly.

'Monsieur Tardivel has become the first victim of our irrepressible bomb! Now, I hope the message will get to the British authorities that their days are numbered! From now on, whoever dares to oppose the will of the people will have to pay a heavy price!' Then sobering down visibly, he changed the topic to personal matters. 'But what are you doing here and who are these people with you?'

Just then, one of the local boys signalled the arrival of the ferry from the other side of the river. And the three youths from Calcutta swiftly climbed onto it on their way to Shyamnagar. Indraneel breathed a sigh of relief. He realised that after catching a train for Sealdah, Barin and his boys would be safely back at the garden later in the evening.

But Tardivel's luck was as good as Kingsford's and Fraser's. For only the bomb's detonator had blown and not the picric acid charge. As a result, Madame Tardivel merely fainted and her husband received a few insignificant injuries.

At about 9.30 p.m. on the night of the attack, an adjutant of the Chandernagore police received a call from the mayor's house and answered it in person. He was given a half-exploded bomb to be handed over to Major J A Black, the British army expert on explosives, in Calcutta. The findings later revealed that the bomb was powerful enough to wreck a large room and kill everyone in it. The next day, Commissioner Halliday sent two officers to the French mayor's house to investigate and the case was handed over to the CID, Bengal.

Later, the commissioner met Leonard Frederick Morshead, the officiating inspector general of police, Bengal and Cecil Plowden, the deputy inspector general of police. Once again, while the commissioner advocated immediate action and arrests, the other two officers preferred to watch the situation. Ten days later, the commissioner and the IG paid a courtesy call to the governor of French India, the administrator of Chandernagore and its mayor, and promised to do everything to help catch the culprits.

The incriminating role played by Kishori Mohan Shampui in smuggling firearms in through the French territory was soon established and the British police took up rigorous investigation to find out how French revolvers found their way into British India. What worried the British most was the fact that four revolvers were sold to Barin and Abinash through a mutual friend of the boys.

~

'Were they your fellow revolutionaries?' Kusum asked Indraneel while walking along the Ganges after breakfast.

'Yes,' Indraneel replied sincerely. 'When we attempted to blow up the Governor's Special, even its partial success created a forceful impact on the minds of the rulers. Unfortunately, the book-bomb sent to hangman Kingsford didn't explode or else it would have been a big publicity for our society. But this mindless attack on the French mayor is nothing short of juvenile whim! And see the result: the mayor wasn't even hurt.'

'Why not select the victims more sensibly?

'Kusum, give me your word that you won't speak about this to anybody, and I'll tell you something that will please you. Recently, Barin sent two boys to Muzaffarpur on a reconnaissance mission to kill Kingsford. You may not know this, but after promoting Kingsford to the post of judge, the government has transferred him to that remote place explicitly to protect him against terrorist attacks. Meanwhile, having made independent observations of the judge's movements in the new environment, the two boys have come back to discuss their final plan with Barin. My feeling is that this time they'll get him. So in a matter of a week or so, you'll hear the good news of Kingsford's elimination.'

'The good news will surely reach me before you because Pishima and I are returning to Deogarh next week.'

By then they had moved away from the inhabited parts of the sprawling estate. As a gentle breeze blew from the south, the bright cerulean light of the sky gently danced across the opaque ripples of the Ganges.

'I don't know why I feel so free whenever I am with you,' Kusum said happily, changing the subject. 'Yet being hurt by your indifference four months ago, I had vowed never to speak to you again!'

'Please don't say that,' Indraneel protested mildly. 'Haven't I explained the painful circumstances that took me back to the city urgently? It was an awful torture for me to bear because I had no way of communicating with you.'

'You know, when I met you for the first time, I had the clear feeling of having seen you somewhere before. But the fact is, I always dreamt of a shy young man with sensitive eyes who would rescue me from my depressing loneliness. That person would be a beacon in my friendless world, a bridge between my gloomy past and the indistinct future.'

50

A Prophecy

Quite typically, Horace had not disclosed his fatal illness to his son. In letter after letter, he had showered his love and good wishes for Harimohan's prosperity but he had hardly ever talked about himself. Harimohan was also very regular in his replies and whenever old friends left for England, he sent his father something typically Indian, such as Darjeeling tea, which he knew his father liked. He had also kept Horace informed about Aurobindo's rise in Bengal politics and regularly sent cuttings of moving editorials from *Bande Mataram*.

Upon returning from Surat, Harimohan was happy to find among his pile of correspondence an envelope addressed to him by Horace. There was also another envelope bearing the postmark of London, which bore an unknown handwriting. Out of curiosity, he opened the latter first. It was a letter from Herbert John Reynolds. Harimohan wondered what had suddenly spurred Herbert Uncle to write to him and quickly began reading the letter. His father was critically ill, Reynolds' letter announced, and he was suffering from cancer. Reynolds took it upon himself to inform Harimohan and solicited Hurry to pay an early visit to England if he wanted to see his father alive. Quickly Harimohan opened Horace's letter and read it. Characteristically, there was no mention of his illness. However, towards the end of his letter, Horace did refer briefly to something that betrayed some signs of emotion. 'How long has it been since we last met?' he wondered.

Harimohan could not leave for England as early as he would have liked to. Many important cases were pending before the high court and his friend had entrusted him with a special assignment. Every morning, he had to read all the major English dailies and choose the most interesting articles, news items or investigative reports, for reproduction in the columns of *Bande Mataram*.

He communicated the sad news of Horace's illness to Aurobindo and informed him about his decision to leave for England.

'You see, Auro,' Harimohan elaborated, 'I haven't met him since I visited England during your ICS exam. I realise how lonely he must be since my mother passed away. I should have done more for him than merely writing letters. I should have stayed with him and been more active in my duties towards him.'

Aurobindo remained silent for sometime, steadily looking at a point above the horizon. He spoke after a long silence.

'Go prepared to stay there for a long time,' Aurobindo said firmly, 'for, you will have to visit many places before you return.'

'I don't know what you mean. How can I abstain from work for too long?'

'I am sorry to learn about Mr Cockerell's illness,' Aurobindo said evenly, as if he had not heard Harimohan's last words. 'It is indeed imperative that you should sail at once.' Then with a half smile he added prophetically, 'I suppose it is God's wish that you should be away when I shall need you the most.'

Lele came to Bengal through Barin's invitation around the middle of February 1908. He spent some time with the young men at the garden and in Deogarh. He also lived with Aurobindo at Scott's Lane. Upon his arrival, Barin felt happy to have at last found a spiritual guru to lead the members of the society in their mission. But when Lele learnt the true goal of the society, he vehemently declined to play the role of its spiritual mentor. He even warned Barin and the boys about facing a severe backlash if they did not forsake the path of violence. A work like this demands clean hearts, he explained, otherwise it will end in useless bloodshed. Convinced that India could never gain independence without the use of force, Barin resolved to ignore Lele's advice. Lele then enquired of Aurobindo about his *sadhana*. Aurobindo said that he had stopped regular meditation, finding himself constantly in a state of deep concentration. Unable to understand this, Lele concluded that the devil had taken hold of him. But Aurobindo was unconcerned. From that moment he became convinced that he would not need a guru any more.

Around this time, Aurobindo had a distinct premonition of the impending danger that was stalking him and the other boys of the garden. He advised Sudhir Sarkar to write to Sil's Lodge in Raidi, asking Upen and some others to return to Calcutta. Disguising his words, Sudhir wrote that the condition at the garden was bad and that monkeys were entering it. By monkeys he evidently meant police spies. Indeed, precaution was the biggest need of the hour. And it was Barin who began feeling it more than anybody else.

What was worrying everyone was that the boys seemed to be followed wherever they went. And they were right in their suspicion. Also, the innocent visits of the unsuspecting, local police sub-inspector were making the society members jittery. In fact, the naïve man was so fascinated by the outward show of Upen's spiritual discourses that he attended the sittings regularly.

Sub-Inspector Suresh Ghose of the Calcutta Police was on the wrong side of his twenties. He was a clever and ambitious young man seeking quick promotions. One day, his colleague Satish Banerjee informed him about the formation of a special team to monitor the movements of some dreaded terrorists in the capital. Following his enrolment, Suresh soon received summons from the senior inspector of police, Soshy Bhushan De.

Earlier, De was given full authority to form a dependable fact-finding group for further investigations when he had reported about the existence of a secret society to his superiors. In consequence, De created a three-tier team under the command of Inspector Purna Chandra Biswas, who was given charge of co-ordinating a group of five sub-inspectors and three head constables. But also quite independently, two ex-criminals were employed to gather information. And the biggest breakthrough came when one of De's men discovered that the secret society's headquarters were located at a garden in Muraripukur. Meanwhile De met his new team and briefed them about Barindra Kumar Ghose, allegedly the ring leader of the gang of terrorists. He also gave them a vivid physical description of the main suspect.

As soon as Suresh heard this piece of information a shiver ran down his spine. He vividly remembered Barin, his former classmate at the Deogarh High School. Even the physical description fitted him down to the last detail except the round spectacles and an imposing moustache, which obviously were new additions. In a flash, his memory raced back to the scene on top of the Nandan Hills where Barin had so spiritedly spoken about his elder brother, Aurobindo. He wondered whether it would be discreet not to inform De about this past connection. However, prudence pressed him to wait till the meeting was over. As the inspector ordered their dismissal at the termination of the meeting, Suresh stepped forward and stood at attention.

'Sir, I have something confidential to report to you. I was in school with your main suspect and was also his classmate. Barin Ghose is the younger brother of Aurobindo Ghose of the *Bande Mataram* case. I thought that the information about my past association with Barin ought to be communicated to you as it may hamper the investigation.'

'On the contrary!' the inspector exclaimed. 'This is indeed a favourable advantage for our investigation. If you can successfully shadow this criminal and help in the investigation surrounding his team of terrorists, you will make me proud.'

'Thank you, Sir, for the trust you repose in me.'

Slowly, more and more information about the society trickled in. Sub-Inspector Satish Banerjee reported having seen Barin coming out of Hem Das' house, mentioning Hem by name. Satish later followed Barin to Muraripukur Garden. This vital link that Barin's secret society bore with Hem was passed on to DIG Cecil Plowden.

Interestingly, Barin failed to spot Suresh even though he passed within inches of his old classmate on the very first day of his surveillance at 4 Harrison Road. Like all De's men, Suresh was neatly disguised as an unassuming low class man. However, Suresh was fated to meet Barin again later that day on a far more incriminating errand. Following the establishment of the vital link between Hem and the secret society, the entire team geared up for one of the biggest raids in the history of Indian surveillance. The same day, a head constable watching the garden, noticed three familiar men coming out of it. He followed them to Hem's house. Later, when Barin, Indu and Gossain, left Hem's house in a tram, the sleuths followed them to the Howrah Station. As the three suspects started by the Loop Passenger, the detectives journeyed in the same train up to Mankundu Station where Barin separated from the group and went towards Chandernagore. While Suresh managed to keep pace with Barin up to a certain point, Banerjee also managed to keep Indu and Gossain in sight for a while but, ultimately, lost sight of them in the darkness.

Luckily, the unsuspecting Barin had inadvertently foiled his ex-classmate's chances of following him on the previous evening for he was busy contacting Professor Charu Chandra Roy's men on an incriminating errand to assassinate Mayor Tardivel of the French territory. However, the bid to kill the mayor had to be put off by a day.

Two days later, however, Inspector Biswas wrote about the Chandernagore misadventure to Plowden but inexplicably failed to link the Calcutta revolutionaries with the later attempt on the life of the mayor.

Meanwhile, when Barin and Abinash unconsciously led the sleuths from the Sealdah Station to nearby 23 Scott's Lane, Aurobindo's name became implicated for the first time with that of the society. Soon the bomb factory at 15 Gopi Mohan Dutt's Lane was unearthed. Five days later, another official tracked down Upen, Paresh and three others as being connected with the bomb factory and gathered the names of Bejoy, Nolini, Hrishikesh, Hem and five others in connection with the garden in his report. The ever-vigilant Suresh then took Inspector De to show him the house at 15 Gopi Mohan Dutt's Lane.

As the boys were jolted out of their innocence by the sudden attention they were receiving from the detectives, they realised that their playful involvement with the revolution had turned sour and threatened to spill into a deadly adventure of war. Although mentally prepared for the worst, no one seemed to be prepared to face such an eventuality so soon. Clearly, time was running out fast and something had to be done to dispose of the incriminating material they had accumulated. But first the dangerous material had to be shifted from Hem's uncle's house at Naba Krishna Street to Gopi Mohan Dutt's Lane in order not to implicate the other members of his maternal family.

Soon one of the constables noticed two bullock carts being brought in front of Hem's house. Some boxes were loaded into them and taken away to Gopi Mohan Dutt's Lane. By then it was clear that the house in Gopi Mohan Dutt's Lane was one of the society's biggest hideouts, requiring special round-the-clock surveillance. Accordingly, the department leased a house diametrically opposite.

Evidently, this was a lucky day for the detectives; sub-inspectors Banerjee and Suresh observed a third-class hackney enter the lane and pull up in front of the house. The sleuths then saw Ullaskar bring down a bag and two steel trunks and get into the coach as Asoke Nandi sat down on the dickey box. Suresh followed it for three miles from Baghbazar to College Street through Cornwallis Street, before pulling up in front of 134 Harrison Road, where he was on time to witness Nagendra and Dharani Gupta take in the basket and the two steel trunks. The next day, under the pretext of buying ayurvedic medicine, the cunning Suresh once again visited the shop and surreptitiously took note of the two trunks peeping out from under a wooden bench, where they had been shelved.

One of the ex-criminals was keeping his attention fixed on Hem Das' house. He stuck on to his hawk-like vigil by turning a nearby grocer's shop into a safe observation post. And, quite undaunted, he then went to a prostitute's den, on the opposite side of the road, to peep into Hem's house, passing himself off as a school boy who had run away and wanted to spend some time in her house.

Interestingly however, the head constable and an associate of the Maniktala police outpost, paid nearly a dozen routine visits between them to Muraripukur but never doubted that anything unlawful was going on there. They were told by the wily Upen that they were a bunch of sadhus practising yoga and meditation. And the ploy worked convincingly. But the biggest sensation was the continued regular visits to the garden by none other than the sub-inspector of the Maniktala Police Station. He seemed genuinely attracted by Upen's discourses. He did not merely take part in the evening rituals but also spoke to the people there. Yet Upen's eyewash was so perfect that he, like his two undoubting subordinates, felt no suspicion about anything there.

51

The Avatar

Having sailed in mid-February, Harimohan reached the British Isles during the third week of March. Unfortunately, by then his father's case had slipped out of the scope of surgery. The seventy-five-year-old Horace put up a brave front and remained cheerful. Although his eyes had the same old sparkle, he had changed beyond recognition, principally due to his white mane and beard, which made him look like a monk.

'Well my son, we meet for the last time before I depart,' he spiritedly began.

'Father,' Harimohan said, as tears welled up in his eyes, 'you know that you and Mother will forever remain alive in my heart. However, the only regret I have is that we have been separated so long.'

After the reassuring resumption of their old relationship, Harimohan felt no difficulty conversing with his father, informing him of all the latest happenings in India and particularly of the development that had taken place in his village.

'The Block Development Officer's report is formal,' he proudly informed Horace, 'the Polba Block is the most progressive sector in the entire district of Hooghly.'

During the second week of April, Horace's condition worsened suddenly. One early morning he called Harimohan and enquired about Aurobindo. Strangely, in the turmoil of his father's condition, he had forgotten to talk to him about his friend. Then slowly, Harimohan recounted all that he had heard from Indraneel about Aurobindo's unique nirvanic experience with Lele. After finishing his narration, he suddenly remembered his own experience in the little South Indian village of Kodiyalam, about the predicted arrival of the Uttara Yogi. He recounted it with a lot of feeling. When he suddenly looked up, Harimohan saw that Horace was crying silently. For a long time both men remained silent.

'I am happy that God allowed me to live up to now for two reasons,' he began at last. 'First, for letting me witness the end of the Kaliyuga and beginning of the Satyayuga, the cycle of truth, and second, for letting me personally know the avatar who has taken charge of our destinies in this momentous new epoch.' Then astounding Harimohan he asked, 'But my son, how did you miss the point? Didn't you realise that Aurobindo was the Uttara Yogi?'

Horace left his body at the end of April. The eagerness of the mourners for a last glimpse transformed Beaufort Gardens into a peaceful centre of pilgrimage as thousands of people from all over England converged there.

With the death of his foster father, Harimohan realised that an important era had ended in his life. At this time, Martha, the elder daughter of the Mangles, arrived. She was a widow and had mellowed considerably. This sudden meeting after nearly eighteen years naturally rekindled the past euphoria. Martha suggested that they make a trip together to America where her sister Cynthia had settled with her husband and children. Horace had bequeathed

Harimohan seven thousand pounds. Now with the inheritance in hand, Martha's offer of the overseas trip was too tempting to let go. Somehow he instinctively felt this would be his last trip abroad. Therefore, in the beginning of May, Harimohan sailed off for America.

52

The Bombing and Its Aftermath

Aurobindo was in a deep financial crisis during this period. In spite of engaging him for a pittance, the authorities of National College were at times paying him half his salary; neither had the affairs of *Bande Mataram* sufficiently improved to allow Aurobindo to overdraw from its account. Fifty rupees a month was all he could benefit from it. Moreover, so much bickering was going on among its office bearers that the future of the daily seemed bleak.

After returning from his long tour of west India, Aurobindo made a last effort to recover the financial position of *Bande Mataram*. He contemplated changing the paper's management into a joint stock company and went to various wealthy men and tried hard to sell its shares. But the scheme did not work out as well as expected.

Meanwhile, Manoranjan Guha Thakurata's *Nabashakti* was also facing an acute crisis and had stopped appearing following its conviction for sedition. Guha Thakurata was unable to pay salaries to many of his employees, including Debabrata Bose and Ramchandra Majumdar. Not only was the printer awarded a sentence of six months, but a staggering fine of one thousand rupees was imposed on him. He also had had to settle arrears of rent for the premises at 48 Grey Street, where the *Nabashakti* press was located.

Coincidentally, wishing to make a new start in these times of distress, Aurobindo was also planning to acquire the defunct *Nabashakti* and edit it himself. He sent Abinash Bhattacharya to Giridih to negotiate the takeover of the paper directly with its owner. Guha Thakurata was so pleased to learn about Aurobindo's initiative to restart his paper that he readily handed over the last of his capital to Abinash. Thereafter, Aurobindo shifted to his new lodging at 48, Grey Street along with Mrinalini, Sarojini and his youngest aunt, Lajjavati Basu. As usual, Abinash, the manager of the household, also moved in with Sailen Bose, his associate from Arbelia.

Plowden's detectives noted this change of address and took down the names of the various members of the society, including Gossain, who paid an early visit to Grey Street.

Earlier, Barin's choice of the assassin fell straight away on Sushil Sen as he had been one of Kingsford's principal victims. But it was inconceivable that the inexperienced Sushil should be assigned such an important task alone. Hence, the veteran Prafulla Chaki and Sushil left on their first reconnaissance mission in the beginning of April. On arriving in Muzaffarpur, they stayed in a cheap guesthouse run by Kishori Mohan Banerjee. Unfortunately on their way Sushil had inadvertently lost his money, forcing Prafulla to write for more from the garden. He finished off his letter humorously, saying, he had seen many places here, but they had not yet seen the bridegroom. Bibhuti promptly sent him twenty rupees by money order, solving their financial difficulties. A couple of days later, the two mercenaries returned to the garden to talk things over with their elders.

After their second reconnaissance, Sushil learned that his father was close to death in Srihatta. After a keen mental tussle between his duty to his country and obligation to his family, Sushil chose the latter. When a replacement for Sushil had to be found, Hem strongly recommended the name of the nineteen-year-old Khudiram Bose, one of his favourite protégés. Khudiram was the most zealous revolutionary of the Midnapore society ever since he had been recruited.

Finally, one day around the end of April, Barin took Prafulla from the garden to Gopi Mohan Datta Lane where Hem and Ullaskar had finished preparing their bomb for Kingsford. Although smaller than a tennis ball, the deadly tin sphere was packed with six ounces of dynamite, a detonator and a black powder fuse. Then Barin and Prafulla travelled to Hem Das' house where Khudiram was waiting. Barin introduced Prafulla to Khudiram as Dinesh Chandra Roy to safeguard his real identity in case they were caught. And the same day, the two left for Muzaffarpur. After reaching Muzaffarpur, the two young men stayed once again at Kishori Mohan's guesthouse.

Around the middle of April, coinciding with Prafulla's and Sushil's second reconnaissance mission to Muzaffarpur, Abinash proudly bragged of the scheme to an acquaintance and an avowed spy of the Calcutta police. The spy immediately passed on the information to his contact who communicated it to deputy superintendent Ramsadoy Mukherjee. The same day, Halliday wrote an urgent letter to J E Armstrong, superintendent of police, Muzaffarpur, of the pretty strong rumour that a Bengali man probably accompanied by a Bengali youth, had left Calcutta three days earlier in order to make an attempt on Kingsford's life. However, the information was so shadowy that he refrained from writing directly to Kingsford. He urged the superintendent to make discreet enquiries and warn the judge. Although Kingsford did not attach much importance to the news, the superintendent thought it fit to assign two constables to watch his house and two to follow him when he went to the club.

One evening towards the end of April, Hrishikesh Kanjilal came unannounced as Indraneel was getting ready to leave his office.

'Neel,' he gasped, handing a sealed envelope and clumsily collapsing into a chair. 'You have an urgent message from Barin … along with this packet.'

Obviously, the steep stairs had taken their toll on the portly man and he was panting for breath.

'How often I've vowed to eat less, but this goddamn greed for food won't die!' However, he felt a lot better after drinking a glass of water.

'Now please excuse me,' he said getting up abruptly after consulting the wall clock, 'unless I leave at once, I will miss the evening passenger to Serampore.'

Indraneel accompanied Kanjilal and saw him off at the main gate of Temple Chambers before reading Barin's message.

'You must leave immediately for Muzaffarpur,' the terse note began. 'I cannot trust anyone else for this urgent mission. The packet that I am sending must be delivered to PC. It is very important that you catch the next train to ensure its timely delivery. The success of the mission now lies entirely in your hands.'

Surely, there was an unforeseen emergency or else Barin would not have summarily summoned him. He understood PC to be an abbreviation for Prafulla Chaki and his instinct warned that Barin had entrusted him with the delivery of a firearm to the lad. After carefully destroying the note, Indraneel quickly went out to the high court terminal to catch a tram bound for Park Circus. He had to go home to make preparations.

As a result, Indraneel called at Kishori Mohan's guesthouse in Muzaffarpur on the morning of the second day. It was around eleven o'clock and the place looked deserted as its boarders had gone out for work. Indraneel met Prafulla who, he was told, was to be addressed as Dinesh Chandra Roy in Khudiram's presence. But as the boy from Midnapore had gone for his bath, Indraneel took advantage of his absence to hand over the packet from Barin. He explained to Prafulla that among the three pistols that had been given to him, the Perrin was classified as defective.

'You would have found yourselves in a tight situation,' Indraneel explained. 'The gun would have betrayed you, forcing you to surrender without firing a single shot.'

'Thank God!' Prafulla exclaimed. 'But this one is a fine specimen of the Belgian .32 calibre Browning,' he said authoritatively, while inspecting the firearm from all angles. 'But I hope Abi-da didn't forget to send matching bullets?'

'No, you will find them in the packet. By the way, today being *amavasya*, Barin wants you to carry out the attempt tonight.'

'All right, but then how safe is it for you to be seen with us on the very day of the attempt? Aren't you exposing yourself?'

'Yes, but for entirely valid reasons. What you are attempting to do for your motherland is unparalleled. I feel greatly honoured to play this small role in your sacrifice. Anyway, I expect to be out of town within a couple of hours.'

'Do you have plans to return directly to the city?'

'No, not directly. I shall halt at Deogarh for a day before returning to Calcutta.'

'Good. After fulfilling our mission the new boy and I propose to split up. So we could travel together from Madhupur onwards on our journey back to Calcutta.'

'Done,' Indraneel assured him, understanding Prafulla's loneliness. 'I shall definitely join you the day after tomorrow at Madhupur. Just lean out of your coach and wave to draw my attention.' Looking into Prafulla's eyes, Indraneel added, 'May God be with you, Brother!' Then hugging him feelingly, he added, 'See you soon.'

Just then a young stranger entered the hall and Prafulla introduced him to the older man. Indraneel was stunned by Khudiram's boyish looks. He wondered how the call of patriotism had turned these two teenagers into hardcore terrorists. He greeted Khudiram briefly and wished him success. Indraneel left for the station.

'Farewell,' Prafulla said from behind. 'Please pardon me if I can't keep the appointment.'

Khudiram and Prafulla had passed the evening of the day preceding the new moon rather conspicuously in the open field opposite Muzaffarpur Club. The two revolutionaries' restless pacing finally drew the attention of a police constable. Ultimately, on the day of reckoning, Prafulla and Khudiram returned to the field with their small deadly tin box. Then they waited under cover of the lightless night.

At the same moment, Douglas Kingsford and his wife were playing bridge at the club with the wife and daughter of their friend, advocate Kennedy. Mrs Kennedy and her tall and good-looking young daughter Grace were popular with the local English society. At around eight-thirty, the Kennedys and the Kingsfords finished their game and started for home in similar, single bay horse-drawn carriages.

It was the advocate's family that preceded the judge's by some distance. As the first carriage passed, Khudiram hurled the deadly bomb into the carriage, thinking it to be the judge's. A deafening blast and a blinding flash overpowered everyone. The two boys ran after throwing the bomb at the carriage. Initially, the two constables posted at the Club gate gave them chase but the fugitives managed to escape in the dark. Another constable, who ran into them on the way, also called out but, naturally, they did not stop. Eventually, Prafulla and Khudiram split up near the guesthouse, choosing to go in different directions.

As a result of the blinding explosion that followed, Miss Kennedy suffered fatal injuries, having absorbed most of the blast. Her mother had been hurt no less. Many neighbours assembled soon and together they carried the ladies into Kingsford's bungalow. By then the Kingsfords had also arrived unaware of what had taken place. However, Grace succumbed to her wounds within the hour while her mother was still fighting for life.

Kingsford immediately reported the attack to the magistrate. And after speaking to J E Armstrong, he left hurriedly for Motihari. The superintendent sent an emergency summons to Sub-Inspector Charturvedi Ramadhar Sarma and nine other constables, including Seusankar Singh, the head constable. He instructed them to catch the first train and proceed to Samastipur and Mokameh.

His advice was to drop plain-clothed constables at all stations, covering the approximate distance of about thirty-five miles between Muzaffarpur and Samastipur. Considering the Mokameh Station to be the vital destination that the terrorists would attempt to reach before proceeding to Calcutta, Armstrong asked Sharma to take up posts there.

Depending on the description gathered from the constables on duty at the Club gate, the police were now on the lookout for two Bengali youths aged about nineteen, probably barefooted, as their shoes were found abandoned near the site of the misdeed. Sharma was also advised to look for any Bengalis dressed in obviously new clothes, as they were expected to supply themselves with a new outfit en route.

In another development, the local magistrate promptly issued a proclamation offering five thousand rupees for any information leading to the detection of the offenders. The reward was expected to spur even the ordinary people in taking part in the manhunt.

And, not too far away from Muzaffarpur, young Khudiram continued to run for his life. He was hurtling through the jungles of north Bihar, a plain terrain well fed by small rivers such as the Burhi Gandak and the Lakhandai. Sweating profusely, he slowed down his pace to catch his breath. After covering twenty-four miles through the night, Khudiram reached the little town of Waini in the early hours of the next day. Feeling hungry, thirsty and exhausted, he hurriedly entered a grocer's shop near the railway station and asked for some parched rice and water.

In the meantime, after catching the one o'clock train from Muzaffarpur, constables Fateh Singh and Shew Pershad Missir got down at the Waini Station at around 3.30 a.m. and straight away started their work in earnest. They were aware that one of the revolutionaries sported longish hair and wore a coat and the other was dressed in a white shirt. Unfortunately, no one answered this description in the station or the train by which they had come. Hence, the two policemen waited patiently for four hours for the next train, but again searched it in vain when it pulled in at the Waini Station.

Following their failure to nab the culprits at the station, the constables tried their luck outside by combing the surrounding shops. Going over to Jitu Taher's grocery shop, the two men peered inside and instantly, their suspicion fell on an innocent-looking lad with longish hair and a slight frame, eating parched rice.

The broad-shouldered Fateh Singh then accosted the lad and enquired of him where he was going and from where he had come. Sensing the young man's discomfort, he began cross-questioning him with gusto. At this point, Khudiram bolted when his eyes accidentally fell on Fateh Singh's ammunition boots. But as a result of the sleepless night and the tiresome march, his limbs could hardly obey his wish and the constables soon caught him. With the inevitable jerk, a loaded pistol fell out from his bundle on the ground. But undaunted by the helpless situation, Khudiram pulled out another smaller pistol from under his dhoti with an intent to shoot. However, the constables proved more than a match for the tired youth and they swiftly wrested the weapon from his hand.

After securing Khudiram by his hands and waist, the policemen now began their routine search of his person. The coat, which had rightly been described by the men on duty at the club gate, was kept neatly folded in the bundle that Khudiram was carrying. Then following strict procedural norms, those things were tied up in a sheet and taken with the prisoner to the station. Following the prize catch, the jubilant constables sent a telegram to Muzaffarpur. And Superintendent Armstrong personally came down to Waini with Mr Hedan, inspector of the armed reserve, to escort the dangerous desperado back to Muzaffarpur.

On the same day that Khudiram was apprehended, Prafulla reached Samastipur Junction and was waiting on the platform of the station to catch the evening train bound for Mokameh. When it pulled in, a smart looking young Bengali gentleman got down to take a stroll. Quite predictably, the stranger's keen sixth sense was instantly aroused as soon as his eyes fell on the lad. The discrepancy between the teenager's new urban clothes and plain rural appearance was far too evident to escape the hawk-like eyes of an ambitious sub-inspector. For, not only had Nandalal Banerjee, the off-duty-officer of the Singbhoom Police, been to Muzaffarpur and heard of Miss Kennedy's murder, he was also aware of the proclaimed reward of five thousand rupees for catching the culprits. Convinced about the dubious qualifications of his prospective catch, he discreetly slipped into the station's telegraphic bureau and sent off an urgent message to his grandfather at Muzaffarpur, asking him to acquire the permission of the local magistrate or the police superintendent as to whether he could make an arrest on suspicion alone. He further requested that the reply be sent to Mokameh.

On returning, Nandalal boarded the same compartment along with his new acquaintance. During the journey, the older passenger cleverly drew the younger one into conversation.

'You see, I had been to Muzaffarpur on a short holiday to my grandfather's house. But then, have you heard the sensational news about the murder of a European lady by unknown assailants in Muzaffarpur last night?'

'No, I haven't heard,' Prafulla replied evenly, without betraying any emotion.

'Kingsford must've got a real fright. The two teenagers threw a bomb into a carriage in which an English advocate's wife and daughter were travelling, mistaking it for the judge's. For, it seems that the carriages of Kingsford and the advocate are quite identical in appearance and the mishap occurred principally due to confusion in the darkness. And while Miss Kennedy died within an hour of the incident, Mrs Kennedy is still fighting for life!'

'How ghastly!' Prafulla exclaimed. Secretly however, he was cursing himself for failing in his duty. He wondered why providence was so bent upon protecting the public enemy. How else could Kingsford survive yet another attempt?

'Yes, they're indeed a desperate lot. By the way, the good news is that one of the murderers was caught this morning at Waini, not too far from here. And I've little doubt that before long the other accomplice will also be arrested. I even have an uncanny feeling that he's lurking somewhere around.'

Elsewhere, on receiving the news of the attempted murder of Kingsford, Commissioner Halliday's attention turned fully to the predictable big crackdown on the dens of the revolutionaries and his sundry duties were beginning to irritate. He knew that applications for the search and arrest warrants could only be started after receiving clearance from the governor in Darjeeling. He asked Head Constable Parayag Missir to quickly summon the hearing while entering his Lalbazar office. Very soon, a mass of people began gathering in the long corridor outside.

As the commissioner grew busy with his regular duties, he noticed a visitor waiting to meet him.

'Sir, I'm the reporter of *Empire*,' the young visitor said walking in briskly with self-assurance, not suspecting that he was causing an interruption. 'May I have your view on the recent bomb outrage at Muzaffarpur for this evening's edition?'

Halliday's head began to throb while the reporter continued.

'Our correspondent stationed in Muzzaffarpur informs that following the death of Mrs and Miss Kennedy, Mr Kingsford has revealed to him your warning about two assassins being sent from Calcutta!'

The commissioner held up his right hand in protest.

'Oh God, how awfully foolish and indiscreet of Kingsford to have revealed my warning!' he lamented. For, leakage of this piece of news in the press would inevitably ruin his carefully laid-out plans. It would show the terrorists how closely the police were watching them and would provide them with the opportunity to take precautions to avoid arrests.

That evening *Empire*'s headlines read: 'Bomb Outrage in Behar. European Lady killed. Attempt to assassinate Mr Kingsford.'

The paper further reported that while confirming the tragic report, the commissioner had declined to give details. However, he did authenticate one important fact.

'The perpetrators are believed to be well-known terrorists,' he said.

Sitting in his *Bande Mataram* office, Aurobindo took note of the commissioner's broad hint. Having a premonition that things were getting out of hand, he immediately left for home. Aurobindo made a quick mental assessment of the incriminating articles or documents that might be lying within the house. To the best of his knowledge there was nothing to worry about. Almost instantly he heard some voices in the ground floor. He went down quickly and found it to be Abinash unloading some heavy bags. Abinash revealed that he had brought five rifles and five bags of cartridges for safekeeping. Aurobindo quickly ordered him to get rid of the articles and tell Barin to do the same at the garden. Abinash then rushed to the garden and brought back Barin and half a dozen boys who took away the arms.

However, getting rid of the arsenal proved more difficult than they imagined. So Barin got holes dug in the vast space in his open yard and had the guns, bombs, cartridges, chemicals and the mould for casting iron, buried. At the same time, he asked some other boys to burn papers in the house, which did not prove easy in the darkness. Everyone did his best and by the time all the work was finished it was late in the night. Now, leaving the garden was considered impractical. A speedy consultation between Barin and Upen determined that everyone would scatter early next morning after spending the night there.

53

The Arrests

Without any culpable proof in connection with the Muzaffarpur murders, the only course of action open to the government was to arrest the members of the secret society and imprison them without trial. This would have to be done under the statute of an existing draconian law—the State Prisoners Regulation III of 1818.

Therefore, Sir Andrew Fraser had his chief secretary draw up a request to the Government of India asking permission to deport five men, namely, Aurobindo, Barin, Satyen, Abinash and Hem. The authorities believed that these men were the prime movers and the principal culprits of the recent outrages. The lieutenant governor was quick to point out that owing to the absence of an adequate law of conspiracy, the administration could not take any legal sanctions against the secret society whose existence was known but no involvement of any specific offence or culpability could be proved. In case the Muzaffarpur assassins desisted from implicating others, their link with their parent society would not be easy to establish.

Meanwhile, the decision to search places frequented by these suspected men and arrest them in Calcutta and its surrounding areas was taken late in the afternoon. Hence, Commissioner Halliday, accompanied by Plowden and Purna Chandra Biswas, appeared in Chief Metropolitan Magistrate T Thornhill's court where Biswas applied for search warrants. After obtaining the warrants, officers had to be appointed to arrest the suspected men and search the eight places that they frequented.

At seven o'clock, Commissioner Halliday called an emergency meeting at his official residence which was attended by nearly all the bigwigs of the Calcutta police. The principal agenda of the evening was to discuss the elaborate arrangements for the next day's secret operation. The services of several veteran British officers with more than twenty years' experience in service were mustered. At last the commissioner's opportunity to take action against the bunch of known terrorists had arrived. He had been advocating this crackdown for months.

Appropriately, the next morning's big drama began to unfold with unusual pomp and dignity. At about 4 a.m., amidst tight security at the garden, Inspector Frizzoni and Sub-Inspector Roy began their operations. Fifty armed constables now stood guard around the garden house and escape was out of the question.

Finally, the hour of reckoning had arrived for Barin and his boys. Upen and Barin were the first to be awakened by the snapping of branches and the creaking of boots. They peered through a crack in the door and could make out in that first break of light, the silhouette of dozens of policemen taking up their position with their usual well-drilled efficiency. A shadow descended upon the two friends as they silently exchanged glances. A sense of guilt and misery brought tears into Barin's eyes.

But with the firm knock on the front door his features hardened. There was no time now left for weakness or sentimentality. He opened the door with courage and dignity and found himself facing the hawk-eyed Inspector Frizzoni.

Simultaneously, the police rounded up twelve boys, namely, Ullaskar, Nolini, Indu, Paresh, Bejoy, Bibhuti and six others. Their sleepy eyes betrayed disbelief. Afterwards search of the house and ground began. But even after two hours, nothing worthwhile, except a few spent cartridges, was found. However, the discovery of a copy of the previous day's *Empire* brought some cheer among the policemen. The Muzaffarpur article in *Empire* had been incriminatingly encircled in blue!

Barin's heart bled and he could no longer remain still as the constables resorted to using filthy language and bullying the younger boys, in particular Sachin. In a flash, he made up his mind to take the entire blame upon himself and shield the younger boys. Barin bravely declared to the officers that the youngsters knew nothing and that he alone was responsible for everything. He was even willing to make a statement. The wily inspector immediately sent an officer to fetch a magistrate, as he realised the uselessness in court of a written document. But when after a couple of hours the officer came back with the news that no magistrate was available, the search resumed with Barin's voluntary guidance. And within minutes the society's dangerous arsenal was uncovered.

The officers were dumbstruck by the size of the society's collection of arms. In all, four sporting rifles, one double-barrelled shotgun, as many as eleven revolvers, fourteen boxes of cartridges and three bombs were unearthed. Besides dynamite, dynamite-cartridges, large quantities of picric acid and other chemicals, bombshells and a forge were also dug out. A copy of the Paris explosive manual and several other textbooks on the same subject and books on military training were also found. Among other compromising papers discovered were some organisational plans, Prafulla's letter mentioning Kingsford as the bridegroom and a notebook belonging to Indu, showing the exact date and time of his attempt to kill the mayor of Chandernagore. A record book for the repair of revolvers carried the name Indra, with obvious reference to Indra Nandi, was also found. Presumably, the darkness of the night before had been instrumental in saving from destruction these incriminating pieces of evidence.

Elsewhere, Superintendent Griffith Bowen was also lucky with his search operation. At 134 Harrison Road, the chemists shop owned by Ullaskar's friends, Nagendra and Dharani Gupta, where, besides arresting these two men, the police also rounded up their three companions Ashok Nandi, and two others. Combing through a storeroom they found the three locked trunks and basket that Ullaskar had brought the previous week. These revealed a big quantity of lethal chemicals for manufacturing bombs. However, at 38/4 Naba Krishna Street, where Hem was arrested, Superintendent Merriman's hopes were largely betrayed as only Hem's chemical apparatus and books on chemistry could be seized. Deputy Commissioner Feeny was given charge to search and make arrests at 15 Gopi Mohan Datta's Lane. He was quite as unlucky, but he arrested Kanailal and Nirapodo.

Meanwhile, Satyen Bose received word about the Calcutta arrests and reacting briskly, destroyed all the papers he could lay hands on. The next day, however, Satyen and his brother Gyan and two others were arrested. But the police could only find an old gun and two swords at his premises.

~

When the policemen entered Aurobindo's room like heroes, pistols in hand, as though they were besieging, with guns and cannon, a well-armed fort, they found him sleeping peacefully on the floor. He sat up instantly, half-asleep. The superintendent gave an order to a policeman to arrest him.

Aurobindo was asked to stand up. At this point he asked to be allowed to go to the toilet but was refused. A tiff arose when Richard Creagan used an extremely objectionable expression. Heated words were exchanged after which Aurobindo asked to see the search warrant, which he read and signed. Under instructions from Creagan, he was handcuffed and a rope was tied round his waist, which an upcountry constable held from behind.

Abinash and Sailen also were brought up to the first floor. From Creagan's words it seemed as if he had entered the lair of some ferocious animal, as if they were a lot of uneducated, wild lawbreakers and it was unnecessary to speak or behave courteously towards them. But somehow, after the sharp exchange with Aurobindo the sahib had grown a little milder.

The superintendent asked, 'It seems you are a BA. Is it not a matter of shame for an educated person like you to be sleeping on the floor of an unfurnished room and in a house like this?'

Aurobindo did not even make an attempt to reply, knowing how impossible it was to explain to such an insensitive man what the love and sacrifice for one's motherland meant.

Meanwhile in a fit of despair, Mrinalini was silently praying to God to put an end to the barbaric behaviour of the police.

The search went on through the following six hours! All Aurobindo's exercise books, letters, papers, scraps, poems, plays, prose, essays and translations—nothing escaped the clutches of the detailed search. The police made two remarkable discoveries—one was a small box containing some powder that resembled a powerful explosive and the other was a letter written by Barin to

Aurobindo. Among the two, the first item lamentably turned out to be some sacred earth from Dakshineswar collected by Mrinalini. But the second find, to be known as the infamous 'Sweets Letter', would become the most incriminating document against Aurobindo's involvement and knowledge about Barin's secret society. It was none other than the letter that Barin had innocently written during the Surat Congress.

On receiving information about the police search at Grey Street, Krishna Kumar Mitra rushed there. Sensing great trouble, he even fetched Attorney Bhupendra Nath Basu from his nearby ancestral house.

Quite accidentally that morning, Abinash's brother, Upendra, took the early morning train from Arbelia to come to Sealdah. From College Street he caught a tram bound for Shyambazar and got down at the Grey Street junction. Here tension was palpable as a big crowd had gathered. Upendra arrived just in time to witness Aurobindo, Abinash and Sailen being led away by the police. The handcuffs and ropes tied around their waists drew his attention. Two hackneys had been hired and the three men were being led into them. Attorney Bhupen Basu was furiously arguing with Creagan about the indignity brought on Aurobindo by tying a rope around his waist. The swelling crowd, too, was reacting angrily on seeing their beloved leader being led away like a common criminal. Upendra was struck by the composure of the one whose arrest was causing so much commotion all around. It was as if Aurobindo's meditative eyes were engrossed in the search of an unseen light above the tumult of the world around. And, as soon as the police left with the prisoners, shouts of *Vande Mataram* rent the air.

Quite expectedly, to the simple-hearted Mrinalini, the day's happenings were the preamble of a far greater catastrophe. Ultimately, her mental torture became so unbearable that she fainted! When she regained consciousness, she found herself in the house of Krishna Kumar Mitra.

~

In due course, Indraneel boarded the Howrah-bound passenger from Muzzaffarpur. To reach Deogarh, it was necessary to disembark at a railway station called Jasidih. But as he was used to coming from Calcutta, Indraneel got confused in approaching the station from the opposite direction. As a result he missed getting down at the right station. He later learned to his dismay that the train's next major halt would be at Madhupur, where Prafulla and he were scheduled to meet. Although he alighted at Madhupur, his spirit sank visibly when he realised that his much-vaunted meeting with Kusum was annulled. Admittedly, it was inconceivable to travel to Deogarh and be back at Madhupur to keep the appointment with Prafulla in such a short while. Feeling despondent, he lost all enthusiasm to meet Prafulla. The torture of being so close to Kusum and not being able to see her raised many questions in his mind. Since his presence was not likely to affect Prafulla's return to the city in any way, why on earth did he agree to meet the boy midway? Besides, he suddenly realised how injudicious his planned encounter with Kingsford' assassin might be in the event that the imperial police force was tracking Prafulla!

However, as the circumstances seemed to strongly endorse a tryst with Prafulla rather than Kusum, Indraneel decided to stay overnight at a guesthouse and have dinner at a wayside eatery. But sleep eluded him that night. He helplessly lay awake remembering the feeling of Kusum's head on his shoulder and the mild perfume of hibiscus oil in her hair. After tossing about in his hard bed for a long time, he eventually fell asleep in the wee hours of the morning. The sun was high in the sky when he awoke. That was when a stray piece of conversation entered his ears.

'Have you heard the sensational news?' a fellow-boarder was asking another. 'Last evening a young memsahib died in a bomb attack! Her mother was badly wounded and is now fighting for her life.'

'Oh, what awful times we are living in,' the other man commented dryly. 'But how would the death of two memsahibs benefit the murderer?'

There was something sinister yet familiar about the whole affair that sent a chill down Indraneel's spine. He sat up quickly and looked straight at the two men conversing in the other corner of the dormitory.

'I beg your pardon,' he asked politely, 'may I know where this incident took place?'

'In Muzaffarpur, Babu,' explained the first man excitedly. 'It seems that a team of assassins hurled a bomb at the carriage before running away.'

'So then, what went wrong?' Indraneel pondered hard. 'Wasn't Kingsford alone in the carriage? Why wasn't there any mention about the judge's death? Surely, the demise of such a notorious public servant would have been too sensational to suppress.' But prudence prompted him not to ask further questions.

Although Prafulla's train was not expected to arrive before 2 p.m., he reached the station an hour earlier and began restlessly pacing the platform. Finally, when the train pulled in, Indraneel desperately hoped to see Prafulla's familiar form waving at him from his coach. But when there was no sign of anyone signalling even after several minutes, he frantically ran from one end of the platform to the other, calling Prafulla's name. At last when it became evident that the boy had not come, he dejectedly entered a coach, trying hard to overcome his grief. That was when the true meaning of Prafulla's last words suddenly dawned on his mind: 'Farewell,' he had said, 'please pardon me if I can't keep the appointment.' Incapable of holding back his tears, Indraneel wept freely.

Coinciding with the police crackdown at Muraripukur Garden and the other locations in Calcutta, another drama was unfolding on the platform of a small railway station called Mokameh Ghat, two hundred and eighty-four miles from the city. Earlier, Nandalal Banerjee had promised to treat Prafulla to breakfast at the Samaria Ghat Station. Then, on the steamer when breakfast was served, he shared a happy moment with his host.

On reaching the other bank, Prafulla and Nandalal went straight to the Mokameh Ghat Station. But an unexpected thing happened as soon as Prafulla joined Nandalal on the platform. An unknown gentleman delivered a telegram to the older man, which he immediately opened and read. As Nandalal turned around holding the telegraphic message from his grandfather, his face hardened suddenly. 'I'm sorry,' he said sombrely, 'I must place you under arrest.'

Although it was late morning, the sun was not high in the sky. Suddenly there was absolute silence all around. Nothing stirred. In a flash, Prafulla's world turned upside down! For a fraction of a second he cursed himself for being so gullible and stared at his benefactor in disbelief. And then, he began to run for his life.

Prafulla had so far not noticed the plain-clothed policemen deployed for action on the platform. As he started running down the length of the platform, they followed quickly. The deliverers of the telegram were none other than Sub-Inspector Chaturvedi Ramadhar Sharma and his companion, Constable Seusankar Singh. Now these two police officers energetically raised a hue and cry while chasing the dangerous outlaw, hearing which, another constable ran in from the opposite direction and made a rush at Prafulla who fired a shot from his Browning narrowly missing him.

By then the other two constables had closed in on Prafulla and a scuffle began. The spirited teenager struggled hard to free his right arm. He quickly fired a shot at his own chest, but the shot did not prove fatal. Prafulla had very little time now. Using all his might, he somehow managed to raise the barrel of the gun to his chin. Again he pulled the trigger. This time the bullet pierced his brain.

Later Prafulla's body was taken to Muzaffarpur for identification by Khudiram. However, Khudiram recognised it only as that of Dinesh Chandra Roy. As Prafulla's head had nearly been severed from the trunk, the authorities cut it off and immersed it in spirit for sending it to Calcutta for further identification.

It had fallen on Inspector Benode Gupta to escort Aurobindo first to Lalbazar and then to the Royd Street police station. It was here that Aurobindo came to know the sly detective Maulvi Shamsul Alam. In the evening the redoubtable Ramsoday Mukherjee appeared on the scene. He expressed words of unusual kindness and sympathy and told everyone present to be careful about Aurobindo's food and bed.

Later at Lalbazar, two Englishmen entered Aurobindo's room. He was told that one of them was Commissioner Halliday. Finding Sailen Bose and him together, Halliday was wrathful with the sergeant, and pointing towards Aurobindo he said, 'Take care that nobody stays or speaks with this man.'

Sailen was at once removed. When the others had left, the commissioner asked him, 'Aren't you ashamed of being involved in this cowardly, dastardly activity?'

'What right have you to assume that I was involved?' Aurobindo replied spiritedly. 'I wholly deny having any connection with these murderous acts.'

The whole of the next day passed in the lock-up. After this, Aurobindo, Abinash and Sailen were produced before Thornhill. Earlier, all the three had refused to make declarations before the commissioner. At the court, Aurobindo met the senior partner of the firm of attorneys, Manuel and Agarwalla and later learnt that according to the police a good deal of suspicious literature had been recovered from his house.

Barin also was escorted by a young sergeant to the detective department and was made to wait. About an hour-and-a-half later, Ramsadoy made his appearance and, feigning ignorance of Barin's long wait, became instantly solicitous.

'Ah, there you are!' he said with an air of utmost concern. 'So they've made you wait here, haven't they? Come in, my son, come in. You are the jewel of the country. What terrific work you've done! And after all this how can the *Firinghee* scoundrels call us cowards? Come in this way, please.'

After that Barin was served tea and snacks. For a while Ramsadoy became the epitome of courtesy and hospitality. However, under the guise of warm bonhomie, he kept up his clever interrogation throughout the evening. There were occasional breaks whenever someone came in.

'Here is Barindra, come and meet him,' Ramsadoy would say, or 'I say, Jones, here is Barindra!'

As a result, many curious police officers and ordinary civilians cast Barin furtive, oblique, glowing and sympathetic looks. Hand-in-hand with this outpouring of paternal concern, Ramsadoy's questioning persisted till one o'clock in the morning.

That evening, using all his worldly wisdom, Barin managed to resist the tide by repeatedly giving the same stock reply. 'Call my associates and let us confer together. Only then, shall I decide about how much to reveal to you.'

Finally, following a prolonged session of questioning, Barin was allowed to sleep. An armed constable was posted throughout the night at his feet. However, the previous morning's unforgettable noise preceding his arrest caused by the policemen's boots crushing the dry leaves of the garden kept haunting him. It became a nightmare that terrified Barin throughout his long prison life.

~

As expected, the Muzaffarpur killings and the subsequent arrests of the revolutionaries electrified the situation of the country. The citizens of Calcutta, in particular, were severely jolted by the arrests and the sensational discoveries. The British became hysterical over the news of the violence, expecting a resurgence of the sentiments that led to the 1857 mutiny.

Throughout the month of May, Calcutta was rocked by bomb explosions. The College Street area of North Calcutta was startled by an explosion in the house of Colonel Nandi, whose son, Indra, was closely connected with Muraripukur Garden and had links with the earlier Jamalpur riots. Indra Nandi inadvertently blew up a bomb while trying to defuse one. The bomb ripped away his left hand, carrying it to the roof of the neighbouring house. Four people were injured when a municipal conservancy cart accidentally ran over a bomb on the Grey Street tramline. A couple of days later, the police removed a live bomb from the steps of a native Christian church. After this, the people of the city talked of nothing else but bombs.

Inspector P C Biswas of the CID submitted an FIR related to five distinct crimes against the thirty-one revolutionaries arrested so far. These included the two attempts to blow up the lieutenant governor's train near Chandernagore, the one at Narayangarh, the attempt to murder the mayor of Chandernagore as well as the Muzaffarpur killings. Of these, the gravest charge was to wage war against the King, attracting death penalty or transportation for life. As this was a heinous conspiracy against the Government, all the accused were to be collectively prosecuted in a single trial by the Alipore sessions judge. Sir Andrew Fraser despatched two letters to Viceroy Minto, including a confidential note, summarising the history of the secret society. Giving prominence to Aurobindo, who appeared to be the ringleader of the gang, he laid special emphasis, in the strongest possible terms, for his banishment.

'He is regarded and spoken of by all as the disciples regard a Master,' he wrote wrathfully. 'He has been at the forefront of all, advising seditious writing and authorising murder. But he has kept himself, like a careful and valued general, out of the sight of the enemy.'

Then with certain reference to the 'Sweets Letter', the governor wrote: 'We've been fortunate enough to get papers, quite sufficient to justify deportation. I earnestly hope that no sentiment would be allowed to prevent this.'

But Fraser's impassioned plea fell on deaf ears. Weary of the recent deportation fiasco of Ajit Singh and of Lala Lajpat Rai in the Punjab, the move had boomeranged by turning the two deportees into national heroes. To the viceroy, Aurobindo's case seemed to fall in the same category. One of the viceroy's chief advisers, however, thought that there was a good chance of obtaining Aurobindo's conviction in court, particularly if one of the prisoners could be induced to turn approver.

54

An Interlude

Returning to Calcutta a day after the political arrests, Indraneel heard all about the fate of his fellow revolutionaries. Revealing deep insight into the rebels' secret activities, the authorities had not only searched the right places frequented by them but made it evident that they were well informed about the link between their gang and the planned murder of Kingsford. But the question was how long it would take the police to establish Indraneel's connection with the delivery of the Browning to the killers.

The next day, the sad news of Khudiram's arrest and Prafulla's suicide reached the capital, plunging Indraneel into further depression. Confirming the rumours he had earlier heard, it was shocking to learn that despite the death of two innocent ladies the despotic Kingsford lived on! Indraneel was also upset by the thought that he had unknowingly waited for the dead Prafulla on the platform!

Although the police raids were not entirely unexpected following the painful developments at Muzaffarpur, Indraneel felt angered and frustrated by the arrest of his friends. Interestingly, it was Aurobindo himself who had warned him against visiting the garden at about the same time that the note from Sudhir had reached Upen at Sil's Lodge. Luckily, Indraneel had blindly heeded Aurobindo's warning even though he was unable to understand why. As a result, no order of arrest was issued in Indraneel's name, although such a warrant stood in the name of Bhababhusan Mitra who had disappeared.

A couple of weeks later, Indraneel summoned his father's assistant Amulya Ratan Burman for some enquiries connected with official work.

'Baba has asked me to hand over these papers to you,' he explained. 'For the moment he has asked you to file them in Dadu's file relating to a certain Bowbazar house.'

'Oh, you mean the prostitute's house?' Burman asked with a twinkle in his eyes.

'What are you talking about?'

'I am sorry. I thought you knew about it. But tell me, what are these papers?'

'I don't know. Apparently, these are money receipts pertaining to some annual commissions paid by a doctor named Pradyumno Sarkar to … Now wait a minute!' Indraneel exclaimed suddenly remembering the good physician who had come to Shakuni's rescue after his accident. 'I think I know this man.' Then as he read on, his expression underwent a change. 'Now, why is Dr Sarkar paying such a fat sum of money to Motimala Dassi?'

'That's a long story, but suffice it to say that she has a right to it. It's interest on money advanced to his nursing home and a cut from his earnings.'

'But if the interest alone is equivalent to three thousand six hundred rupees, then the principal must be around twenty thousand rupees!' Indraneel was flabbergasted. From where did Motimala get so much money? Indraneel knew something was fishy. Obviously, he was ignorant of a secret that everybody else in the office knew and which seemed to have a scandalous ring about it. Besides, Indraneel felt intrigued because of Motimala's involvement in the matter. 'Now, Burman Babu, please tell me everything.'

'I shall tell you if you insist but don't blame me if you don't like the truth. Years ago, your Dadu had kept this woman. Afterwards Gourmohan Datta gifted her the house in question. Later, on realising his mistake, he asked your father to get back the house for him, and he did it by paying twenty thousand rupees.'

This was the most incredible story that Indraneel had ever heard. His Mashima was a prostitute! 'But then,' he asked himself, 'why did she donate those heavy gold bracelets to the society? Be what may, she had not imposed any conditions. But of all people, to be his Dadu's mistress!' The very thought was repugnant. He damned his fate for leading him so treacherously to her house. Then in a mood of derision and contempt, he vowed never to see Motimala again.

Consequently, Motimala was unable to recover from her mental shock about Indraneel's cessation to visit her house even after a long penance at the Thanthania Kali Bari. Destiny had played a cruel game ever since it had brought the soft, sensitive, Indraneel. The boy had a glow of innocence and nobility written over his youthful face that had awakened in her *mamata*, a mother's natural love for her offspring. Motimala grew more and more despondent in her friendless world as weeks passed and Indraneel did not come back to her. She began losing hope and her anguish turned into a mental depression, making her totally withdrawn.

Then one day, a lady came to offer puja to the goddess at the Kali Bari. As Motimala was sitting right beside the priest facing the image, she could not help overhearing her.

'My husband's name is Harimohan Datta,' the woman said. 'At present he is in faraway England. And my son's name is Indraneel. I would like to offer puja in both names, for their welfare.'

Motimala could not help glancing up at the lady. What a coincidence! 'My God!' she silently reflected, 'here is Mrs Datta, the wife of the renowned barrister and lucky mother of Indraneel!' Just then, a thought struck her and she instinctively turned and looked back. Indraneel was standing hardly three yards away with eyes closed and hands folded in deep prayer.

Motimala was moved to tears by the happy coincidence and wiped her eyes delicately with the end of her sari. For, her ardent prayers to see Indraneel had at long last been fulfilled. Slowly, she got up and headed home with resolute steps. Her determination was unshakeable. According to her secret vow, she would now have to dedicate herself unrestrictedly to the Mother's cause.

Commonsense suggested that Indraneel should maintain a low profile and desist from visiting the rebels' hideouts. But soon, an idea occurred, opening a safer line of action. Why not temporarily take exile in Deogarh since it was unsafe to live in the city? He could take his mother for a pilgrimage and discreetly introduce her to Kusum. Surely, Kusum would be happy to interact with his mother and he, too, could take her into confidence about his feelings for the girl.

Consequently, Saraju and Indraneel reached Deogarh after a fortnight. Having dropped a postcard to Kusum to make sure that she would come to the temple in the afternoon, Indraneel took his mother for Baba's darshan at four o'clock. Kusum came punctually and stood beside Indraneel with a smiling face while Saraju was immersed in adoration. He took her hand and gave it a fond squeeze. Responding warmly, Kusum stood close to him so that no one could make out that their hands were intertwined. He made a sign with his eyes pointing to his mother and Kusum automatically followed his gaze.

When Saraju turned around, wanting to offer Baba's *prasad* to her son, she was surprised to see two happy faces intently smiling at her. She was smart enough to guess the rest. She first gave the *prasad* to Kusum and then to her son. Then she took her son aside and fondly pulled his ear.

'I wondered why my son came to Baidyanath so often,' she whispered. 'But I now realise that he has mastered the art of drinking stealthily while swimming underwater!'

Planning to live for a month in Baidyanath, Indraneel and Saraju rented a house at Karnibagh, near Balananda Ashram. To the pious Saraju the twenty-two temples housed within the sacred complex were the source of immense solace and she spent most of her time going from one temple to the other. As for Saraju's son, this relaxed period was the best interlude he had known in his twenty-seven years. Although not as devout as his mother, he nevertheless paid frequent visits to Baba's temple during *sandhyarati*. However, the most attractive part of his days was the late afternoon when, together with Kusum, he would walk along the Darowa or the Yamunajor rivulets, sometimes going as far as the low Nandan Hills or the Data Jungle on the northern edge of the town. Deogarh boasts of a unique backdrop of verdure and variety, surrounded by the Trikut, Nandan and the Dighiria Hills, which form part of the larger Rajmahal Range.

One afternoon, Kusum happily snuggled against Indraneel as they sat atop the Nandan Hills.

'Have you wondered what will happen to us in ten years?' she asked. 'Shall we still be around to enjoy this pristine beauty? I'm sure you will be a family man by then.'

'Do you seriously believe that your life will remain the same as now?' Indraneel replied. 'You're so young. Why don't you move forward and consciously break the impasse that your life has prematurely reached?'

'But how can I change my fate? Did I not dream of founding a family and a home? Every woman wants to become a mother. Besides, the stigmas attached to widowhood are unbearable! One is not allowed to socialise, laugh or mix with men freely, leave alone eating meat or fish. One isn't even allowed to consume onion because it adds taste to the vegetarian food.'

Then, growing aware that the discussion was spoiling the sanctity of the moment, Kusum went back to the earlier subject. 'Will you promise me something? Will you remember this special day forever?'

'I promise,' he answered solemnly, 'not only to remember this unique day but also this blue sky, these green fields, the song of the birds and in the midst of it all—my dearest Kusum! The truth is this place holds a special value in my heart because of your presence, because I'm sharing this unforgettable moment with you.'

'I know as a widow I've no right to say this, but I want to live. I don't want to lose you. I want to be forever near you.'

'Neither do I want to lose you, Kusum,' he said cupping her face with his hands. And as their eyes probed each other's hearts for confirmation, he fearlessly added, 'I therefore see only one solution: marry me.'

Kusum hugged him spontaneously, hiding her face in his chest. Holding her tightly to himself, Indraneel wondered in amazement how he could propose to her so easily. Then as his heart pounded harder, he added, 'I hope your parents would approve of me as their future son-in-law.'

'I don't see why they should have any objection when socially and culturally you're much superior to us. But wouldn't your parents oppose their only son's marriage to a widow?' Kusum asked without looking up.

'I think you're forgetting that my father died before I was born. My mother would have remained a social outcast but for her remarriage to my stepfather. Besides, I have talked to my mother about you and she has readily given her blessings. As for my stepfather, he's the most wonderful man on earth! I don't see why he should disapprove of the person I choose. But at the moment he's away in England and I don't know when he'll return.'

Then after a moment's hesitation, Indraneel added, 'Now, let's talk of some serious matters. You know I share with my fellow revolutionaries the dream of an independent India. And my activities may lead me to stay away from home for long stretches of time. Will you endure the separation?

'Make no mistake,' Kusum replied firmly. 'I wouldn't be so much interested in you had you not made the freedom of the country your noble ideal. I want to feel proud of being the wife of someone who has made an uncommon goal his life's cherished mission. Besides, I'm reconciled to my fate. A life of pleasure isn't meant for me. Married or unmarried, I know I would be as companionless as your Sejo Bouthan.'

One day, after returning to Calcutta, Indraneel discovered to his dismay that a detective was following him after coming out of the *Bande Mataram* office. Walking through Creek Row, Indraneel cleverly led the inquisitive man into the crowded Sealdah Station where he managed to give him the slip. But Indraneel was in a fix. It suddenly dawned on him that for reasons of security, the revolver that he had so impulsively bought could not be kept at home, for if discovered it might compromise the public image of his father and threaten the peace of the household. It also occurred to him that it would be unsafe to keep the weapon in the village house throughout the week in the absence of any family member. Then an idea struck him. But he instantly recoiled at the thought of exploiting someone's goodness. Besides, had he not vowed never to visit her again? Yet he had to get rid of the weapon fast. Although it would be purely selfish and mean on his part to imperil a woman's safety, there seemed no other option.

The following day, sad news was awaiting Indraneel. When he arrived at Hartukibagan, Shakuni informed him that Motimala had disappeared some time ago without leaving a trace. Indraneel also came to know that in her terrible mental state, she had repeatedly taken his name and silently wept for him. As Shakuni spoke on fervently, a dreadful sense of guilt gnawed at Indraneel's heart.

For the first time, he realised the kind of persecution that Motimala had been subjected to throughout her life. The irony was that while it had all begun with her physical abuse by Gourmohan, followed by an extreme act of legal redress by his father, it had ended miserably with his own rejection. He touched the bulging object tucked at his waist and cursed himself for thinking of taking further advantage of Motimala. That evening, Indraneel hid the firearm once again among his things. And, tormented by thoughts of his own insecurity and Motimala's depression, Indraneel lay tossing in bed. He blamed himself for his sudden decision not to meet her again, which upset everything. Indraneel took the solemn vow that he would find Motimala, wherever she was.

55

Life in Prison

The prisoners were taken to Alipore Central Jail where they were remanded to custody.

Actually, what lured Barin into confessing was self-glorification. When he realised this would be his last chance to publicly proclaim his deeds, he tried to impress Upen and Ullaskar too. Why not then avail this last opportunity and show the countrymen how to tread upon the path of revolution and pursue the task of preparation or draw the battlelines against the alien government? But later, Barin noted with some remorse how the inadvertent revealing of Gossain's name nearly upset their plans and threatened to compromise the fate of the entire gang. Barin's faux pas came as a rude shock not only to his senior colleagues like Hem, but to Aurobindo as well.

For, reacting in disbelief, Aurobindo was said to have asked, 'Has Barin gone off his head?'

Following legal advice, by the time the confessions were retracted, they had already formed the solid basis of the prosecution's case. And yet, had Aurobindo not left standing instructions with Barin in the event of their possible arrest? 'We live to fight another day,' was according to Aurobindo, a true soldier's motto.

After the confessions of Barin and his associates, Gossain was the first man to be arrested and brought to court. Under the circumstances, Gossain had to confess his role in the attempted murder of the mayor of Chandernagore. Thereafter, Hrishikesh Kanjilal, Sudhir and some others were also arrested. Finally, the three Sen brothers—Hem, Biren and Sushil of Srihatta—were apprehended. Following the new arrests, the preliminary hearing began at the Alipore Court for committing the accused to the sessions court.

Two police carriages drove up with the twenty-six prisoners. What struck the onlookers was the absence of any sign of worry or anxiety on the faces of the prisoners. They all looked bright, cheerful and smiling, as though conscious of their innocence.

As it took three months to commit the case to the sessions, which the government had earlier expected would take barely three days, it became evident that the case would take an inordinately long time to conclude for the political implications of the bomb case were immense. Right from the start, the Alipore Bomb Case assumed a great importance in the minds of the members of parliament as well as the Liberal government in England. Not only did the government have to justify dragging so many people to court but it also had to prove everyone's involvement in the plot to overthrow it. Therefore, the number of exhibits involved rose to over a thousand documents and objects, and there were two hundred and twenty-two witnesses and an unending length of corresponding depositions. The prosecution counsel, in particular, along with his team of assistants, had a tough time coping with the stupendous pressure that the case was generating.

Unwilling to take any chances, the government appointed J Eardley Norton of the Madras High Court, one of the most successful trial lawyers in India. Norton was assisted by attorneys Withal and Upton and public prosecutor Ashutosh Biswas. These four men were aided by scores of police officers, including a superintendent of the CID named L H Barton and the familiar Maulvi Shamsul Alam, at a later stage.

In view of the gravity of their charges, the thirty-four bomb case detainees were kept in an old ward of the Alipore Central Jail where they were completely cut off from the rest of the two thousand-odd prisoners. While most of the bomb case prisoners were lodged in groups of three, Aurobindo and Hem Das—the two men that the government feared the most—were placed in solitary confinement in an independent wing. All the cells were of the same dimension—nine feet in length and six feet in breadth. There were no windows but only barred doors in front. The bland, tasteless food, quite unworthy of human consumption, was brought in twice daily by other convicts. And while at night the prisoners were sadistically roused from their sleep with every change of guard, the prison siren wailed every morning to jolt them out of their restless slumber. As a result, the fortnight preceding the hearing in the magistrate's court became a psychological nightmare for all the prisoners.

Even Aurobindo, accustomed to solitary life, was finding it extremely hard. And so he entered his tiny prison cell where the walls seemed to come closer, eager to embrace, like the all-pervading Brahman. Being totally alone, Aurobindo understood why even firm and well-developed intellects broke down in such a state of detention and became insane. At the same time, he could realise God's infinite mercy and the rare advantage offered by these same conditions. He tried to meditate for long periods. Afterwards, devoid of human conversation and an insufferable listlessness due to absence of any subject of thought, his mind gradually lost its capacity to think. In this state, he suffered an intense mental agony. Aurobindo prayed intensely to God to prevent his loss of intelligence and, soon, the suffering lessened. Just as a child sleeps, secure and without fear, on the lap of his mother, so he remained on the lap of the 'World-Mother'. The sufferings seemed as impermanent as water drops on a lotus leaf.

He recited the deeply moving, ageless, powerful mantras of the Upanishads and tried to realise the basic truths of the immanent Godhead, God in every form. All this was the Brahman. As he went on doing this, sometimes the prison ceased to appear to be a prison at all. The high wall, those iron bars, the white wall, the green-leafed tree shining in sunlight—all these seemingly commonplace objects appeared not at all unconscious, but that they vibrated with a universal consciousness, and that they loved him and wished to embrace him. Always it seemed as if someone was embracing him, holding him close to his bosom. The manifestation of these emotions overpowered his whole body and mind. A pure and wide peace reigned everywhere.

Leonard Birley took up his magisterial responsibilities with commendable zeal. In the normal course of affairs, any case arising within the eastern suburbs of the city would have been heard in the police court of Sealdah. But it was entirely under Birley's initiative that the case was transferred to his court in Alipore.

The prisoners recovered their high spirits as soon as they were allowed to see one another when the hearings began in Birley's court. They chatted, joked and sang every morning while being driven to court. Inside the courtroom, they were made to stand within a fenced enclosure—about fifteen feet long and twelve feet wide—throughout the magisterial hearing. Finally, they were allowed to sit on the floor when it transpired that the hearings were getting too lengthy. Curious spectators and reporters covering the event for prestigious dailies were appalled by the high spirit of the under-trial prisoners, manifesting utter disregard for the outcome of the litigation.

A landmark event brought about all the happiness that the prisoners could expect under the strained circumstances of their confinement. As the jail authorities realised that the revolutionaries were after all not as dangerous as they were initially thought to be, they were transferred to a ward consisting of a large hall and two attached smaller rooms. Now the prisoners could move freely between the three rooms, the courtyard and the veranda. Very soon a pattern emerged and the large crowd fell into three distinct groups. One group followed Aurobindo into a side room, determined to meditate and contemplate; another group moved to the other smaller chamber with Hem. It was left to Upen and Ullaskar to entertain the rest in the vastness of the central hall.

Gossain joined the contemplative group solely to be in Aurobindo's company. But to Aurobindo it was clear that being faint-hearted and weak, it was impossible for Gossain to put up with the minimum suffering of prison life. Within a few days his father began to visit him frequently. Eventually, detective Shamsul Alam also started holding long conversations with him.

Significantly, Gossain developed a tendency to be curious and asked all kinds of questions to his fellow detainees, during this period of Shamsul Alam's visits. He would ask questions such as: Who were the big men of India? Who was helping the secret society with money? Who would now run the society after the leaders' arrest? And where were its branches? The news of Gossain's sudden curiosity soon reached everyone. There was a good deal of comment about the fact that new questions were sprouting in Gossain's mind following every visit from the police. One day, Gossain admitted to Aurobindo that the police were trying to persuade him to turn into a King's approver.

At first no one allowed Gossain to guess that his designs were known to all. He was so stupid as to be unaware of this and thought he was helping the police quite secretly. Eventually Gossain was kept in comfort with two European convicts as bodyguards. But one day, Norton dropped a virtual bombshell.

'I have the honour to apply to the court,' Norton solemnly announced, 'to tender pardon to Narendranath Gossain for his turning approver.'

The disbelief in the eyes of the accused was complete. When Gossain was produced before the magistrate, all the prisoners stood up in one body and listened in oppressive silence to whatever Gossain had to say. Although his connection with the police had become evident, his ignominious betrayal was unbelievable!

In his narration, Gossain spared no one—not even Aurobindo. Talking at length, he recounted how he had learnt about the existence of a secret society whose avowed leader was Aurobindo Ghose. He also revealed Hem Das' mission to France and his own association with Subodh Mullick and Charu Chandra Dutt. He described his aborted mission of the failed robbery in Rangpur and the planned dacoity at Bankura.

As a direct result of the approver's revelations, Indra Nandi and Nikhileshwar Ray Moulick were rounded up on the very first day of the deposition. Soon, one by one, Jatin Banerjee and four others were detained. These seven men along with Debabrata Bose and Charu Chandra Roy formed the second batch of the accused. However, Professor Roy of the Dupleix College, Chandernagore, was soon released under the French Government's pressure. Satyen Bose, who was earlier apprehended under the Midnapore Arms Act, was also hauled up at the Alipore Jail.

The jail authorities now realised that the space that the hall with its two side rooms offered was quite inadequate for sheltering this multitude of prisoners. Hence, they were shifted to a larger hall known as Ward 23. Here, all forty detainees were lodged together much to their happiness.

The entertainment in the prison now began in earnest. Besides, the more mentally engaging pastime of word-making, there was acting, caricature and Ullaskar's ventriloquism. In the evenings there was singing. The jail doctor, Daly had allowed fruits and sweets to be brought in as many of the prisoners complained to him about the insipidity of the food. As a result, Sachin Sen's father began sending sweets, mangoes and jackfruit regularly. The members of the Calcutta Anushilan Samiti also frequently sent rice, ghee and meat, which Hem Das would turn into *pulau* at the hospital kitchen.

Hem Sen of Srihatta often hid some food that he got from outside. In the middle of the night some of the boys took the food out and had a lot of fun sharing it with those who were still awake. Once when Abinash was handing out some of Hem's biscuits, he noticed that Aurobindo was awake. He stuffed some biscuits into his hands. Aurobindo chortled with delight like a child, then stretched out on the floor and started munching them.

Observing Aurobindo meditating, many others including Probhash Deb and Bejoy Bhattacharya started to meditate at night. Once seeing Probhash meditate, Bejoy took a palm-leaf fan in hand and holding it like a flute in the pose of Lord Krishna, stood before Probhash. 'Here I have come!' he whispered insolently. Pandemonium broke out! Probhash jumped up and chased Bejoy through the whole length of the big hall. Finally, the panic-stricken Bejoy took shelter under Aurobindo's wings. Probhash threatened to kill himself if justice was not delivered at once! So a mock court was set up at two o'clock in the morning! Ullaskar became the judge and Aurobindo the counsel for the defendant. The court began with Upen and Hem Das and some others as counsels for the accused, while the rest of the prisoners acted as witnesses for one side or the other.

Watching the behaviour of the boys, Aurobindo could clearly feel that a new age had dawned. That fearless and innocent look in their eyes, their carefree delighted laughter, the undaunted courage even in the midst of great danger were symptoms not of the inert Indians of those days, but of a new age, a new race and a new stir. Indeed, the boys did not care about the outcome of the trial.

Later, a strange phenomenon began in the courtroom. While the fate of thirty or forty accused persons was being wrangled over, ending perhaps in hanging or transportation for life, some of these accused persons without as much as glancing at what was happening around them, were absorbed in reading the novels of Bankimchandra, the writings of Vivekananda, the Gita or European philosophy.

Elsewhere, the trial of Kingsford's sole surviving assailant, Khudiram, opened with much fanfare. The teenager showed no interest in the legal proceedings expecting to receive the worst sentence for his wicked deed. Even though Khudiram pleaded guilty to the charge of attempted murder and expressed remorse in accidentally killing two innocent ladies, he was quick to reiterate his desire to annihilate the heartless Kingsford. Otherwise, Khudiram's indifference was so complete that he was often seen to doze off during the court trial. As a consequence, he put on two pounds during the trial!

Oddly, coinciding with the general merriment in the Alipore Jail due to the prisoners' reunion, the verdict of death for Khudiram was also read out in mid-June. Khudiram's reaction was so remarkable that the confused judge enquired whether he had properly understood the sentence. Khudiram then brightened up and nodded and smiled.

Later during the course of an interview with his lawyer, Khudiram revealed the real reason behind his calm. It was the message of the Gita, which had given him the inner strength to combat and surmount the fear of death. However, an appeal was preferred by his councillor before the high court, but as was to be expected, the sentence of the lower court was firmly upheld. Khudiram was to be hanged in mid-August in the Muzaffarpur Jail. Khudiram mounted the gallows resolutely and cheerfully and even smiled when the cap was drawn over his head. Thus a quiet and peaceful funeral on the banks of the Gandak brought a premature end to a dedicated career.

'Khudiram Bose was executed this morning,' wrote *Empire*. 'It is alleged that he mounted the scaffold with his body erect. He was cheerful and smiling and when his pleader visited him in the jail the day before the execution, Khudiram told him that he would die as fearlessly as the Rajput women, in the past, did on the funeral pyre.'

Khudiram's hanging, probably the first ever to be so widely publicised, was to leave an indelible mark on the minds and imagination of his people that time would not be able to erase or greater events dampen.

Although everyone was very pleased at the prospect of living together, Aurobindo was clearly unwilling to be in the midst of a crowd, for at that time his spiritual life was proceeding at a rapid pace. He feared that by remaining in company, this new state of being might suffer, or even be washed away. In fact, that is exactly how it happened. But then realising the greater truth behind the outward events, he did not understand that for the fullness of his spiritual experience it was necessary to evoke opposite emotions.

During the Alipore Bomb Trial, the national press was busy leading a concerted campaign against political extremism that was on the rise. Distressed and aggrieved by their gross misconceptions, Aurobindo secretly took up the cause from his prison cell and penned his defence in support of the bomb. He wrote four articles: 'The Morality of the Bomb', 'The Message of the Bomb', 'The Psychology of the Bomb' and 'The Policy of the Bomb'. Nolini, to whom his mentor gifted these articles, somehow managed to smuggle them out of jail. Fearing police searches at home, the person responsible for their safe-keeping had no other alternative but to bury them under the earth in the hollow section of a bamboo. And as was only to be expected, the valuable manuscripts were lost forever, destroyed by termites!

Aurobindo went into meditation in the evenings and before dawn. He never said anything, even if the boys shouted around him. In the afternoon he would recite verses from the Upanishads or some religious texts while pacing up and down for two or three hours at a stretch. But in the evenings he had to join others in their games. Sometimes there would be a mock court in which Ullaskar would be the judge and Aurobindo himself would imitate public prosecutor Norton. Sometimes, speaking with great lucidity, he would expound subjects such as the philosophy of British law and justice, the morality and immorality of anarchism, imperialism, revolution, the morality of political dacoity, bombing and political killing.

After his bath, Aurobindo would spend hours with his head on the floor and feet in the air. One day, when Sir Edward Norman Baker, the new governor of Bengal, came to their ward, Aurobindo was suspended in that pose with his feet upwards. Sir Edward reportedly remained standing there for half-an-hour without uttering a word. He left dejected when Aurobindo did not respond in any manner.

56

The Plot to Assassinate Gossain

Suffering from a bronchial disorder, Satyen had been kept in the jail hospital since his arrival from Midnapore. Being the indisputable head of the Midnapore secret society, Satyen was a man of method and deep insight. From the beginning, he had rightly foreseen that no part of the approver's evidence could be used against any accused till the approver could be cross-examined. Hence, uncorroborated evidence would be disqualified in court. After reaching this crucial conclusion in his hospital bed, Satyen secretly got in touch with Hem Das. He wanted to know if Hem knew of a viable way of killing Gossain. Satyen proposed to act as Gossain's accomplice and corroborator in order to get in touch with him. Being a patient of fatal bronchial asthma whose days were anyway numbered, Satyen took it upon himself to slay the betrayer.

At this point, Barin became obsessed with the thought of making a daring escape. Through intermediaries he sent word to his trusted friend, Indraneel, to come and meet him urgently. Indraneel, who had been keeping a low profile ever since the May arrests, was taken aback at being suddenly summoned to the Alipore Jail. He was even more surprised to see the big change in his friend. Gloomy and depressed, Barin seemed the ghost of his cheerful old self. After warmly hugging through the iron bars, the two friends stood facing each other in the little meeting room of the jail.

'Neel,' Barin suddenly whispered, 'I want you to do me a special favour. But first let me explain my plan to you. I'm fed up with prison life. I want to escape!'

'What?' Indraneel exclaimed. 'Are you out of your senses?'

'Of course not! Look, I've given it sufficient thought. You have to get in touch with the Chandernagore gang and smuggle in ten or twelve revolvers. As you see, importing things to the jail isn't as difficult as you imagine. I've been receiving money and letters endlessly from our associates at large.'

'Yes, I understand, but money and letters are not the same things as firearms!'

'I tell you, it won't be difficult! You also must arrange for a motorcar to come to the other side of the boundary wall just beyond the kitchen and the toilets. We shall overpower the sentries with the help of the revolvers then we'll make our daring escape with the help of ropes lowered from outside!' The absurdity of the plan was so bewildering that no sound came out of Indraneel's open mouth. Then realising that his friend seemed far from convinced, Barin continued in a more serious tone.

'You must understand, my friend, as things stand, we lose nothing by attempting an escape. As interned revolutionaries, our fates are sealed anyway! By the way, I've already convinced a friendly warder to deploy sympathetic sentries on duty on the fateful evening of our escape. And believe it or not, he has promised me cooperation.'

It was not said in vain that Barin was a dreamer who possessed the uncanny ability to realise his fantasies. Even though the whole plan seemed absolute madness from beginning to end, Indraneel could not dismiss the argument that attempting to escape from jail made more sense than tamely staring into death's ugly face. And if there existed even an infinitesimal chance of success in this absurd plan—he was duty-bound to come to his friend's rescue.

'All right,' Indraneel said assuredly. 'I shall do whatever is possible within my means.'

'Good boy! Here, take this letter then,' Barin said lowering his voice. 'I've written to my friends in Chandernagore, asking their help in acquiring arms.'

~

Finally, on 15 August 1908, Magistrate Birley took the decision to commit the case to sessions. Meanwhile, two pleaders of the defendants had applied for the cross-examination of Gossain. But Birley passed an order refusing their request. As the defence advocates felt that the approver could later be examined in the sessions court, they desisted from pressing the matter.

As a sidelight to the trial, a small but not so insignificant event occurred at the dock on Aurobindo's thirty-sixth birthday. A reporter of *Empire* who frequently came to the courtroom took courage and entered the enclosure earmarked for the desperados and took an interview sitting beside Aurobindo! Three days later an article titled 'Arabindo Ghose, A Remarkable Interview, Birthdays and Coincidences' was published. 'The Arabindo of Saturday was quite another being,' wrote *Empire*. 'His personality, hitherto grave and prepossessed, had been metamorphosed into one of sprightliness and sunniness.' The cause of all this 'jollification' as Aurobindo clarified, was to a certain extent remarkable. 'In the first place,' he explained, 'today is my birthday; and we are celebrating it as best we can under the circumstances. I was born on 15 August 1872, and on that anniversary in 1906 the National College opened its doors to teach among other things the principles of Swadeshism. It was either the day before or the day after my birthday, 1907, that I was arrested in connection with the first *Bande Mataram* sedition case. And more remarkable still my birthday is round again today and the magistrate has given definite assurance that he will commit on the evidence given in this, a case not of sedition but revolution.' Aurobindo's facetious parting shot to the interviewer was: 'You can add to those coincidences the fact that I shall be very probably coming back from the Andamans on my birthday next year.'

The following Sunday, Indraneel went to Uttarpara. After discussing Barin's plan of escape with Amar Chatterjee, the two friends proceeded to Chandernagore. Arriving in the French enclave, the two young men walked up to Charu Chandra Roy's house. Although Amar knew the addressees of Barin's letters, he did not know their house. Therefore, they thought it best to contact their leader. Amar was received with warmth by the professor, as he knew him through Upen. Amar introduced Indraneel to Charu Chandra and the newcomer quickly bent down to touch his feet.

'We've come on behalf of Barin,' Amar explained. 'He has sent a letter to Sudhangshu Jiban Roy. I think Barin has plans for breaking out of jail.'

'What? And he wishes us to help him realise this wild dream? Well, following my meeting with Aurobindo in jail, I'm now convinced that there's a streak of insanity in their family. Both the brothers are downright lunatics. For one, mixing politics with religion is the sure and unhealthy sign of a fermenting brain. And second, Aurobindo is a totally unfit politician to lead Bengal. I must own that men who come in contact with him are charmed and fall prey to his holiness. But unfortunately, his spirituality does not improve his politics! As for Barin, he too is unfit to lead. In a revolution one has to be circumspect. The police came across a notebook containing names of his party members. In it Indu Bhushan Roy Chowdhury was supposedly referred to as Charu Chandra Roy, as he was also known by that name. Just think, to leave such notebooks lying around! And how I had to suffer for his blunder! As for this jail-break—let's forget it.'

'Sir,' Amar said with dignity, 'please tell us how to contact any of these three gentlemen, Sudhangshu Jiban Roy, Shrish Ghose or Basanta Chatterjee.'

'Take these gentlemen to Shrish,' Charu Chandra shouted indifferently in the direction of the door.

Accordingly, Amar and Indraneel were escorted through the neighbourhood and luckily, the short boy of eighteen of Fatakgora proved more helpful than his mentor and promised to provide as many revolvers as he could. As a result, two revolvers reached the jail shortly. Out of the two revolvers that were smuggled into the Alipore Jail, the first one was brought by Sudhangshu Roy dissimulated in a packet which was handed over to Barin and hidden in some blankets; the smaller revolver was brought a week later by Shrish who handed it also to Barin.

The under-trial prisoners now got a long holiday following the commitment of the bomb case by the magistrate to the session's court. This was because some procedural time was needed for the new case to come up before the sessions judge. With nothing worthwhile to do, they once again spent their energies laughing and playing around. Sometimes they would discuss the final result of the trial.

One day Kanailal said, 'Forget any chance of acquittal. Everyone will get twenty years of deportation. But whether the country gets its independence or not, I shall be free. I shall not bear twenty years of imprisonment.'

A couple of days after this, Kanailal lay down in the evening complaining of stomach ache. The doctor sent him to the hospital after examining him. From then on Kanailal remained at the hospital where Satyen was lodged.

Preceding the arrival of the second revolver by a day, Satyen formally entered in contact with Gossain and expressed his willingness to depose before the court as a King's approver. For this, Satyen informed Gossain that several meetings between them were necessary and arranged to meet Gossain at the jail hospital. Two instructive encounters followed between the approver and his would-be-corroborator and the third and final one was fixed for the morning of the last day of August. According to an earlier plan, on the morning of the 31 August 1908, Gossain accompanied by Higgins, a European warder, came to see Satyen in the hospital. After climbing up to the first floor they reached the dispensary located right beside the wide staircase. Kanailal had pretended of stomach ache in the previous evening and had been allowed to be with Satyen. The three prisoners then went out on the adjoining front veranda where they began to converse softly.

Suddenly, a gunshot was heard and Gossain came running into the dispensary. Fear was written all over his face. 'For God's sake Mr Higgins,' he screamed hysterically, 'save me, they will shoot!' But before Higgins could react Kanailal rushed in like a panther. Trying to protect Gossain, Higgins was himself shot through the palm of his hand. The shattering pain momentarily disabled him. Meanwhile, as Gossain was shivering in the corner of the room, Kanailal took quick aim and wounded him in the hip.

Taking advantage of this confusion, the panic stricken Gossain and Higgins scampered down the stairs as fast as their injuries allowed them. Then on coming out onto the wide two hundred-feet-long passage, they tried to make their way to the jail gate. Kanai and Satyen also gave them a hot chase. On reaching the gate, the hunted and the hunters turned to the left where the passage led northward towards the six-degree cells. Fortunately, the jailer and some assistants were coming through this jail gate accompanied by another European convict, Linton. All except Linton panicked and allowed Gossain and Higgins, closely followed by Kanailal and Satyen, to pass them. Only Linton grappled with Satyen. But as Satyen fired a shot close to his ears, he was startled and looked up in horror to see Gossain spin round and fall. Satyen seized the opportunity and shot at Gossain. By now the frightened traitor lost his balance and fell face down into the three-foot-wide and the three-foot-deep open drain.

Meanwhile, the robust Linton wrested the revolver out of Satyen's hand and threw it away. Seizing this opportunity of Kanailal's distraction Linton sprang forward and held him. Distraught, Kanailal forcefully pushed the muzzle of his R.I.C. 450 Webley revolver against Linton's forehead, causing a triangular cut. The few seconds of respite that this wound caused allowed Kanailal to fulfil his mission.

He fired at Gossain from a point blank range. Then in a mood of suppressed jubilation, he waited to be apprehended.

At around seven-thirty – the time for the prisoners' morning stroll out in the courtyard – everyone was startled by the sound of unexpected gunshots from the side of the hospital. Finally, their apprehension became frenzied with the sound of the alarm and the wailing of the jail siren. Evidently, something very dangerous had occurred. But when an upcountry convict came running in their direction shouting, '*Naren Gossain thanda ho gaya*! [Naren Gossain is finished!],' the screaming not only felt like sweet music to the ears of the prisoners but strangely rejuvenated their flagging morale. But who had done it?

Meanwhile Gossain was rushed to the hospital. The attending doctors did their best but he expired within a few minutes.

The accused were driven back at gunpoint by a squad of policemen. After the ward was thoroughly searched, the prisoners were marched off to their cells. However, this time, everyone was lodged separately and their cells were changed every five or six days. The inefficient warders were supplemented by the gun-toting Gordon Highlanders.

The irony behind Gossain's murder was that while the traitor was assassinated with the weapons smuggled in by Barin, the other leaders thought it unnecessary to keep him informed about their secret plot. This was done with the belief that Barin would oppose such carnage within the jail premises. Even Nolini, the keeper of the first revolver, had not been notified of the removal of the firearm from his armoury.

And mysteriously confirming Nonilal Dey's earlier prediction, Kanailal had completed his twentieth year on the day preceding Gossain's murder. He was not destined to live beyond this limit.

57

Alipore Bomb Case

Judge Charles Porten Beachcroft woke up with the first song of the birds. He had a hunch that this day would be a fateful one. Now, in the middle of the festive season, Beachcroft had fewer cases to attend to.

Coming out onto the terrace from his bedroom, he took a deep breath. The air was fresh and pleasant. Looking over some smaller buildings from his Penn Road residence he could see the sprawling estate that housed the Alipore Court across the arterial Judge's Court Road at a distance. He wondered absently how his association with its hallowed walls had mysteriously combined with destiny. In a few hours from now, Judge Beachcroft would hear a case against Aurobindo, whom he clearly remembered from his days in Cambridge. Together, they had appeared for the open competitive examination for the ICS in 1890. They had not met since passing the ICS exam two years later. This, however, did not stop him from following Aurobindo's political career with more than mere objective interest.

This day, Beachcroft went out earlier than usual. Protocol forbade him covering even the few hundred yards between his residence and the court on foot. He however felt reassured to see that uniformed white sergeants were controlling the large crowd that had already gathered around the main court at nine o'clock in the morning. An uneasy hush fell as soon as his carriage came into view but the tension was quite palpable.

At nine-thirty, the prisoners were brought into court amidst tumultuous excitement. The crowd spontaneously broke into a Bengali song. The judge could only follow the melody without understanding its meaning. Just then the usherer arrived.

'Good morning, Milord,' he said politely. 'They're singing one of Tagore's recent patriotic songs. It says: "From deep within Bengal's heart, you have appeared today, O Mother, mesmerising our eyes with your radiant beauty; You hold open your golden temple's gate."'

'Have all the prisoners arrived?' the judge asked, duly stressing the word 'all'.

'Yes,' replied the usherer. 'The police have escorted them to the courtroom.'

The judge looked up at the wall-clock as it struck ten. The formalities were complicated and it would still take a fairly long time to start the proceedings. By the time he had completed these and got up it was about half-past-eleven.

'Oyez' shouted the usherer.

The whole court rose to greet the judge. His handsome mien and suavity instantly endeared him to the Indian crowd. The judge was only thirty-seven but his greying hair, a natural result of chronic illnesses, elicited a sense of deep respect. So far Beachcroft had carefully avoided looking in the direction of the docks. It was there that a drama now exploded. A loud thud and the sudden clanging of shackles caught everyone's attention. A panic stricken sentry was crying for help as a burly prisoner shook his cuffed hands threateningly above his head. The other prisoners were pulling him from behind, trying to prevent what could become a courtroom murder. However, the aggressor was strong as a bull and no force seemed able to stop him. He went on shouting and gesticulating excitedly: 'How dare he touch Sejda. I'll kill him.'

At last the prisoners gained control over him and the elders rebuked him: 'Sudhir stop, have you gone mad? Get a hold on yourself, Sudhir!'

Slowly everything became clear. The sentry, noticing Aurobindo's faraway, unconcerned look, had been a trifle annoyed and had shaken him up roughly. This had angered Sudhir. He had jumped down and would have hit the sentry with his chained hands had the others not stopped him in time. Sudhir's respect for Aurobindo was so strong that he could not tolerate the slightest misconduct against him. The judge, who at first had mistaken Sudhir's intention, was now touched by this sense of respect and solidarity with Aurobindo. The incident left a strong imprint on the judge's mind inasmuch as it was an unusual introduction to the prisoners.

However, one thing still puzzled Beachcroft. The person around whom the drama was taking place remained completely unmoved. It was not plain indifference but complete detachment that he saw on his face and in his general appearance. Beachcroft felt a strange mystical magnetism in this new Aurobindo he was seeing after so long. What had happened to him?

'Let the proceedings begin,' he announced evenly as a matter of routine as the court sat down to transact the day's business.

As many as fifteen barristers, pleaders and advocates appeared for the defendants on the first day. The most senior among them was undoubtedly Byomkesh Chakravarty who had been appointed to defend Aurobindo. Chakravarty's stature and fees were not in any way less than Eardley Norton's. This was the occasion when Aurobindo's friends missed Harimohan Datta the most. They remembered with sadness his friendship and brilliance. Not only would he have led Aurobindo's defence with authority and diligence, but would have been instrumental in guiding all the junior advocates in their arguments. But Harimohan was stuck elsewhere and there was no news when he would return to India. The defence team comprised another familiar stalwart, P Mitra.

In early November, the question of admissibility of the evidence given by the assassinated approver, Narendranath Gossain came up before Judge Beachcroft. Remaining characteristically unbiased, the judge declared that as sufficient opportunity was not given to the accused to cross-examine the approver, Gossain's testimony was invalid. As expected, this landmark ruling changed the entire complexion of the trial.

However, the judge ruled favourably on the prosecution's argument that although the withdrawal of confessions by the accused affected their value, they did not lessen their admissibility. Hence, these statements remained the main substance of the government's case. But what posed the biggest problem to the prosecution was proving the case against those like Aurobindo, who did not confess. Linking them to the conspiracy became a veritable ordeal as no evidence or record existed of their participation in any conspiracy. The protracted proceedings, therefore, rolled on through the entire winter. In all two hundred and six witnesses were cross-examined and a staggering fourteen hundred and thirty-eight exhibits were filed.

As the stakes of the case were much higher at the sessions court than at the magistrate's court, Krishna Kumar Mitra was working tirelessly to collect money for his nephew's defence, which was expected to cost an astronomical sixty thousand rupees. Krishna Kumar had judiciously published appeals for funds for Aurobindo under Sarojini's signature through the nationalist papers. Although the initial response was encouraging, the aggregate never exceeded the sum of twenty-three thousand rupees for which again the police was responsible. Owing to repeated searches at Krishna Kumar's house, the wealthy citizens of Calcutta desisted from donating for the cause of anarchists fearing official reprisals.

On the afternoon after Gossain's murder, Kanailal and Satyen were produced before the district magistrate of the 24 Parganas. While Kanailal confessed to the killing, Satyen reserved his statement. When asked by the magistrate how he had procured his revolver, Kanailal astonished everyone by saying, 'Khudiram's ghost gave it to me.' The magistrate had no difficulty in charging the two with murder and committed them to the sessions court. Although Kanai did not appeal against the magistrate's sentence, his case came up before the high court bench. The judgement was read out in the third week of October. While upholding the lower court's verdict of death for Kanai, the high court also found Satyen guilty of homicide and sentenced him to be hanged.

Prafulla's death, Khudiram's hanging and Gossain's dramatic assassination triggered off a sensation that had not been felt in Bengal before. The might of the bomb assumed a larger-than-life-proportion. Suddenly Bengal woke up to a new strength that spectacularly altered the psyche of the Bengalis and introduced an element of exaltation that upheld public morale. As news of the traitor's death spread, a thanksgiving service was held in a small village where women joyfully blew conch-shells to celebrate the victory of good over evil. The entire country was perplexed by the sudden change of mood in Bengal.

Unexpectedly, the death of the traitor also brought a respite to the beleaguered editors of *Bande Mataram*. Tested severely by a financial crunch, they now found themselves face-to-face with a decent solution. They adopted a defiant posture and wrote a highly provocative editorial named 'Traitors in the Camp'.

'No more shall the wretch of an Indian who kisses away the heads of his comrades reckon himself safe from the avenging hand,' it warned. 'Beware of traitors!'

As a result, the Government of Bengal ordered the confiscation of *Bande Mataram*. Therefore, instead of dying tamely in misery and in debt, the newspaper finally ended with some éclat and in all honour.

Sir Andrew Fraser, the outgoing lieutenant governor of Bengal, survived an attempt on his life when a young student took out a pistol and pulled the trigger from pointblank range. The defective arm missed fire. But it has not been said in vain that the Bengalis were deadly accurate in exterminating their own compatriots, even though they missed their British targets. Two days later, gun shots rang out again—this time in the darkness of Serpentine Lane. Nandalal Banerjee, who had been presented a cash award of one thousand rupees upon successfully nabbing Prafulla Chaki, was residing with a relative. As he went out to post a letter, an unknown assailant fired four shots and killed the sub-inspector.

Barely four days later, an informer and member of the Dacca Anushilan Samiti who had agreed to give evidence against Pulin Das was brutally decapitated. In both cases the police were clueless. Unable to catch the culprits, Viceroy Minto once again asked John Morley to grant permission to deport suspects without previous sanction. This time, a reluctant under-secretary had no way but to concede in view of the reforms he was planning for India, to be shortly known as the Morley-Minto Reforms.

Kanailal's execution was slated for mid-November. And on the last evening of his life, the warders granted him leave to meet his fellow prisoners. Like Khudiram, Kanailal had found the full value of his life after selflessly sacrificing it. It was evident that a sense of fulfilment had filled the hearts of both these heroes as Kanailal also had put on weight after he was sentenced to death. Barin was moved beyond words on beholding Kanailal's radiant face, bearing an expression of deep quietude. Kanailal stopped in front of Barin's cell to smile and bow down one final time.

While Kanailal was bidding farewell to his fellow conspirators on that fateful evening, Motilal Roy of Chandernagore reached Calcutta with some friends, following an understanding with Kanailal's elder brother, Dr Ashutosh Datta. Without wasting time, the men from Chandernagore went around buying items for the typical Bengali funeral, according to the doctor's instruction. After creasing the dhoti to make Kanailal look more refined in death, the procedure was repeated on the chaddar to be hung around his shoulders. As the young men's fingers kept working mechanically, the full irony of the situation stung them for the first time. They were preparing for Kanailal's funeral even though he was still alive. Hoping against hope, they expected the execution to be put off by some unforeseen miracle.

Very early the next morning, Kanailal's friends hired a carriage and headed for the Alipore Jail. On their way they met a newspaper hawker with an enormous banner that announced in bold crimson letters the sensational murder of Sub-Inspector Nandalal Banerjee the previous evening. Even in their gloom Motilal and the other men reacted with alacrity to the exciting news and exchanged warm looks of appreciation. The revolutionaries had struck again to protest against Kanailal's execution.

More unexpectedly, a welcome development at the prison gate brought instant cheer to their hearts. An overflowing crowd had gathered to take part in Kanailal's last journey. As the visitors' horse-carriage approached, cries of *Vande Mataram* rent the air. Dr Ashutosh Datta had arrived ahead of them. Motilal and his group were received at the gate by the district magistrate and Commissioner Halliday.

In the cell, they found Kanailal's body wrapped in a blanket. Strangely, the Irish warder in charge of the prisoner also joined Dr Datta in shedding tears as he broke down in front of his brother's body. While Dr Datta momentarily lost control over himself on seeing his dead brother's face, he was rudely shaken by Halliday's warning. 'Hurry up,' the commissioner said, 'the body can't remain here forever!'

Halliday once again intervened, as they were about to pick up the bier on their shoulders. He ordered that Kanailal's face be covered and forbid them to exit by the front gate. Halliday cleverly suggested the use of the small backdoor in order to deny exposure of the dead body before the vast multitude. He obviously wanted to avoid any public demonstration of sympathy leading to Kanailal's martyrdom.

But destiny did not let Kanailal down in death. When the restive crowd got wind that the body was being taken out by the rear gate, they quietly regrouped on Hazra Road near the intersection with the narrow lane and received the body with full honour. As soon as the cortege came out on Hazra Road, the sea of humanity unexpectedly engulfed it from all sides and the men from Chandernagore lost control over Kanailal's bier as well as the proceedings. It went from shoulder to shoulder as an endless mob surged forward to touch it in the midst of lusty cries of *Vande Mataram* that rent the air as never before.

One of the English sergeants accompanying the body was so overwhelmed by the public sentiment that he ordered the removal of the cover from Kanailal's face. A virtual rain of flowers started pouring in on the cortege from all sides. People came forward in masses to get a glimpse of the hero who had slain the betrayer and retrieved the motherland's lost dignity. As the procession inched forward through the more densely populated areas, housewives came out in overwhelming numbers on their balconies and blew conchshells. Even many European families were seen eagerly waiting to get a glimpse of the corpse. At places, servants openly brought flowers on behalf of their European masters to decorate the body. The unbelievable turnout carried also the tacit approval of the multitude for Kanailal's and Satyen's bold act of revenge.

As the bier was lowered after reaching the crematorium, people spontaneously lined up to touch their head against Kanailal's feet. This went on for hours. At this point, hundreds of copies of the Gita along with the heaps of flowers and garlands poured in ceaselessly over the body. The excitement began to die down only towards two in the afternoon—seven hours after the body had left the jail premises.

At last the pyre was made ready. And, the large amount of sandalwood brought by the crowd was set alight. It was kept alive for hours by the endless feeding of ghee. When the cremation was over, Kanailal's ashes were collected by the vast multitude of grateful admirers in gold, silver and ivory containers. It was quite late in the evening when the ceremony ended. The tired mob returned home with the memory of the departed hero, who first strove to free the country, but having failed, redeemed its honour.

Deeply shaken by the overwhelming response and public sentiment, the government took no chances when Satyen's turn arrived. When Satyen was hanged, the authorities uncharitably forced his relatives to cremate the body in the jail courtyard.

~

Indraneel's arrival in Deogarh coincided with the Mahakal Bhairav Puja at Baba's Temple as autumn was spreading over the Hindi-speaking parts of Bengal. But he was taken aback by the sudden change in Kusum's behaviour. He received a jolt when she refused to go out with him the next afternoon and for the first time in over two years he found her sullen and depressed. She finally agreed to meet him outside the temple complex but made it clear that the meeting would last only half-an-hour. She came as promised but Indraneel had a hard time making her talk.

'What's the matter with you,' he asked patiently. 'Did your parents forbid you to meet me?'

She remained speechless for a long time and avoided looking in his eyes.

'I hate people who are selfish,' she said at last. 'I feel so ashamed. I can't allow this immoral marriage to take place. It may ruin your life. I recently learnt that my parents had all along been plotting to engineer our marriage. They didn't dare to speak to you directly as you come from a rich family. So they laid bait and waited for the results.'

'What rubbish! How could your parents know that I was coming to Deogarh with my mother? Moreover, it all happened so spontaneously!'

'Actually, they were expecting you to propose to me in Chandernagore during the month of *Baisakh*. Doesn't it disgust you? Doesn't it reek of corruption? Doesn't it make you feel like being pawns in their hands, replete with the evils of betting?'

'Be what may,' Indraneel answered evenly, 'your parents plotted to make things happen only because they ignored my true feelings for you. They had no way of guessing how madly I was in love with you. The pleasure of spending a few days with you was too tempting to refuse.'

'I'm amazed! Don't you hate me now that you know the whole truth? Doesn't it bother you that my parents connived to make you assume the burden of their ill-fated daughter? I gave them a good piece of my mind! I even told them that it was ignoble on their part to dream of such a superior match for me.'

'Now, now, please calm down. I suppose it's every parent's wish to see their children happily settled in life.'

'My God, how noble it is of you to see it in that light! But don't you fear dying in case there's a real curse of death on whosoever marries me?'

'That's not the rational Kusum talking! But let me warn you too. There's a prediction prevailing since my birth that I shall cause a lot of hardship to the people around me but in spite of these predilections, I shall unbelievably be famous. Frankly, in the context of the recent developments,' he added laughingly, 'I wonder if my fate is not going to be akin to that of Khudiram and Prafulla.'

Kusum looked at him admiringly. This evidently was not the same introverted character that he had projected himself to be.

'I beg your pardon, but it could well be like that of Naren Gossain,' she suggested mischievously. 'There's no denying that Gossain will one day be as famous as his executioners—although for the wrong reasons.'

Indraneel laughed openly in appreciation of Kusum's sense of humour. He was happy that at last she had come around and was taking part in the conversation. 'I hope you'll grant me a year's time,' he pleaded sincerely. 'For, I have lots of work to do to avenge the arrest of my brothers. I'm now in the process of drawing up my plans and once this work is fulfilled, I shall be ready for matrimony.'

~

It was more than a month since Byomkesh Chakravarty had withdrawn from the bomb trial and in the absence of a senior counsellor the case could be lost. Although Chittaranjan Das, who was associated with Aurobindo in England, in the Anushilan Samiti and *Bande Mataram*, knew he had the ability to defend his friend, he was reluctant to ask for the brief on his own, without it being offered to him. But as Aurobindo's release was essential for the survival of the freedom movement, he felt that something urgent had to be done.

Meanwhile, Krishna Kumar Mitra had a vivid premonition of his pre-ordained imprisonment. Krishna Kumar was terribly worried about Aurobindo's future, as he was alone in supervising his defence. Chakravarty's turnaround put Krishna Kumar in a quandary. Not only had he to organise Aurobindo's defence in the face of depleting funds, but the frantic search for a competent pleader now became another burden. Besides, the police suspected Krishna Kumar to be an associate of the anarchists.

And then, the name of Chittaranjan Das flashed in his mind. Sometime during the second week of December, Krishna Kumar met his ex-pupil, Dhannulal Agarwala, who was already associated with the Bomb Case. Dhannulal was a partner in the firm of Manuel and Agarwala, attorneys-at-law, whose senior partner had met Aurobindo after his arrest at the Lalbazar police headquarters. Krishna Kumar judged it safer and prudent to approach Chittaranjan through Dhannulal.

'*Arey! Jayramjiki Mastermosai!*' Dhannulal exclaimed amiably on meeting his former teacher after a long time. The seasoned attorney warmly welcomed Krishna Kumar. Dhannulal spoke Bengali with a thick Marwari accent, often throwing in words and expressions in his mother tongue.

'Thank you, Dhannu. But I have not come to sit and chat,' cautioned Krishna Kumar. 'Are you aware that Aurobindo is my nephew? Now, there are still six thousand rupees left from the fund, and I was wondering if someone honest, trustworthy and intelligent could be found ...' Krishna Kumar hesitated. 'I thought if Chittaranjan could be persuaded ...'

The astute attorney came to a quick decision. 'Sir, you please wait here. I'll go to the Bar Library and be back in a few minutes. Now that the lunch break is on I'll be able to catch him.'

Dhannulal quickly put on his black coat and went out. When at last the attorney returned his face was gleaming with excitement.

'He agreed, Sir. He says he'll accept six thousand rupees on condition that whatever money is collected in the future would be given to him. He may be an inexperienced barrister but he has brains!'

The next day Krishna Kumar was arrested and deported to Agra. Viceroy Minto used this opportunity to vent his frustration at his government's inability to curb the political upsurge in Bengal. He deported not only Pulin Das and Ashwini Kumar Dutt, but strangely, the viceroy's eyes fell also on the familiar mass leaders such as Shyamsundar Chakravarty, Subodh Mullick, Manoranjan Guhathakurata and Krishna Kumar Mitra.

Chittaranjan Das threw himself into the case, tirelessly working till early hours of the morning. Although he had appeared alongside the senior Byomkesh Chakravarty since the middle of November, the case reposed entirely in his hands after Krishna Kumar retained him. Das' legal strategy was plain. While he challenged the legitimacy of the evidence, he endeavoured to prove that the allegation to wage war was the government's false imagination, and that, instead, each isolated act of terrorism was perpetrated with the view of redressing private wrongs. Chittaranjan applied for the censure of any dubious writing that did not match the handwriting of any one or the other of the accused. Barin's infamous 'Sweets Letter' was consequently ascribed to this category.

But the more the prosecution tried to implicate Aurobindo, the more unconvincing it sounded. All that Norton succeeded in achieving was to enthrone Aurobindo as the indisputable leader of the Bengal extremists. However to Norton's cunning it appeared that an evil conspiracy to overthrow the government had spread in Bengal consisting of *Chhatrabhandar*, the student's store, the two most seditious papers *Jugantar* and *Bande Mataram* and Muraripukur Garden, and Aurobindo, the ring-leader, was closely associated with all these organisations. Besides, the property at Muraripukur was partly owned by Aurobindo himself and run by his younger brother along the lines specifically set by Aurobindo in the Bhavani Mandir.

Earlier, answering the call for funds to defend Aurobindo, two students started from Maharashtra on their way to Calcutta. One of the boys, destined to become the Shankaracharya of the Saradamath, revealed that as the address for sending contributions was mentioned in the appeal, he along with his friend called on the advertisers. Aurobindo's asceticism had stirred them very deeply. After delivering the money raised for the defence fund, they enquired if they could be useful in Aurobindo's cause. The boys finished their errands as fast as they could and spent the rest of the day in the Alipore Court. During the period when the counsels for prosecution and defence were cross-examining the various witnesses, a longish brown envelope arrived at the fund collection office. The envelope only contained two full page typed sheets of serialised statements relating to the Alipore Bomb Trial and no letter was found inside. The boys from Maharashtra were entrusted with the delivery of the envelope to Chittaranjan Das.

The barrister was stunned on reading them.

'Who has sent these?' he enquired incredulously.

But the boys did not know the answer. In fact, no one at the *Sanjibani* office knew who had sent the envelope.

'These sheets,' Chittaranjan explained, 'contain valuable legal references that would have taken a minimum of seven days to find. Whoever has sent these is well-versed in the intricacies of the expansive Alipore Bomb Case.'

The two boys then went back to College Square and excitedly informed the others about Chittaranjan's reaction. In the absence of any other name that suited the account, the lengthy debate yielded only one probable name—Judge Beachcroft himself!

Following Gossain's murder, Aurobindo found himself once again in the same solitary cell where he had spent his initial days at the jail. His was the first one in a row of six cells called the 'six degrees', a little to the south of the 'forty-four degrees' where most of the other boys were kept. The separation from the rest of the accused bode well for Aurobindo as his *sadhana* had entered a decisive phase. In fact, the pressure had become so intense that he was sleeping only once in three nights. This was also the period when he received a deep insight into the all-pervasive Brahman, a state of the mind that allows envisioning godhead in every living being and in the most inert objects.

During this time, an army officer named Afsan received transfer orders to assume charge as a European warder of the Alipore Jail. One night, he had a strange experience during his duty at the jail gate. At around three o'clock in the morning, Afsan heard a series of urgent knocks on the wicket gate. As soon as he approached it, the head warder of the night round informed him in a chilled voice that the Swadeshi accused of cell number one of the six degrees had escaped. He further informed him that Aurobindo was seen conversing with an invisible person below the banyan tree. On recognising Aurobindo, the jail warder called him but did not get any response. Then he noticed that the door of the first cell was wide open and the sentry on duty was sleeping in a sitting position. Afsan rebuked the head warder for having quit his post and reminded him that he should have blown the whistle in such an emergency as per rules laid down in the jail code. The head warder acknowledged his mistake and ran back to his spot after requesting Afsan to follow him.

Afsan then ran towards the banyan tree where Aurobindo was reportedly seen. But he found no one there. Then he went to the degree gate where a strange sight awaited him. Inexplicably, Aurobindo was meditating within his cell, sitting on his rug, indrawn, unperturbed. Afsan called the accused several times but received no response. He checked the lock on the door of the cell but found it properly fastened. He scolded the sentry for sleeping during his round and also reprimanded the warder for giving him a false report. But the enigma remained. Who were the mysterious persons under the tree? Not willing to leave anything to chance, Afsan took his warder along and together they inspected the whole area within the jail premises. They also interviewed all the sentries on duty about seeing any suspicious person. But nobody had seen anyone.

Uncannily, Aurobindo's night errands did not stop with this first reported episode—it was only the beginning of a whole series of others. Afterwards, Aurobindo would often be spotted at night under the big banyan tree and his nocturnal escapades continued in spite of posting a sentry there. But on inspection, the prisoner would invariably be found meditating in his cell. Occasionally, he could even be heard conversing with someone within his cell.

No one ever succeeded in extracting an explanation from Aurobindo about these strange happenings.

However, as there was very little the jail authorities could do about it, the matter was left at that. But it gave birth to a lot of speculation. Inevitably, word went around that Aurobindo had become insane due to the stresses of prison life. Then the religious-minded Chief Medical Officer Dr Daly, who held the accused in great respect, checked him and concluded that he was perfectly sane—only profoundly obsessed with the praise of God. Ultimately, the speculations died down when the jail administrators accepted the fact that Aurobindo was not an ordinary being.

Even before Gossain's murder, and in particular since their collective life had come to an abrupt end, Aurobindo's *sadhana* was going on in earnest. He remained perpetually indrawn and contemplative night and day. But what perplexed his jail mates was his strange behaviour, veering towards insanity.

'Do you know what the night warder says about him?' Upen asked his companions within the cage of the courtroom.

'Apparently, he doesn't sleep and remains standing the whole night while his bedding lies folded in a corner. The jail authorities are worried. For instance, a warder has complained that he feeds ants, cockroaches and lizards from his share of the food. What astonishes me the most is the oil that drips down his hair. From where does he get it?'

'You notice only some small things,' Sudhir interrupted. 'Another time Sejda fasted for ten days. He lost several pounds but otherwise seemed fit. But what is worrying me now is his silence. He is withdrawn and totally unconscious of his surroundings. At the same time he continues to look upon the world with a childlike wonder, a happy smile perpetually brightening up his carefree features. And his eyes! Oh, what peace and tranquillity they communicate! Whenever I approach him, the comforting fragrance of a baby's tender body welcomes me.' Glancing in the direction where Aurobindo was sitting inattentively, he continued, 'You know when Chittaranjan Das comes to discuss his defence, he just stares back blankly. I've even witnessed the moving scene when the pleader broke down in utter despair and left dejectedly.'

To the others, Sudhir's emotional outburst was something new. His anxiety was becoming contagious and his fellow prisoners felt their throats dry up too.

'I'm really confused,' he continued. 'Haven't you noticed how uncontrollably he laughs during court proceedings, till his face grows red? God alone knows what he sees there. I can't bear to behold such a noble man like him wearing his dhoti above his knees like an ordinary labourer. Remember what happened during the other day's identification parade—he failed to move even after he was asked to. During lunch break, he unwittingly puts the puris, sweets and betel leaves all at once into his mouth. And have you noticed the present state of his fingernails? They're half-an-inch long at least. His hair and beard are also growing wild.'

Upen put his arm lightly round Sudhir's waist, sensing he was on the verge of tears. Then a hush fell on the group as they noticed a little movement from Aurobindo's direction. At first Aurobindo half opened his eyes, and to their pleasant surprise, looked straight at them. Were they dreaming? Wasn't there a faint sign of recognition in his eyes? Expecting he might need something, Sudhir quickly rushed to his side. Spontaneously the others followed and sat down in a semi-circle before Aurobindo. Sachin opened the conversation.

'What have you achieved in your *sadhana*?' he asked.

Aurobindo smiled sweetly at his young interviewer and placing his hand on his shoulder answered, 'I've found what I was searching for.'

'We were wondering about the mystery of your gleaming hair,' Upen said casually, 'How much oil do you use before bathing?'

'But I've stopped bathing totally—why should I use oil?' Aurobindo answered, amazing everyone. 'I'm noticing changes within my body as a result of my *sadhana*. My hair is now sucking out oil from my fat.'

'I've also observed,' Upen said, 'and even showed some of the boys in the courtroom how your eyes had once become glassy-still while remaining fully open. I've heard that this is one of the principal symptoms of a quietened mind.'

'Yes, one feels a perpetual calm,' Aurobindo replied after a short pause. 'And then one has the consciousness of the One in all. For instance, as I look around I see everything as Brahman. No, it is not mere thinking, it is concrete experience; even the wall and the iron-gate is Brahman. I see you no more as Upen, Sachin or Sudhir, but as the Divine living in the Divine. It's a wonderful experience! During the court proceedings, I see Vasudeva in all beings. The counsel for the Crown, the judge and even the prisoners appear to me as Lord Krishna.'

'Sudhir tells us that you fasted for ten days. But didn't you feel weak?'

'I can draw as much vital force from the universe as I require,' Aurobindo explained. 'I only slept every third night, and at the end of the tenth day I felt much stronger. I could lift weights, which I could not lift before, but I lost eleven pounds. My flesh shrivelled up, hence the necessity of taking material food.'

'And have you achieved any physical realisation?'

'At one time I thought that physical *siddhi* was impossible. But I found once after meditation that my body had occupied a position, which was physically impossible—it was actually raised some inches above the ground, what is known as levitation. Then again, I was practising to raise my hands and keep them suspended in the air without any muscular control. Once in that condition I fell asleep. The warder saw me and reported that I was dead. The authorities came and found that I was quite alive. I told them that the warder was a fool.'

'Ah, now I understand,' Sudhir cried joyfully. 'That was the time when the warder went crazy. He picked you up on his shoulders and started dancing wildly in front of our cells. But you were totally still. There wasn't a trace of smile or annoyance on your face. You didn't resist at all. It seemed to me that only your body, separated from your consciousness, was held on the shoulder of the warder.'

Everyone, including Aurobindo, laughed. It was a great relief for the entire group. Only Sudhir remained quiet, his eyes fast filling with tears of intense joy. He was silently thanking God for answering his prayer to make his mentor normal again.

Established in the heart of the European quarters, the United Service Club of Bengal was undoubtedly one of the most elegant clubs in India. It boasted of the highest number of government dignitaries as its members.

One bright morning, a couple of days before Christmas, as Philip Sergeant was sipping a dry martini at the United Service

Club, he accidentally met Arthur Wood, another acquaintance from his student days in England.

'Arthur, ol' chap!' Philip called out excitedly. 'What a pleasant surprise! What are you doing in Calcutta?'

Arthur stared in disbelief.

'Good old Philip, is that you really? How much you've changed! We haven't met for years.'

'Tell me aren't you posted in some district of Bombay?'

'Yes, I am the district collector of Kaira,' Arthur confirmed with pride.

'Fancy that!' Philip exclaimed. 'But wait till I introduce you to a very close friend of mine who has suddenly shot to fame. I expect him to arrive any moment now. In the meantime, what about a drink?' he waived Arthur to a chair.

Philip grew a little agitated as he caught sight of the friend he was expecting.

'This way Charles,' he shouted excitedly across the hall. A smile of recognition lit up his guest's handsome features.

'Philip, how nice to see you again,' he said, warmly shaking hands. Philip introduced Arthur to Charles.

'This is Arthur Wood with whom I was at school,' he said with a touch of nostalgia.

'Yes, that's true,' Arthur said, extending his hand. 'Philip and I studied together at the St. Paul's School in London, 1884 to 1889, to be precise.'

'Then you must have surely known Aurobindo Ghose in the same school?' Charles Beachcroft enquired surprising them.

The two men exchanged glances.

'Oh! By the way, Arthur,' interrupted Philip, 'Charles is the sessions judge of Alipore and is presently conducting one of the longest and protracted enquiries in the history of the Indian judiciary.' Then turning towards Charles he said apologetically, 'And, we haven't met since you took up the Bomb Case. But anyway, it was my intention to tell you that your main accused and I were classmates. That's precisely why I fixed the appointment.'

'Yes, I've read about the Alipore Bomb Trial,' said Arthur. 'I've been following it closely because of my personal knowledge of Aravinda Akroyd Ghose.'

'But, will you believe me if I were to tell you that Aurobindo and I appeared together for the ICS exam?' butted in Charles. Philip and Arthur looked incredulously at the judge. 'Now isn't that quite a coincidence?'

'I've often wondered how from that shy schoolboy Aurobindo could become the manufacturer of bombs,' commented Arthur.

'Well, at this stage of investigation it's indeed hard to say whether the accusation is true or false,' confided the judge. 'There's very little evidence against Aurobindo actually but that does not rule out his involvement.' The judge was lost in thought.

'You two haven't seen Aurobindo lately,' Charles suddenly resumed, 'But there's a very big change in him now. The look in his eyes defies explanation. Yet, I know he's unconcerned. And I wonder sometimes even if he understands who I am—does he remember me? By the way, have you ever read his political writings? His love for his country is unshakeable and he worships her as the Mother.'

'Isn't that a typically Hindu sentiment?' wondered Arthur.

'May be, but the poet Bankim Chandra Chatterjee preached it, and Aurobindo adopted it,' replied the judge.

'I think, Charles, you're being carried away by the romanticism of the concept of deification of the motherland,' Philip said dryly.

'Can you really equate self-sacrifice with some kind of vague romanticism?' Charles wondered aloud.

'Who on earth is laying down his life for his motherland?' Arthur asked in awe.

'All those forty boys,' the judge replied confidently. 'I assure you, they're neither afraid nor bothered by physical hardship. Their spirit understands no captivity. And even while their fate hangs by a thread, they're reconciled to their destiny—what will be, will be.'

'Are you then suggesting they aren't a group of misguided youth? Philip speculated. 'You're surely not saying that they've deliberately chosen the cult of violence as a faith?'

'I am,' Charles confirmed assertively. 'I'm even professing that they're fully aware of their doom. And knowingly they've accepted to follow the philosophy of self-sacrifice. In this path, they're led by the best possible man.'

'But fancy, being tried in court by a former classmate!' Arthur remarked with a hint of derision.

'Quite to the contrary, my friends,' Charles replied pensively. 'I feel as if I'm being tried by Aurobindo rather than the other way round.'

One afternoon, in mid-February 1909, as the unpopular public prosecutor, Ashu Biswas, was leaving the magistrate's court, an unassuming youth fired at him. Having overcome his initial shock, Biswas began running for his life. The youth caught up easily with the bulky advocate and placing his Belgian-made revolver against Biswas' back, fired another shot that pierced his body.

Even though the police constables on duty grappled with him, the attacker was able to fire a third shot. Biswas managed to reach the court sub-inspector's office and died within a few minutes. The assailant Charu Chandra Bose's act was more creditable because his right hand was deformed from birth. The cripple, therefore, had strapped the gun onto his bad hand and used the other to pull the trigger.

From the time of his appointment as public prosecutor for the Crown, Biswas knew he was a condemned man. On being asked to explain the motive of his crime, Charu explained that he had killed Biswas because he was an enemy of the country who conducted cases against innocent men and tried his best to secure a conviction. Three weeks after the attack, Charu was hanged in the Alipore Central Jail.

While political retribution was confined mostly to small riots and petty acts of vandalism in the northern and western sectors of the country, its manifestation had become more violent in Bengal. The sedition unleashed by the secret society was manifesting in almost every district. Bombs had been unearthed in Nadia, Midnapore and Chandernagore.

Two days after the public prosecutor's murder, Charles Beachcroft formulated the charges against the thirty-six accused. Norton closed his evidence in March and began his two-week-long elaborate conclusion. Understandably, the thrust of his argument hinged around the complicity of the most important accused, Aurobindo, the man who was possessed of qualities far above the ordinary run. His complicity would not have been in doubt had Gossain not been tactically murdered. It was hard to believe that Aurobindo was unaware of the unlawful activities being carried on at Muraripukur. Besides, a notebook was found at the garden with the incriminating initials AG. Then there was the compromising 'Sweets Letter' and another notebook with scribbling reportedly in Aurobindo's own hand in which the names of some of the accused and a judicial 'use of the stuff' were mentioned. Further, Abinash Bhattacharya, one of the admitted conspirators, was Aurobindo's home manager.

58

Behind the Scene

One day, Madhusudan Dasgupta's clerk brought a sealed envelope for Indraneel. Asking him to wait, Indraneel quickly tore it open and began reading the letter. As expected, the short note was from Kusum informing him of her sudden arrival and urging him to pay her a visit.

'Thanks,' he told the clerk. 'Please convey my regards to your employer and tell him that I shall visit his residence this evening after work.'

The thrill of meeting Kusum temporarily drowned the boredom that Indraneel had lately been experiencing at his office. Work had steadily been accumulating in the absence of his father and there was no news from him of his return. The letters sent to Martha Solomon's address had remained by and large unanswered, suggesting that Harimohan was on an extensive tour of America.

Kusum looked radiant. She informed him that the members of her family had gone out and that they would be back only at seven o'clock. After the servant served him tea, she sat down to talk.

'Actually, Pishima and I decided to come to the city to attend a cousin's wedding. In fact, my parents have gone to pay a courtesy call to my Mashi's family before the event. But tell me, how are you and how far are you with your plan to avenge the arrest of your associates?'

'I'm fine. Things are looking bright for the execution of my first plan in a couple of months. The implementation of such tall schemes cannot be carried out without assistance from others and requires extensive preparation and execution. And I'm glad to say that the measures are ready in both spheres.'

'Then you have formed a team of committed workers.' Kusum looked surprised. Earlier, Indraneel had never spoken to her about his secret activities. This meant that he was functioning independently, without assistance from Barin or anyone else in the post-arrest scenario of the rebels. She was quite amazed by his leadership qualities. 'May I know what you plan to do?' she asked candidly.

'There are two aspects of a revolution. One is the acquisition of arms and the other, the acquisition of money to fund further growth of the movement. First, firearms have to be procured and as an initial step, I've planned to raid a police armoury. Then I shall work out a detailed scheme to attack a government convoy transporting tax money. Unless my activities are directed against the government, alien rule will forever remain unchallenged in our country. So by looting arms and money from the state I also wish to strike a mighty blow at the foreign citadel!'

'Would that involve bloodshed?' she earnestly asked, fearing for his safety.

'Not if things go according to my scheme,' he acknowledged with a smile. 'I promise there won't be a scratch on anybody.'

Accordingly, in the district of Hooghly, an intensely trained and agile band of mercenaries was enacting a daredevil adventure. Ever since the inception of the Bajra Samiti, literally meaning Lightning Group, Indraneel had worked untiringly to train his young band of guerrillas, closely following the methods of Jatin Banerjee. Although Indraneel himself had never taken part in the Anushilan Samiti's training, he had often witnessed the instructions for the preparation of soldiers.

Judging that his revolution could begin only after the acquisition of proper arms, Indraneel had carefully formulated, over the months, a plan to raid the police armoury at Chinsura. With this aim in mind, he had befriended the middle-aged officer-in-charge of the barrack. Although small in comparison to the others in Bengal, this armoury held over a hundred antiquated Martini-Henri rifles, over four dozen unsophisticated .380 bore Osman pistols, besides a fairly large quantity of ammunition. But Indraneel needed only a few arms and some ammunition to begin work.

In the absence of a big number of participants in the raid, Indraneel had to depend on stealth, speed and co-ordination. Having matured his scheme after prolonged scrutiny and observation of the daily routine at the armoury, Indraneel came to the conclusion that the best time to lay siege would be around noon when the police vigil appeared to be slack. Accordingly, the Bajra Samiti decided to act on the day of Dol Jatra. Insisting from the beginning that unnecessary tension and bloodshed be avoided, Indraneel had asserted that the group's action be rehearsed meticulously, step by step.

On the appointed day, Indraneel moved in early, aware that the officer-in-charge would be elsewhere in the district. Feigning ignorance of his absence, Indraneel started a conversation with the dozen or so constables, whom he knew by their first names. The constables readily joined in the discussion, flattered by the attention they were getting. Indraneel noted with satisfaction that the remaining eight constables were on leave. At about 12.30 p.m., Haran, Khitin and Dolu arrived with a hand-drawn cart heaped with cowdung cakes, wearing labourers' clothes. A couple of minutes later Bhupati and Kailash came pushing a similar cart containing more cowdung cakes. Earlier, Indraneel had helped his boys to clinch the deal for supplying this useful item at the barrack kitchen at an appreciably lower than market price. As a result, this was their fourth delivery.

The armoury was adjacent to the kitchen where cooking was already over for midday and the place bore a deserted look except for the presence of Ataur Rahman, the lone, bulky sentry. While three boys were emptying their cart-load in a small storeroom beside the kitchen, Haran and Dolu surreptitiously approached the unsuspecting constable from behind. Dolu hit him on the neck and, as the sentry fainted, the two men quickly carried him into the store and locked the door. Meanwhile, using a small crowbar, Bhupati broke open the heavy lock at the armoury gate as noiselessly as he could. The distance from the barrack and other daytime noises from all around made the sounds of the cracking metal almost inaudible. Then, while the other three men carried on the unloading, Bhupati and Kailash slipped into the armoury facing the Ganges. They helped themselves to a dozen long-muzzled revolvers and two sacks of matching ammunition that they had been taught to select. They then put these in gunny bags. Bhupati and Kailash shut the door and proceeded to hide the stolen items under their carts where provision had been made to carry the firearms out of sight. The entire operation took barely five minutes. Soon the boys re-emerged before the unsuspecting group of constables chatting with Indraneel. Innocently pushing the empty carts, they halted momentarily and demanded to be paid.

Indraneel pretended to get angry and snapped back, 'Baro sahib is on leave. Haven't I given the assurance to pay you on Monday?' After the boys left with a salaam, Indraneel hung around for a quarter-of-an-hour, and then left for his village. Thus, the operation was carried out without any hitch, devoid of any bloodshed or gunfire from Indraneel's loaded revolver that was tucked under his belt.

To get rid of their loot, Indraneel had had a deep hole dug and covered with loose earth at a deserted spot below a banyan tree. After taking a detour to this spot, Indraneel's soldiers put the haul into a brass pot and lowered it into the pit, covering it up again with earth. They also destroyed all evidence of the use of their carts' under-carriages for carrying the firearms. Then the boys returned home, proud at the success of their first major mission for the motherland.

The robbery was detected at around two o'clock when a constable went to urinate on the bank of the Ganges. He grew suspicious at not finding Ataur Rahman on duty at the armoury gate and searched the surrounding area. He found the portly man lying unconscious in the storeroom. Then on discovering the break-in, he instantly sounded the alarm and gathered all the constables present to check what was missing. Meanwhile, one man called on the district magistrate to inform him about the robbery. But the latter had gone to deposit the money collected during the week at the treasury office in Calcutta.

However, with the return of the district magistrate, a search party was rushed to Seiya where Indraneel was waiting quietly. On being informed of the robbery, he readily led the police party to Harit, a nearby village and put it in touch with the five youths who were all found in their homes. Each one of them denied any involvement with the theft and gladly accompanied the policemen back to the armoury. In the absence of witnesses and Ataur's inability to identify his assailants, the whole affair was reduced to a farce. As a result, the enquiry had to be dropped at the instance of the district magistrate. Besides Indraneel's testimonial about the good nature of the boys, the deposition of the ten constables, who were the principal witnesses, confirmed that the suspected men had hauled away only their empty carts. Evidently, as in all such developments, a head had to roll and the officer in charge of the armoury was transferred to an insignificant post in a remote town of Hooghly to make him pay for the serious lapse of security at the armoury.

Judging it imprudent to stay in the city following the armoury raid, Indraneel decided to leave for Deogarh on the very night of his return from Seiya. On his arrival at Baidyanath, he was happily surprised by the festivities of Holi and Chhapan Bhog, traditionally held on the occasion of Phalguni Purnima. In Bihar, the arrival of spring is marked with fervour and rendered memorable by the endless splashing of colours.

Indraneel anxiously waited for Kusum as he had had no time to announce his arrival. But by the time Kusum reached the temple, her sari was so full of colours that it was impossible to recognise its whiteness. Holding coloured powder within his fists, Indraneel unexpectedly sprang on her and used it freely to smear her face. Protesting nervously, Kusum tried to resist him thinking it to be an ill-intentioned stranger. Her face grew radiant as soon as she recognised him.

'You couldn't have come at a better time. I'm so happy you are here!' Then growing serious and lowering her voice, she asked,

'And what about the attack you had planned? Did everything go according to plot?'

'Yes,' he answered while bringing his face near hers, 'it was a great success!'

Kusum peered into his eyes with admiration. Although mobbed from all sides, they strangely felt like an island in that mad melee of turbulence. Possessed by that spiritual frenzy, the revellers wildly danced all around them as the beats of drums, the clanging of cymbals and the melody of the flute grew shriller and louder. Indraneel and Kusum held hands as their hearts pounded faster. Finally, in a fit of spontaneous excitement Indraneel impulsively lifted her off the ground and turned in circles like the other young men were doing. The animation went on for hours. Tired and weary, they ultimately came out of their dream-like state as the celebration lost its momentum and stopped at the fall of night.

Indraneel then recounted the entire episode of the burglary. Midway, through his narration they left the temple and began walking towards Kusum's house. The streets were dark except for the silvery glow of the full moon, which delightfully bathed the town. Strangely, not a soul stirred although it was hardly nine o'clock. And no sooner had they arrived in front of Kusum's house than she whispered: 'Leave me here and go now. Can you guess what will happen if Pishima sees us together at this time of the night? I noticed one of the old widows of this neighbourhood ogling at me from amidst the crowd at the temple. I hope she won't report about it to Pishima.'

'I can imagine the situation if she does,' Indraneel replied while leaving. 'Take care.'

Leaning lightly against the railing of the steamship, Harimohan peered into the turquoise waters of the Arabian Sea. He was silently cursing himself for the thousandth time for being so selfish and letting his friend down when he needed him the most. The past two months had been the longest in Harimohan's life and their slow passage had caused him agonies such as he had not experienced before.

Earlier, after reaching America, he had visited Cynthia Solomon in Norfolk. Cynthia was the younger daughter of Ross Lewis Mangles, Harimohan's first guardian in England. Then leaving Martha with her sister, he had set off on a touring spree. He had practically visited the entire eastern coast of the United States, from Miami to Boston. Ultimately his tour brought him back to New York where he knew Bhupen Dutt had recently settled. Bhupen was advised by his well-wishers to summarily leave the country to thwart any chance of a re-arrest as the end of his imprisonment had coincided with the intense session of the Alipore Bomb Trial. Consequently, he fled to America and got himself admitted as a junior pupil at New York University.

As Harimohan knew he would shortly visit New York and was aware of Bhupen's address, he had requested Saraju in his last letter to send her next message at the New York University. Bhupen was extremely happy on meeting a former acquaintance from his country. The two men spent a very happy day together as Bhupen proudly showed the visitor around. Most of the seventy-eight-year-old buildings of the university were scattered across a squarish area surrounding the Washington Square Park, adjacent to Broadway.

Later, while leisurely sharing an Italian lunch in a way-side open restaurant, the two Bengalis got down to talking about Calcutta.

And the inevitable happened as soon as the Alipore Bomb Case came up for discussion. The news touched Harimohan to the quick as he was rudely shaken out of his ignorance. Aurobindo's prophecy about him being unavailable when he would need him most, flashed in his memory. Remorse and anxiety about his friend's predicament began to gnaw at his heart from the moment he heard about it. The biggest question that began tormenting his mind was who was conducting the case in his absence. Then he suddenly remembered that Saraju was supposed to send him a reply at Bhupen's address. So both of them rushed back to the University. As expected, an envelope bearing his name was waiting in the reception office. He hurriedly tore it open and began reading the letter. Finally towards the bottom, he found a reference to what he was so desperately looking for. 'Thakurpo's case has been dragging on for the last nine months,' Saraju wrote, 'and, we hope everything would be well with the pronouncement of the verdict before the end of the month of *Chaitra*.'

Harimohan made a quick mental calculation. If the verdict was to be delivered within the month of *Chaitra* then there was just three weeks left. But there was a much bigger problem facing Aurobindo. In case the prosecution proved him guilty and he was decreed to be hanged, the time for filing a challenge before the higher court might expire well before he reached Calcutta! There was only a thin chance of saving his friend from the gallows if he immediately started back to India. Reacting promptly, Harimohan booked a cabin on the first available ship for London. Then he sent a telegram to Cynthia and Martha asking them to pardon him for abruptly changing his original plans of going back to Norfolk before sailing to India. After this began the greatest anxiety in Harimohan's life! The long delay without any news from India was as nerve-wrecking as the slow pace of the ship. In London he was lucky to get a cabin on a mail ship which was about to sail directly to Calcutta via Colombo.

Ultimately, after what seemed like eternity, the steamship was circumnavigating the western coastline of India on its way to Colombo and would, he hoped, take him to his destination in a little over a week's time. But would he be on time to see his friend again?

59

The Verdict

Chittaranjan Das had been leading the case on behalf of his friend with deep commitment, method and aptitude. The counsel for the Crown was not finding it easy to counter his contentions. In the absence of direct proofs, Norton spent entire days trying to establish Aurobindo's connection with Barin, Upen, Ullaskar, Abinash, Sudhir, Hem and the others. Ultimately, Norton finished his address in the third week of March. A couple of days later, Chittaranjan began his address on behalf of Aurobindo. He used his adroitness to turn the tables on both the police and the prosecution.

Noticing some confusion in the classification of the voluminous documents seized, he added fearlessly, 'There is just another point about the "Sweets Letter". Your Honour will find that the number of the bundle was subsequently added to. There were sixty-four letters and only twenty envelopes.' By this contention Chittaranjan swiftly and conclusively established that the 'Sweets Letter' was a forged document slipped into the main bundle at a later stage of investigation. It not only glorified Chittaranjan's own case but inevitably tarnished the image of the police force by his insinuation—that having failed to obtain honest results, the law-keepers had stooped low and unlawfully fabricated a document to malign a leader of national stature.

After this, Chittaranjan rose to his eloquent best. Using the rhetoric of his formidable adversary of the bar, he managed to undermine Norton's contention by locking horns, issue by issue. He seemed to have become possessed by a higher will. His moving speech in the first person is a living proof.

'If it is suggested that I preached the ideal of freedom to my country, which is against the law,' he began, 'I plead guilty to the charge. But do not impute to me crimes that I am not guilty of. It's for that I came to Calcutta to live for it and to labour for it. It has been the one thought of my waking hours, the dream of my sleep. I felt I was called upon to preach to my countrymen to make them realise that India had a mission to perform in the committee of nations. You will never get out of me a denial of that charge.

'My appeal to you, therefore, is that a man like this who is being charged with the offences imputed to him stands not only before the bar in this court but stands before the bar of the high court of history and my appeal to you is this: That long after this controversy is hushed in silence, long after this turmoil, this agitation ceases, long after he is dead and gone, he will be looked upon as the poet of patriotism, as the prophet of nationalism and the lover of humanity. Long after he is dead and gone, his words will be echoed and re-echoed not only in India but also across distant seas and lands. Therefore I say that the man in his position is not only standing before the bar of this court but before the bar of the high court of history.'

Following Chittaranjan, the other defence counsels pleaded their clients' cases till the middle of April, which marked a record 125th day of the proceedings. The court then rose and the judge informed everyone that he would take a month to write his judgement.

The court reassembled again in early May 1909. Without even bothering to make a preliminary speech, Charles Beachcroft read out the names of those he had convicted.

'Accused Barindra Kumar Ghose and Ullaskar Datta,' he opened gravely, 'are sentenced to death under sections 121, 121A, and 122 IPC and they are informed that if they wish to appeal they must do so within one week.' He also sentenced Hem, Upen, Bibhuti, Hrishikesh, Biren, Sudhir, Indra, Abinash, Sailen and Indu to transportation for life. Six others were given between one year to ten-year terms of deportation or imprisonment. All the others were acquitted and set at liberty.

In Beachcroft's mammoth 354-page judgement, Aurobindo's case alone occupied fifty sheets. He dealt with every document that the prosecution had put up to extract a negative verdict against Aurobindo. Naturally, the prosecution's case would get a big boost if it could safely establish that Aurobindo, like its other members, frequented any of these places. But what remained to be refuted were the visits to his own residence, namely at 23 Scott's Lane. Das had masterfully pointed out that as Abinash resided there, the visitors in fact came to see Abinash and not Aurobindo. And the judge upheld this contention.

Concerning the 'Sweets Letter' the judge gave his opinion.

'The letter,' he ruled, 'is of so suspicious a character that I hesitate to accept it. Experience tells us that in cases when spies are employed, documents do find their way into houses of suspected persons in a manner, which cannot be explained by the accused.'

Another important document found in Aurobindo's house was a page containing a few scribbled notes, mere incoherent rambling.

It suggested that there will be success next time with the use of a 'small charge of the stuff' if the writer is present instead of trying to hide himself. Aurobindo contended that the scribbling was not in the book while in his possession, suggesting that it was forged later. The judge looked upon this piece of evidence as the most difficult point in this case.

'In Aurobindo's favour we have the fact that he has in the columns of *Bande Mataram* deprecated violence,' Charles Beachcroft wrote. 'And taking all the evidence together, I am of the opinion that it falls short of such proof. No Englishman worthy of the name will grudge the Indians the ideal of independence; no Indian of decent feeling will deprecate the methods sought to attain it. The danger of a conspiracy such as this lies not so much in its prospect of success as in its fruition.'

Earlier, Upen had enquired whether Aurobindo knew his own fate in the Bomb Trial.

'I shall be released,' Aurobindo had emphatically stated, adding that Vasudeva Narayana has spoken to him. As Beachcroft's verdict took everybody, including the government, by surprise, it strangely vindicated Aurobindo's prophecy to the last detail. Earlier, Aurobindo had also told Barin that he would not be hanged and predicted Abinash will return soon. Getting his opportunity, Sudhir had soulfully asked his mentor what he should do if he became weak and started to falter due to his young age while bearing the days in prison? Aurobindo's answer had equally moved him as it had all the others. 'Think of me,' he lovingly reassured, 'I shall always be with you.'

While imposing the death sentence on Ullaskar and Barin, Beachcroft had momentarily stopped reading and cast a closer look at the two. He probably expected the condemned men to swoon because of excessive emotion. Defying the judge's anticipation, Ullaskar publicly acknowledged, 'Thank you very much.' Upon returning to jail, the irrepressible Ullaskar laughed uproariously and added, 'I have at last gained freedom from all liabilities!'

Seeing Hem Das' reaction, a senior police officer felt that he was disappointed at not being sentenced to death. In stark contrast, Kanjilal responded philosophically, lamenting his deportation. To him it amounted to nothing more than a bad dream.

Forgetting their fate, everyone gathered around and unanimously acclaimed Aurobindo's acquittal. Soon the farewells began. As each one in turn embraced the prophet of nationalism, they realised how destiny had brought them in such close contact with this great man.

The following day, Charles Beachcroft proceeded on a long, well-deserved furlough. He would be promoted in absentia to the rank of district and sessions judge in full recognition of the commendable work he had done.

Meanwhile, embroiled in licking its wounds, the government pored over the Alipore Bomb Trial judgement. The government had, in fact, three choices to subdue Aurobindo. First, to bring a fresh charge of sedition against him or re-open the Alipore Bomb Trial itself by filing an appeal in the high court. Or, simply deport Aurobindo under Regulation III of 1818 without issuing any warrant. But each of these contingencies had its drawback. Filing a new case against him would prove extremely difficult unless he committed a decisive blunder. Some dignitaries felt that even if the Crown succeeded in implicating Aurobindo Ghose, the inevitable result would be to turn him into a myth. Besides, both the legal remembrancers of Bengal and Bombay were of the opinion that appeal against the Alipore Bomb Trial judgement would not be fruitful. Finally, Governor Baker himself backed out of the third option and wrote to the Government of India that he was against the deportation of Aurobindo Ghose.

60

God's Purpose

After their release, the prisoners came to Chittaranjan Das' residence on Russa Road. As news of the arrival of the freedom fighters spread, the women of the neighbourhood spontaneously converged at the gateway. In an unexpected scene enacted with nostalgic fervour and devotion, they sprinkled flowers and incense on the heroes while ululating loudly in the same traditional way they would receive deities. Interestingly, the first thing that the free men did was to dive into the pond at the centre of the holdings for a refreshing bath. The cry of *Vande Mataram* repeatedly rent the air. And while this memorable scene of impromptu merriment carried on for an hour, Chittaranjan sent his men to the market to buy dozens of new dhotis for the celebrities.

Meanwhile, the air of festivity increased as the women of the house got busy cooking a worthy lunch, the men's first free meal since their internment a year ago. The children also got their share of responsibilities. They were asked to clean the dozens of green banana leaves and earthen pots, meant to serve as plates and glasses. The long veranda in front of Chittaranjan's office room was temporarily converted into a dining space.

Chittaranjan sat down to lunch with Aurobindo. Appropriately, Aurobindo was the cynosure of everyone's eyes, receiving all the attention that he genuinely was wary of. Even the little girls, including Chittaranjan's daughter, Aparna, and his niece Sahana, were vying with each other over the serving of some special item to the most honoured guest. Finally, Aparna earned the distinction of serving a sweet to Aurobindo, an act that would remain etched in her memory forever. Similarly, Aurobindo's light and charisma remained engraved in little Sahana's heart ever since that memorable day of May. Sahana, who would turn twelve within eleven days of Aurobindo's release, received the distinction of serving ghee to the guest of honour. The lingering influence of this little service that she rendered was enough to change the course of her life.

Aurobindo's release was just as surprising to his countrymen as it was shocking to the government. So much rejoicing and jubilation broke out in Calcutta that at one point an attack on the European quarters seemed imminent. Sifting through the articles published by the native press, the government agencies found out that Aurobindo's acquittal remained their main focus for days. In numerous editorials, the local press had consistently acknowledged the nation's indebtedness to the godlike being who had sought to glorify the country by risking his life. *Basumati* movingly wrote: 'Who else has served the Mother, heart and soul, like you? Come, then, O most wise ascetic in tattered prison garb, let us fulfil our status as brothers by putting on thy golden person the beautiful dress made by the Mother. Come, O saintly Aurobindo, who has seen the Truth! Come O Aurobindo, who is like a God.' *Bangabandhu* professed: 'A change of scene brings before our gaze that Mahayogi lost in meditation. When the sound of the foot fall of that great man was heard at the solitary prison entrance, the prayers of the entire population of the country were, as it were, present there in an incorporeal shape to welcome him. Those iron chains have been converted into gold by having paid worship at the feet of this god-like guest whom the whole of India has paid obeisance, whom young Bengal worships as a sage by sitting at whose feet the present-day civilisation can attain real humanity.'

From Russa Road, Aurobindo went straight to College Street, where he stayed with Krishna Kumar's family. Soon Mrinalini and Sarojini joined him.

A few days after his release, Aurobindo himself sought to thank his countrymen through the columns of *Bengalee* and *Amrita Bazar Patrika* for the solidarity shown at his hour of distress.

Earlier, Amar Chatterjee had come in contact with Rajendranath Mukherjee, also known as Misri Babu to his inner circle of friends. He was the older son of Raja Peary Mohan Mukherjee of Uttarpara. Misri Babu had taken the vow of Swadeshi and got down to earnest work. This was the time of radical changes. Kumar Rajendranath was made the president of a religious organisation called Dharma Rakshini Sabha. In consequence, Misri-Babu's fate underwent the change that he had sincerely hoped for. Soon a mammoth meeting of the Sabha was planned in Uttarpara and Aurobindo was to be its chief guest and speaker. Amar was given the responsibility of bringing Aurobindo to Uttarpara.

Accordingly, on the penultimate day of May, Amar went to the *Sanjivani* office to fetch Aurobindo. Amar found him absolutely quiet as if in meditation. Soon afterwards, they left by train, arriving in Uttarpara around three o'clock in the afternoon. The old Raja

Peary Mohan Mukherjee and his son, Rajendranath, had come to the railway station to garland Aurobindo. After that Aurobindo was taken in a procession through the town.

Earlier, Barin and Upen had come over to Uttarpara and held a discussion with Rajendranath with a request to support their party with his wealth and he had promised to do all that he could. Now, Aurobindo expressed his satisfaction at the lead given by Misri Babu.

'God willing,' Misri Babu replied with sincerity and frankness, 'I shall certainly prove worthy of your trust, for I have confidence in myself.'

Of the heaps of garlands made of jasmine flowers that Aurobindo got at his extraordinary reception at Uttarpara, the biggest one was offered by Misri Babu himself. As Aurobindo left without the garland it was picked up by an admirer as a sacred memento. Misri Babu aired his anger freely. Fearfully, the culprit brought back the trophy the next morning and begged for forgiveness. 'Ask God to pardon you,' a subdued Rajendranath said, 'for I have already done so.' Had the man met Misri Babu the previous evening he would have received a serious thrashing. But the culprit was spared from any violence now because Rajendranath's iron hand had turned into gold. 'Yes,' Misri Babu admitted frankly, 'I can feel the remarkable effect that Aurobindo Ghose's speech has had on me.'

The historic meeting, which was attended by almost ten thousand people, was held in the immense adjoining courtyard of the Joykrishna Library, on the picturesque western bank of the Ganges. Aurobindo rose to address the meeting amid deafening cries of *Vande Mataram*. A hush fell on the whole crowd as soon as he stood before it. The audience was overwhelmed by the speaker's spiritual depth and remained in a state of meditation throughout.

'The year of detention was meant only for a year of seclusion and of training' Aurobindo emphasised. 'How could anyone hold me in jail longer than was necessary for God's purpose? He had given me a word to speak and a work to do, and until that word was spoken I knew that no human power could hush me, until that work was done no human power could stop God's instrument. I looked at the jail that secluded me from men and it was no longer by its high walls that I was imprisoned; no, it was Vasudeva who surrounded me. I walked under the branches of the tree in front of my cell but it was not the tree, I knew it was Vasudeva, it was Sri Krishna whom I saw standing there and holding over me His shade. I looked at the bars of my cell, the very grating that did duty for a door and again I saw Vasudeva. It was Narayana who was guarding and standing sentry over me. Or I lay on the coarse blankets that were given to me for a couch and felt the arms of Sri Krishna around me, the arms of my Friend and Lover. This was the first use of the deeper vision He gave me. I looked at the prisoners in the jail, the thieves, the murderers, the swindlers, and as I looked at them I saw Vasudeva, it was Narayana whom I found in these darkened souls and misused bodies.

'When I approached God at that time, I hardly had a living faith in Him. Yet something drew me to the truth. I felt there must be a mighty truth somewhere in this yoga, a mighty truth in this religion based on the Vedanta. So when I turned to the yoga and resolved to practise it and find out if my idea was right, I did it in this spirit and with this prayer to Him, "If Thou art, then Thou knowest my heart. I ask only for strength to uplift this nation, I ask only to be allowed to live and work for this people whom I love and to whom I pray that I may devote my life."'

By the time Aurobindo resumed his seat, the first stars had begun to flicker in that huge expanse of the eastern sky across the Ganges. The sound of tiny waves breaking on the banks of the Ganges is all that pervaded everyone's ears.

Renewing the special bond of love that he shared with his aunt, Aurobindo stayed with her and her three children after his release from jail. During this time Krishna Kumar was still languishing in the Agra prison. As Lilavati was suffering from a constitutional weakness, the family physician had recommended for her regular baths in the Ganges as a natural measure for maintaining good health. Lilavati would sometimes ask Aurobindo to accompany her as it was unthinkable of going there alone. Leaving all his work, even without as much as completing the sentence he had begun to write, the nephew would obediently follow her. Sometimes the poor printer waiting to take the matter for composing was kept waiting until Aurobindo returned after his aunt's bath. Aurobindo's sense of obedience amazed his cousin, Basanti.

Krishna Kumar's youngest daughter also recalled how on one occasion her mother put on Aurobindo's sandals and went up to the terrace for her daily walk. As people came to meet Aurobindo and he was unable to find his sandals, he had to keep his visitors waiting for a long time, but he soon discovered that his aunt had them on her feet. As Lilavati serenely gave them back to him, Basanti was struck by his composure. That she took away his sandals, she observed touchingly, that he had to wait—nothing of this ever irritated him.

This happy period allowed Mrinalini to once again share her life with her husband. Although she had briefly visited Aurobindo at the Alipore Central Jail a few times with her father, she had had to remain calm and composed. She had indeed not seen him close for a very long time. During this period, Rabindranath Tagore paid a visit to Aurobindo.

It was evident that the British had once again successfully curbed any semblance of a rebellion. Besides the nine deportees from Bengal, most of the prominent extremist leaders such as Bipin Chandra Pal were in self-imposed exile. Although Aurobindo worked hard to revive the past enthusiasm, even men like Satish Bose or Pulin Das showed a lukewarm interest. Even when all the leaders were jailed and some deported, he continued to hold his political meetings in College Square. In all there used to be about a hundred persons and he had the honour of presiding over several such meetings!

Aurobindo had the satisfaction of returning to his profession of editorship. In June, *Karmayogin* hit the stands. This English weekly review of national religion, literature, science and philosophy was edited practically single-handedly by Aurobindo. He not only wrote all its articles and editorial comments, he even published in it a number of his poems and translations.

A little over a month later, the Bengali weekly, *Dharma,* appeared. Aurobindo wrote most of the editorial content for this paper as well. But with time, Suresh Chakravarty, also known as Moni, younger brother of Prafulla who perished at the mishap in the Dighiria, Ramchandra Majumdar and Nolini Kanta Gupta, joined as junior contributors.

Earlier, following his release from jail, Nolini had once attempted to renounce life and become a monk at the Belur Math where Debabrata Bose and Sachin Sen had already found refuge. After being disheartened by Sarat Maharaj, he and Bejoy began frequenting their mentor at 6 College Square. Aurobindo suggested that they accompany him to Jalsuka and to the Surma Valley Conference in East Bengal and Assam, which he was scheduled to attend during the middle of September of that year. Aurobindo attended the Jalsuka and the Surma Valley Conference accompanied by fifteen of his followers to preach the basics of self-government and national institutions.

Meanwhile, Barin had managed to make Ullaskar see reason and a challenge was filed in the high court against their death sentences. Soon the rest of the victims followed suit. Towards the end of November, the high court delivered its judgement.

Barin and Ullaskar's sentences were modified to transportation for life, the same as that of Hem and Upen whose terms remained unaltered. While Bibhuti, Indu and Hrishikesh had their sentences diminished from life imprisonment to ten years, Sudhir's and Abinash's terms were changed from life to transportation for seven years. Three others also had their sentences reduced considerably while the teenaged Balkrishna Hari Kane was released.

However, following a difference of opinion between the two judges about the fate of the other four, the case was referred to a third judge for a final assessment. Unfortunately, as Ashok Nandi died around this time, he was the only accused who did not benefit from the re-appraisals.

Ultimately, Justice Harrington read out his judgement in mid-February 1910. While upholding the conviction of Biren and Sailen, he reduced their previous sentences from seven and five years, respectively. But he was to let three others off, for want of evidence. Out of the thirty-eight accused initially committed before the magistrate, only half had been convicted by the sessions judge. And out of them fourteen men were convicted to serve sentences. But the final eleven had been condemned to the fearful islands of Andamans.

'What is Aurobindo's fate?' was the first thing that Harimohan asked on reaching home.

And Saraju pleasantly countered, '*Rakhey Hari marey ke*?' [How can anyone punish God's instrument?]'

Not satisfied, he asked where Aurobindo was staying. Saraju then explained that he was living at his aunt's house with Mrinalini. Harimohan heaved a big sigh of relief on realising that the improbable had happened; Aurobindo had been acquitted of all charges!

As Harimohan's return to India coincided with Aurobindo's launching of *Karmayogin*, he got the right opportunity to atone for his unintended negligence. He donated freely for the launching of Aurobindo's two new papers—*Karmayogin* and *Dharma*. Realising that he had very little money in hand, he secretly sold the Gaekwad's pearl ring that fetched him a handsome price and offered the entire amount to Aurobindo. At least he had the satisfaction of doing a selfless act for his friend.

But he was surprised to see how much Aurobindo had changed. His aura of peace and tranquillity now engulfed whoever came in contact with him. It was the distant look in his eyes that puzzled Harimohan the most. Quite characteristically, Aurobindo did not show any sign of impatience or hardness of feelings for his absence. Secretly, Harimohan kept asking himself how long it would be before his friend would leave for South India.

During the final period of Harimohan's absence, his father had suffered a paralytic stroke that had incapacitated him completely. Gourmohan was now confined to bed. Like a dutiful daughter-in-law, Saraju was doing whatever she could to pull him out of his stupor.

Harimohan was happy to learn that during his absence, Indraneel had wholeheartedly taken up the work in the village and it was entirely due to him that the work of social welfare was proceeding well. This made him feel proud. One Saturday, after Indraneel had left for Seiya, Harimohan needed to consult a property deed that he had given to Indraneel. As the client was waiting in the drawing room he rummaged through Indraneel's belongings. Suddenly, his hand touched a cold object in the far end of the cupboard. He pulled it out and to his utter amazement realised that he was holding a revolver! Although he was overwhelmed, Harimohan quickly put it back. But the episode left a lasting impression in his mind.

Around Rath Jatra, Gourmohan suffered a heart attack and lay unconscious. By now it was clear that he had very little time to live. One day, Gourmohan suddenly opened his eyes while Saraju was sponging his body.

'Bouma,' Gourmohan mumbled, fully conscious, 'after I die, please throw coins on the path of my bier for the poor. That's my last wish.' Dropping coins for the needy along the path of the bier was believed to be the ultimate good act, leading to the deliverance of the soul of the deceased.

Ultimately, Gourmohan died at the age of sixty-nine, in early *Sravan* of that year. He had the good fortune of having his three sons, three grandchildren and one step-grandson near him when he breathed his last. As the bier was lifted by Gourmohan's three sons and Indraneel, someone suggested that coins would have to be procured for the last journey. This reminded Saraju of the old man's last wish. She ran up as fast as she could as the pallbearers waited. She frantically searched in her cupboard and suddenly her hand landed on a pouch that jingled softly at her touch. Saraju pulled it out and opened to see whether there were enough coins in it. Although it vaguely reminded her of something, she could not entirely recall what it was. She ran down and handed the pouch to one of her nephews-in-law.

Destiny had clearly overtaken old Gourmohan in his death. For the money meant to ensure his edict of exterminating Saraju was uncannily being used for paving his own way to heaven.

A fortnight later, Harimohan sat chatting with Saraju after breakfast. 'There's a big surprise for you,' she eagerly informed. 'Can you guess what it is? I'll give you a hint. It's something that'll make you and me equally happy.'

'I've guessed it,' Harimohan said, looking towards Indraneel who quickly hid his face behind the newspaper. 'Now, who found the girl, you or Neel?'

'It's he. But I must admit that the boy has taste. Your would-be daughter-in-law is the offspring of an advocate living in North Calcutta's Simla area. She's so pretty that you'd think she's Goddess Lakshmi incarnate!'

'She's the daughter of Advocate Madhusudan Dasgupta of the city civil court,' Indraneel intervened for the first time. 'He knows you well. Theirs is the big house at the junction of Cornwallis Street and Maniktala Spur, the one with a handsome portico on the northwestern corner of Cornwallis Street.'

'I gather you knew her for a couple of years before my departure,' Harimohan commented, feigning surprise, 'and we were not even informed about it!' Saraju laughed merrily as Indraneel got up and left the room to avoid further embarrassment.

'Now that we're alone,' Harimohan said, bringing down his voice, 'tell me all that you know about this girl. I can see that you too have fallen under her spell. Doesn't she have any defect?'

'Doesn't even the moon have blemishes? Is there anyone in the world without a single defect? On the other hand, the girl has a lot of character. On the whole, I feel she's the person to make Neel happy. I found her smart, elegant and intelligent.'

'How did the affair begin?'

'Neel told me that they met on the day of the great deluge. In fact, it was in her house that he stayed the night. Then they accidentally met again in Deogarh when Neel took those medicines for Thakurpo. Apparently, it was love at first sight for him and it was he who kept up the connection after that.'

'But how eager is our son to get married?'

'He hasn't yet asked me to fix the date of wedding, if that's what you mean.'

'You must understand that I need some time to arrange things. My long absence from office has completely dried up the flow of money. And I need some time to revive my income. So in case Neel approaches you about arranging dates ask him to speak directly to me. I don't think such a big event can take place for a year.'

61

Going South

In July, Aurobindo met S Parthasarathi Iyengar who explained to him the nationalist movement in South India, emphasising that they were publishing the Tamil weekly *India* in the politically safe French enclave of Pondicherry because the journal had been prosecuted in Madras.

As a personal rapport developed between Parthasarathi and Aurobindo, the Madrasi began teaching Tamil to the Bengali. The lessons were given in one of the rooms at the *Karmayogin*'s office. Aurobindo soon realised that the shortcoming of the Tamil alphabet lay in its small number of letters. This further meant that Tamil has only the first and the last letters in each of the first five groups of Sanskrit consonants and did not seem to recognise in its alphabet the existence of the other three, nor did it have the conjunct consonants. Aurobindo immediately realised the potential for mischief and he eagerly looked for a name to suit his prank. He settled on the name of one of his associates. Then beaming like a school boy of fourteen, he comically asked his companions, 'Do you know what is *Pirentir Nat Tattakopta*?' Naturally, everyone was left speechless in their ignorance. Then after a hearty laugh,

Aurobindo explained, 'That is how Birendra Nath Datta Gupta is pronounced in Tamil!'

In the beginning of September, Rangacharya, a correspondent of *India*, visited the *Sanjibani* office and interviewed Aurobindo, mainly on his spiritual experiences in jail. Aurobindo spoke at length on his jail life and made some remarkable prophecies. These predictions dealt with upheavals, which would be one of a revolutionary change following the end of five thousand years of Kaliyuga, the Dark Age, three years earlier, in 1906. 'The upheaval will have developed well enough to be visible to all,' Aurobindo declared.

Intriguingly, Aurobindo cast his own horoscope after learning Indian astrology. He also revealed that the dynamic planetary combinations of the horoscope made it the most remarkable yet possessed in this *yuga*. He further predicted that because of some of the occult planetary combinations, death by old age became impossible.

More than seven years had passed in Ayanar Gounder's life since that fateful night at Kodiyalam Iyengar's ancestral house. Although he was now in his early eighties, he still looked just as energetic and healthy as before. In fact, his remarkable physical fitness enabled him to travel to Tanjore in late September to attend a family wedding.

Coincidentally, Gounder also went to pay homage to the century-old temple where Harimohan and Saraju had earlier met the Kodiyalam Iyengars. It was while offering his obeisance to the deity that old Gounder received the divine command to visit the other three Shaivaite shrines around Tanjore. Accordingly, Gounder and his retinue set off on a pilgrimage. But the simple journey was fated to culminate in a far more significant event. The seed of this uncanny happening was sown at the Brihadishwara's imposing outer gateway, where traditionally an elephant stands to bless devotees in exchange for a few coins. Just as the elephant's trunk touched Gounder's head and he gave the animal a pice, the old man's attention was drawn by a young newspaper vendor's shouts. 'Apocalypse!' he was screaming, '*Mahapralaya* predicted by ascetic!' As Gounder's curiosity was aroused, he impulsively bought a copy of *India* from the boy. However, Gounder did not have time to read the paper then but remembered to take it with him on his long and arduous trek. It was on the evening of the second day, surrounded by the delicately carved sculptures of the Airavateshwara Temple of Darasuram in Kumbakonam that Gounder asked Elangovan, his grandson, to read out the interesting article predicting the *mahapralaya*.

The young man leafed through the copy of *India* and began reading the article named, '*Sriman Aravinda Ghosetan sampakshanei*', meaning 'A conversation with Sriman Aravinda Ghose'. He glanced at the older man relaxing on the granite floor under the cool shade of the chariot-shaped pulpit, the carved pillars of which depicted the familiar events of Lord Shiva's marriage to Parvati. 'A few days ago,' Elangovan read, 'one of our correspondents went to Calcutta and spoke to *Mahajnani* Sriman Aravinda Ghose on several topics. On seeing him our correspondent could only wonder, "Is this the Yogi born to redeem us through an upheaval, showing a new way to India?"'

Old Gounder's eyes opened wide as he sat up with an agility that astonished his grandson.

'Will you read that again,' he impatiently asked.

The reader fumbled as he tried to find the passage once again and read it out. 'It was when he saw the eyes that our correspondent felt reassured. Oh! How knowing those eyes were! What grace in them! What peace! *Mahashanti! Mahashanti!*'

Then noticing his grandfather's excitement, Elangovan could not help asking him, '*Ungalakkey avarei theriyooma?* [Do you know him?]'

Gounder smiled significantly. His eyes had become moist with unshed tears of joy as he remembered Kodiyalam Vasudeva Iyengar's description of the Uttara Yogi of whom he had dreamt. 'Although his eyes smouldered with the fire of power, nobility and chastity, his face bore an expression of limitless compassion,' he had said.

'Yes, indeed,' Gounder spoke with eyes half-closed, 'it seems as if I have known him for ages! But don't stop. Please read on.'

'Our correspondent,' continued the grandson, 'asked a few questions about the Narayana darshan, which Aravinda Babu had experienced when he was in prison. But when he listened to his reply, all his doubts vanished. When our correspondent saw the humility, the peace, the solemnity, the innocence and the light that appeared on his face when he answered, it was very clear to him that he was indeed a *Mahasiddha*. Aravinda Babu continued to answer with great grace: "There will be an upheaval. The year 1906 completes 5,000 years of Kaliyuga, and a new age has begun with the year 1907. The upheaval will have advanced well enough to be visible to all. It will be complete in a further period of four to five years. The upheaval will be one of a revolutionary change, a great step; the low will be raised and the high brought down. There will be change, change, everywhere—change in government, change in our people; new resolves, new thoughts, new ways for all actions.'"

After the reading was over, Gounder sat still for a few minutes. Then he got up and slowly walked towards the sanctum sanctorum. In a trance-like state, he bowed respectfully from outside Lord Airavateshwara's chamber and rang the big brass bell, marking the end of his prayer. Immediately after that he re-assembled his family members and to the dismay of the ladies and children, announced his decision to send them off to Ariyalur, along with his son and nephew. He explained that he had received a higher 'command' to proceed at once on an even more significant pilgrimage. Taking along only Elangovan, he set off for an unknown destination.

A strange sense of fulfilment had taken over Gounder. It was as if the great wheel of time had come full circle and the all-important event that he had been waiting for had arrived at last. He could tangibly feel the fulfilment of the epoch-making event predicted thirty-nine years earlier to be hardly days or months away. Suddenly, the old man's heart pounded with a new passion. Like Iyengar, he too wanted to behold the Uttara Yogi with his own eyes. Would destiny grant him that rare opportunity?

But before that Ayanar Gounder had one last duty left. When he reached Kodiyalam, he was informed that Vasudeva Iyengar had died three years earlier. The zamindar's two sons had grown up, Rangaswami was now twenty-two and Srinivasa, twenty. The two men instantly recognised Gounder and took him and Elangovan in, overwhelming the old man with their warm hospitality. After a short rest Gounder went to meet the brothers again.

'I find it hard to conceal my joy in sharing a secret with you,' he began. 'I think I've identified the Uttara Yogi!'

The two brothers quickly exchanged looks but said nothing. Gounder handed over the precious copy of *India* he had brought along. The old man felt deeply rewarded as they read the article with great concentration and interest.

'We thank you for this illuminating article,' said Rangaswami. 'In the beginning we were not sure who you had identified as the Uttara Yogi, but as soon as we read the title of the article we understood that you too, had come to the same conclusion that we have reached. We have been aware of the Uttara Yogi's identity for more than a year now.'

Then noticing the bewilderment on Gounder's face, Rangaswami promptly asked, 'I guess you haven't heard about the Alipore Bomb Trial?'

'No,' admitted the old man. 'But let not my ignorance stand in the way. Please tell me all about it.'

Briefly, the two brothers informed Gounder about the charges brought against Aurobindo and the final outcome of the trial. Then they explained the most poignant part of the story of how Aurobindo's personal letters to his wife, seized by the police during his arrest, were unexpectedly made public. These intimate letters were written in Bengali and were obviously meant to be secret but saw the light of the day only through the happy stroke of destiny. For, had these letters not been made public, Aurobindo's deep mysticism and an important side of his nature, which had to culminate in his great spiritual work, could not have become known to others.

'In a long letter of August 1905,' Rangaswami elaborated, 'Aurobindo had touched upon the important subject of undertaking spiritual life.' Then taking the copy of the paper that had published Aurobindo's letters out of an iron safe, Rangaswami read it out with feeling. He covered point by point all the three madnesses of Aurobindo as explained to Mrinalini and looked up to see the old man's reaction.

'But these are the very three utterances that were predicted!' Gounder exclaimed.

'Indeed, they are,' agreed the brothers. The two younger men were thrilled by the older man's excitement. 'We arrived at the same conclusion on learning about the three madnesses. And, quite expectedly, Aurobindo's mysticism has made a deep impact on the public mind. I am sure that no reader has previously read such a moving correspondence between husband and wife. The *India* interview also confirmed that he is indeed the Yogi who will show us the path of salvation. Do you realise,' Rangaswami exclaimed, suddenly struck by a new thought, 'he's a freedom fighter too! Don't you remember what the Nagai Swami said?'

'Oh yes!' recalled Gounder. '"He will not only deliver India from the bondage of colonialism but free the world from the darkness of the Kaliyuga."'

'My God, I can't believe it's happening at last,' said the shy Srinivasa. 'We knew all through that the Swami's predictions could not be false.'

'And what is stopping you now from getting in touch with Aurobindo Ghose?'

'We already have done so, Sir. You'll be pleased to know that we have established contact with him through an agent named Sir Sharma of Mavoor, who is a great Kali devotee and who lives in Calcutta. I shall give you his address.'

'I am planning to go to Calcutta to meet Aurobindo Ghose personally and request him to come here.' The two Iyengar brothers were stunned by Gounder's disclosure. 'However,' continued the old man, 'when I left my village I had no plans to come here or go to Calcutta. So I have to go back there first.'

'There's no hurry. But we shall be glad to do whatever we can for your noble endeavour. However, do you realise the odds? You have to cover a distance of fifteen hundred miles to reach there. I mean, is it wise for someone of your age?'

'God shall be my guide and look after me,' countered Gounder. 'I would much rather pass away nobly, trying to meet Him, than die an ordinary man's death doing nothing for my own salvation.'

Rangaswami got up abruptly and disappeared inside the house. He returned a little later holding an envelope and a piece of paper.

'Here,' he said respectfully, placing the little card on which there were two addresses. One was of Sir Sharma, the other Harimohan Datta. Rangaswami reverentially placed the envelope at Gounder's feet.

'Please accept these five hundred rupees as expenses,' he said. 'You don't have to repay me. Promise me only one thing: bring the Uttara Yogi to the land where he belongs.'

One morning towards the end of November 1909, a distinguished member of the British Parliament and later the first Labour prime minister of Great Britain, James Ramsay MacDonald and his wife called on Aurobindo at 6 College Square, during a visit to India.

'I called on one whose name is on every lip as a wild extremist across whose path the shadow of the hangman falls,' recalled MacDonald. 'He talked of things, which troubled the soul of man. He was far more a mystic than a politician who saw India seated on a temple throne. The *Matri Puja*—the worship of the Mother—had become a political rite. For, there was no India without its faith and no faith without India.'

As repression by the government continued almost unabated, Aurobindo saw little hope of carrying out his ideas. He thought it necessary to proclaim the broad lines along which the nationalists must continue to work in case he should be imprisoned. Following fresh rumours of his arrest, he wrote a signed article in *Karmayogin* titled, 'An Open Letter to My Countrymen' with this aim in mind. But as the government was determined to get rid of Aurobindo, the only considerable obstacle left to the success of their repressive policy, they decided to deport him following their inability to prosecute him.

When Nivedita came to know about this nefarious conspiracy, she advised Aurobindo to leave British India and work from outside. Following this pointer, Aurobindo contented himself with publishing another signed article in which he wrote about the government's design to deport him and he consciously left the nation what he called his last will and testament. He foresaw the possibility of outplaying the government and its idea of deportation by exposing the malevolent plan. And that is precisely what happened.

Leaving aside their option to deport him, the administration had to wait for some opportunity to prosecute him for sedition. Following the publication on Christmas day of Aurobindo's second signed article reviewing the political situation, the government belatedly swung into action even though the editorial was moderate.

Towards the end of January 1910, another sensational drama was enacted in the heart of the high court at Calcutta. Inspector Shamsul Alam had been proudly involved in steering the Alipore Appeal Reference. Judge Jenkins had earlier commended his industry and perseverance in mastering the details of the case.

As Alam stepped out of the courtroom and emerged onto the spacious veranda, a young man named Birendra Nath Datta Gupta leapt out of the usual crowd and shot Alam in the back. As the unpopular detective tumbled down the steps fatally wounded, Biren quickly strode down into the sprawling courtyard and made a desperate dash for the exit. He fired wildly on being surrounded by mounted policemen. As expected, he was soon overpowered and arrested.

In the mean time, Satish Sarkar, an accomplice who had taken upon himself the task of identifying the detective, managed to run away to safety. And for his brave exploit, Satish was soon to be nicknamed *Kanistha Papistha*—Junior Sinner—by his party colleagues! Satish called on Bagha Jyotin and reported to him the success of their mission. Then on Jyotin's instruction, he also called on Aurobindo at Shyampukur Lane and briefed him before leaving Calcutta.

As an interesting sidelight to the Shamsul Alam murder case, the venerable Surendranath Banerjea, who traditionally kept aloof from the violent agenda, dropped his mask momentarily when news of the murder reached his office. The old Congressman surprised everyone by an impromptu display of wild revelry and dancing. Unsatisfied with that little display of joy, Surendranath had sweets bought and distributed to express his happiness.

The Tamil month of *Pourathasi* was nearing its end when Ayanar Gounder reached Ariyalur after his second visit to Kodiyalam. Back home, he found his wife, Pattammal, in a rebellious mood because he had forced her to return home, giving up her pilgrimage midway. Predictably therefore, she openly opposed his plans to go to Calcutta when she came to know about it. For her it was a useless errand in search of an illusory character. Her husband's sudden obsession with the Uttara Yogi went against her orthodox religiousness. Ironically, it was this new obsession that brought Pattammal the missing lever to exert her feminine force over her husband's refusal to take her to Sabarimalai. Now she made her opportunistic move, 'Either take me to the abode of Lord Ayyappa within this year or give up all your other travel plans.'

Much to his regret, with the inevitable delays caused by his family obligations, Gounder reached Calcutta only around mid-February. By then the worst part of winter was over, although it still affected the old man appreciably. After resting for a day in a distant niece's house, Gounder set out to meet Sir Sharma in the Kali Temple at Kalighat where he supposedly came to pray every day.

Saraswati Puja began on a bright, chilly morning. Gounder marvelled at the wide-eyed young boys and girls in light orange dresses in honour of the goddess, the harbinger of spring. The pandals were decorated with chrome orange marigolds. The clay images of Saraswati were covered with garlands of marigolds too. A pleasant mood of festivity was in the air as Gounder strolled down the wide Hazra Road wrapped in a shawl.

At the gate of the temple he was accosted by an old *panda* who seemed to know Sir Sharma quite well and promised to introduce Gounder to him as soon as he arrived. Gounder waited for a couple of hours before he finally turned up. On reading the letter of introduction given by the Iyengar brothers, Sir Sharma immediately took Gounder aside and whispered: 'If you want to meet Aurobindo Ghose you must act fast,' he said. 'There's fear of his re-arrest.'

'My God, can't we go and meet him right now?'

'No. But how about tomorrow? Come let's first offer prayers to the Mother.'

The strong presence inside the temple touched Gounder profoundly. An instant prayer welled up from his heart, 'Mother, please make the Uttara Yogi come to South India.' And significantly, when the priest reassured him that the Mother would fulfil his desire, Gounder's heart filled with joy.

The following day, Sir Sharma arrived at ten as promised.

'Did you eat anything in the morning?' he earnestly asked after offering obeisance.

'How could I eat before offering my prayers to the Mother?' Gounder replied.

'But there'll be no opportunity to eat for several hours!' Sharma did not insist. Hiring a carriage both men climbed in. Gounder sat motionless throughout the journey with his entire consciousness focussed on his mission—to meet the Deliverer of whom he had heard forty long years ago.

At 6 College Square, all the male members of the family had had their lunch with the exception of Aurobindo. At two o'clock, Basanti went to the sitting room to call her cousin. She was surprised to find the room overflowing with people. As soon as Aurobindo spotted his cousin, he raised his hand.

He seemed to be saying, 'I am coming to eat shortly.'

Basanti went in satisfied and began to lay the table. However, minutes ticked by but he did not come. Finally, when the big wall clock struck two-thirty she peeped into the sitting room once again. But where had all the men disappeared? Even her 'Aurodada' was gone. She was baffled as such a thing had never happened before. She wondered what was so urgent that he had to go out without eating.

When Gounder's hackney reached College Square and the two elderly men walked up to its entrance they saw some men assembled there. As a small crowd unexpectedly surged out of the house, Sir Sharma's eyes immediately sighted the familiar figure of Aurobindo at the head of the group and he called out excitedly: 'Mr Ghose, Mr Ghose.' But no one heard. The men went past hurriedly while talking among themselves.

'Which is Aravindar?' Gounder asked urgently. 'Quick, show him to me.' Unfortunately, by then the group had boarded three separate hackneys parked a little away and left instantly. 'Oh! How sad!' Gounder muttered dejectedly. 'He was right in front of me and now he has vanished!'

'Don't be so upset. Come let's find out when he's expected to return.' Sir Sharma asked to see someone of the family. Within a couple of minutes an attractive but shy young lady in her mid-twenties stood before them. It was Basanti. 'We came to meet Mr Ghose,' Sharma explained briefly.

'But he left quite suddenly,' Basanti replied. 'He has still not had lunch.'

Sir Sharma then looked at the wall clock. 'I will have to leave. Can this gentleman please wait here? You see, he is quite elderly and has travelled all the way from Tanjore just to meet him.' Then turning towards Gounder, he instructed him how to get back home.

Following Sir Sharma's departure, Basanti could not remain still. She was strangely drawn to the visitor sitting in the hall. After half-an-hour, she walked in holding a brass plate in one hand and a big brass tumbler in the other.

'Sir, please come and eat,' she requested sweetly. 'The food is getting cold.'

Gounder could not believe his ears. No one in the house knew that he had not eaten since the night before. Then had God sent him this food? Under pressure, Gounder had no choice but to give in. Afterwards, Basanti asked the visitor about the purpose of his visit. 'Is it for some political work?' she enquired sweetly.

'Not politics,' he replied, 'but another very important mission.' Gounder hesitated a little. 'My child, a great saint has predicted the coming of a saviour of the world,' he explained, pointing towards the sky with both hands. Then with great fervour, Gounder began his story right from Sri Vasudeva's prediction about the advent of the saviour till his death within a short time, and from Gounder's meeting with the Iyengar family to his own decision to come and contact Aurobindo in Calcutta.

Basanti was stunned. There was no doubt in her mind about Aurodada's mysticism but she had never thought him to be someone of such high spiritual stature. She too strongly felt that his three madnesses were unmistakably the three utterances that were predicted by the Nagai Swami. Everything else also coincided marvellously. She recollected vividly the interview Aurodada had given to *India*.

'It's strange,' Basanti observed. 'Now that you say so, all that he has said seems to assume a new significance and fits wonderfully. "Wait and see," he emphatically asserted the other day during a discussion on Swadeshism, "I shall free India through the power of my *sadhana* alone."'

'Ah, you see, that's another missing piece of the complex puzzle. Aurobindo himself has left clues of his spiritual genius. But how old is Aurobindo?'

'About thirty-seven or thirty-eight, I think.'

'My God! That means the prediction was made before his birth,' Gounder murmured softly. 'It is all happening exactly as in the great epic Ramayana which was said to have been written before Lord Rama's advent.' Realising that it was quite late, Gounder got up to leave. 'Please give me any old object used by Aurobindo,' the old man requested.

A while later, Basanti came back holding something wrapped in a piece of newspaper. 'I'm sorry I couldn't find anything that he is not using other than this pair of worn-out shoes. These he doesn't use any more.'

As tears of joy rolled down, Gounder touched the shoes to his forehead. 'Nothing could be a worthier gift than these,' he exclaimed. 'But,' the old man hesitated a little, 'a devout Hindu's prayer is fulfilled only by sacred *prasad*.'

'Rejoice, then. The food you ate just now was meant for the Uttara Yogi.'

62

On the Run

The steamer carrying Shyamsundar Chakravarty docked at Chandpal Ghat at four o'clock that afternoon. It came from Burma where Shyamsundar had been kept in the Mandalay Jail during the past fourteen months. Shyamsundar looked pleased by Aurobindo's gesture of coming to receive him personally. The same group of people, who had earlier assembled at 6 College Square, had also accompanied Aurobindo to the Ghat. Foregoing his lunch, Aurobindo went straight to Shyampukur Lane from Chandpal Ghat, reaching considerably later than usual. The streets of Shyambazar bore a deserted look with the exception of the two ever-familiar CID men responsible for shadowing Aurobindo. They were at their habitual spot—the open field facing the Laha Colony, hardly sixty yards south from the *Karmayogin* office.

A couple of hours later, Aurobindo was conducting a séance of automatic speech. Every evening, about half-a-dozen young men assembled around him. Besides Nolini, Bejoy and Moni, a few others such as Mrinalini's cousin Saurin, Ramchandra Majumdar and Biren Ghose were regular attendants. That evening, while Ram was absent, Hem Sen had taken his place. Everybody became quiet as soon as the lights were put out. Then suddenly, following the usual pattern, Aurobindo spoke out in a strange voice.

The séance would have continued well into the night had Ramchandra not burst in unexpectedly. 'Mr Ghose, Mr Ghose,' he exclaimed. 'I came to warn you!'

The urgency in his voice surprised everyone. One of the boys lit up a lamp and held it near Ramchandra's face, highlighting the scar on his forehead. 'My father was told by our usual contact that an arrest warrant has been issued in your name.'

This unexpected announcement took everyone's breath away. And no sooner had the communication been made that wild suggestions began to fly. 'Let's quit this place immediately,' someone said. 'Let's escape from the back door,' suggested another. But Ramchandra was not in a mood to run away or give in meekly to the police party. 'Come on, friends,' he said haughtily, 'let's give the police a fight. Let us show them who we are!' Many such ideas were thrown about at random until a familiar voice unexpectedly spoke out.

'No,' Aurobindo said calmly. 'I shall go to Chandernagore.'

Aurobindo sent no word to anyone, not even to his wife or uncle. He only left a message in writing for Nivedita to look after the two journals during his absence.

Soon Aurobindo and Ramchandra went out ahead, followed by Biren. Moni formed the rear of the silent parade, keeping a safe distance behind Biren. Moni looked back to see if they were being watched. Surprisingly, the two omnipresent detectives were not there! Instead of using the main roads, Ramchandra now led Aurobindo through the labyrinths, principally to thwart any design of the police catching them. They reached the bank of the Ganges in about ten minutes.

Discerning the lone form of a boat in the silvery light of a faint moon, Ramchandra called out, 'Hey, will you take a fare?' And, one by one, Biren and Moni followed Aurobindo into the boat which glided smoothly northwards. And unknown to anyone, Aurobindo's life had entered another new phase.

On reaching Rani Ghat on Chandernagore's strand, Aurobindo sent Biren to Charu Roy's residence to seek refuge. Biren returned with the message that the leader of the Chandernagore revolutionaries had flatly refused to provide shelter.

When Shrish Ghose met Charu Chandra early in the morning, he learnt the shocking news of his leader's refusal to provide shelter to Aurobindo who had come to seek it. Shrish and his friend Narendranath Banerjee were already in close league with the *Karmayogin* officebearers and had previously discussed the possibility of Aurobindo's withdrawal into the French territory whenever the eventuality would arise. For this reason, Aurobindo's unannounced arrival bewildered them. Shrish and Narendranath got down to discussing the various possibilities of sheltering Aurobindo. The two men decided to ask the late Kanailal's friend, Motilal Roy, to put up Aurobindo for some time.

It was past 6.30 when Shrish reached Motilal. Aware of Motilal's highly emotive temperament, Shrish purposely gave a moving description of Aurobindo's sudden arrival. The ploy worked. In a few judicious words, Shrish was able to involve his friend in his scheme. Reacting along predictable lines, Motilal dashed off to Rani Ghat at lightning speed. Motilal noticed someone sitting at the edge of the boat and asked, 'Are you from Calcutta? Is Aurobindo Babu in this boat?' The youth called him in. As he entered the low, half-cylindrical roof, Aurobindo's reclining figure became visible. When Aurobindo enquired whether it would be possible for Motilal to offer him shelter, he said, 'Indeed, I've come to fetch you.' Motilal then instructed the boatman to row his boat about half-a-mile further north and lay anchor at Boraichanditala Ghat.

As Aurobindo disembarked, he made it clear that he wanted his stay to remain a secret. In the mean time, Moni and Biren had to go back to Calcutta as the presence of new men was bound to arouse suspicion in the minds of the local residents.

Aurobindo followed Motilal through an unused portion of the house into an abandoned room on the first floor. A little later, hiding the fact even from his wife, Motilal brought Aurobindo his own portion of refreshment. Then he took his guest down again to the small parlour beside the main entrance and made arrangements for Aurobindo's bath inside the room by bringing in two buckets of water. However, when it came to using the toilet that was located outside the house, there was no other way than using the narrow public lane through which they had entered the house. Luckily, there was no one there. At noon, Motilal purchased food for him from a wayside restaurant. But how could he let Aurobindo sleep in that dark room with insects crawling all over? After a brief consultation with Shrish, Motilal decided to take Santosh Dey of Khejurtala into confidence. Although Aurobindo spent the night at Santosh's house as planned, he wished to be brought back the next evening.

After bringing back Aurobindo to his residence Motilal put him up in the out-of-repair, small lumber room stacked with furniture. Motilal hung a mosquito net and stacked some chairs compactly all around the makeshift bed. Aurobindo appeared happy with the arrangement and Motilal realised that, above all, he loved solitude. The next morning, Motilal's wife, Radharani, inadvertently entered the lumber room and was shocked to discover a stranger living there. Mercifully, besides feeling scared she neither screamed nor mentioned it to anyone else. Although Motilal was happy to make a clean breast of it to his wife, he sadly realised that the time had come to shift Aurobindo elsewhere again to avoid compromising his safety.

Accordingly, the three friends made arrangements to transfer him to Gondalpara. During the three or four days that followed, Aurobindo was led from the coolie lines to Narendranath's house at regular intervals. However, when the owner of the hut unexpectedly discovered Aurobindo, it was again time to transfer him elsewhere.

At this juncture, when Naren was looking for an alternative, it suddenly occurred to him to put up Aurobindo in the unoccupied Karer Bagan. In order to discuss the matter of Aurobindo's transfer, Naren met Shrish in Charu Chandra's house. But an unexpected and disagreeable situation arose, as he did not wait to think how the professor would react to the news of Aurobindo's continued presence in Chandernagore. Shrish and Naren left hastily, deciding that Aurobindo would be housed at Karer Bagan without Charu Chandra's knowledge.

Next evening, after dinner, Naren and Aurobindo set out on foot for Karer Bagan. As the two were walking through Padripara, Naren got the first taste of Aurobindo's keen sense of humour. In one of the two-storeyed houses someone was throwing a party and the sound of merrymaking could be heard.

'If only some specimen of their dishes could be procured!' Aurobindo said jokingly, 'then your expenses for tonight's dinner could've been spared!' Whenever he would pass that way, Naren would inevitably remember Aurobindo's witty remark.

As they approached Karer Bagan, Naren was reminded of Shrish's warning not to enter the garden through its front entrance on the main road. While creeping in through a portion of the wall, which was broken down, Aurobindo and Naren clumsily fell over one another.

Aurobindo was quick to recover and mischievously commented: 'I see that we are doomed to die an unnatural death on account of these English.'

Here again, Aurobindo's stay was cut short because the house was considered to be too exposed. Finally, Aurobindo was moved to a place called Nichupatti near Jagannath Bari. It is said that the dilapidated shed, which he occupied, was sometimes resorted to by opium addicts. Interestingly, he remained there undisturbed by dopers or detectives and spent the greater part of his stay here alone, immersed in his *sadhana*. Sudarshan Chatterjee, the revolutionary responsible for him, locked the place from outside whenever he went out to work.

By now, a month had passed since Motilal had last met Aurobindo. Yet, due entirely to Motilal's peculiar disposition, he had not once thought it necessary to call on Aurobindo. Quite predictably, therefore, when he received summons through Shrish, Motilal was jolted back to his senses. Aurobindo lovingly enquired about his health and said, 'You've made yourself scarce; business engagements perhaps?' After a prolonged discussion on yoga, when Motilal was about to take leave, Aurobindo stunned him by saying, 'Come tomorrow, if you can. I'm leaving very shortly.'

Realising that Aurobindo was not willing to share the secret entirely with him, Motilal left it at that. However, he soon received instructions to prepare for his journey out of Chandernagore to the principal town of French settlements in India—Pondicherry.

63

Destiny Unfolds

'Namaskar, I am Harimohan Datta and here, this is my wife Sarajubala.'

'Please take your seat. I am Madhusudan Dasgupta and this is my wife, Jaya.'

After Harimohan discreetly left the packet of sweets on the table at the centre of the hall, Saraju went up to Jaya and they both sat down on a long sofa. Likewise, the men sat down on another sofa facing their wives. The Dasguptas were handsome and well-bred. Harimohan could see it from his host's manners and speech that he was no upstart. The big room was tastefully decorated and although some of the items on display were old and discoloured, they were the relics of better days.

'Your son is a gem of a person, Mr Datta,' Madhusudan said sincerely. 'When I came to know him on the evening of that deluge, I didn't hesitate to invite him to stay the night. It's entirely the boy's credit. But I must admit that I never imagined then that this acquaintance would mature into such a cherished bond for life.'

'Madhusudan Babu, there's something I must discuss with you before finalising anything. I hope you are aware that Indraneel is involved with a secret society whose primary aim is to overthrow the British Government. In fact, some of his comrades were recently convicted in the Alipore Bomb Trial. As the groom's father I thought it was my duty to inform you about it.'

'Yes, Mr Datta, and I appreciate your honesty. By the way, I hope you have heard all about Kusum's first marriage?'

Just then, Kusum entered the hall with tea and snacks. She stooped before Harimohan first and also touched her father's feet, seeking their blessings. She then bent down before Saraju who spontaneously gave her a warm embrace.

'Don't you like this Lakshmi?' she enquired of her husband, cupping Kusum's face in her hand. 'Didn't I tell you that my son has very good taste?'

Everyone heartily laughed at Saraju's simplicity. Although it was Kusum's beauty that appealed to Saraju, it was the young woman's poise that impressed Harimohan. And instinctively, he understood why the shy Indraneel felt so naturally drawn to her strong magnetism. It was the typical appeal of opposite poles that drew them together.

'Now then, Mr Dasgupta,' Harimohan said aloud, 'would it suit you if we were to fix the date of the marriage towards the end of *Phalgune* corresponding to mid-March in the English calendar? That would allow us two months to prepare for the big event.'

Madhusudan Dasgupta readily gave his approval after a quick consultation with his wife.

Indraneel had to resort to a secret meeting with Kusum at Hedua, realising that it would be preposterous for the would-be-groom to meet his fiancée at home. He was aware that even this would not be easy for her as she would be restricted from going out alone. Understandably, therefore, Kusum came with her sister, Sushama, after dark. Indraneel explained that the matter was delicate and that he needed to consult her urgently. Conscious that it was difficult to hold an open discussion about such a sensitive matter before Sushama, Indraneel began to speak in a soft tone.

'Do you remember the attack on a convoy that I had planned? When I planned it for the last Saturday of February there was no talk yet of our marriage. Now everything is in place and the boys are trained for the assault and they'll feel morally upset if I put it off! Besides, as the collector transports the tax money only once a month, our next opportunity would come well after our marriage. And I would hate to do it after you move in.'

'Look, there's no point vacillating after taking a decision. Just do it confidently and please hope for the best. Besides, don't you need to avenge the deportation of your friends?'

'But if I'm arrested our marriage might be in jeopardy!'

'When I decided to marry an outlaw, I did so consciously. So I refuse to be cowed down now. I could ask Baba to postpone the distribution of invitation cards until a few days after the middle of *Phalgune,* which will correspond to the beginning of March.'

Indraneel was baffled by Kusum's callousness. 'You sound so uncaring, Kusum!' he remarked in desperation. 'Don't you realise that our wedding could be put off indefinitely … or may be forever … in case I'm caught?'

'Yes, I do realise that our marriage may be put off indefinitely if you're jailed,' she said confidently. 'But I'm ready to abide by the rules of the game and wait for your return. The alternative of settling down tamely by calling off the attack isn't acceptable to me because it's tantamount to asking the tiger to change its stripes—the prime feature of the wild cat that I adore! Look, you have freely chosen to tread this path. And even your aged parents have dignifiedly accepted that decision. I would much rather see you act bravely and face the consequences than lead a mundane life like the millions of insensitive people of this country. Unless the British are forced to depart, do you imagine they will give up their empire?'

Kusum's irresistible smile was visible even under the scanty light of the oil lamps placed at strategic points of the park. Indraneel stealthily took her hand in his to let its warmth bring comfort to his restless heart. She made no effort to retract it and instead gave his hand a loving squeeze.

'I'm leaving shortly for Seiya,' Indraneel solemly said, his heart suddenly flooding with confidence. 'Please be with me in spirit. I shall miss you very much.'

'Be cautious in whatever you do. My best wishes will always be with you.'

Indraneel bent down to pinch Sushama's cheeks. 'Knowing that you would come I brought you these,' he told the girl and gave her a packet of toffees.

'May God protect you,' Kusum whispered, melting away in the darkness. 'I shall eagerly wait for your return.'

As Indraneel was associated with the boys at the *Karmayogin* office, Harimohan had gathered through him information regarding Aurobindo's unexpected departure for an unknown destination. One of the boys had further assured him that Aurobindo was safe. That indeed was a big solace for the whole family.

Earlier, on the afternoon of the third Sunday of February, the doorman announced the arrival of an old man. As Harimohan went down to meet the visitor, Saraju heard an exclamation of joy. 'Saraju,' he screamed, 'see who has come!'

Unable to meet Aurobindo even after a week's delay, Ayanar Gounder had come on a surprise visit to his old acquaintances whom he had accidentally met at Kodiyalam. Gounder disclosed the sad news of Vasudeva Iyengar's death. Then unable to suppress his excitement, he shared with them the identity of the Uttara Yogi. Harimohan and Saraju exchanged glances.

'I've known it ever since Thakurpo's malarial fever,' she said happily. Turning to her husband, she enquired, 'Don't you remember that I told you that Thakurpo would ultimately have to settle down in some unknown land?'

'Now, now, wait a minute,' Gounder interrupted. 'Are you Aurobindo's friends?'

'Well, yes,' Harimohan explained, 'I have known him since his childhood.'

'Oh! Just think of it! You knew Aurobindo even before we met at Kodiyalam!'

'Yes. But I only knew him as Aurobindo Ghose—not as the Uttara Yogi.'

Gounder explained briefly about how the Iyengar brothers had conclusively identified Aurobindo as the Deliverer and about his second journey to Kodiyalam. Finally, he spoke about his trip to Calcutta to meet the Uttara Yogi.

'No,' Saraju said emphatically, 'if he must go to South India, then the circumstances will inevitably lead him there. No one can stop him. What is decreed by God is final—nobody can interfere with His work.'

Harimohan was overwhelmed. Gounder's narrative had only confirmed all that his foster father had told him about Aurobindo's clear-cut destiny as the Deliverer.

Subsequently, arrangements were made for Gounder's stay at Rawdon Street.

By now, Indraneel's life had entered a decisive phase. So having acquired some firearms, his present objective lay in procuring money to fund his further exploits. Underlining the basic principle of self-sufficiency, Indraneel felt compelled to obtain by coercion all that was indispensable, but not available for the cause. In order to spend a prolonged period of time in Seiya, Indraneel informed his father that in view of the accumulating work regarding their properties it had become imperative to spend an entire week at their village. Before leaving, Indraneel went up to his mother and informed her of his departure. As Indraneel bent down and touched her feet, his mother looked surprised, as he had never done this before. When Indraneel went to see his father, Harimohan looked at him intently. 'If you have planned any dangerous action for the coming week,' he said, surprising Indraneel, 'then I would advise utmost restraint even though you must fulfil your mission. May God be with you, my son.'

Although Indraneel wondered how his father had guessed, he did not fail to admire his ingenuity and deep insight. He quickly bent down and touched Harimohan's feet. 'I am glad that you guessed, Baba,' Indraneel said candidly. 'I feel reassured by your blessings. But please don't tell anything to Ma yet. Although what I have planned is dangerous, you've my assurance regarding caution.

You know how important this work is for me, for the society and for all my doomed friends!'

Harimohan understood perfectly how important it was for Indraneel to assume the leadership in the absence of any other responsible member. Harimohan held Indraneel in a close embrace. 'I'm proud of you, my son,' he said emotionally. 'Please be careful.'

After reaching Seiya, Indraneel met his five-man team and geared up for action. He had secretly planned to rob the district collector's carriage on its way from Arambagh to the headquarters in Chinsura. On the last Saturday of each month the collector was said to carry the monthly tax paid by the handloom weavers of the Dhoniakhali division, amounting to over five thousand rupees. Only four guards armed with antiquated Martini-Henri rifles were said to accompany the tax collector.

For a long time, Indraneel and his boys had been doing target practice with their stolen firearms in the deep woods faraway from Seiya. This little forest, located in an area about four miles south of Seiya, was surrounded on three sides by the rivulet Kedarmati and punctuated by the peripheral villages—Badinan, Erenga and Karicherbheri. Although Indraneel kept the revolvers hidden in the hollow of a big tree, in the safety of the forest, the big haul of ammunition was kept elsewhere as a precaution. For this, Indraneel had had holes dug in the big wooden beams of the only room on the second floor of their house. Feeling confident and satisfied with his men's progress, Indraneel planned to attack the convoy several blocks away near Tamila in order to confuse the police. This would suggest that the raiders were local men of that region. He made arrangements to procure three bicycles from the villagers for a whole day. His idea was to ride the cycles in pairs, leaving in the early hours of the day.

After reaching a lonely spot on the main road, the men felled a small tree and transformed it into a log to block the road. As the carriage was not expected to arrive before noon, one of the boys kept watch over the road. Finally, at around two o'clock, a lone carriage was spotted coming from the side of Arambagh. Everyone tied a piece of cloth over his face below the eyes as soon as the announcement was made. Indraneel had arranged that they all wore the same kind of city clothes in order to confuse the witnesses, making it look like one more political dacoity.

Just as the carriage rolled within twenty yards, three boys hurriedly pulled up the trunk of the felled tree to obstruct its way. The driver frantically pulled the reigns, causing the twin horses to neigh in panic as the carriage ground to a halt. No sooner had the alarmed constables caught their breath that they were thrown off their seats. A hush fell as soon as they realised that they were surrounded by a gang of six armed men. While the leader of the attackers ordered everybody to climb down with hands raised above their heads, one of the attackers climbed into the carriage and brought down the four loaded rifles. Soon the frightened tax collector, the four sepoys and the coachman had their hands tied behind their backs and were made to stand at a safe distance away from the road. The coffer containing the money was then brought down and the leader calmly inspected its content by opening it with the collector's key. Next, while the six captured men were being blindfolded, the loot of silver coins was transferred into three gunny bags.

But at this point something unexpected happened. As the tax collector panicked and suddenly began running for his life, one of the boys shouted an order to halt but he did not listen. Indraneel turned his gun and pulled the trigger in a flash. The shot narrowly missed the man. The second shot hit him in the back of his thigh and the poor man fell face downward. The red hot blood trickling down his wound had an instant sobering effect and everyone froze with fear. After tying the six men, including the coachman, inside the carriage, the light-footed Dolu drove the carriage back nearly a mile and abandoned it conspicuously by the side of the road. Then half-an-hour later, as one of his companions drove him back on his cycle, the full reunited group of the Bajra Samiti ecstatically shouted *Vande Mataram*, standing at attention. This was their proudest moment since the arms seizure nearly a year earlier.

The group left the main road and pedalled down an unfrequented mud road. Here, they stopped for a while to change to their usual, village dresses. They also split up the booty, the four rifles and the ammunition on their three cycles. By now only the weak rays of the setting sun illuminated the countryside. As the heavy sacks containing the coins were being removed, one of the cycles accidentally tilted over to one side and overturned. With the tearing of the gunny bag at its sudden impact with the hard ground, a large quantity of coins spilled out with a loud jingle. After putting back the fallen coins into another sack, Indraneel proposed to sit down for a well-deserved meal. In their tension they had forgotten all about their lunch.

In the end, the four rifles and the three heavy gunny bags were lowered into a deep pit dug in the midst of thick undergrowth and tall trees of their familiar forest. At about nine o'clock the tired men rode back to their village after dropping Indraneel at Seiya. Indraneel advised the boys not to panic or to reveal anything, even if they were caught. They were neither to divulge anything about their collective activities nor confess their involvement with any dacoity to anyone.

When the tax money did not reach Chinsura even after eight o'clock in the evening, the district magistrate summoned the superintendent of police. The men escorting the convoy unexpectedly showed up a quarter-of-an-hour later.

'Where's the tax collector?' the district magistrate enquired.

'He was shot at Sir. And, we were also attacked by bandits on the highway!'

The superintendent and the district magistrate looked at each other. Their expression of disbelief seemed to suggest that they thought the head constable was drunk. But one look at the bulky tax collector was enough to show that he was writhing in pain. Then on realising the daring nature of the attack, the district magistrate decided to refer the case to the CID. That is how the wily Yasubuddin Ahmed stepped in.

Arriving promptly the next day, Ahmed lost no time in going to the spot of the daring robbery. He immediately searched for the empty shell of one of the two shots fired, as reported by the victims. When his men found the empty shell, his trained eyes recognised it as belonging to the .380 bore Osman class pistols.

'Oh! how interesting!' he reflected. 'Weren't a dozen of these pistols burgled from the Chinsura armoury a year earlier?'

Realising that it was an important evidence, he quickly inferred that the culprits of both these crimes might belong to some place half-way between this scene of robbery and the big town. So he concentrated his scrutiny around the main road, looking for further clues. He discovered a mud path leading eastward towards the district headquarters bearing unmistakable marks of cycle tyres. 'The cycles were heavy,' Yasubuddin chuckled, 'with the weight of an extra rider and perhaps a third of the burden of those five thousand coins and an additional Martini-Henri rifle.'

He analysed the other possibilities. Trying to outsmart the investigators, the assailants had driven back the carriage nearly a mile westward along the main road before abandoning it. This classic ruse to confuse also led Yasubuddin to conclude rightly that the fugitives must have taken the opposite direction eastward towards Chinsura.

Before dusk, searching along the mud path, the detective came to a place where scattered puffed rice was being blown in circles by the breeze. After examining the area more thoroughly, one of his assistants showed him a spot where a silver coin was lying. The place also bore clear marks of three heavy sacks. Now, Yasubuddin was absolutely certain of being on the right track. Whoever was foolish enough to drop a silver coin without realising his loss had to have too many to keep an exact count.

Resuming the search the next day, his attention was drawn by a thick jungle some distance from the mud road. He did not have to enter further to discover evidence of target practice on the trunks of some big trees. On closer examination, the ground under the undergrowth revealed empty cartridges of the same .380 bore Osman pistols. The detective was certain that his culprits lay within a striking distance.

Right from the start, Yasubuddin had a hunch about the involvement of at least one educated man in the robbery as too many details pointed to that fact. First, all six men were wearing masks. The villagers may not have thought of hiding their faces, nor would they have had the courage to rob so much money on their own. Also, all the victims were unanimous about the leading Babu's role whose polished Bengali was in utter contrast with the thick intonation of the villagers. But this crucial fact could also complicate matters. For by now the city man may have decamped and hidden the money in Calcutta.

At this point, Yasubuddin committed two monstrous errors. After flawlessly arriving so far, the detective foolishly abandoned his search for the buried guns or the money within that thick jungle in his eagerness to arrest the culprit. Hoping that the leader may still be lurking in one of the surrounding villages, he sent spies from his enquiry party to investigate and report back. He argued that an imposing entry into the villages with his entourage would inevitably send warning signals to the culprit.

Ironically, the very decision to send an investigator to each neighbouring village assured the escape of the fugitive. For, Yasubuddin's secret agents were all constables from the local Polba Thana who knew Indraneel Gupta personally and respected him too. So, when Constable Gobardhan Santra called on Indraneel and casually informed him of the impending search in the village, Indraneel was totally bewildered. He could not understand what had given him away, allowing the sleuth to track him down so easily. Obeying his instinct, he hurriedly left the village.

Being aware that his connection with the Muraripukur gang would soon be established, Indraneel refrained from going back to Rawdon Street. It was at that point that he remembered with alarm and regret that he had left his French revolver in his cupboard. That small metallic object would become the source of infinite trouble for his parents, jeopardising their safety and compromising their honour.

In his brief introduction, Constable Santra had revealed the exact spot where the police party was camping. This eliminated Indraneel's chances of hiding in the woods. So he chose the only other option open to him and made a dash through the tall grass of the northern fields. After sprinting for half-an-hour Indraneel stopped to rummage his side-pockets. To his dismay, he discovered that after the tipping of the constable he had no money left except some small coins. This put him in a dilemma. How could he live without money? That evening, ignoring hunger, Indraneel headed towards the northwest where fate seemed to guide him. After trudging through the night, feeling weak and exhausted, he reached the outskirts of a very small town the next morning. There he satisfied his hunger by eating parched rice and water.

In the mean time, on hearing from Constable Santra that a Babu named Indraneel Gupta had hurriedly left the village that morning, Yasubuddin descended upon Seiya with his entire group. After learning that Indraneel was a resident of Calcutta and was the foster son of Barrister Harimohan Datta, he despatched one of his attendants to his headquarters. He wrote a letter requesting Superintendent Montague Bugden Ellis to send an officer to apprehend Indraneel at his residence. Oddly again, it was Yasubuddin's assumption about his Calcutta link that saved Indraneel. No one looked for him around the village, presuming he had made a straight dash for the city.

However, more evidence soon piled up against Indraneel. Other than his association with the Muraripukur boys, a thorough search of the village house soon revealed the hollows in the beams and their damning contents of ammunition.

But the most unbelievable part of the story was the police's failure to arraign the boys in spite of their prompt rounding up on the basis of their earlier supposed involvement in the armoury raid case. Their clever alibis also received full corroboration from the villagers. Even though the old armoury raid case was reopened with fanfare, the boys once again came out unscathed in the absence of witnesses! But to save their credibility, the administration mounted pressure on the local magistrate trying the boys. He was coerced into issuing a verdict of a month's rigorous imprisonment for the five young men and a simple fine of twenty-five rupees for their suspected involvement.

Simultaneously, some twenty-odd miles to the southeast, another long-drawn tale was coming to a close. Happily, this was to be Aurobindo's last phase of preparation for the epoch-making task that awaited him in South India. But independent of his will or that of the eager disciples of the Nagai Swami, his transfer was being arranged by a higher power that transcends human comprehension. And, however much the Iyengar brothers may have tried to make things happen, Aurobindo's predicted arrival in the southern peninsula would be made possible through the threat of a warrant of arrest that was never served. Nevertheless, the threat of the warrant did stop Aurobindo's outer activities and caused his total withdrawal from public life. As his reliance on God's will was confirmed, his transfer to South India simply required one more *adesh*.

In a masterly stroke, the Almighty had removed Aurobindo from his family, friends and politics, never to join them. Already there were signs that showed that he obeyed a higher will. His eating, for instance, seemed to be performed mechanically, as if by a third agency. His look, too, seemed not to be that of a human being; it was as if someone behind the eyes elongated the sight.

Once, taking courage in hand, Motilal enquired what he saw with his strangely fixed regard. Aurobindo replied, 'A multitude of letters comes trooping down in the air. I try to decipher.' What he meant was *akasha lipi*, the etheric writing that keeps the record of all things past, transcribes all that is in process in the present, writes out the future. He further explained to Motilal another common occurrence, *rupa drishti*, the vision of significant forms. 'Gods of the invisible worlds become visible. They are as significant as the alphabet and want to communicate something, which I endeavour to discover.'

Among the divine forms seen by Aurobindo at Chandernagore were those of three Vedic goddesses. His first contact with Vedic thought came indirectly while pursuing certain lines of self-development in the way of yoga, which, without his knowing it, were spontaneously converging on the ancient paths followed by the spiritual forefathers. At this time there arose in his mind an arrangement of symbolic names attached to certain psychological experiences which had begun to regularise themselves; among them came the goddesses Ila, Saraswati and Sarama, representing three out of the four enegies of the intuitive reason—revelation, inspiration and intuition.

Through these spiritual experiences, Aurobindo was slowly moving towards his real yoga.

In late March, he wrote from Chandernagore to Sukumar Mitra to make arrangements for his departure to Pondicherry. He also expressed the wish to have Bejoy Nag as his companion. A comprehensive plan was drawn up to lead Aurobindo out of British India, although its execution was not going to be easy for Sukumar. His house was under the constant surveillance of half a dozen, plain clothes policemen, camping round-the-clock in the facing College Square. However, as Aurobindo had given him a free hand in the planning and execution of the whole mission, he had total control over the choice of people or the mode of transport to be used.

The most that Sukumar himself could do was to collect money for the scheme from people Aurobindo had suggested, but he had to rely on friends for the actual running around. He chose two members of the Anti-Circular Society—Nagendrakumar Guharay and Surendrakumar Chakravarti. Displaying unusual circumspection, Sukumar always spoke to the two men separately, not allowing them even the chance to talk to each other about the mysterious work they were engaged in. As a first step, he asked Nagen to take two steel trunks to the nearby students' hostel where he stayed.

As it was inconceivable for Aurobindo to travel by train and evade the attention of the whole gauntlet of detectives between Calcutta and Pondicherry, Sukumar's only choice lay in one regular steamer that connected the two capitals. This was the *S.S. Dupleix,* belonging to a French company named Messagerie Maritime. As Calcutta's major English dailies regularly advertised the schedule for the company's steamers, Sukumar had no trouble finding out that the *Dupleix* was due to leave on 1 April from Calcutta's Esplanade moorings for Colombo, with a halt at the French enclave.

As it would be impossible to let Aurobindo and Bejoy travel under their own names, Sukumar found two aliases for them from the long list of subscribers of *Sanjivani*—Jotindra Nath Mitra of Uluberia and Bankim Chandra Bhowmik of Nilphamari. This was necessary as the names and addresses of the second class passengers had to be disclosed on the application forms. Sukumar felt that it would be safer to use names of real individuals living in remote areas that were traceable but time- consuming, rather than entirely fictitious ones that would betray the plot instantly. He hoped that by the time the police got scent of the plot, Aurobindo and Bejoy would have entered the international waters of the Bay of Bengal.

With the objective of reducing the chances of immediate official scrutiny, Sukumar advised Nagen to procure two second class tickets in one double cabin from Thomas Cook & Company, instead of the Messagerie Maritime's regular counter at Hare Street.

Nagen had been directed to leave instructions that both passengers would take their meals in their cabin as one of them was suffering from malaria. This was aimed at eliminating whatever chance there was of being recognised by fellow passengers on board the ship. Further, they were to board the steamer directly from the riverside instead of the regular gangway. By this manoeuvre Sukumar hoped to outwit the police at the time of boarding.

An even more elaborate arrangement had been worked out by Sukumar and Motilal to bring Aurobindo back to the city. Once again, the safer waterway had been preferred rather than the easier train route. But this time, Aurobindo was not to be brought directly. Sukumar feared that in case the boatmen were identified and grilled by the police, they would naturally disclose the exact destination of the men they had transported and then the Government could try to stop the departure of the steamer, or try to arrest Aurobindo midway. Therefore, he recruited the services of three different groups for this crucial phase of the journey. Initially, Motilal's men would bring Aurobindo to Agarpara's Dumurtala Ghat. This place was to serve as the point of rendezvous between them and a second group led by Amar Chatterjee. The second boat would then pick up Aurobindo and lead him to a ghat on the western side again. This was to be either Bali or Uttarpara. From there, a third boat consisting of Sukumar's men, Nagen and Suren, would take Aurobindo and Bejoy to the Esplanade moorings, where they would finally board the steamer by climbing the rope ladder and shut themselves in their cabin, where their baggage would be waiting.

Despite all these elaborate arrangements, hoodwinking the sensitive intelligence network of the British police was not going to be easy.

~

Harimohan was interrogated in his house by Superintendent Ellis. The shrewd barrister excused himself and went up to his room professedly to put on a more dignified dress in honour of his venerable guest. He quickly ransacked his son's cupboard and discovered to his horror that the French revolver was still there! Removing it instantly, he hid it under his wife's intimate things in her boudoir. Even before the detective could bring up the topic, Harimohan suggested that the police make a search of his house and particularly his son's belongings. The ruse worked and, in the absence of a search warrant, the veteran policeman had to backtrack. But within a couple of hours, Ellis' assistants were back again armed with a search warrant and they ransacked the house. Mercifully, by then the revolver had been safely smuggled out.

Three days after the daring attack, all the major dailies carried prominent coverage of the sensational burglary amounting to a record haul of five thousand rupees. But bigger headlines were to follow a couple of days later when police investigations revealed that the Arambagh dacoity was closely linked to the hitherto unsolved Chinsura armoury raid. In no time everyone was talking about Indraneel Gupta! His notoriety reached dizzy heights when the unnerved government put a price of ten thousand rupees on his head. Suddenly, Indraneel had become a dreaded terrorist, authenticating old Kedarnath's prediction that in spite of bringing tragedy upon himself and all those around him, he was destined to earn extraordinary fame.

However, all was not well with the Datta family. Harimohan was gradually losing his prestigious government briefs. His close links with Aurobindo on the one hand and the recent outcry against the renegade Indraneel was the last straw for the government, which unceremoniously stripped him of the post of public prosecutor.

At first Saraju lost her appetite and energy, ruminating fearful thoughts about Indraneel. She would often wake up in the middle of the night shrieking and screaming after recurring nightmares. But miraculously, it all stopped one day just as suddenly as it had begun. Saraju regained her composure and even resumed her activities. Harimohan was intrigued by this change and one day followed her quietly to the puja room where she spent most of her time. He was surprised to see her clutching a neatly folded dhoti while praying. Then suddenly turning around, suspecting someone to be in the room, she smiled happily as soon as she realised it was her husband.

'Neel is well protected,' she cheerfully said. 'You see, I too initially felt worried at Thakurpo's disappearance. But feeling convinced that wherever he is, he must be well, I entered into a communion with him. And it is he who instructs me not to worry. Neel is safe.'

'Saraju, how on earth do you know it is Auro who is answering your prayers?'

'Well, I have total faith in him. I know that if he gives an assurance it's bound to come true. Just wait for another week. Neel's news will reach us.'

Harimohan shook his head in disbelief. His wife was showing clear signs of disorientation.

'Tell me, where is your Thakurpo now?' he asked guardedly.

'That I don't know. But don't you understand that he has to resurface in South India? Even if he isn't, he'll soon be. What's the hurry?'

'And what's that dhoti doing in the puja room?'

'Ah! This is a gift that Thakurpo gave me for taking care of him! This is my most coveted treasure, dearer than my life.'

After walking for a fortnight, Indraneel at last reached the outskirts of Indas. Afflicted by hunger and thirst, and feeling feverish from physical exhaustion, he kept trudging ahead with determination, ever vitalised by the thought of beating the police. There was on the eastern edge of Indas a burning ghat where Hindus cremated their dead. Drawn from far by the lustre of a funeral pyre in that otherwise lightless night, Indraneel put in a last effort before collapsing at about fifty yards from the ghat. Luckily, one of the three guards on duty noticed a shadowy figure tottering before clumsily dropping on the ground. He drew his fellow workers' attention and the three men swiftly ran to the spot. On touching him they realised that he had high fever. After a brief discussion, one of the guards ran to fetch Jogini Ma, the tantric practitioner who lived in a small hut beside the ghat.

In front of Jogini Ma was a two feet-high statue of Smashana Kali, the Goddess of the Crematorium, behind which stood a row of neatly arranged reddened human skulls. Jogini Ma was making mudras, while reciting from the immortal verses of the *Markandeya Uvacha*. As one of the guards called, Jogini Ma awoke from her deep meditation. There was dignity and nobility written on her features.

'A young stranger has arrived, Ma,' the guard said. 'He fell unconscious probably due to exhaustion. He is running a fever. Will you please come and see?'

Jogini Ma rose and collected her *trishul* in her right hand. Her red robe and the *tilak* on her forehead shone brightly in the flickering chiaroscuro of the burning ghat. After examining the young man, she poured some sacred water into his mouth from her *kamandulu*. Miraculously, the stranger opened his eyes. Under instructions from Jogini Ma he was transferred to her hut. She then prepared hot rice in the middle of the night and fed him as best as she could. After that she asked him to sleep. By now, slumber benumbed Indraneel's limbs and he peacefully fell asleep. He felt a lot better after the invigorating meal.

Indraneel woke up at around noon the next day. Inside the hut it was cool and dark. Although he had some vague memories of the previous night, Indraneel had still not realised that he was in a burning ghat. He was a little surprised to find Jogini Ma sitting beside him with her back turned towards the door. And much as he would have liked to see her face, he could only discern her silhouette. After trying hard to get up, Indraneel lay exhausted, realising how weak he was. Jogini Ma advised him to rest.

'You needn't strain, son,' she reassured him. 'Get back your strength first.'

'My name's Indraneel Gupta,' he introduced himself. 'Although I live in Calcutta, I have come here from a far off village. It's a very long story.'

'All right, let me begin it for you,' Jogini Ma said. 'You're a political fugitive running away from justice after looting five thousand rupees of government money. The whole nation has heard about your heroic deeds. You are a national hero now. The government has put a price of ten thousand rupees on your head.'

The revelation made Indraneel inhale sharply. He had no idea that he was being so desperately sought by the police. And what if Jogini Ma and her accomplices turned him in to the police for getting the reward?

'Don't worry, my son. You are safe here,' she added, calming his fears. 'Now, in order to protect you from the prying eyes of the police, my men will help you put on these clothes,' she said, handing him a red dhoti and a piece of cloth for tying around his head. 'And let your beard grow.'

'All right,' Indraneel said gratefully, touching the clothes to his head. 'But I must somehow contact my parents and let them know that I am well.'

'I have already done so my son. I have sent word to Harimohan Datta at his office in the high court. I have informed your father that you are under my care. I have also apprised him that you are to stay with me for as long as your safety requires it. But he is not supposed to know where you are.'

'Ma,' Indraneel asked while peering into her eyes, 'how do you know so much?'

'Oh! You still have not been able to guess who I am?' Motimala said, grinning happily. 'Don't you know your father rendered me a lot of selfless help in the past? And, it is now my turn to protect his son as my own.'

Indraneel was pleasantly surprised to see Motimala. He could not believe that fate had brought him so unexpectedly back to her. Suddenly, he felt happy to be with her again and eagerly stretched his arms. As Indraneel looked with moist, indebted eyes, Motimala leaned forward and gathered him in her arms.

'It's so comforting,' she whispered softly, 'to hear you address me as Ma. To me you were my child from the very first day that we met.'

64

Many Journeys

After Aurobindo's departure from Calcutta, Saurin, Biren, Nolini, Bejoy and Moni dispersed from Shyampukur Lane and stayed separately. During this time, Moni had taken up lodgings in a mess in Bowbazar. It was at this address, towards the end of March, that a messenger delivered a cryptic message to Moni written on a tiny piece of paper in Aurobindo's hand. It asked him to proceed to Pondicherry to arrange a house for Aurobindo's stay. Moni was informed that the responsibility of making arrangements for his journey had fallen on Saurin who would personally put him on the train. All that was asked of Moni was to go to the Howrah Station and board the Madras-bound mail train. Although Moni left without luggage, his host, Kanistha Pandava, gave him two invaluable gifts. One was a novel by Guy Boothby named *Love Made Manifest*, and the other a silver-plated nickel pocket watch, which Moni proudly hung round his neck. This, he felt, would be his most effective talisman to ward off the plebeian secret police.

At the station Moni was able to spot Saurin easily, waiting in front of a second class coach overflowing with Europeans. Moni received three ten-rupee notes and a few coins for his expenses. He pushed his belongings brought by Saurin underneath the bench and sat down beside a man who, despite his European clothes, looked like a Bengali. As the train left, the suffocating crowd began to thin out with each halt, and at Kharagpur, hardly five or six long-distance passengers remained in the coach. Moni's long journey would have been a fiasco had there not been that portly, warm-hearted, suited and booted compatriot, who had a formidable stock of *luchi*s and *sandesh*.

As acquaintance turned into friendship, it brought in its trail a frown of worry. When asked about his destination Moni cautiously informed the engineer that he was going to Madras to learn tannery, trying his best to throw him off the scent. Although the quick reply made Moni feel proud of himself, it later became another source of worry. He soon discovered that for going to Pondicherry he would have to catch the same train from Madras as the engineer. A sudden idea struck the teenager. Moni informed the engineer employed at Trichenapolly that although he was going to Madras, he would first visit Pondicherry. Since Paris was one of the most beautiful cities in the world, he argued, the French town, too, must have some similarity with it. The undoubting engineer expressed his joy that they would continue the journey a little farther together. At this point, the engineer dozed off. Out of sheer boredom, Moni casually opened *Love Made Manifest* and began reading it.

As time passed, the unhappy truth dawned on Gounder's mind that he was not likely to meet Aurobindo again—that brief encounter was all that was fated for him. Slowly, the month of March came to an end. It was now over a month-and-a-half since Gounder had arrived at the capital. Finally, the circumstances forced Gounder to take the hard decision to return home as his family would be unduly worried. With a heavy heart, he ultimately boarded the Madras Mail.

That a second class coach could be so congested was beyond his imagination. What struck him most was that the coach was overflowing with European and Anglo-Indians. But mercifully, practically the entire crowd got down at Kharagpur. Gounder realised with relief that only five or six passengers had remained on board and he began to scrutinise them. His attention was instantly drawn by a young man barely out of his teens reading a book with a very colourful cover. There was something in the boy that roused the paternal instinct in Gounder.

'Where are you going, my son?' Gounder asked.

'To ... to Madras,' stammered Moni. 'I suppose you came to Calcutta to visit relatives?'

'No, not relatives, Aurobindo Ghose,' Gounder said, lowering his voice.

Was the old man a spy? Moni looked intently into his eyes but could not find any sign of mistrust. 'And were you able to meet him?' he asked cautiously.

'Yes and no. I saw him once from very close but couldn't talk to him. Immediately afterwards he disappeared mysteriously.'

Moni's heart was pounding furiously. 'Aren't you returning empty-handed following your inability to meet Aurobindo?' he asked figuratively.

'Not quite. I was in fact able to acquire something of immense value—these,' Gounder replied, proudly displaying Aurobindo's discarded shoes.

'Where did you get these from?' Moni asked excitedly, his eyes literally bulging out, as he recognised the pair. 'Please show them to me.' With great interest Moni first took up the right shoe and then examined the left one. He distinctly remembered getting one of them repaired by the cobbler as it had a hole near the small toe, during one of Aurobindo's visits to Shyampukur Lane. Moni looked satisfied after finding the patchwork intact. The shoes did indeed belong to Aurobindo. He returned them to Gounder with a smile of approval on his face.

'I think you owe me an explanation. Aren't you related to Aurobindo Ghose? For, I distinctly felt that you recognised these pair of shoes.'

Moni was appalled. He felt ashamed at having betrayed himself so carelessly. How much could he reveal to the old man without telling the rest? On the other hand, he was sure that if he lied he would be caught instantly. After an uneasy silence he spoke at last. 'Indeed I do. I have known him closely for over three months now.'

'Then tell me, my friend, is he safe or in police custody?'

'He's all right. You have my assurance on that.'

'Then he must surely be in South India,' Gounder concluded in a whisper, stunning Moni into silence. 'And you're on your way to visit him. Now wait. I don't think you are going to Madras but my guess is that you are actually bound for French-ruled Pondicherry, where some other political refugees are also domiciled. I've heard of one such man, Srinivasa Acharya, who is the owner of *India*.'

'But you've put me in a quandary! I'm not supposed to tell you all this.'

'You needn't. Let me guess. You know Acharya, don't you?'

'No. But I'm going to know him soon.'

A long silence followed thereafter as Gounder examined all the possibilities.

'I think I've got it fairly clear now. You're the messenger on your way to arrange the great leader's stay. You have Srinivasa Acharya's contact address and, therefore, going straight to meet him and arrange things. Right?'

Moni did not reply, but smiled at the old man's astuteness.

By the way,' Gounder asked, 'isn't Pondicherry a port? My God, then everything seems to fall into place,' Gounder added ecstatically. 'Iyengar had dreamt of Him standing by the sea!'

'I beg your pardon?' Moni asked in bewilderment.

'Never mind,' Gounder added hastily. 'But don't you think travelling by train is too risky for him? Since you say Pondicherry is a port, will it not be easier if ...?'

The discussion was becoming a mental torture for Moni not so much due to Gounder's brilliance in the art of inference, but because there lurked the possibility of the police discovering the plot by using the same logic. If a rustic commoner could guess so much from so little, why could the British spies not unearth more?

'Don't panic, my boy,' Gounder reassured Moni, as if reading his thoughts. 'If Aurobindo Ghose's arrival in South India is decreed by God, then no force in the universe can stop it, leave alone the British!'

Following the search of his house, Harimohan decided to call off Indraneel's marriage. But another thing worried him. What if his son returned home just before the scheduled date of marriage and unwittingly walked into the trap laid by the police? Was there no way of informing Indraneel that detectives in plain clothes were guarding his house round-the-clock? Harimohan peeked through the northern window of his bedroom and sure enough the sleuths were there at the corner of the graveyard. Saraju's prediction that they would soon hear from Indraneel and that he was well protected brought him some consolation.

Harimohan requested Saraju to get ready to go out with him. 'I want you to accompany me to the Dasgupta mansion,' he told her. 'We must inform them immediately that the wedding is postponed.' Then her husband gently led her to the window so that she could see through its shutters. 'See those men over there?' he pointed out, 'they're policemen in plain clothes mounting vigil day and night to arrest Neel! Do you understand what would happen if Neel returned now? Are you convinced that we've no other option but to postpone the marriage? The wedding needs to be put off until the atmosphere clears and more favourable times return. As a first step we must immediately communicate our decision to Neel's in-laws.'

Half-an-hour later, the barrister's carriage was speeding towards the high court as on all week days. The sleuths let the phaeton pass ignoring that a lady was crouching on its floor with all the shutters deliberately left open. After turning on Park Street, Harimohan quietly pulled down the shutters and Saraju assumed her seat. He took a furtive look backwards to make sure that they were not being followed. Soon the phaeton was hurtling towards Shyambazar.

'Have you heard from Indraneel?' Jaya enquired anxiously as she met them on the top of the stairs. 'But please come in and tell me what you have decided.'

'We've no option but to call off the marriage at present. Can we see Kusum?'

'Sure, you can meet her. But what will happen to her now?' Jaya asked, soliciting Saraju's sympathy. 'After this cancellation, will she ever be able to remarry?'

'We're not annulling but merely postponing the date of the marriage,' Harimohan explained. 'We value our son's choice and have nothing against your daughter.'

As Jaya wiped her tears and went out to prepare some snacks for her guests, Kusum quietly walked in and sought the blessings of her prospective in-laws. She smiled dignifiedly and sat down beside Saraju.

'Aren't you disheartened?' Saraju asked a little perplexed.

'Is there anything to worry about when he has willingly gone out on a mission?' countered Kusum. She looked towards the door to make sure that her mother was not listening and added in a low voice, 'Your son and I discussed this a week before he left but my parents don't know anything about it. I let him go because what he was attempting to do would not be possible soon after our marriage. He and his boys had been preparing for the assault for a long time but were caught off guard by the sudden announcement of the dates of our marriage. Besides, I didn't deem it right to interfere with his ideals as I value them greatly.'

Harimohan and Saraju exchanged looks of astonishment. 'We are seeking the postponement of the wedding simply because the time is not right,' Harimohan said consolingly. 'It's as simple as that.'

'I understand. We may have to wait for a long time now.'

'May not be as long as you think but I'm amazed at your level of understanding! Aren't you feeling helpless because your plans are ruined?'

'If you are referring to my happiness as a newly-wed, then, I must say, as a widow I've no moral ground to seek it, much less dream of it. I'm grateful that your son chose me to be his wife. But in the context of his association with the secret society long before meeting me, I think it would be wrong on my behalf to expect the joys of a normal married life. And I assure you, I've no difficulty in accepting his first choice of liberating the country over his duty towards me or his family. I only pray for his safety.'

After cruising through thick forests and hilly terrains and over the Mahanadi, the Godavari and the Krishna, the Madras Mail eventually entered the picturesque Coromandel Coast on the third day of its seemingly unending journey. By then, however, Moni's dress was so completely covered with coal dust from the steam engine that it was difficult to recognise its newness. The train reached the Madras Central at around eleven o'clock on the penultimate day of March. Moni and the engineer went over to Egmore, to catch the Boat Mail. Moni was to get down at Villupuram and board the midnight passenger bound for Pondicherry, and the engineer would go further up to Trichenapolly. But as their train was to leave only later in the evening, the two friends spent an uneventful day in the armchairs of the waiting room. After the Boat Mail left Egmore, Moni walked through the corridor to call on the engineer to finish whatever remained of his *luchi*s and *sandesh*. Then they finally bid each other farewell.

Moni's train reached Pondicherry in the early hours of 31 March. The next morning, he hired a *pousse-pousse*, a strange four-wheeled vehicle that existed only in French India. Moni's contact address was 10 Rue Valdaour, which turned out to be a printing press where no one lived. Instructed by someone who worked there, the *pousse-pousse* continued its way to a house about half-a-mile away, on Rue Mouttoumariammane Kovil.

Srinivasa Acharya, a medium-built, orthodox Brahmin of around thirty, had the typical sharp features and fair complexion of the Aryan-looking South Indian Brahmins. He received Moni with warmth and invited him to stay in his house. The same day, at about noon, a slightly younger gentleman with a moustache sauntered in, munching betel leaves. This was Subramaniam Bharati, the greatest Tamil poet of his time. Bharati, a political refugee, was living in Pondicherry following the issuing of an arrest warrant because of his seditious poetry that earlier regularly appeared in *India*. After Bharati arrived in Pondicherry, Acharya followed him into the French territory to continue publishing *India* from there.

~

When Harilal announced the arrival of a new visitor, Harimohan was unprepared for the shock he was about to get. For, the stranger was a middle-aged tantric, a worshipper of Kali, dressed in red with a prominent smudge of vermillion on his forehead. Even his headgear matched the colour of his dress. Sporting long hair and a cropped dark beard, the black liner around his eyes seemed to enhance the fire of his penetrating gaze. 'Please make sure that no one overhears our conversation,' the visitor began in a husky voice. 'What I have to say is very confidential. Do you recognise this article?' the stranger asked without introduction, while handing him a shiny ring. 'Your son is safe,' the stranger assured, while putting back the ring in his wallet. 'He sends you his regards and asks his mother not to worry.'

Harimohan noted with pleasure that Saraju's predictions were coming true to the last detail. Earlier, he had received an anonymous note about Indraneel's well being exactly a week after her premonition and now he had the pleasure of hearing his news from someone who had direct access to him. 'May I know where my son is?' the barrister asked cautiously.

'No, you may not,' the stranger replied curtly. 'There's no question of meeting him either. But I can tell you this much: he is under the care of Jogini Ma, who sent you the anonymous letter a couple of days back.'

'I see. But has he sent word about an imminent event?'

'Yes, Jogini Ma sends you her advice concerning the event.'

'You mean your Jogini Ma knows me?' Harimohan asked in astonishment, causing an involuntary smile on the visitor's face.

'Yes, she knows you. But I can't give you any other information. She asks that your son's marriage be postponed by a month.'

'But Bengalis don't get married during the inauspicious month of *Chaitra*!'

'Jogini Ma advises that a simple marriage be held at Kalighat Temple on the eighteenth *Chaitra* during *godhuli lagna*. Don't you know that weddings can take place on any day during the propitious transition of the day and night? Another thing that Jogini Ma insists on is that there should be no invitees—only the members from both families.'

Harimohan was about to raise another objection but good sense prevailed. At least, this would bring the opportunity for him and Saraju to meet their son. Besides, Jogini Ma seemed to recognise the need for secrecy and Indraneel's need of protection from prying eyes. And that was probably the reason why she wanted to hold the ceremony at a public place such as Kalighat where no one would notice him in the midst of the vast multitude. Besides, the dim light of the evening would also offer the perfect cover. Now, Saraju and the Dasguptas would have to be convinced.

'All right,' he said at last. 'Both parties would be present on the appointed day. But please make sure that my son comes too. In the meantime, convey my deep regards to Jogini Ma and please don't forget to give her these two hundred rupees for Indraneel's expenses as well as your travelling fare. And, above everything, thank her on my behalf for taking care of my son.'

In the early hours of 31 March, coinciding with Moni's arrival at Pondicherry, Aurobindo was standing by the Ganges, beside a small boat that was to take him away from Chandernagore. Noticing that Motilal was not there, he asked Shrish Ghose to fetch him. Motilal immediately rushed to the ghat and bowed at Aurobindo's feet. Aurobindo held him in a warm embrace that expressed his gratitude for all that Motilal had done for him during the last month-and-a-half. 'I must get going,' he said, while settling into the boat. 'We shall meet again.' As Motilal stood dejectedly, he realised that his life would never be the same again.

Aurobindo's little boat slowly sailed through the long first leg of the journey and by the time day broke, it was nearing Serampore where a palatial mansion with big Roman pillars attracted the eyes. This was the late Narendranath Gossain's family house. A little ahead, on the left, lay the beautiful, verdant army barracks of Barrackpore. This is where, fifty-three long years ago, a gunshot against the British Raj had rung out to herald India's first war of independence—the Sepoy Mutiny.

Sadly, the more recent second war had also ended disgracefully because of clumsy errors. Even if outward signs presaged a backward step, an inextinguishable desire for independence now burnt in every Indian nationalist's heart. This was principally because of the inspiring leaders in *Bande Mataram* on the one hand, and the indirect publicity gained through the Alipore Bomb Case, on the other.

As the river bent to the right and then to the left, the Dumurtala Ghat lay exposed through the morning haze. Soon the men accompanying Aurobindo were able to spot a banner, similar to their own, fluttering atop another boat. The familiar figure of Amar Chatterjee now became clear with that of his right-hand man, Manmatha Biswas. When the men from Chandernagore, Shrish Ghose and Sudarshan Chatterjee, took leave after bowing before him, Aurobindo entered the other boat brought from Uttarpara. As the day progressed, the second and the shortest of the three planned boat rides began. Within less than two hours the group was skirting past the imposing Joy Krishna Library of Uttarpara, on the adjoining maidan of which, hardly a year ago, Aurobindo had held a ten-thousand-strong crowd enthralled with his tales of prison life. As the boat approached Balighat, there was no sign anywhere of the third boat.

Meanwhile, Nagen and Suren had hired a dinghy from Baghbazar and sailed towards Bali but somehow they failed to locate the boat in which Amar was bringing Aurobindo. They became worried as their search ended in frustration. Having hastily brought their boat back to Calcutta, they contacted Sukumar at around six in the evening.

After initially drifting around in mid-stream for a couple of hours, Amar's entire plan seemed threatened by failure. At this point, when he and his assistant were at their wit's end, Amar too realised the need to contact Sukumar. Accordingly, he instructed the boatmen to set sail towards Calcutta's Chandpal Ghat.

Finally, as evening descended, Amar left the boat and hired a carriage at the ghat. He drew the curtains, shut the door and took Aurobindo northward through Calcutta's potentially dangerous thoroughfares where uniformed policemen were out patrolling in large numbers. Obviously, these were the last places through which a political fugitive would ever want to pass. After reaching the vicinity of 6 College Square, Amar sent Manmatha to Sukumar's house. Unfortunately, Sukumar was not at home.

Earlier, when Nagen and Suren had reported about their fiasco, Sukumar was compelled to take a hard decision. After dismissing Suren he instructed Nagen to get the two steel trunks down that were earlier put in the cabin of the steamer. For, if the trunks were discovered, the police would have found out a great deal. At this point, he concluded that something had held back his Aurodada in Chandernagore and he was not coming.

Soon after Nagen left for the Chandpal Ghat, Manmatha's second visit to the *Sanjibani* office enabled him to meet Sukumar. From Manmatha Sukumar learnt that Amar had brought Aurobindo to Calcutta. Although the news brought Sukumar relief, his instruction to get the trunks back from the steamer made him feel nervous. Sukumar told Manmatha to take Aurobindo immediately back to the Chandpal Ghat where he would be sending the two trunks again.

Shortly after this, Nagen put back the luggage in his mess and immediately came to give his mentor another piece of bad news that further demoralised Sukumar. The doctor, whose medical certificate was essential to clear the passage of the men travelling by the *Dupleix*, had already finished his round and gone home.

However, Nagen had met the captain and obtained the doctor's address. The only way open to them was to take Aurobindo and Bejoy to the doctor's residence and if the doctor was not asleep by the time they arrived, they could have their medical clearance there. Nagen further informed him that the coolie who had helped him to carry down the trunks had told him that he knew the doctor's house and was willing to accompany them there.

For young Nagen this was a very trying day indeed. He was again asked to rush back to the Chandpal Ghat with the two trunks as Aurobindo and the three men would be waiting there. But this time, Nagen was able to contact the other men with comparative ease. When he saw a carriage with all its shutters down parked on the wayside, he immediately understood it to be Aurobindo's. After briefly explaining the situation to Amar, Nagen urged them to hurry. So quickly dismissing his own hackney and putting the luggage on the roof of Aurobindo's carriage, the five men and the coolie drove straight to Theatre Road. Mercifully, the doctor was awake and was willing to meet them in exchange for a fat fee of thirty-two rupees. At this juncture, Nagen gave Aurobindo and Bejoy their tickets as well as the thirty-two rupees required as fees. Aurobindo was also briefed to pose as a malaria patient undertaking a voyage with his attendant to convalesce at the sea resort. After half-an-hour, the servant welcomed them. As expected, the doctor was impressed by Aurobindo's English and enquired if he had acquired it in England. The doctor then issued the certificates without further ado.

When the carriage was finally speeding away towards Chandpal Ghat, the three men accompanying Aurobindo and Bejoy were openly wondering how Aurobindo had throughout remained so calm. He whose safety was causing them so much restlessness was himself untroubled, unshaken, motionless like a statue. The day's misfortunes had caused everyone innumerable worries.

One more hurdle remained to be overcome. The captain had warned that the passengers had to get their medical certificates and board the ship by 11 p.m., failing which they could not travel the next morning. While passing through the maidan, Amar kept constantly checking his watch and urging the coachman to drive faster. Fortunately, they were able to reach the ghat on time and the staff allowed them to embark.

After loading the luggage onto the coolie's head, the four men entered the *Dupleix* by the gangway and headed straight for the second class cabin where Bejoy made Aurobindo's bed while Amar and Nagen waited at the door. It was now time to bid farewell. Amar handed over the money that was Misri Babu's final gift to Aurobindo and did a namaskar. Nagen bent down and touched his forehead to Aurobindo's feet and, in the touch of the body, felt fulfilled. Ironically, it was entirely due to the inordinate delay caused by the various mix-ups that Aurobindo was able to board the ship safely.

Harimohan impressed on Saraju that maintaining secrecy and observing a healthy detachment from the preparations of their son's wedding were vital for Indraneel's welfare. The fact that the marriage was being held in the backdrop of intense political repression warranted discretion, he explained. At last, the big day arrived and Saraju stepped out of her room at four o'clock in the afternoon wearing a simple *Dhakai* sari. Harimohan was waiting for her in the spacious ground floor drawing room. He noticed that she was carrying a cloth bag but said nothing.

Realising that dodging the omnipresent sleuths was almost impossible, Harimohan loudly instructed the coachman to drive them to Kalighat, making sure that the spies heard him. They would be shadowed in any case but at least no unnecessary alarm would be raised.

Half-an-hour later, while coursing through the bustling Chowringhee Road, Harimohan noticed that Saraju was clutching the cloth bag to her chest. Out of curiosity, he asked her what was in it and Saraju readily held it out to him. 'It's Thakurpo's dhoti,' she said, brightening up considerably. 'Wherever he may be, it's he who is looking after Neel. For the whole of last month I've been in touch with him. He asks us not to worry.'

'Ah, I also earnestly wish he were here to meet our beautiful daughter-in-law.'

'But Thakurpo says he has seen her already. He assures me that he has seen Neel and Kusum together. He also affirms that Kusum would bear a positive influence over our son and he approves of the match.'

By now, the carriage had reached the crossing of Hazra Road and turned right towards Kalighat.

'Now, now,' Harimohan said sceptically, 'how could Auro meet Kusum?'

'My guess is that he saw them together in Deogarh when Neel went to deliver the medicines. Thakurpo also told me that he knows the benefactor under whose care Neel is living. Apparently, he had once received a valuable gift from her through Neel. He also said that he saw a great aspiration for change in her heart.'

'Now, wait a minute!' Harimohan exclaimed incredulously. 'That definitely reminds me of someone! Neel once showed me a pair of gold bangles that someone had presented him for the liberation of the country. But who was it? It happened four or five years ago. Yes, yes, I remember now: it was during Shakuni's accident that Neel had received the gift. My God, how can it be possible? But we shall soon find out.'

Saraju was not listening because at that instant the carriage was entering the temple complex. And no sooner had the phaeton come to a halt that it was mobbed from all sides by noisy priests. 'Leave them alone,' a hefty priest named Kalicharan Panda threatened from behind. 'They are my customers.' And the dozen irksome priests disappeared miraculously. 'You'll have to wait a little,' Kalicharan said, 'the doors of the temple will open at five o'clock.'

Just then another carriage arrived and the barrister made a gesture with his eyes to the priest to receive it. Kalicharan had been meticulously instructed by the barrister about the plans. In consequence, instead of letting the Dasguptas mingle with the Dattas, they were led to another side of the temple. This was deliberately done to avoid raising doubts in the minds of the detectives. Meanwhile, Harimohan's keen eyes spotted the familiar sleuths keeping vigil on them from under a distant tree.

As Saturdays are considered auspicious by the followers of Kali, the turnout at the temple was exceptionally high. Harimohan appreciated Jogini Ma's ingenuity in selecting this public place on a busy day. This would drastically reduce the chances of Indraneel being recognised by the police. Eventually, a brass bell rang, causing a mild flutter among the devotees. Soon, they were led in for darshan in single file. A few minutes later, Kalicharan took the Dattas inside the *garbha griha* and made them stand on one corner of the hall. From there they silently offered their obeisance to the deity. Harimohan noticed from the corner of his eye that the two detectives had remained rooted under the tree. 'This bodes well,' he thought. 'Rather than losing us in the crowd, they're keeping an eye on our carriage, an arrangement that would keep them outside the temple. This would shield Neel from their prying eyes during the ceremony.'

Harimohan felt the warmth of Saraju's hand on his and followed her gaze. He discovered the Dasguptas clustered on the opposite end of the moderate hall. He noticed Kusum gazing at them and cautiously smiled back. This was the first time that she was not wearing her customary white sari. She was looking ravishing in her red bridal sari glowing under the orange radiance of the torches.

Harimohan looked more worried with the passing of each minute. But Saraju was totally indrawn in the sacred presence of the deity, whose awesome dark image, with three red eyes and golden tongue, overwhelmingly presided over the surrounding.

Suddenly, a commotion was felt when a stunning Jogini appeared at the gateway. Robed in red with long matted hair, she calmly surveyed the scene from the entrance. Then she walked in impressively with an entourage of four young men. Lifting her trident lightly, she touched it to her own forehead in veneration of the goddess. Saraju tugged at her husband's sleeve on recognising her son among the four accompanying disciples. But what a change there was in him! He was sporting an impressive beard that closely matched those of his associates. Wearing a prominent *tilak* on his forehead, he also held a human bone like his other three fellow disciples. Belonging to the same age group, the four men were also attired in red with matching headgear. Obviously, there could be no better disguise for a political fugitive attempting to pass incognito.

But Harimohan's attention was turned elsewhere. He was impatiently waiting to catch a glimpse of the Jogini's face to test the veracity of Saraju's prediction. And he did not have to wait long. Soon Jogini Ma walked up and stood before him. 'Datta Babu,' she whispered, 'your son will remain with me as long as he needs my protection. But he will return when the danger decreases. The place where we live is far away from human habitation and is ideally suited for harbouring him.'

'We are indeed grateful to you for taking care of our child,' Harimohan replied sincerely. 'I don't know how to repay you.'

'It was your generosity that brought about this big change in my life.'

'My intervention may only have helped in breaking your shackles but it was your own generosity that catapulted you to the present position. Let me explain. The gold bangles that you generously offered my son for the freedom movement reached the hands of his leader, Aurobindo Ghose. If you scrutinise the events following your donation you will realise how Aurobindo's blessings brought about this phenomenal change in your life, which, no doubt was sparked off by your aspiration for a higher life.'

Jogini Ma was stunned by the revelation. 'I didn't realise that,' she said, touching her forehead with folded hands. 'But yes, I now understand how eventually I was led to serve Ma Kali and gradually got initiated into her spiritual order.' She touched Harimohan's and Saraju's heads with her trident and walked back to her disciples.

And as if on cue, the evening prayers began with exceptional pomp and clamour. Preparations had been made in advance to hold the simple ceremony of Indraneel's wedding with Kusum

Kumari at the holy transition from day to night. And as an old priest performed the rites, his utterances were drowned under the din of tolling bells and the beats of drums. To the habituated public, the ceremony held no novelty as it was regular fare. And all that they saw from behind was the exchange of garlands made by the marrying couple and mechanically prayed for their welfare.

When the prayers ended and the restive crowd headed for the gate amid a mild chaos, Jogini Ma serenely brought the newly-wedded couple to Harimohan and Saraju to seek their blessings. A pat on the head was all that Saraju could offer her son while her husband held open a small box containing two gleaming diamond rings. Happily surprised, she first offered one to her daughter-in-law and the other to her son. Then Saraju astonished them by touching their heads with an old piece of cloth. 'I'm blessing you on behalf of your Sejda,' she explained. Betraying his emotions for the first time, Indraneel respectfully kneeled down, holding the dhoti to his chest.

After this, Jogini Ma took the couple to the Dasguptas. Then, passing right under the scrutiny of the detectives, she departed with her disciples, without leaving any trace of the ceremony that was performed.

Shortly after this, Madhusudan walked up to Harimohan. 'I don't know what wicked deed my daughter has performed to merit such punishment,' he said emotionally. 'Isn't it ironical that in spite of getting married twice she's unable to share a home with her husband?'

Unable to find words to console him, Harimohan embraced him spontaneously. 'I'm taking Kusum back to our house because yours is under surveillance,' Madhusudan added sadly.

'Remain calm and everything will be all right,' Harimohan said compassionately, 'Don't ever underestimate the force that is at work.'

65

Pondicherry, 1910

Since the *Dupleix* carrying Aurobindo and Bejoy was not due to arrive before 4 April, Moni had nothing to do except sit around and wait. However, communicating with his new friends was not proving easy for Moni, as his spoken English was far from adequate. During this period it had become a daily routine for Moni to remind Srinivasa Acharya to find a house for Aurobindo's stay, but he received only evasive answers. To the eighteen-year-old this was turning out to be a desperate situation.

At last, with hardly a day left before the much-awaited arrival, as Moni made an especially strong request, he was taken along to see a tiny garret in a dirty out-of-the-way part of the town. Framed pictures of revolutionaries, including that of the late Kanailal Datta, looked down from its walls. Clearly, no place could have been more inappropriate for Aurobindo's stay. However, Moni held his tongue and continued to wait.

But the *India* men were not as naïve as they seemed to be. For, they had secretly approached a wealthy businessman named Calve Shankara Chettiar who had agreed to put up the Calcutta leader in his own house, ideally suited for keeping him away from the public eye. The precaution taken against leaking this information to Moni was an obvious safeguard to keep it away from the British, in case the unknown teenager turned out to be their spy. If Aurobindo failed to arrive by the *Dupleix*, the Bengali stripling would be given a lesson that he would find hard to forget.

The *Dupleix* reached at around four o'clock on 4 April and dropped anchor off the coast of Pondicherry. Srinivasa and Moni were already waiting on the quarter-of-a-mile long metal pier. From there the two men got down into a waiting oar-driven boat and headed for the mail-ship.

The *Dupleix* was a 2,600 ton, medium-sized steam ship, carrying passenger as well as freight, with two thin masts and a chimney marginally inclined backward, over its main central structure. As their boat approached the ship, Moni felt relieved on beholding the familiar figures of Aurobindo and Bejoy staring intently at them from its deck. The two visitors soon found themselves in the cabin below the deck, in the august company of Messieurs Jotindra Nath Mitra and Bankim Chandra Bhowmik. It was teatime on board, and they were served tea along with the passengers who were about to disembark. But Acharya, an orthodox Brahmin and a strict vegetarian, would have neither tea nor the fish-shaped biscuits on board the foreign ship.

Soon the four men climbed down the rope-ladder into the waiting boat, where Aurobindo's four-levered steel trunk, with the smaller paraphernalia, had been lowered by the steamer's cabin crew. Calve Shankara Chettiar and the poet Bharati met them as the boat reached the pier.

Epilogue

The Deliverer

When the Boat Mail reached Villupuram Junction early in the morning of 31 March, a familiar octogenarian alighted stealthily behind a solitary teenager from a second class coach and quietly slipped into the Pondicherry-bound midnight passenger behind him. But Gounder's plans were well chalked out before his arrival at Pondicherry.

He enquired from the station master the name and address of the local shipping agent and headed for its office beside the tall lighthouse, on the beautiful Cours Chabrol overlooking the Bay of Bengal. The adjacent *Place de la République* with the lighthouse on one side, and the *Douane* with its massive flag-staff flying the French tricolour on the other, was a breathtaking sight opposite the long pier proudly jutting out into the sea. But though the simplicity of the French colonial architecture was very pleasing to the eyes, Pondicherry seemed dreadfully dead after Gounder's recent experience of Calcutta.

At the Messagerie Maritime, he learnt that their next ship was due to arrive from Calcutta on the afternoon of 4 April. The Tamil clerk also confirmed that there was no booking in the name of Aurobindo Ghose. This was as expected, reasoned Gounder, as it would be foolish for a political fugitive seeking asylum in a foreign territory to travel under his own name.

On the morning of 4 April, Gounder paid one more visit to the Messagerie Maritime to check whether their ship was on schedule. After receiving confirmation, he offered a special puja at the Manakula Vinayagar Temple and fasted the whole day. He was at the beach well before Moni arrived. As the minutes ticked by, and a hazy trail of smoke became visible on the northeastern corner of the horizon where the land mass, dotted with lush verdant coconut groves, bends out into the sea, Gounder watched with eager eyes a tiny dark speck gradually grow into a medium-sized steam-ship.

As the Deliverer stepped out onto the holy soil of South India, old Ayanar Gounder was the only man to witness the fulfilment of the prediction made forty long years ago by the Nagai Swami. Although this was an exceptional moment for the residents of Pondicherry as no other leader of national fame had ever visited the town, the Uttara Yogi seemed strangely detached from the excitement that his presence was causing. Quietly, he exchanged greetings with the people waiting to welcome him.

As the old man surveyed this moving scene with the tranquil eyes of a devotee, something unusual was happening within him. Suddenly, everything around seemed to come to a stand still. Even the sea appeared to hold back its breakers. The rays of the effulgent sun, bathing the town and the bright turquoise blue ocean from a cloudless sky, appeared to glow brighter.

When Aurobindo approached the carriage meant to take him to his new lodging, he was stopped by a tall old man whom he vaguely remembered having seen somewhere recently. To his astonishment the stranger touched his feet and sought his blessings. Aurobindo held the man's shoulders and gazed into his eyes. The old man's strength and nobility struck everyone around. No one spoke. The exchange of glances said it all. Then slowly Aurobindo smiled reassuringly and boarded the horse-drawn carriage to go, as the old man stood lost in a reverie.

A little later, Aurobindo left for the Rue Comoutty and Acharya, Chettiar and Bharati accompanied him. Moni did a respectful salutation as he recognised Gounder. The next moment he followed Bejoy in a *pousse-pousse,* along with a guide.

Gounder was standing alone on the seafront, his heart alight with intense fulfilment. The Uttara Yogi's loving touch had blessed and purified him. It was as though he had waited all his life only to live this tremendous moment. All that existed now were the Deliverer and the world he had come to transform.

It was not just the fulfilment of an extraordinary prediction; it was the beginning of a New Age.

> In Matter shall be lit the spirit's glow,
> A few shall see what none yet understands;
> God shall grow up while the wise men talk and sleep;
> For man shall not know the coming till its hour
> And belief shall be not till the work is done.
>
> – Sri Aurobindo, *Savitri*

Members of Ghose Family and their Relatives:

Dr Krishna Dhone Ghose	:	doctor and philanthropist
Swarnalata (Basu) Ghose	:	Krishna Dhone's wife
Benoybhushan Ghose	:	Krishna Dhone and Swarnalata's eldest son
Manomohan Ghose	:	Krishna Dhone and Swarnalata' second son
Aurobindo Ghose	:	Krishna Dhone and Swarnalata's third son
Sarojini Ghose	:	Krishna Dhone and Swarnalata's only daughter
Barindra Kumar Ghose	:	Krishna Dhone and Swarnalata's youngest son
Mrinalini (Bose) Ghose	:	Aurobindo's wife
Rajnarayan Basu	:	Swarnalata's father
Nistarini Basu	:	Rajnarayan's wife
Jogendranath Basu	:	Rajnarayan's eldest son
Monindranath Basu	:	Rajnarayan's youngest son
Lajjavati Basu	:	Rajnarayan's youngest daughter
Lilavati (Basu) Mitra	:	Rajnarayan's fourth daughter
Krishna Kumar Mitra	:	Lilavati's husband
Kumudini Mitra	:	Krishna Kumar and Lilavati's eldest daughter
Sukumar Mitra	:	Krishna Kumar and Lilavati's son
Basanti Mitra	:	Krishna Kumar and Lilavati's youngest daughter
Bhupal Chandra Bose	:	Mrinalini's father
Golapkamini Bose	:	Mrinalini's mother
Sisir Bose	:	Mrinalini's brother

Saibalini Bose	:	Mrinalini's sister
Abinash alias Hoopo	:	a cousin of Aurobindo
Saurin Bose	:	a cousin of Mrinalini
Biren Ghose	:	- do -

Historical Personalities:

Baker, Sir Edward Norman	:	lieutenant governor of Bengal (1908–11)
Banerjea, Surendranath	:	veteran politician and moderate Congress leader
Bose, Abala	:	wife of Jagadish Chandra Bose
Bose, Jagadish Chandra	:	scientist
Chapekar, Balkrishna	:	revolutionary of Poona
Chapekar, Damodar Hari	:	-do-
Chapekar, Wasudev	:	-do-
Chatterjee, Bankim Chandra	:	author, deputy collector of Hooghly
Cockerell, Horace Abel	:	British administrative officer, officiating lieutenant governor of Bengal (11 August–17 September 1885)
Cockerell, Julia	:	wife of Horace Cockerell
Curzon, George Nathaniel, (Lord)	:	viceroy of India (1899–1905)
Deuskar, Sakharam Ganesh	:	Barin's former teacher, instructor of economics to the revolutionaries
Dravid, Ganpatrao	:	police informer of Poona
Dravid, Ramchandra	:	- do -
Drummond, Sir Edmond	:	lieutenant governor of the N-W Provinces (1863–68), father of Julia Cockerell
Dutt, Ashwini Kumar	:	nationalist Congress leader of Barisal
Dutt, Charu Chandra, Judge	:	brother-in-law of Subodh Mullick, Aurobindo's friend

Dutt, Lilavati	:	wife of Charu Chandra
Fraser, Sir Henderson Leith	:	lieutenant governor of Bengal (1903–8)
Fuller, Sir Bamfylde	:	lieutenant governor of eastern Bengal and Assam (1905–6)
Gaekwad, Sayajirao III	:	ruler of Baroda, Aurobindo's employer
Ghosal, Sarala	:	niece of Tagore, founder of an *akhara* in Calcutta
Kimberley, Lord	:	secretary of state for India (1882–85, 1886, 1892–94)
MacDonald, Ramsay	:	member of parliament of the Labour Party
Minto, Gilbert John Elliot Murray-Kynynmond Earl of, Lord	:	viceroy of India (1905–10)
Mitra, Pramathanath	:	bar-at-law, president, Anushilan Samiti
Morley, John	:	secretary of state for India (1905–10)
Mukherjee, Peary Mohan	:	Raja of Uttarpara
Mukherjee, Rajendranath	:	(alias Misri-Babu) Kumar of Uttarpara
Mukherjee, Satish Chandra	:	promoter of Dawn Society and national education
Mullick, Nirod	:	aristocrat, cousin of Subodh Chandra
Mullick, Subodh Chandra	:	aristocrat, Aurobindo's host and associate
Nivedita (Margaret Noble)	:	disciple of Vivekananda, mentor of revolutionaries
Pal, Bipin Chandra	:	nationalist leader of Congress Party
Rai, Lala Lajpat	:	nationalist Congress leader and Arya Samajist
Ranade, Mahadev Govind	:	ex-judge connected with *Induprakash*
Ranade, Mahadev Vinayak	:	revolutionary of Poona
Roosevelt, Theodore	:	President of the United States of America (1901–9)

Russell, George William Erskine	:	under-secretary of state for India (1892–94)
Tagore, Rabindranath	:	poet and nobleman
Tagore, Surendranath	:	poet Tagore's nephew, treasurer of Anushilan Samiti
Tardivel, Léon	:	mayor of the French settlement of Chandernagore
Thakur Ramsingh	:	revolutionary leader of Bombay
Thakur Saheb	:	prince of small state, revolutionary leader
Thompson, Sir Augustus R	:	lieutenant governor of Bengal (1882–87)
Tilak, Bal Gangadhar	:	nationalist leader of Congress Party
Upadhyay, Brahma Bandhab	:	political leader and satirist, editor of *Sandhya*
Vidyabhushan, Jogendra Nath	:	ex-magistrate, Sanskrit scholar
Wadiar, Krishnaraja	:	ruler of Mysore

The Revolutionaries of Muraripukur:

Banerjee, Upendra Nath
Bhattacharya, Abinash
Bose, Debabrata
Bose, Dindayal
Bose, Khudiram
Bose, Sailen
Bose, Satyen
Buxi, Narendra Nath
Chaki, Prafulla
Chakravarty, Prafulla
Chandra Sen, Purna
Das (Kanungo), Hem Chandra

Datta, Kanailal
Datta, Ullaskar
Ghose, Biren
Ghose, Hemendra Nath
Ghose, Sishir Kumar
Gossain, Narendranath
Gupta, Nolini Kanta
Kanjilal, Hrishikesh
Mullick, Poresh
Nag, Bejoy
Nandi, Asoke Chandra
Nandi, Indranath
Rai, Niarapada
Roy, Indu Bhushan
Saha, Kunjolal
Sanyal, Krishna Jibon
Sarkar, Bibhuti Bhushan
Sarkar, Sudhir Kumar
Sen, Biren
Sen, Hem
Sen, Sachin
Sen, Sushil

Bibliography

Primary Sources (unpublished)

Alipore Bomb Trial Records. Collection of original records in Additional District and Sessions Judge's Court, Alipore, Calcutta.

Amarendranath Chatterjee Papers. Source: Sri Yogabrata Chatterjee, Uttarpara. Now in Sri Aurobindo Archives and Research Library, Pondicherry.

Biren Sen Papers. Source: Sri Aurobindo Archives and Research Library, Pondicherry.

Government of India, Home Department Political Proceedings, Home Department (Jails). Source: Sri Aurobindo Archives & Research Library, Pondicherry.

India Office Records, London, Judicial and Public Department. Source: Sri Aurobindo Archives and Research Library, Pondicherry.

Police Commissioner's Order Book No. 46 (from 9.3.08 to 17.6.08) entries Nos. 1032 to 1099 corresponding to 1.5.1908. Source: Lalbazar Police Head Quarters, Calcutta.

Records of Baroda State, comprising Confidential files, Ordinary files of various departments, Baroda College Records. Source: Sri Aurobindo Archives and Research Library, Pondicherry.

Statement of Political Sufferer Jogendra Chandra Bhattacharya, Bundle No. 22, Paper No. 125 (xxvii), *History of the 'Sadhana Samaj' at Mymensingh*. Source: West Bengal Sate Archives, Writers Buildings, Calcutta.

Statement of Political Sufferer Nirvan Swami alias Satish Chandra Sarkar, Bundle No. 22, Paper No. 125, (x). Source: West Bengal Sate Archives, Writers' Building, Calcutta.

Official Reports

Armstrong, J.E. Superintendent of Police on special duty, 1917, *An Account of the Revolutionary Organisation in Eastern Bengal with Special Reference to the Dacca Anushilan Samiti*, Vols. I and II, [Armstrong Report] as reproduced in *Terrorism in Bengal*, Vol. II, Calcutta 1995.

Daly, F.C. DIG Special Branch, Calcutta, *Notes on the Growth of the Revolutionary Movement in Bengal (1905-1911)* [Daly Report] as reproduced in *Terrorism in Bengal*, Vol. I, Calcutta 1995.

________. *First Rebels*, Calcutta 1911, reprinted Calcutta 1981.

Ker, J.C. *Political Trouble in India 1907–1917*, reprinted Calcutta 1973.

Nixon, J.C. *An Account of the Revolutionary Organisations in Bengal other than the Dacca Anushilan Samiti*, Calcutta 1917, as reproduced in *Terrorism in Bengal*, Vol. II, Calcutta 1995.

Tegart, Charles. *Terrorism in India*, Calcutta 1993.

Primary Sources (published)

Bose, Bijoy Krishna. Ed. *The Alipore Bomb Trial*, Calcutta 1922.

Bengal Civil List, 1880, 1883, 1885, 1899, 1905–1910. Source: West Bengal Secretariat Library, Writers' Building, Calcutta.

Bengal Past & Present, December 1909.

Buckland, C.E. *Dictionary of Indian Biography*, London 1905, reprinted Varanasi, 1971.

Dictionary of National Biography, (Vols. I– IV), Institute of Historical Studies, Calcutta 1972.

McCluskie's Calcutta Directory 1906 and Guide. Source: Sri Thankappan Nair, Calcutta.

Politico-Criminal Who's Who, Govt. of India, 1914.

Thacker's Calcutta Directory 1906-1911. Source: National Library, Calcutta.

The India Office List 1887, 1909, 1935. Source: West Bengal Secretariat Library, Writers' Building, Calcutta.

The Statesman, An Anthology 1875–1975, Calcutta 1975.

Sangsad Bangali Charitabhidhan, Calcutta 1998.

Sri Aurobindo Archives and Research, (reprints in bi-annual journal) 1977–94, Pondicherry.

Who Was Who, 1897–1915, 1916–1928, London 1916 and 1929. Source: National Library, Calcutta.

Newspapers and Other Periodicals

Bande Mataram, reprinted in Sri Aurobindo Birth Centenary Library (SABCL), Vol. I, Pondicherry 1972.

Karmayogin, ibid.

Sri Aurobindo Mandir Annual 1944, from Calcutta, containing 'Salutation', original poem by Rabindranath Tagore translated by Khitish Chandra Sen, on pp. 1–2.

The Statesman. Source: Statesman House, Calcutta.

The Hindoo Patriot. Source: National Library, Calcutta.

Mother India, 1952, May p. 8; June p. 18; August; September pp. 10–11.

Writings by Participants and Eyewitnesses

Aparna Devi. *Manush Chittaranjan*, Calcutta 1362 B.S.

Aurobindo, Sri [Aurobindo Ghose]. *On Himself*, SABCL Vol. 26.

________. *Speeches*, Pondicherry 1974.

________. *Tales of Prison Life*, Pondicherry 1997.

________. *Sri Aurobindo Archives and Research* (original unpublished writings in the bi-annual journal) 1977–94, Pondicherry.

Banerjea, Surendranath. *A Nation in Making*, London 1925.

Banerjee, Narendranath. *Rakta Biplaber Ek Audhyay*, Chandernagore 1361 B.S.

Banerjee, Upendranath. *Aurobindo Prasanga*, *Dainik Basumati 20 Augrahayan* Calcutta, 1357 B.S.

________. *Nirbashiter Atmokatha*, Calcutta 1333 B.S.

Basu, Sailendranath. *Sri Aurobinder Sahadharmini Mrinalini Debir Smritikatha*, Calcutta 1971.

Basu, Bhupal Chandra. *Mrinalini Ghose*, Statement of 26th August 1931, reproduced in Sri Aurobindo Archives and Research, December 1978.

Basu, Satish Chandra. *Anushilan Samitir Utpatti Bishaye Satish Chandra Basur Bibriti*, in Bhupendranath Datta, *Bharater Dwitiya Swadhinatar Sangram*, 1st part, Calcutta 1983.

Basu, Sisir. *Sri Aurobindo's Marriage*, Statement of 25th November 1941, reproduced in Sri Aurobindo Archives and Research, December 1978.

Bhattacharya, Abinash. *Aurobindo, Galpo Bharati 6,* 1357 B.S.

_______. *Baiplabik Samitir Prarambha Kaler Itihas*, in Bhupendranath Datta, *Bharater Dwitiya Swadhinatar Sangram*, 1st part, Calcutta 1983.

_______. Ed. *Mukti Kon Pathey*, Calcutta, 1314 B. S., pp. 167-69.

Bhattacharya, Upendrachandra. *Amar Elomelo Jiboner Kauyekti Audhyay*, Calcutta 1369 B.S.

Chakravarty, Basanti. *Amader Aurodada, Galpo Bharati 6,* 1357 B.S.

Chakravarty, Suresh Chandra. *Smritikatha*, Pondicherry 1962.

Chatterjee, Ramananda. *Selected Writings & Tributes*, New Delhi 1979.

Chaudhurani, Sarala Devi. *Jibaner Jharapata*, Calcutta 1879 Sakabda.

Chirol, Valentine. *Indian Unrest*, London 1910.

Das (Kanungo), Hemchandra. *Banglay Biplab Prachesta*, Calcutta 1984.

Das, Pulin Behari. *Amar Jiban Kahini*, Calcutta 1987.

Datta, Bhupendranath. *Bharater Dwitiya Swadhinatar Sangram*, 1st part, Calcutta 1983.

Datta, Charu Chandra. *Purana Katha Upasanghar*, Calcutta 1952.

De, Bishwanath. Ed. *Nibedita Smriti*, Calcutta 1972.

Ghose, Barindra Kumar. *Agnijug*, Calcutta 1355 B.S.

_______. *Atmakatha*, Calcutta 1403 B.S.

_______. *Barindrer Atmakahini*, Calcutta 1390 B.S.

Guhathakurata, Manoranjan. *Manoramar Jiban-Chitra Vol. II*, Calcutta 1978.

Gupta, Nolini Kanta. *Smritir Pata*, Calcutta 1988.

Macdonald, James Ramsay. *The Awakening of India*, London. (n.d.) as reprinted in Dilip Kumar Roy. *Sri Aurobindo Came to Me*, Bombay 1969, p. 161.

Mitra, Krishna Kumar. *Atmacharit*, Calcutta 1381 B.S.

Mitra, Saibalani. *Mrinalini Smritikatha*, Srinvantu, Sravan 1381.

Mitra, Sukumar. *Sri Aurobindoke Jemonti Dekhiachhi*, in *Agnijug*, ed. Sailesh De, Calcutta 1986, p. 137.

Mukherjee, Jadugopal. *Biplabi Jibaner Smriti*, Calcutta 1983.

Nandi, Indranath. *Atmonnati Samitir Itihas*, in Bhupendranath Datta, *Bharater Dwitiya Swadhinatar Sangram*, 1st part, Calcutta 1983.

Nevinson, Henry W. *The New Spirit in India*, London 1908, reprinted (in part) in Manoj Das, *Sri Aurobindo in the First Decade of the Century*, Pondicherry 1972 and as reprinted in Dilip Kumar Roy, *Sri Aurobindo Came to Me*, Bombay 1969, pp. 50–51.

Nirodbaran. Ed. *Talks with Sri Aurobindo*. 3 volumes, Calcutta, Madras, Pondicherry, 1986, 1985, 1989.

Pal, Bipin Chandra. *Indian Nationalism: Its Principles and Personalities*, 1918, reprinted in Manoj Das, *Sri Aurobindo in the First Decade of the Century*, Pondicherry 1972.

Purani, A.B. Ed. *Evening Talks with Sri Aurobindo*, Pondicherry 1982.

Roy, Dinendra Kumar. *Aurobindo Prasanga*, Calcutta 1379 B.S.

Sardesai, Govind Sakharam. *Sri Sayaji Rao Gaekwar yancha Sahavasant*, Poona 1956.

Sarkar, Nolini Kanta. *Asha Jaowar Majhkhaney*, Vol. I, Calcutta 1389 B.S.(?)

Sergeant, Philip W. *The Ruler of Baroda*, London 1928.

St. Nihal Singh. *Glimpses of Baroda*, The Modern Review, March 1924.

Upadhyay, Brahmabandhab. *Rachana Sangraha*, Calcutta 1987.

Secondary Sources

Aurobindo, Sri. *Life Divine*, SABCL Vols. 18, 19.

________. *Savitri*, SABCL Vols. 28, 29.

Bagchi, Kironendu. *Bonhi Biplab*, Calcutta 1386 B.S., pp. 470–71.

Bhattacharya, Amitrasudan. *Bankimchandra O Bangadarshan*, Calcutta 1971.

De, Amalendu. *Raja Subodh Mullick and His Times*, Calcutta 1996.

Chatterjee, Satyabrata. *Biplabi Amarendranath Chattopadhyay*, Calcutta 1392 B.S.

Cronin, Richard Paul, *British Policy and Administration in Bengal, 1905–1912*, Calcutta 1977.

Danino, Michel and Sujata Nahar. *The Invasion That Never Was*, Auroville 1996.

Gaekwad, Fatehsinghrao. *Sayajirao of Baroda, The Prince and the Man*, Bombay 1989.

Ghosh, Anuradha. *Biplabi Bhupendranath Datta, Sankshipta Parichiti*, Calcutta 1992, p. 3.

Ghosh, Kali Charan. *The Roll of Honour*, Calcutta 1965.

________. *The Footprints on the Road to Indian Independence*, Calcutta 1975.

Ghosh, Yatindrakumar. *Echo of Aswinikumar's Deportation*, Calcutta 1980.

Haldar, Jibantara. *Anushilan Samitir Sankhipta Itihas*, Calcutta 1356 B.S.

Heehs, Peter. *The Bomb in Bengal*, Delhi 1993.

James, Robert Rhodes. *The British Revolution, British Politics 1880–1939*, London 1978.

Joshi, Kireet. *The Portals of Vedic Knowledge*, Auroville 2001.

Keer, Dhananjay. *Lokmanya Tilak Father of the Indian Freedom Struggle*, Bombay 1969.

Koley, Asru. *Rajnarayan Basu: Jiban O Sahitya*, Calcutta 1975.

Majumdar, R.C. *History of Modern Bengal*, Calcutta 1981.

Mitra, Radharaman. *Kolikata Darpan*, Calcutta 1988.

Mukherjee, Dr Amitabha. *Fifty Years of National Education*, Calcutta 1992.

Mukherjee, Uma and Haridas. *Bharater Swadhinata Andolane Jugantar Patrikar Dan*, Calcutta 1972.

________. *The Origins of the National Education Movement (1905–1910)* Calcutta 1957.

________. *Sri Aurobindo and the New Thought in Indian Politics*, Calcutta 1974.

________. *Swadeshi Andolan O Banglar Nabajug*, Calcutta 1961.

Mukhopadhyay, Prithwindranath. *Sadhak Biplabee Jyotindranath*, Calcutta 1990.

________. Ed. *Samasamoyiker Chokhe Sri Aurobindo*, Calcutta 1969.

Nair, P. Thankappan. *A History of Calcutta's Streets*, Calcutta 1987, pp. 824–26.

Nirodbaran. *Mrinalini Devi*, Pondicherry 1988.

Pal, Prashantakumar. *Robijibani, Vol. V*, Calcutta 1990, pp. 375–76.

Pradhan, G.P. and Bhagwat, A.K. *Lokmanya Tilak*, Bombay 1959.

Purani, A.B. *The Life of Sri Aurobindo*, Pondicherry 1987.

Ray, Rajat Kanta. *Social Conflict and Political Unrest in Bengal 1875–1927*, Delhi 1984.

Roy, Dilip Kumar. *Sri Aurobindo Came to Me*, Bombay 1969, pp. 50–51, 161.

Roy, Motilal. *Amar Jibansangini*, Calcutta 1968.

________. *Amar Dekha Biplab O Biplabi*, Calcutta 1984.

________. *Biplabi Shaheed Kanailal*, Calcutta 1973.

Samanta, Basantakumar. *Shaheed Kanailal Natun Tothther Aloke*, Calcutta 1990.

Sarkar, Mona. Ed. *A Spirit Indomitable*, Pondicherry 1989.

Sen, Surendra Nath. *Eighteen Fifty Seven*, Calcutta 1957.
Vidyabhushan, Jogendranath. *Jogendra Granthabali,* Calcutta 1286 B.S.
Warner & Marten. *The Groundwork of British History*, London 1934.

Glossary

adesh	order
akhara	gymnasium
alur chop	savoury made of mashed potato and spices, fried in oil
amangalam	inauspicious
amavasya	new moon
annaprashan	rice ceremony; a child's first morsel of solid food
Ashar	third month in the Bengali calendar
Audrishto Bharat	destiny of India
Augrahayan	eighth month in the Bengali calendar
Baba Baidyanath	alternate name of Lord Shiva
Benarasi	sari made in Benaras, also known as Vanarasi in Uttar Pradesh
Bhadra	fifth month in the Bengali calendar
Bhai	brother
bhakti	faith
bilait	England
Bitiya	daughter
Borho Mama	elder maternal uncle
Bouthan	sister-in-law, elder brother's wife
brahmachari	bachelor
Chaitra	twelfth month of the Bengali calendar
Chhorda	youngest older brother
Chhoto Mama	youngest maternal uncle
coolie	porter
Dadu	grandfather

darshan	vision
dehati	rustic
dewan	prime minister
dhoti	a full-length, long piece of cloth worn round the waist by men
Didi	elder sister
Dol Jatra	Holi festival marking the arrival of spring
Durga	ten-armed goddess symbolising victory over evil
ekadasi	the eleventh day of a lunar month
esraj	a stringed instrument played with a bow
Firinghee	white man
garbha griha	sanctum sanctorum
Gauri Shankar	combined aspect of Lord Shiva and his consort, Parvati
godhuli	the mystical transition between day and night
goonda	hooligan
gowala	milkman
grihapravesh	house warming ceremony
hateykhori	the chalk ceremony marking the beginning of education
Jagaddhatri Puja	the adoration of Goddess Jagaddhatri
Kali	an aspect of Durga, the Goddess of Destruction
Kaliyuga	the age of falsehood
kamandulu	a receptacle containing holy water
Kartamoshay	the person in charge
kaviraj	a naturopath
Kayastha	a caste lower in status than the Brahmin
khol	a type of drum
khabardaar	beware
kirtan	devotional song
Krishna	a Hindu god who delivered the famous sermons at Kurukshetra
lagna	the sacred conjunction of the planets
Lakshmi	Hindu Goddess of Wealth and Beauty
lota	small metal pot

*luchi*s	puris, flat piece of unleavened bread
Magh	tenth month in the Bengali calendar
mahajnani	the enlightened
mahapralaya	destruction, upheaval
mahashanti	profound peace
mahasiddha	realised soul
Mashima	aunt, mother's sister
math	temple
Meshomoshay	Mashima's husband
mohur	gold coin
moshay	mister
namaskar	a sign of greeting with folded hands
Narayana	alternate name of Lord Vishnu, the Protector of the Universe
Nau Mashi	fourth maternal aunt
pala	red bangles worn on the wrists by married women
panda	priest
Phalgune	eleventh month of the Bengali calendar
Pishima	aunt, father's sister
pitha	place of worship
Poush	ninth month in the Bengali calendar
pranayama	the discipline of breathing
prasad	food offered to a deity
pucca	permanent
pugri	a headgear
rajasic	dynamic
rakhi	band of friendship
Rath Jatra	the chariot festival of Lord Jangannath of Puri
rudraksha	sacred seeds of a tree
sadhana	spiritual pursuit
sahib	usually a foreigner, a respectful way of addressing a man
sandesh	Bengali delicacy made out of milk and sugar
sandhyarati	worship of deity in the evening
Saraswati	Goddess of Music and Knowledge

Sejda	third elder brother
Sejo Bouthan	third sister-in-law
shamla	a round cloth hat that noblemen used to wear till the turn of the twentieth century
shankha	cross-sectioned slices of conch shell worn on the wrists by married women
sherbat	a flavoured drink
shikar	hunting
shradh	obsequies
siddhi	spiritual realisation
Sonar Bangla	the endowed land of Bengal
Sravan	fourth month in the Bengali calendar
Sri Panchami	another name for Saraswati Puja
taluk	estate
tamasic	lethargic
tantrik	a spiritual seeker of the *Tantra* sect of Hinduism
tapasya	penance
Thakurpo	brother-in-law (husband's brother)
thana	police outpost
tilak	a sacred smudge of vermilion on the forehead
trishul	trident
tulsi	basil
tyaga	sacrifice
Vasudeva	alternate name of Lord Krishna
yantra	a form of occult significance
yuga	cycle, age
zulum	oppression